The practice of comparative politics

A Reader

The Practice of Comparative Politics

A Reader

edited by
Paul G. Lewis, David C. Potter and Francis G. Castles
at The Open University

Second edition

Published by
Longman in association with
The Open University Press

Longman Group Limited London

*Associated companies, branches and representatives
throughout the world*

*Published in the United States of America
by Longman Inc., New York*

Selection and editoral material
© The Open University 1973, 1978

First published 1978

British Library Cataloguing in Publication Data
The practice of comparative politics.
  — 2nd ed.
    1. Comparative government – Addresses, essays, lectures
    I. Lewis, Paul Geoffrey II. Potter, David
    III. Castles, Francis Geoffrey
    320.3   JF111   78-40212

ISBN 0-582-49033-2

Printed in Great Britain by
Whitstable Litho Ltd., Whitstable, Kent

Contents

vi   *Contents*

Acknowledgements

We are grateful to the following for permission to reproduce copyright material:

The author and The American Political Science Association for article 'Concept Misformation in Comparative Politics' by Giovanni Sartori from *American Political Science Review*, Vol. 54; American Sociological Association for article 'Towards a Theory of Revolution' by J. C. Davies from *ASR*, Vol. 27, 1962; Cambridge University Press for adapted excerpts from 'Ideas, Institutions and the Politics of Government: A Comparative Analysis' Parts I, II and III by Anthony King in *British Journal of Political Science* 1973/1974; The City University of New York (The Graduate School and University Center) for excerpts from 'Transitions to Democracy: Towards a Dynamic Model' by Dankwart A. Rustow in *Comparative Politics*, April 1970, and 'Types of Democratic Systems and Types of Public Policy: An Empirical Examination' by B. Guy Peters, John C. Doughtie and M. Kathleen McCulloch in *Comparative Politics*, IX:3, April 1977; The Economist for article 'Parkinson's Law' by C. Northcote Parkinson from *The Economist* Nov. 19, 1955; MacGibbon & Kee for excerpts from 'National Profiles' in *Exploitation* by R. Jenkins; Macmillan Publishing Co. Inc. for excerpts from *The Methodology of Comparative Research* by R. T. Holt and J. E. Turner, 'Comparative Politics' by Gabriel A. Almond in *International Encyclopedia of the Scoial Sciences*, Vol. 13, Macmillan 1968 and 'The Utility of Quantative Methods in Political Science' by A. Hacker in *Contemporary Political Analysis* ed. J. C. Charlesworth, Collier Macmillan, London 1967; McGraw-Hill Book Co. for excerpts from *Approaches to Development: Politics, Administration and Change* ed. J. D.

Montgomery and W. J. Siffin, Copyright © 1966 by McGraw-Hill
Inc. By permission of McGraw-Hill Book Company; Oxford University
Press for excerpt from 'Politics as a Vocation' in *Max Weber*
eds. H. H. Gerth and C. Wright Mills; Penguin Books Ltd for
excerpts from *Comparative Government* by S. E. Finer (Allen Lane
The Penguin Press, 1970), pp. 37–40, copyright © S. E. Finer 1970
and excerpts from Aristotle *The Politics* translated by T. A. Sinclair
(Penguin Classics, 1962), pp. 55, 101–2, 115–16, 171–6, 189–97,
copyright © the Estate of T. A. Sinclair, 1962; Prentice-Hall, Inc.
for excerpts from *Modern Political Analysis*, 3rd Edn. by Robert Dahl,
© 1976, pp. 1–11. Reprinted by permission of Prentice-Hall, Inc.
N.J.; Princeton University Press for article 'Comparative History
and the Theory of Modernization' by L. M. Salamon in *World
Politics*, Vol. 23, Oct. 1970; Random House, Inc. for excerpt from
'The Nature of Comparative Analysis' in *The Study of Comparative
Government* by Roy C. Macridis. Copyright © 1955 by Random
House Inc. Reprinted by permission; Schoken Books Inc. and
Gerald Duckworth Co. Ltd. for essay 'Is a Science of Comparative
Politics Possible?' in *Against the Self-Images of the Age* by A. C.
MacIntyre © 1971; Social Forces for article from 'Old Regime
Legacies and Communist Revolutions in Russia and China' by
Theda Skocpol, reprinted from *Social Forces,* 55 Dec. 1976, pp. 284–
315. Copyright © The University of North Carolina Press; the
authors and John Wiley & Sons, Inc. for adapted excerpts from
'Comparative Research and Social Science Theory' and 'Formulat-
ing Theories Across Systems' in *The Logic of Comparative Social
Inquiry* by Adam Przeworski and Henry Teune.

General introduction

Politics refers broadly to patterns of human relationships that involve, to a significant extent, power, rule, or authority. Comparative politics can be referred to in an introductory way as one of the techniques of inquiry by which one can understand or answer questions about such relationships. A celebrated illustration of the practice of comparative politics is found in Aristotle's *Politics*, and it is appropriate in a book with this title to note at the outset how (as far as we know) Aristotle and his students conducted their inquiry.

Aristotle lived at a time when the politics of Greek city-states were turbulent and unstable, and his attention was drawn to the causes of instability; by implication he also wanted to know what form of constitution, or polity, was most stable. As a scientist, his first step was to formulate his problem in the form of a question amenable to comparative analysis (e.g. what are the causes of political instability?). Then he dispatched his students to collect case histories of city-state constitutions. Having obtained these case histories, he proceeded to classify them in terms of three relevant (to him) criteria:

1. number of rulers: kingship, aristocracy, polity (corresponding deviations being tyranny, oligarchy, democracy);
2. modes of operation: oligarchic or democratic;
3. class structure: types of distribution of power among classes.

He then related the results of his classification to stability and instability, to see which types of polities, in terms of number of rulers, mode of operation and class structure, were most or least stable. He found, on the basis of the evidence as classified, that the least stable forms of city-state government were either pure democracies or pure oligarchies, whereas the most stable city-states were those in which power was either held by a strong middle class, if there was one, or shared between classes, as in democratic oligarchies or oligarchic democracies. After further analysis of his results he came up with generalisations consistent with his evidence which provided an explanation for the causes of stability and instability. There are at least half a dozen ways to compare, but the basic logic of the enterprise of comparative politics as a technique of inquiry is clearly illustrated in Aristotle's work. This is so despite the fact that his *Politics* also contains argument (especially with Plato) and assertions unsupported by evidence, and it is frequently unclear where empirical evidence stops and assertion begins.

The formulation of a question or research project, the collection and classification of relevant empirical data, and correlation and analysis leading to explanatory generalisations have remained important features in the practice of comparative politics to the present day. Those who engage in the exercise are not without their critics, and indeed there is considerable discussion in the current literature on a wide range of problems involved in doing such analysis well, or the folly of attempting it at all. The volume of such discussion and lively polemic on comparative methodologies and alternative theoretical approaches is such that one sometimes feels that political scientists are more preoccupied with thinking about how to approach political problems than in actually working on them. One is reminded of A. G. Keller's jibe about the man who is endlessly packing a suitcase for a journey that never takes place.

These reflections were uppermost in our minds as we prepared this Reader. We wished first to give special attention to examples of scholars actually doing comparative analysis of a fairly straightforward kind; these examples serve as a means of entrée, for beginning students, to a consideration of the very real problems of method and theory that can be encountered in such work. It is usual to reverse this order, to start with theory and method (frequently divorced from practice). The fact that our way of introducing the subject of comparative politics is unusual (probably unique) is our main justification for adding yet another Reader to the dozens already in existence. This approach to the subject is also the main consideration behind the title of this book and its table of contents.

The book opens in Section 1 with brief considerations of the meaning of two words: politics and comparison. It then touches in a preliminary way on the nature of comparative government and politics as a discipline of study. The Reader as a whole is, in an important sense, exploring the question: what is comparative politics? This first section is meant to serve as an opening shot, a means of getting one's bearings.

Examples of the practice of comparative politics are found in Section 2. We have ranged rather widely to find appropriate selections, and in the end we had to interpret our self-imposed brief more loosely than we would have liked. The fact that we had difficulty finding appropriate examples is due in part to the constraints of a Reader format; much of the practice of comparative politics is located in more lengthy books or monographs (a fact that points up the difficulties and complexities of comparative political analysis) whereas Readers are, by nature perhaps, collections of shorter pieces. But the main reason, as we said before, is the current preoccupation in the literature with packing suitcases rather than going on trips.

The selections in Section 3 identify and discuss some of the problems, particularly of data and method, that crop up in comparative politics. Problems that receive attention include non-comparability, bias, subjectivity, faulty classification and concept misformation. Critiques of method inevitably raise larger issues, such as whether or not one can or should be neutral or objective when doing comparative analysis and, even more generally, whether or not a science of comparative politics is possible. There is a vast literature on the collecting of data and scientific method, and the selections here are meant to serve only as illustrations of a few of the problems and issues involved.

Section 4 opens with two essays specially commissioned for this Reader. The first outlines major strategies and theories in the field. Two important points are made: first, questions of correct approach are an integral part of comparative analysis; second, some approaches are more useful than others for certain types and levels of problems. The second essay mounts a broad critique of main-stream comparative politics as practised in the Anglo-Saxon world. This essay points to limitations and biases within the field by comparing its strategy and theory to Idealist, Weberian, and Marxist approaches. The other two selections in Section 4 bring out additional issues about strategy and theory that are discussed between political scientists in the literature.

Finally, we want to stress that the division of the Reader into four sections is artificial and meant only to serve the purposes of exposition. The practice of comparative politics cannot be separated from discussions of method and theory. Most political scientists do both. Nor can problems of method and theory be usefully examined in isolation from each other. Theory and method come together when one is engaged in the practice of comparative politics.

SECTION I

What is comparative politics?

There is no snappy answer to this question. If forced to provide one, we would say that it refers to a combination of appropriate method, strategy and theoretical approach by which one seeks generalisations that provide explanations related to particular problems or questions about politics. But this is inadequate. There is in principle no limit to methods, strategies and theoretical approaches that could be used. The reason is that the appropriate ones depend on the kind of question being asked. Since there is virtually no limit to the questions about politics that can be asked, there can be no clear boundary drawn round the field of comparative politics. And where there is no boundary, there can be no definition.

Although we can offer no formal definition of comparative politics, we can give examples and indicate the kinds of things that get talked about in the literature. This is what the Reader as a whole does, without, of course, claiming to cover all the ground or arrange the material in order of importance.

The selections in Section 1, which are quite straightforward, deal in an introductory way with politics and comparisons, and then with the two notions in combination. It is perhaps worth noting that Dahl's definition of politics, although a standard one, is only one of many. He mentions several others, and there are other ones not mentioned. Nevertheless, his discussion of the central concept in this Reader provides a useful beginning; further discussion of the meaning and nature of politics occurs frequently at various points throughout the Reader. Many political scientists (including Dahl), when discussing the nature of politics, refer explicitly to the influence of Max Weber's earlier formulation on their thinking. That is why we have included the selection from Weber. The piece by Macridis on the nature of comparison and Almond's 'Comparative politics' entry in the new *International Encyclopedia of the Social Sciences* (almost always a useful place to begin, by the way) are what they say they are and require no comment here. Finer's discussion of the comparative study of government reveals that comparative politics and comparative government share common ground. We take the position that there is not much point in trying to separate them. Hence government and politics come together in this Reader. The last two sentences in Finer's piece, and Section 1, make the point that the comparative study of government has always been a complicated undertaking and its findings fluid, and the best one can do in the circumstances is to try. Section 2 contains examples of people who did just that.

I

R. A. Dahl   What is politics?—I

Excerpts from 'What is politics?', in *Modern Political Analysis*, 3rd edn, Prentice-Hall, 1976, Ch. 1, pp. 1–11.

NATURE OF THE POLITICAL ASPECT

What distinguishes the political aspect of human society from other aspects? What are the characteristics of a political system as distinct, say, from an economic system? Although students of politics have never entirely agreed on answers to these questions, they tend to agree on certain key points. Probably no one would quarrel with the notion that a political system is a pattern of political relationships. But what is a political relationship?

On this question, as on many others, an important, though not always entirely clear, place to start is Aristotle's *Politics* (written ca. 335–332 BC). In the first book of the *Politics,* Aristotle argues against those who say that all kinds of authority are identical and seeks to distinguish the authority of the political leader in a political association, or polis, from other forms of authority, such as the master over the slave, the husband over the wife and the parents over the children.

Aristotle takes for granted, however, that at least one aspect of a political association is the existence of *authority* or *rule*. Indeed, Aristotle defines the polis, or political association, as the 'most sovereign and inclusive association' and a constitution, or polity, as 'the organisation of a polis, in respect of its offices generally, but especially in respect of that particular office which is sovereign in all issues' (1962, pp. 1, 110). One of Aristotle's criteria for classifying constitutions is the portion of the citizen body in which final *authority* or *rule* is located.

Ever since Aristotle's time, the notion has been widely shared that a political relationship in some way involves authority, ruling or

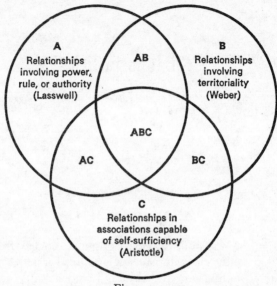

Figure 1.1

power. For example, one of the most influential modern social scientists, the German scholar Max Weber (1864–1920), postulated that an association should be called political 'if and in so far as the enforcement of its order is carried out continually within a given territorial area by the application and threat of physical force on the part of the administrative staff'. Thus, although Weber emphasised the territorial aspect of a political association, like Aristotle he specified that a relationship of authority or rule was one of its essential characteristics (1947, pp. 154, 145–53).

To take a final example, a leading contemporary political scientist, Harold Lasswell, defines 'political science, as an empirical discipline, [as] the study of the shaping and sharing of power' and 'a political act [as] one performed in power perspectives' (1950, pp. xiv, 240).

The areas of agreement and disagreement in the positions held by Aristotle, Weber, and Lasswell on the nature of politics are illustrated by Figure 1. Aristotle, Weber, and Lasswell, and almost all other political scientists agree that political relationships are to be found somewhere within circle A, the set of relationships involving power, rule or authority. Lasswell calls everything in A political, by definition. Aristotle and Weber, on the other hand, define the term 'political' so as to require one or more additional characteristics, indicated by circles B and C. For example, to Weber the domain of the political would not be everything inside A or everything inside B (territoriality) but everything in the area of overlap, AB, involving both rule *and* territoriality. Although Aristotle is less clear than either Weber or Lasswell on the point, doubtless he would limit the domain of the political even further—e.g., to relationships in associations capable of self-sufficiency (C). Hence, to Aristotle, 'politics' would be found only in the area ABC.

Clearly, everything that Aristotle and Weber would call political, Lasswell would too. But Lasswell would consider as political some things that Weber and Aristotle might not: a business firm or a trade union, for example, would have 'political' aspects. Let us therefore boldly define a political system as *any persistent pattern of human relationships that involves, to a significant extent, control, influence, power or authority.*

THE UBIQUITY OF POLITICS

Admittedly, this definition is very broad. Indeed, it means that many associations that most people ordinarily do not regard as 'political' possess political systems: private clubs, business firms, labour unions, religious organisations, civic groups, primitive tribes, clans, perhaps even families. Three considerations may help clarify the unfamiliar notion that almost every human association has a political aspect:

1. In common parlance we speak of the 'government' of a club, a firm and so on. In fact, we may even describe such a government as dictatorial, democratic, representative or authoritarian; and we often hear about 'politics' and 'politicking' going on in these associations.
2. A political system is only *one* aspect of an association. When we say that a person is a doctor, or a teacher or a farmer, we do not assume that he is *only* a doctor, *only* a teacher, *only* a farmer. No human association is exclusively political in all its aspects. People experience many relationships other than power and authority: love, respect, dedication, shared beliefs and so on.
3. Our definition says virtually nothing about human *motives*. It definitely does not imply that in every political system people are driven by powerful inner needs to rule others, that leaders passionately want authority or that politics is inherently a fierce struggle for power. Conceivably, relationships of authority could exist even among people of whom none had a passion for power, or in situations

where people who most ardently thirsted for authority had the least chance of acquiring it. Thus the Zuni Indians of the American Southwest are reported to have had a very strong sense that power-seeking was illicit and power-seekers must not be given power (Benedict, 1934). Closer to our own experience is the not uncommon view among members of various American private organisations that those who want most intensely to head the organisation are least suited to do so, while the most suitable are among those who least want the job. But whatever the evidence from anthropology or folklore may be, the central point is this: our highly general definition of a political system makes practically no assumptions as to the nature of human motives. Despite its breadth, the definition helps us make some critical distinctions that are often blurred in ordinary discussions.

Politics and economics

Political analysis deals with power, rule or authority. Economics concerns itself with scarce resources or the production and distribution of goods and services. Politics is one aspect of a great variety of human institutions; economics is another aspect. Hence an economist and a political scientist might both study the same concrete institution—the Federal Reserve system, for example, or the budget. But the economist would be concerned primarily with problems involving scarcity and the use of scarce resources, and the political scientist would deal primarily with problems involving relationships of power, rule or authority. Like most distinctions between subjects of intellectual inquiry, however, that between politics and economics is not perfectly sharp.

Political systems and economic systems

Many people indiscriminately apply terms like 'democracy', 'dictatorship', 'capitalism' and 'socialism' to both political and economic systems. This tendency to confuse political with economic systems stems from the lack of a standardised set of definitions, from ignorance of the historical origins of these terms, and in some cases from a desire to exploit a highly favourable or unfavourable political term like 'democracy' or 'dictatorship' in order to influence attitudes toward economic systems.

It follows, however, that the political aspects of an institution are not the same as its economic aspects. Historically, the terms 'democracy' and 'dictatorship' usually have referred to political systems, whereas 'capitalism' and 'socialism' have referred to economic institutions. From the way the terms have been used historically, the following definitions are appropriate:

1. A democracy is a political system in which the opportunity to participate in decisions is widely shared among all adult citizens.
2. A dictatorship is a political system in which the opportunity to participate in decisions is restricted to a few.
3. Capitalism is an economic system in which most major economic activities are performed by privately owned and controlled firms.
4. Socialism is an economic system in which most major activities are performed by agencies owned by the government or society.

Each pair of terms, democracy–dictatorship, capitalism–socialism, implies a dichotomy, and dichotomies are often unsatisfactory. In fact, many political systems are neither wholly democratic nor wholly dictatorial; in many countries private and governmental operations are mixed together in all sorts of complex ways. These mixtures not only demonstrate the shortcomings of the dichotomy 'capitalism–socialism' but also emphasize the fact that some institutions and processes can be viewed as part of the economic system for certain purposes and as part of the political system for others. The point to remember is that in spite of, or even because of, this intermixing it has proved to be intellectually fruitful to distinguish some aspects of life as 'economic' and other aspects as 'political'.

Government and state

In every society, people tend to develop more or less standard expectations about social behaviour in various situations. One learns how to behave as a host or a guest, a parent or grandparent, a 'good loser', a soldier, a bank clerk, a prosecutor, a judge, and so on. Patterns like these, in which a number of people share roughly similar expectations about behaviour in particular situations, are called *roles*. We all play various roles and frequently shift from one role to another rapidly.

Whenever a political system is complex and stable, political roles develop. Perhaps the most obvious political roles are played by persons who create, interpret and enforce rules that are binding on members of the political system. These roles are *offices*, and the collection of offices in a political system constitutes the government of that system. At any given moment, of course, these offices, or roles, are (aside from vacancies) filled by particular individuals, concrete persons . . . But in many systems the roles remain much the same even when they are played by a succession of individuals. To be sure, different actors may—and usually do—interpret the role of Hamlet or Othello in different ways, sometimes in radically different ways. So, too, with political roles . . .

But—a reader might ask—in defining 'government' as we have just done, don't we create a new problem for ourselves? If there is a great variety of political systems—from trade unions and universities to countries and international organisations—what about *the* Government? After all, the United States, as in most other countries, when you speak of *the* Government everyone seems to know what you mean. Of all the governments in the various associations of a particular territory, generally one is in some way recognised as *the* Government. How does the Government differ from other governments? Consider three possible answers:

1. *The* Government pursues 'higher' and 'nobler' purposes than other governments. There are at least three difficulties with this proposal. First, because people disagree about what the 'higher' or 'nobler' purposes are, and even whether a given purpose is or is not being pursued at any given moment, this criterion might not be very helpful in trying to decide whether this or that government is *the* Government. Second, despite the fact that people often disagree over how to rank purposes or values and may even hold that *the* Government is pursuing evil ends, they still agree on what is and what is not the Government. An anarchist does not doubt that he is being oppressed by *the* Government. Third, what about bad Governments? For example, do democratic and totalitarian Governments *both* pursue noble purposes? That point seems logically absurd.

Our first proposed answer, then, confuses the problem of defining Government with the more difficult and more important task of deciding on the criteria for a 'good' or 'just' Government. Before anyone can decide what the *best* Government is, he must know first what the Government is.

2. Aristotle suggested another possibility: *the* Government is distinguished by the character of the association to which it pertains— namely, a political association that is self-sufficient, in the sense that it possesses all the qualities and resources necessary for a good life. This definition suffers from some of the same difficulties as the first. Moreover, if it were strictly applied, we should have to conclude that no Governments exist! Aristotle's idealised interpretation of the city-state was very far from reality even in his day. Athens was not self-sufficient culturally, economically or militarily. In fact, she was quite unable to guarantee her own peace or independence; without allies,

she could not even maintain the freedom of her own citizens. What was true of the Greek city-states is of course equally true today.

3. *The* Government is *any government that successfully upholds a claim to the exclusive regulation of the legitimate use of physical force in enforcing its rules within a given territorial area.*[1] The political system made up of the residents of that territorial area and the Government of the area is a 'State'.[2]

This definition immediately suggests three questions:

1. Can't individuals who aren't Government officials ever legitimately use force? What about parents who spank their children? The answer is, of course, that the Government of a State does not necessarily *monopolise* the use of force, but it has the exclusive authority to set the limits within which force may legitimately be used. The Governments of most States permit private individuals to use force in some circumstances. For example, although many Governments forbid cruel or excessive punishment of children, most permit parents to spank their own offspring. Boxing is permitted in many countries.

2. What about criminals who go uncaught? After all, no country is free of assault, murder, rape, and other forms of violence, and criminals sometimes escape the law. The point is, however, that the claim of the Government of the State to regulate violence and force is successfully upheld, in the sense that few people would seriously contest the exclusive right of the State to punish criminals. Although criminal violence exists, it is not legitimate.

3. What about circumstances of truly widespread violence and force, such as civil war or revolution? In this case no single answer will suffice. (Remember the disadvantages of dichotomous definitions.) For brief periods, no State may exist at all, since no government is capable of upholding its claim to the exclusive regulation of the legitimate use of physical force. Several governments may contest for the privilege over the same territory. Or what was formerly a territory ruled by the Government of one State may now be divided and ruled by the Governments of two or more States, with grey stateless areas where they meet.

[1] Adapted from Weber (1947), p. 154, by substituting 'exclusive regulation' for 'monopoly' and 'rules' for 'its order.'
[2] Capitalized here to avoid confusion with constituent states in federal systems.

We can be reasonably sure of one thing: When large numbers of people in a particular territory begin to doubt or deny the claim of the Government to regulate force, then the existing State is in peril of dissolution.

REFERENCES

ARISTOTLE (1962) *The Politics of Aristotle,* ed. Ernest Barker, Oxford University Press.
BENEDICT, R. (1934) *Patterns of Culture,* Houghton Mifflin.
KAPLAN, A. (1964) *The Conduct of Inquiry,* Chandler.
LASSWELL, H. D. and KAPLAN, A. (1950) *Power and Society,* Yale University Press.
WEBER, MAX (1947) *The Theory of Social and Economic Organizations,* trans. A. M. Henderson and Talcott Parsons, Oxford University Press.

2

Max Weber   What is politics?—II

Excerpt from 'Politics as a vocation', in *From Max Weber*, ed. H. H. Gerth
C. Wright Mills, Routledge and Kegan Paul, Paperback Edition 1970,
pp. 77–8.*

What do we understand by politics? The concept is extremely broad
and comprises any kind of *independent* leadership in action. One
speaks of the currency policy of the banks, of the discounting policy
of the Reichsbank, of the strike policy of the trade union; one may
speak of the educational policy of a municipality or a township, of the
policy of the president of a voluntary association, and, finally, even of
the policy of a prudent wife who seeks to guide her husband. Our
reflections are, of course, not based upon such a broad concept. We wish
to understand by politics only the leadership, or the influencing of the
leadership, of a *political* association, hence today, of a *state*.

But what is a 'political' association? What is a 'state'? Sociologically,
the state cannot be defined in terms of its ends. There is scarcely any
task that some political association has not taken in hand, and there is
no task that one could say has always been exclusive and peculiar to
those associations which are designated as political ones: today the
state, or historically, those associations which have been the predecessors
of the modern state. Ultimately, one can define the modern state only
in terms of the specific *means* peculiar to it, as to every political association, namely, the use of physical force.

'Every state is founded on force', said Trotsky at Brest-Litovsk.
That is indeed right. If no social institutions existed which knew the
use of violence, then the concept of 'state' would be eliminated, and a
condition would emerge that could be designated as 'anarchy', in the

*'Politik als Beruf', *Gesammelte Politische Schriften* (Munich, 1921),
pp. 396–450. Originally a speech at Munich University, 1917, published in
1919 by Duncker and Humboldt, Munich.

specific sense of this word. Of course, force is certainly not the normal or the only means of the state—nobody says that—but force is a means specific to the state. Today the relation between the state and violence is an especially intimate one. In the past, the most varied institutions—beginning with the sib [kinship group]—have known the use of physical force as quite normal. Today, however, we have-to say that a state is a human community that (successfully) claims the *monopoly of the legitimate use of physical force* within a given territory. Note that 'territory' is one of the characteristics of the state. Specifically, at the present time, the right to use physical force is ascribed to other institutions or to individuals only to the extent to which the state permits it. The state is considered the sole source of the 'right' to use violence. Hence, 'politics' for us means striving to share power or striving to influence the distribution of power, either among states or among groups within a state.

This corresponds essentially to ordinary usage. When a question is said to be a 'political' question, when a cabinet minister or an official is said to be a 'political' official, or when a decision is said to be 'politically' determined, what is always meant is that interests in the distribution, maintenance, or transfer of power are decisive for answering the questions and determining the decision or the official's sphere of activity. He who is active in politics strives for power either as a means in serving other aims, ideal or egoistic, or as 'power for power's sake', that is, in order to enjoy the prestige-feeling that power gives.

Like the political institutions historically preceding it, the state is a relation of men dominating men, a relation supported by means of legitimate (i.e. considered to be legitimate) violence. If the state is to exist, the dominated must obey the authority claimed by the powers that be.

3

R. C. Macridis — The nature of comparative analysis

Excerpt from 'The nature of comparative analysis' in *The Study of Comparative Government*, Random House, 1955, pp. 1-3.

Comparative analysis is an integral part of the study of politics. The comparative study of politics suggests immediately the laboratory of a scientist. It provides us with the opportunity to discuss specific phenomena in the light of different historical and social backgrounds. It suggests variables of a rather complex order that can be dissociated from the cultural background and studied comparatively. Political parties, for instance, will differ depending upon the economic development of a given system. Political consensus may be functionally interrelated with political ideology, which in turn can be understood only with reference to the economic and social configuration of the country. More specifically, however, the function of comparative study is to identify uniformities and differences and to explain them. Explanation requires the development of theories in the light of which similarities and differences come, so to speak, to life. They then lose their adventitious character and assume a significance that has a causal, i.e. explanatory, character. Phenomena that have mystified men ever since Herodotus observed the variety of human customs and ways tend to fall into place.

Comparative study has also an important role to play in the more traditional approach to the study of politics in which fact and value are interrelated in the scheme of the investigator. Here the parallel comparisons of systems may provide us with important clues about the implementation of values and policies. The need for social legislation, for instance, and its compatibility with political freedom may be studied with reference to political systems which have both, so that the investigation may reveal a clear picture of what such legislation entails and of how it can be related to democratic political institutions. The development of parliamentary institutions and democratic practices in a number of former colonies, when subjected to careful comparative analysis, suggests the conditioning factors that account for the development of such institutions and more particularly for the concrete forms that such a development assumes.

The comparative study of political institutions and systems, therefore, entails the comparison of variables against a background of uniformity, either actual or analytical, for the purpose of discovering causal factors that account for variations. More generally it has a threefold function: (1) to explain such variables in the light of analytical schemes and to develop a body of verified knowledge; (2) to appraise policy measures and to identify problem areas and trends; (3) to reach a stage where prediction of the institutional trends or processes is possible.

This conception of the role of comparative analysis, however, raises the following question: Is not 'comparative government' a very old discipline indeed? Political speculation began with a realisation of contrasts—contrasts between the political institutions and practices of various Greek city-states and between those of the Greeks and those of the barbarians. Long before it was uttered, the Greeks had discovered the truth of Pascal's aphorism that what is true on one side of the Pyrennean mountains may be false on the other. Aristotle was the first student of comparative politics. His study of the various constitutions of ancient Greece was truly comparative, particularly if we recall that Aristotle defined 'constitution' in broad terms: it was the mode of life, which included not only the political institutions of a community but the distribution of wealth, the religious myths, and the education and leisure of its citizens. His approach was also systematic in at least two senses. First, he had a general frame of reference in the light of which he observed his facts—this was his notion that the central phenomenon of politics, or rather the central concept under which political institutions could be studied, was that of citizen participation. Second, Aristotle used the three so-called laws enunciated in the nineteenth century by historians and sociologists—the law of imitation, the law of diffusion, and the law of similar causes—in order to explain uniformities and similarities.

It is equally true that throughout the eighteenth and nineteenth centuries comparison was constantly 'in the air'. It was called for by the works of the *philosophes*; by the founder of modern sociology, Auguste Comte; by the theories of evolution developed by Lamarck and Darwin and adopted by Walter Bagehot (1873) in England and by many others. It was part and parcel of the school of historical jurisprudence founded in Germany by Savigny and was also essential to the philosophic systems of Herder and Hegel, Schiller and others. Rousseauian romanticism had evoked the interest of philosophers in the non-Western societies, while the rapid development of colonialism thrust upon both policy-maker and student of politics new questions that called for investigation. Karl Marx's theories provided a frame of reference for the comparative investigation of political systems in the light of a generalised concept according to which the mode of production in any given system shapes the political and social institutions.

The remarkable thing indeed is that the eighteenth and nineteenth centuries abounded in theories that claimed to be 'explanatory' or 'problem-solving'. They were also based, like all political theories, on certain moral assumptions. Marxist philosophy, for instance, was both scientific in the proper sense of the word, since it postulated a broad frame of reference about human actions in the light of which hypotheses could be evolved and tested and moral, in the sense that it affirmed a desirable goal. Bagehot in his *Physics and Politics* also postulates a frame of reference and introduces a number of hypotheses in the light of which empirical investigation of institutions could take place, but there was an underlying moral theory of progress in his works. The school of historical jurisprudence formulated a theory of law that was suggestive, to say the least, for hypothetical formulations and empirical study. So were the works of Henry Maine (1891). The hypotheses Maine developed as to the origin of the state, the emergence of individual liberty, and the institutional implementation freedom found in the state, were indeed theories that should have been taken more seriously by political scientists. The curious thing is that they were not. Slowly political science, and particularly the comparative study of politics, shifted to the study of institutions of separate countries; it became descriptive; it shied away from theoretical formulations; it scrutinised the formal external paraphernalia of politics—constitutions, legislatures, administration, decisions of courts and the like. It evaded the issue of what the function of politics was in society. Political theory became moral theory and 'political science' became nothing more than an ontology of political forms and institutions.

The comparative study of politics is beginning only now to enter a new stage which reflects in essence the progressive systematic orientation in the study of politics. It is beginning to assume a central role in empirically oriented study.

REFERENCES

BAGEHOT, W. (1873) *Physics and Politics*, Appleton.
MAINE, H. (1891) *Ancient Law*, Murray.

4

G. *A. Almond*   Comparative politics

Reprinted from 'Comparative politics' in *International Encyclopedia of the Social Sciences*, ed. Sills, New York, Macmillan, 1968, vol. 13, pp. 331–6.

The *Encyclopedia of the Social Sciences*, published between 1930 and 1935, contained no special article on comparative politics or comparative government. There is an article 'Government', followed by articles on individual governments; but no explicit comparative themes are treated, nor do they appear elsewhere under other topics. Much of the great tradition of political theory, in contrast, is essentially comparative, classificatory, typological. Comparison is such an intrinsic methodological assumption that it is not separated out as a specific subfield or approach. This background suggests the thesis of this article: that contemporary comparative politics is a *movement* rather than a subfield or subdiscipline.

The case for comparative politics as a movement is quite persuasive. We start from a tradition in which comparison is an intrinsic aspect of political theory, then move to a situation in which it practically disappears along with the creative political theory of which it is a part, and arrive at the contemporary situation, in which it is a salient and separate part of the political science curriculum.

THE THEORY OF DEMOCRATIC PROGRESS

How can we explain this development? Perhaps we may begin by commenting on the fate of the Aristotelian classification scheme and theory of political change in the history of political science. On the surface it would appear that this Aristotelian macrotheoretical tradition continues straight on through subsequent millennia, up to and including Dahl's *Modern Political Analysis* (1963). And yet it would be misleading to say that the Aristotelian approach to comparison continues as a dominant intellectual construct into present-day political science. Enlightenment political theory moved away from the relativistic and cyclical approach of Aristotle to a unilinear approach to political history and political development. This is particularly marked in British, French, and American political theory, where at first democracy was justified as the best form of government on the basis of natural law and social contrast, and then, as the democratic revolution spread, as the inevitable direction of human history. Locke and Rousseau are typical of the first approach to democratisation, while Tocqueville is among the first to view it as historically inevitable. His *Democracy in America* (1835) reflects a growing conviction that democratic politics is the political form of the future. America is the laboratory from which he seeks to derive some sense of the political, social, moral, and cultural consequences of this inevitable democratisation. Ostrogorskii (1902) focused on the development of democracy in Britain and the United States, convinced that this was to be the trend of the future but deeply troubled by the growing elitism and bureaucratism of the mass political party in Britain and America. The important point is that Tocqueville and Ostrogorskii were both concerned with comparisons within the democratic framework and were interested in non-democratic systems principally as base lines against which democratic systems can be evaluated.

The influence of social and political setting on political theory is reflected vividly in the contrasting reactions to democratic development of Woodrow Wilson (1889) and Bryce (1921) and those of Pareto (1916), Michels (1911), and Mosca (1896). Both the Anglo-American theorists and the continental European theorists reject the Aristotelian relativistic typology and cyclical theory of political change. Pareto, Michels, and Mosca argue that all political rule is oligarchical or elitist, regardless of its formal legal or ideological characteristics, while the British and American political theorists see a sweeping historical movement in the direction of constitutional and democratic forms. Woodrow Wilson's *The State* (1889) is an interesting syncretic product. On the one hand, it shows the great influence of nineteenth-century German political theory, with its massive ethnographic and historical learning, and the persistence of the Aristotelian categories, but at the same time the work is suffused with an evolutionary, democratic faith. In Bryce's *Modern Democracies* (1921) faith turns into conviction. He speaks in his introduction of '... the universal acceptance of democracy as the normal and natural form of government'.

Thus, on the eve of the development of American political science as a university-based, professional discipline, the theory of democratic progress dominated the field and justified a loss of interest in the classification and comparison of types of political systems or in the general theory of political change. The answers to these questions were viewed as self-evident, and normative speculation about the relative value of different kinds of political systems, and even empirical study of nondemocratic political systems, were pointless, or at best were useful, in the language employed in W. B. Munro's preface to his *The Governments of Europe* (1925), to make possible the '... comprehension of the daily news from abroad'.

One might say, therefore, that it was the Enlightenment itself, and in particular the parochial American 'populistic' and 'progressive' version of that faith, which resulted in an attenuation of interest in political comparison and typologies, as well as of the political theory of which that interest was a part.

Broadly speaking, this unilinear evolutionary theory of political systems and political development characterised American political science as it began to develop into a substantial university-based discipline in the first decades of the twentieth century. As separate departments of political science began to appear in these decades, the principal stress in the curriculum was on American politics. Research and teaching proliferated around themes having to do with problems of American democracy. The field of public administration was essentially concerned with the development of a professional public service and with the introduction of rational organisational and management practices in American government. Constitutional law was concerned principally with the conservatism of the Supreme Court and with what some constitutional lawyers thought of as the usurpation by the judiciary of law-making and constitution-making functions. The 'real' functioning of the Congress and the executive also were fields of teaching and research interest. But the distinctive development during this period was the study of the informal, or the nonlegal, aspects of politics—the role of political parties, the political machine, the lobby and pressure groups, and the popular press. While students in these various fields were concerned with generalising about these phenomena, their theories were based essentially on American experience, and practically the whole burden of the research effort in the growing profession of political science was on American political institutions and processes.

The older tradition of comparison and political theory survived in the work of such scholars as Carl Friedrich and Herman Finer. Both

Finer's *Theory and Practice of Modern Government* (1932) and Friedrich's *Constitutional Government and Democracy* (1937) are works in the older political science tradition. They are comparative, and they treat varieties of forms of government and of governmental institutions and processes in the context of some of the great themes of political theory. But it is of interest that both of these scholars focus their work predominantly on constitutional, democratic systems.

This approach to political science teaching and research was characteristic of American political science in the first four decades of the twentieth century, roughly until the end of World War II. This was the time when the profession was developing its own departments of political science (or government) and when the membership of the American Political Science Association was expanding from around two hundred at the turn of the century to roughly three thousand at the end of World War II. The American profession consisted in the main of students of American public administration, American public law, American political parties and pressure groups, Congress and the executive, and American state and local government. International relations and European governments were essentially minor themes, and students of non-Western political systems were oddities, working in isolation.

The breakdown of this pattern was the consequence of the frustration of Enlightenment expectations resulting from the spread of fascism and communism in the 1920s and 1930s and increasing with the emergence of communism in the post-World War II period as an unambiguously competing form of modernisation. Another factor making for the rejection of the earlier confidence in democratic development was the emergence in the post-World War II period of the many new nations of Asia, the Middle East, and Africa, with their confusing variety of cultural and structural patterns and developmental processes.

THE COMPARATIVE POLITICS MOVEMENT

Comparative politics as a movement in political science acquired momentum after World War II (Interuniversity Summer Seminar ... 1953; Herring 1953; Kahin, Pauker and Pye 1955; Macridis 1955; Almond 1956; Heckscher 1957; Neumann 1957; Rustow 1957; Apter 1958; Eckstein and Apter 1963). Among the principal intellectual influences which fed into it are (1) the growing body of data on non-Western political systems; (2) the introduction into foreign political studies of concepts and methods that had emerged in research on American political processes; (3) anthropological, psychological, and psychoanalytic theories of culture and personality; and (4) the concepts and insights of historical sociology and sociological theory.

Acquisition of non-Western data

During the 1950s young political scientists streamed into Asia, the Middle East, Africa, and—somewhat later—into Latin America, producing monographic studies often as sophisticated analytically as the best of American and European political studies. The dominance of the political science profession by Americanists and Europeanists began to be challenged by a young generation of political scientists whose field experience was non-Western. The requirements of their research gave them a sensitivity and a sophistication in the use of sociological and anthropological methods and theories that their Americanist and Europeanist colleagues often lacked (Apter 1955; 1961; Binder 1962; Pye 1962; Weiner 1962). Parliamentary institutions, bureaucracies, political parties, and interest groups in these new and developing nations often had quite a different significance than they had in Western nations, particularly the United States. Thus, in their search for the effective policy-making and policy-implementing processes in these nations they were led to look for their *functional* equivalents. 'System', 'process', and 'functional' concepts, anthropological field methods, and anthropological and sociological theory had a natural appeal to these students of non-Western political systems.

The behavioural movement

A second significant influence in the development of the comparative politics movement was the behavioural movement, which had its origins in studies of American electoral and political processes. One significant channel in this process of intellectual diffusion was the Committee on Political Behavior of the Social Science Research Council, which stimulated the organisation of the Committee on Comparative Politics, which in turn played an important role in diffusing into the field research in non-Western and European areas many of the insights and methodologies that had developed in American political studies. The principal contributions from American political studies adapted to studies of foreign areas were the 'process' frame of reference (Herring 1940; Schattschneider 1942; Key 1942; Truman 1951); the emphasis on the nonformal aspects of political processes—political parties, interest groups, media of communication, and public opinion (Ehrmann 1957; Eckstein 1960; Weiner 1962; LaPalombara 1964)—and the newer and more rigorous methodologies employed in the studies of elections and public opinion (Lazarsfeld, Berelson, and Gaudet 1944; Campbell, Gurin, and Miller 1954).

The culture and personality approach

A third influence feeding into the comparative politics movement was the so-called psycho-cultural approach developing out of the work of Freud and some of his disciples and the psycho-analytically oriented social scientists from the 1920s on, including such figures as Harold D. Lasswell (1930; 1948), Ruth Benedict (1934), Margaret Mead (1928–35), Abram Kardiner (1939), Ralph Linton (1945), and Nathan Leites (1948). Their work, particularly in response to World War II problems, on the German, Japanese, Russian, and American national characters, created a sensitivity among students in the comparative politics movement to these aspects of politics and public policy. The political culture approach in comparative politics was greatly influenced by this psycho-anthropological literature. It sought to relate cognitive and attitudinal patterns in national and subnational populations to the characteristics and functioning of political systems, through the use of cross-section survey methods, studies of particular elite groups, and the like (Almond and Verba 1963; Pye and Verba 1965).

Historical sociology and sociological theory

A fourth intellectual current was that of historical sociology and sociological theory. In particular, the work of such sociological theorists as Max Weber (1906–24; 1922), Ferdinand Tönnies (1887), Talcott Parsons, and Edward Shils (see Parsons and Shils 1951; Shils 1959–60) influenced the efforts of some of the newer students of comparative politics to develop theoretical frameworks capable of ordering and codifying the research results and the insights produced by this extraordinary empirical research effort. The system concepts of Talcott Parsons and of the information theorists influenced the work of a group of political theorists and students of comparative politics. These included the theoretical contributions of David Easton (1953; 1965), Karl Deutsch (1963), David Apter (1965), Gabriel A. Almond and James Coleman (1960), and Lucian Pye (1962; 1966).

ACHIEVEMENTS AND PROSPECTS

If one speculates about the future of the comparative politics movement, a number of points are suggested. In the first place, the need to codify the growing accumulation of research on political systems from all of the various culture areas of the world and at all levels of structural differentiation and secularisation has brought about a return to the classic themes of political theory. The classifications of Almond (1956), Shils (1959–60), Dahl (1963), Apter (1965), Almond and Coleman (1960), and others reflect a return to the Aristotelian tradition—but now with greater theoretical sophistication and with more, and more reliable, information. Similarly, the concern with theories of political development among these and other authors is again indicative of a return to the classic theoretical problems of political change. The future of this classificatory and developmental interest would appear to lie with political theory rather than with a special subdiscipline of comparative politics.

A second development brought about by the comparative politics movement is the breakdown in the parochialism of the theories of various special institutions and processes, such as bureaucracy (LaPalombara 1963; Riggs, 1964), political parties (Duverger, 1951; Neumann, 1956; LaPalombara and Weiner, 1966), interest groups, and the like. Here again, one cannot see a future in a comparative politics subdiscipline for these developments but, rather, in the more adequate development of theories of particular processes and institutions in the functioning of political systems.

Third, the studies of specific political systems now broadly grouped under the heading of comparative government and politics in most political science curricula are shifting from a configurative approach to one that employs schemes of classification, generic categories of a functional kind, and is illuminated by comparison. It makes no sense to include these studies of individual political systems under the heading of comparative politics, since all political systems will be treated comparatively, whether within the framework of theoretical courses, which will group them into classes and varieties, or in the more intensive analyses of individual cases, which will draw upon general classificatory and developmental theories, and upon specific institutional and process theories.

Another and more recent development in comparative politics would again seem to have long-run implications for the development of empirical and normative political theory rather than for the development of a special discipline of comparative politics. As political scientists have become increasingly concerned with the adaptation and transformation of political systems, and particularly with problems of public policy relating to the new nations, there has been an increasing tendency to focus on the interaction of whole political systems with their domestic and international environments, since it is at this level that it becomes possible to explain political change. This most recent development among students of comparative politics and political development holds out the prospect of bridging the discontinuity between empirical and normative political theories. As methodologies are developed that will make possible precise characterisation of the interaction of political systems with their environments, the problem of the ethical evaluation of political systems becomes more of a rigorous, empirically based exercise. This, of course, is not to say that empirical performance is the same thing as ethical evaluation. It can, however, provide the information essential to evaluation and can test hypotheses regarding the ethical properties of varieties of political systems.

Finally, the most recent preoccupation in the field of comparative politics—with political development and with the logic of a theory of resource allocation to effect political change—again holds out the prospect for the enrichment of political theory rather than for the future of a particular subdiscipline within the field. Thus, this interest too may be assimilated into a general body of political theory.

It is difficult to see, therefore, that comparative politics has a long-run future as a subdiscipline of political science. Rather, it would appear that, like the political behaviour movement which preceded it, its promise lies in enriching the discipline of political science as a whole.

REFERENCES

ALMOND, G. A. (1956) 'Comparative political systems', *Journal of Politics*, 18.
ALMOND, G. A., and COLEMAN, J. S., eds. (1960) *The Politics of the Developing Areas*, Princeton University Press.
ALMOND, G. A. and VERBA, S. (1963) *The Civic Culture: Political Attitudes and Democracy in Five Nations*, Princeton University Press.
APTER, D. E. (1955) *Ghana in Transition* (rev. edn.), Atheneum.
APTER, D. E. (1958) 'A comparative method for the study of politics', *American Journal of Sociology*, 64.
APTER, D. E. (1961) *The Political Kingdom of Uganda: a Study in Bureaucratic Nationalism*, Princeton University Press.
APTER, D. E. (1965) *The Politics of Modernization*, University of Chicago Press.
BENEDICT, R. (1934) *Patterns of Culture* (2nd edn.), Houghton Mifflin.
BERELSON, B., LAZARSFELD, P. F. and MCPHEE, W. N. (1954). *Voting a Study of Opinion Formation in a Presidential Campaign*, University of Chicago Press.
BINDER, L. (1962) *Iran: Political Development in a Changing Society*. Published under the auspices of the Near Eastern Center, University of California. University of California Press.
BRYCE, J. (1921) *Modern Democracies*, 2 vols., New York, Macmillan.
CAMPBELL, A., GURIN, G. and MILLER, W. F. (1954) *The Voter Decides*, Row, Peterson.

CAMPBELL, A. *et al.* (1960) *The American Voter:* see Michigan, University of, below.

DAHL, R. A. (1963) *Modern Political Analysis*, Prentice-Hall.

DEUTSCH, K. W. (1963) *The Nerves of Government: Models of Political Communication and Control*, New York, Free Press.

DUVERGER, M. (1951) *Political Parties: Their Organization and Activity in the Modern State.* (2nd English ed. rev.), Wiley.

EASTON, D. (1953) *The Political System: an Inquiry into the State of Political Science, Knopf.*

EASTON, D. (1965) *A Systems Analysis of Political Life*, Wiley.

ECKSTEIN, H. (1960) *Pressure Group Politics: the Case of the British Medical Association*, Stanford University Press; London: Allen & Unwin.

ECKSTEIN, H. and APTER, D. E., eds. (1963) *Comparative Politics: a Reader*, New York, Free Press.

EHRMANN, H. W. (1957) *Organized Business in France*, Princeton University Press.

FINER, H. (1932) *The Theory and Practice of Modern Government*, rev. edn., Holt.

FRIEDRICH, C. J. (1937) *Constitutional Government and Democracy: Theory and Practice in Europe and America*, rev. edn., Ginn.

HECKSCHER, G. (1957) *The Study of Comparative Government and Politics*, Allen & Unwin.

HERRING, E. P. (1940) *The Politics of Democracy: American Parties in Action*, Norton.

HERRING, E. P. (1953) 'On the study of government', *American Political Science Review*, 47.

INTERUNIVERSITY SUMMER SEMINAR ON POLITICAL BEHAVIOR, Social Science Research Council (1953), 'Research in comparative politics', *American Political Science Review*, 47.

KAHIN, G. MCT., PAUKER, G. J. and PYE, L. W. (1955) 'Comparative politics of non-western countries', *American Political Science Review*, 49.

KARDINER, A. (1939) *The Individual and His Society: the Psychodynamics of Primitive Social Organization*, Columbia University Press.

KEY, V. O. jr. (1942) *Politics, Parties and Pressure Groups*, 5th edn., New York, Crowell.

LAPALOMBARA, J. G. (ed. 1963) *Bureaucracy and Political Development*, Princeton University Press.

LAPALOMBARA, J. G. (1964) *Interest Groups in Italian Politics*, Princeton University Press.

LAPALOMBARA, J. G. and WEINER, M., eds. (1966) *Political Parties and Political Development*, Princeton University Press.

LASSWELL, H. D. (1930) *Psychopathology and Politics* (rev. edn.), Viking.

LASSWELL, H. D. (1930–51) *The Political Writings of Harold D. Lasswell*, New York, Free Press.

LASSWELL, H. D. (1948) *Power and Personality*, Norton.

LAZARSFELD, P. F., BERELSON, B. and GAUDET, H. (1944) *The People's Choice: How the Voter Makes Up His Mind in a Presidential Campaign*, (2nd ed.), Colombia University Press.

LEITES, N. (1948) 'Psycho-cultural hypotheses about political acts', *World Politics*, 1.

LINTON, R. (1945) *The Cultural Background of Personality*, Appleton.

LOCKE, J. (1690) *Two Treatises of Government*, Cambridge University Press, 1964: see especially 'Of Civil Government'.

MACRIDIS, R. C. (1955) *The Study of Comparative Government*, Doubleday.

MEAD, M. (1951) 'The study of national character', in D. Lerner and H. D. Lasswell, eds., *The Policy Sciences: Recent Developments in Scope and Method*, Stanford University Press.

MICHELS, R. (1911) *Political Parties: A Sociological Study of the Oligarchical Tendencies of Modern Democracy*; repr. Dover, 1959.

MICHIGAN, UNIVERSITY OF, SURVEY RESEARCH CENTER (1960) *The American Voter*, by A. Campbell *et al.*, Wiley.

MOSCA, G. (1896) *The Ruling Class*; repr. McGraw-Hill, 1939.

MUNRO, W. B. (1925) *The Governments of Europe*, New York, Macmillan.

NEUMANN, S., ed. (1956) *Modern Political Parties: Approaches to Comparative Politics*, University of Chicago Press.

NEUMANN, S. (1957) 'Comparative politics: a half-century appraisal', *Journal of Politics*, 19.

OSTROGORSKII, M. I. (1902) *Democracy and the Organization of Political Parties*, 2 vols., Macmillan.

PARETO, V. (1916) *The Mind and Society: A Treatise on General Sociology*, 4 vols., Dover, 1963.

PARSONS, T. and SHILS, E., eds. (1951) *Toward a General Theory of Action*, Harvard University Press.

PYE, L. W. (1962) *Politics, Personality, and Nation Building: Burma's Search for Identity*, Yale University Press.

PYE, L. W. (1966) *Aspects of Political Development: an Analytic Study*, Little, Brown.

PYE, L. W. and VERBA, H., eds. (1965) *Political Culture and Political Development*, Princeton University Press.

RIGGS, F. W. (1964) *Administration in Developing Countries*, Houghton Mifflin.

ROUSSEAU, J. J. (1792) *The Social Contract*; repr. Dent, 1961.

RUSTOW, D. A. (1957) 'New horizons for comparative politics', *World Politics*, 9.

SCHATTSCHNEIDER, E. F. (1942) *Party Government*, repr. Holt, 1960.

SHILS, E. (1959–60) *Political Development in the New States*, The Hague, Mouton, 1962.

TOCQUEVILLE, A. DE (1835) *Democracy in America*. 2 vols., repr. Knopf, 1945.

TÖNNIES, F. (1887) *Community and Society*, trans. and ed. C. P. Loomis, Michigan State University Press, 1957.

TRUMAN, D. B. (1951) *The Governmental Process: Political Interests and Public Opinion*; repr. Knopf, 1962.

WEBER, M. (1906–24) *From Max Weber: Essays in Sociology*, trans. and ed. H. H. Gerth and C. Wright Mills, New York, Oxford University Press, 1946.

WEBER, M. (1962) *The Theory of Social and Economic Organization*, ed. T. Parsons, New York, Free Press, 1957.

WEINER, M. (1962) *The Politics of Scarcity: Public Pressure and Political Response in India*, University of Chicago.

WILSON, W. (1889) *The State: Elements of Historical and Practical Politics*, Heath, 1918.

5

S. E. *Finer*   Comparative government

Excerpts from *Comparative Government*, Basic Books, 1970, ch. 1, pp. 37–40.

What is Government? It is a standardised arrangement for taking decisions affecting the group and for giving effect to them. Most organised human groups have such arrangements, whether they are small primary face-to-face groups like the family, or the territorial state itself. The government of units like the family, the Church, the trade union or the firm may properly be called 'private' government. It is, however, to what might by contrast be called 'public' government, that is to say, the government of the territorial state, that the term 'government' is commonly applied ...

Why have Government? The answer that has been given to this is that government is a response to political predicaments, i.e. to situations where the group in question (in this case the territorial association called the state) *has* to adopt a common policy, but where rival bodies of members advocate policies which are mutually exclusive. To secure a common policy, the condition of self-division must be replaced by one of unanimity. The creation of this admittedly artificial and it may be fragile unanimity is effectuated by the exercise of political power, ranging from affection and persuasion at one end of the spectrum to coercion at the other. Government, as an arrangement for taking the common decision, defines and channels these exercises of power. In the territorial association of the state, various groupings, as we saw, provide the members of that state with rival focuses of authority and with alternative sets of sanctions; the mutually exclusive policies of these groupings are, precisely, what generate the demand for a common public policy and formulate its alternatives—in a word, then, make 'public' government necessary or at least desirable; finally, those who govern these groupings seek to further their exclusive aims either by becoming the governors of the state or at least by getting those governors to espouse their own aims and objectives as opposed to those of their rivals, so as to ensure that their own policies will be translated into general rules that bind the whole of the community with the full moral authority and the penal sanctions of the state behind them. Government, as a set of standardised arrangements for taking and effectuating group decisions, cannot be considered in isolation from these 'private governments' because it is a response to the problem which their conflicting interests and attitudes have created. These interests and attitudes of the groups and associations, the relationships existing between such groups and associations, condition the form of the arrangements, who shall handle them, what support or resistance these persons or the arrangements themselves shall receive, and the issues that are to be decided under or by them. Government is a regulator of society so that its form, its scope and its procedures are all to greater or lesser extent outcomes of that society.

Hence arises the study of 'comparative government'. For the form, the procedures, the scope of government differ from one society to another, often very widely. It is the task of comparative government to establish, first how—and then, as far as possible, *why*.

The 1966 *Statesman's Year Book* listed 122 different independent states and, even as these words were written, no less than four new states were in the process of being formed. Clearly the task of comparing and contrasting all of these in every respect would be difficult —and would be so confusing as not to be rewarding. Fortunately no such extended comparison is necessary. Although each and every one of these states differs from the others, there are family resemblances; and the most direct practical way of going about our business is to group these states into their respective 'families' and compare and contrast these.

Unhappily, though this disposes of some difficulties, it also creates new ones. In one sense all these 122 states are unique—hence there ought to be 122 'families'. In another sense all are identical: all are ruled by a group of influential individuals who are less numerous than those they govern. In this sense all are oligarchies. The problem is to establish categories that are neither so numerous as to make comparisons impossible nor so few as to make contrasts impossible. And how many categories there should be, and of what type, depends upon the initial criteria we select. But what one observer thinks an important or significant criterion of comparison and contrast may appear trivial to another. At one time, for instance, it was common to distinguish states according to whether they were monarchies or republics. Today this appears to be of far less importance than other criteria. In the fourth century BC, Aristotle classified forms of government into three main types, using as criteria the numbers and the wealth of those who held formal authority in the state; then he subdivided each of these three categories into two, according to whether those who held authority were concerned for their own private wellbeing or for that of the community as a whole. So he derived his three pairs, monarchy-tyranny, aristocracy-oligarchy, *politeia*-democracy. And then, when he came to treat each one, he subdivided it further—monarchy ('the rule of one man'), for instance, was subdivided into five distinct types.

What Aristotle did, political scientists are still continuing to do; and it would seem that the best one can hope for is to produce a typology that (*a*) covers all the known varieties of governmental forms with (*b*) the most economical set of distinctions, so as to (*c*) provide the receiver with what he, at any rate, regards as a satisfactory basis for explaining what forms arise in what given circumstances and, (*d*) hence, has some power of predicting what vicissitudes or alterations any given form may undergo should circumstances change in named respects. And even this may be too much to expect. The study of comparative government is as old as Plato and Aristotle but, as its history has shown, is so enormously complicated that its findings and even its basic typology are still fluid. The best one can do, then, is to try.

SECTION 2

Some examples

'All scientific inquiry starts with the conscious or unconscious perception of a puzzle'. This assertion is made by one of the contributors (Rustow, p. 118) in this section, and suggests the main reason for the form of title attached to each of our examples. In each case a puzzle or question about politics or government is posed and a solution or answer suggested (usually provisional or qualified in some way). The particular ways by which the answers are arrived at vary from case to case, but they all involve an element of comparative analysis.

There are eight examples, and they differ considerably from each other. The first, dealing with why M. Rouget votes communist, is hypothetical and therefore is not, strictly speaking, an example of the practice of comparative politics. We include it because it summarises most succinctly, by way of a simple example, the purpose and logic of explanation, particularly of a statistical nature, in social science: it also shows clearly how comparative analysis is central to the discovery of such explanations. The second example, propounding the famous Parkinson's Law, could be dismissed as nothing more than an amusing bit of nonsense. We believe, however, that it is also a good example, very clearly presented, of the use of chronological comparison for the purpose of constructing an explanatory generalisation. In brief, the first two examples show, in a preliminary way, that comparisons can be both across space and through time.

The next example is a short extract from Aristotle's *Politics*. Every translator or editor of this classic feels bound to write a fairly lengthy introduction to it, warning the reader of some of its unusual features. We recommend reading such an introduction, but this is not the place, nor is there space, to provide one. However, two points must be made. First, little of the evidence on which his comparative analysis rests is available; only one of the 158 case histories of city constitutions (that of Athens) has survived, found on papyrus-rolls in Egypt in 1891. There is in addition little explicit reference to these data in the *Politics*. In reading the book therefore, one is for the most part reading a sort of report of the results of Aristotle's research based on evidence and comparative analysis that has since been lost. This limitation should be borne in mind when reading the selection from the *Politics* as an example of the practice of comparative politics. Secondly, Aristotle not only compared the actual working of constitutions: he also made comparisons between actual and imaginary constitutions (imagined by his predecessors, including Plato). This is not surprising, for speculative study of the ideal was predominant in his day. The question 'what is the best form of constitution?' was a standard one at the time. It was also, appropriately, a central concern in the *Politics*. What was new was the way Aristotle treated this question and the related question of instability and change, for he included in his study the analysis of actual constitutions in a scientific way. It is for this reason that the *Politics* has continued to the present day to be an interesting and important example of the practice of comparative politics.

The piece by Rustow involves the use of chronological comparison to investigate the reasons why democracy comes into existence, an eminently sensible approach given the kind of question being asked. (That the nature of the question determines the type of approach employed is a central point developed in Section 4.) Rustow's answer to his question, based on comparisons mainly between Sweden and Turkey, is somewhat more tentative and suggestive than in the other examples. This is so because this particular selection is a report of preliminary work connected with ongoing research. It should be read at least in part, then, as an illustration mainly of an early stage in the practice of comparative politics.

Having arrived at some preliminary conclusions concerning the reasons why democratic institutions come into existence, it is appropriate to examine the variation in types of public policy which may occur in democratic systems. Both Peters and King address this issue, and attempt to locate the major political determinants of diverse public policy outcomes. Peters and his colleagues try to show that different types of democratic political systems have important consequences for the kinds of policy adopted, and the statistical methods by which they arrive at this conclusion constitute an excellent example of modern behavioural research in political science. King's main theme is the difference in the extent of state activity in the United States and other advanced democracies; a divergence which he attempts to explain in terms of the unique pattern of political ideas prevalent in the USA.

The example by Davies, to do with why revolutions occur, is based on comparisons between the Russian revolution of 1917 and the Egyptian revolution of 1952, with brief attention to other revolutions as defined. Certain regularities are discovered in the course of the analysis, which suggest an explanation for the occurrence of revolution. Once again, systematic comparison of cases relevant to the question being asked leads to the identification of generalisations which provide answers, suggest more general explanations, and enhance one's understanding of political life.

The final article, by Skocpol, also examines the Russian case, this time in comparison with the Chinese revolution. In contrast to Davies's essay, Skocpol employs the 'most similar' strategy in studying the development of revolutions. Starting with the experience of communist revolution which was common to both Russia and China she seeks to explain, through comparative analysis, why subsequent developments in those countries differed. Differences in the sociopolitical structures and the patterns of economic development of the prerevolutionary societies are established which, it is argued, exercised a significant influence on the way in which the revolutionary forces achieved state power and used that power for subsequent development.

6

A. Przeworski
and H. Teune

Why does M. Rouget, a French worker, vote Communist?

Adapted from 'Comparative research and social science theory' and 'Formulating theories across systems' in *The Logic of Comparative Social Inquiry*, Wiley, 1970, pp. 18–20, 75–6.

The goal of science is to explain and predict why certain events occur when and where they do. Why was the Kowalski marriage not successful? Why did Smith commit a crime? Why did Napoleon attack Russia? Science is concerned with the explanation of specific events by means of statements that are invariantly true from one set of circumstances to another. But what does it mean to 'explain' or 'predict' a concrete, specific event?

To explain a specific event is to state the conditions under which it always or usually takes place, that is, to cite general statements (laws) from which other statements concerning properties of specific events can be inferred with some reasonable certainty (Hempel, 1965). In the social sciences such an explanation will most often be of a statistical nature. In order to understand why an individual behaved in a certain way in a given situation, we invoke general probabilistic statements that say that, for an individual of a particular type, it is likely that he will behave in this way, given this type of a situation.

For example, why does Monsieur Rouget, age twenty-four, blond hair, brown eyes, a worker in a large factory, vote Communist? To explain the vote of M. Rouget, one must rely upon general probabilistic statements that are relevant for voting behaviour and have been sufficiently confirmed against various sets of evidence. The particular features of M. Rouget must be used as the first premise of the explanation:

M. Rouget is a worker and
works in a large factory and
is young (twenty-four years old).

The second premise consists of a conjunction of general statements describing with a high likelihood the behaviour of skilled workers, employees of large factories, and young persons. (No interaction is assumed.)

One out of every two workers votes Communist; and employees of large organisations vote Communist more often than employees of small organisations; and young people vote Communist more often than older people.

Therefore it is likely that

M. Rouget votes Communist.

This explanation is incomplete. The probability of a French worker, twenty-four, employed in a large factory, and voting Communist is still far from 1·00. Several other factors, such as place of residence, marital status, father's occupation, religiosity, and so forth, might have to be considered if the explanation (prediction) of M. Rouget's behaviour were to approach certainty. Most explanations in the social sciences are incomplete in the sense that the probability of the explained phenomenon taking place does not approach 1·00 (or zero). Since the rules of inference are probabilistic, we cannot expect that, even if the premises are true, the conclusions will invariably follow. As the probability of inferential rules increases, however, the probability of predicting a property also increases—it moves away from what could be expected randomly.

Let us assume that several studies have confirmed that in all systems in which the option of voting for the Left is present, young workers employed in large factories are likely to vote for a leftist party with the probability of 0·60 to 0·70. We are now in a position to explain the vote of young Chilean and Norwegian workers as well. Regardless of the social system in which the behaviour of individuals occur, the same theory is valid; young workers employed in large factories tend to vote Communist. But if an additional explanatory factor is introduced, this theory is no longer equally true. When the sex of a French or a Chilean worker is considered, the explanation of the vote becomes more complete. Males in France and Chile are more likely to vote Communist than females. The introduction of this explanatory factor increases the probability of the Communist vote of young workers employed in large factories to 0·80.

But in Norway voting for the Left is independent of sex. At this stage the explanation must include a statement of the relevant characteristics of France and Chile, on the one hand, and Norway, on the other. An explanatory statement must be logically open to extension to other cases. So instead of specifying names of social systems, a variable operating at the level of systems must be added to the explanation. For example, it may be that wherever the role of established religious organisations is strong, there will be a difference in the voting behaviour of men and women. The explanation of the vote of M. Rouget would then assume the following form:

1. M. Rouget is a young male worker employed in a large factory in a social system in which the church plays an important role, and
2. young workers employed in large factories tend to vote Left with the probability of 0·60 to 0·70 and in those systems in which the role of the church is strong, men vote Left more often than women; *therefore it is highly likely* (probability of 0·80) that
3. M. Rouget votes for a party of the Left.

The premises of the explanation of the vote of Mr Janson, a Norwegian worker, would be the same, but the second premise concerning systemic conditions under which behaviour of men differs from that of women, would not provide any gain in prediction. Thus the behaviour of both individuals, a Frenchman and a Norwegian, would be explained in terms of the same theory, but the explanation of the behaviour of a Frenchman would be more complete—the probability that the conclusion is true would be higher.

REFERENCE

HEMPEL, C. G. (1965) *Aspects of Scientific Explanations and other Essays on the Philosophy of Science*, New York, Free Press.

7

C. N. *Parkinson*   Does the civil service
expand regardless of the
amount of work (if any) to
be done?

Reprinted from 'Parkinson's Law', *The Economist*, 19 November 1955, pp. 635–7.

It is a commonplace observation that work expands so as to fill the time available for its completion. Thus, an elderly lady of leisure can spend the entire day in writing and despatching a postcard to her niece at Bognor Regis. An hour will be spent in finding the postcard, another in hunting for spectacles, half-an-hour in a search for the address, an hour and a quarter in composition, and twenty minutes in deciding whether or not to take an umbrella when going to the pillar-box in the next street. The total effort which would occupy a busy man for three minutes all told may in this fashion leave another person prostrate after a day of doubt, anxiety and toil.

Granted that work (and especially paper work) is thus elastic in its demands on time, it is manifest that there need be little or no relationship between the work to be done and the size of the staff to which it may be assigned. Before the discovery of a new scientific law—herewith presented to the public for the first time, and to be called Parkinson's Law—there has, however, been insufficient recognition of the implications of this fact in the field of public administration. Politicians and taxpayers have assumed (with occasional phases of doubt) that a rising total in the number of civil servants must reflect a growing volume of work to be done. Cynics, in questioning this belief, have imagined that the multiplication of officials must have left some of them idle or all of them able to work for shorter hours. But this is a matter in which faith and doubt seem equally misplaced. The fact is that the number of the officials and the quantity of the work to be done are not related to each other at all. The rise in the total of those employed is governed by Parkinson's Law, and would be much the same whether the volume of the work were to increase, diminish or even disappear. The importance of Parkinson's Law lies in the fact that it is a law of growth based upon an analysis of the factors by which that growth is controlled.

The validity of this recently discovered law must rest mainly on statistical proofs, which will follow. Of more interest to the general reader is the explanation of the factors that underlie the general tendency to which this law gives definition. Omitting technicalities (which are numerous) we may distinguish, at the outset, two motive forces. They can be represented for the present purpose by two almost axiomatic statements, thus:

Factor I. An official wants to multiply subordinates, not rivals; and
Factor II. Officials make work for each other.

We must now examine these motive forces in turn.

THE LAW OF MULTIPLICATION OF SUBORDINATES

To comprehend Factor I, we must picture a civil servant called A who finds himself overworked. Whether this overwork is real or imaginary is immaterial; but we should observe, in passing, that A's sensation (or illusion) might easily result from his own decreasing energy—a normal symptom of middle-age. For this real or imagined overwork there are, broadly speaking, three possible remedies:

1. He may resign.
2. He may ask to halve the work with a colleague called B.
3. He may demand the assistance of two subordinates, to be called C and D.

There is probably no instance in civil service history of A choosing any but the third alternative. By resignation he would lose his pension rights. By having B appointed, on his own level in the hierarchy, he would merely bring in a rival for promotion to W's vacancy when W (at long last) retires. So A would rather have C and D, junior men, below him. They will add to his consequence; and, by dividing the work into two categories, as between C and D, he will have the merit of being the only man who comprehends them both.

It is essential to realise, at this point, that C and D are, as it were, inseparable. To appoint C alone would have been impossible. Why? Because C, if by himself, would divide the work with A and so assume almost the equal status which has been refused in the first instance to B; a status the more emphasised if C is A's only possible successor. Subordinates must thus number two or more, each being kept in order by fear of the other's promotion. When C complains in turn of being overworked (as he certainly will) A will, with the concurrence of C, advise the appointment of two assistants to help C. But he can then avert internal friction only by advising the appointment of two more assistants to help D, whose position is much the same. With this recruitment of E, F, G and H, the promotion of A is now practically certain.

THE LAW OF MULTIPLICATION OF WORK

Seven officials are now doing what one did before. This is where Factor II comes into operation. For these seven make so much work for each other that all are fully occupied and A is actually working harder than ever. An incoming document may well come before each of them in turn. Official E decides that it falls within the province of F, who places a draft reply before C, who amends it drastically before consulting D, who asks G to deal with it. But G goes on leave at this point, handing the file over to H, who drafts a minute, which is signed by D and returned to C, who revises his draft accordingly and lays the new version before A.

What does A do? He would have every excuse for signing the thing unread, for he has many other matters on his mind. Knowing now that he is to succeed W next year, he has to decide whether C or D should succeed to his own office. He had to agree to G going on leave, although not yet strictly entitled to it. He is worried whether H should not have gone instead, for reasons of health. He has looked pale recently—partly but not solely because of his domestic troubles. Then there is the business of F's special increment of salary for the period of the conference, and E's application for transfer to the Ministry of Pensions. A has heard that D is in love with a married typist and that G and F are no longer on speaking terms—no one seems to know why. So A might be tempted to sign C's draft and have done with it.

But A is a conscientious man. Beset as he is with problems created by his colleagues for themselves and for him—created by the mere fact of these officials' existence—he is not the man to shirk his duty. He reads through the draft with care, deletes the fussy paragraphs added by C and H and restores the thing back to the form preferred in the first instance by the able (if quarrelsome) F. He corrects the English —none of these young men can write grammatically—and finally produces the same reply he would have written if officials C to H had never been born. Far more people have taken far longer to produce the same result. No one has been idle. All have done their best. And it is late in the evening before A finally quits his office and begins the return journey to Ealing. The last of the office lights are being turned off in the gathering dusk which marks the end of another day's administrative toil. Among the last to leave, A reflects, with bowed shoulders and a wry smile, that late hours, like grey hairs, are among the penalties of success.

THE SCIENTIFIC PROOFS

From this description of the factors at work the student of political science will recognise that administrators are more or less bound to multiply. Nothing has yet been said, however, about the period of time likely to elapse between the date of A's appointment and the date from which we can calculate the pensionable service of H. Vast masses of statistical evidence have been collected and it is from a study of this data that Parkinson's Law has been deduced. Space will not allow of detailed analysis, but research began in the British Navy Estimates. These were chosen because the Admiralty's responsibilities are more easily measurable than those of (say) the Board of Trade.

The accompanying table is derived from Admiralty statistics for 1914 and 1928. The criticism voiced at the time centred on the comparison between the sharp fall in numbers of those available for fighting and the sharp rise in those available only for administration, the creation, it was said, of 'a magnificent Navy on land'. But that comparison is not to the present purpose. What we have to note is that the 2,000 Admiralty officials of 1914 had become the 3,569 of 1928; and that this growth was unrelated to any possible increase in their work. The Navy during that period had diminished, in point of fact, by a third in men and two-thirds in ships. Nor, from 1922 onwards, was its strength even expected to increase, for its total of ships (unlike its total of officials) was limited by the Washington Naval

Admiralty Statistics

	1914	1928	Percentage increase or decrease
Capital ships in commission	62	20	− 67·74
Officers and men in Royal Navy	146,000	100,000	− 31·50
Dockyard workers	57,000	62,439	+ 9·45
Dockyard officials and clerks	3,249	4,558	+ 40·28
Admiralty officials	2,000	3,569	+ 78·45

Agreement of that year. Yet in these circumstances we had a 78·45 per cent increase in Admiralty officials over a period of fourteen years; an average increase of 5·6 per cent a year on the earlier total. In fact, as we shall see, the rate of increase was not as regular as that. All we have to consider, at this stage, is the percentage rise over a given period.

Can this rise in the total number of civil servants be accounted for except on the assumption that such a total must always rise by a law governing its growth? It might be urged, at this point, that the period under discussion was one of rapid development in naval technique. The use of the flying machine was no longer confined to the eccentric. Submarines were tolerated if not approved. Engineer officers were beginning to be regarded as almost human. In so revolutionary an age we might expect that storekeepers would have more elaborate inventories to compile. We might not wonder to see more draughtsmen on the pay-roll, more designers, more technicians and scientists. But these, the dockyard officials, increased only by 40 per cent in number, while the men of Whitehall increased by nearly 80 per cent. For every new foreman or electrical engineer at Portsmouth there had to be two more clerks at Charing Cross. From this we might be tempted to conclude, provisionally, that the rate of increase in administrative staff is likely to be double that of the technical staff at a time when the actually useful strength (in this case, of seamen) is being reduced by 31·5 per cent. It has been proved, however, statistically, that this last percentage is irrelevant. *The officials would have multiplied at the same rate had there been no actual seamen at all.*

It would be interesting to follow the further progress by which the 8,118 Admiralty staff of 1935 came to number 33,788 by 1954. But the staff of the Colonial Office affords a better field of study during a period of Imperial decline. The relevant statistics are set down below. Before showing what the rate of increase is, we must observe that the extent of this department's responsibilities was far from constant during these twenty years. The colonial territories were not much altered in area or population between 1935 and 1939. They were considerably diminished by 1943, certain areas being in enemy hands. They were

Colonial Office Officials

1935	1939	1943	1947	1954
372	450	817	1,139	1,661

increased again in 1947, but have since then shrunk steadily from year to year as successive colonies achieve self-government.

It would be rational, prior to the discovery of Parkinson's Law, to suppose that these changes in the scope of Empire would be reflected in the size of its central administration. But a glance at the figures shows that the staff totals represent automatic stages in an inevitable increase. And this increase, while related to that observed in other departments, has nothing to do with the size—or even the existence—of the Empire. What are the percentages of increase? We must ignore, for this purpose, the rapid increase in staff which accompanied the diminution of responsibility during World War II. We should note rather the peacetime rates of increase; over 5·24 per cent between 1935 and 1939, and 6·55 per cent between 1947 and 1954. This gives an average increase of 5·89 per cent each year, a percentage markedly similar to that already found in the Admiralty staff increase between 1914 and 1928.

Further and detailed statistical analysis of departmental staffs would be inappropriate in such an article as this. It is hoped, however, to reach a tentative conclusion regarding the time likely to elapse between a given official's first appointment and the later appointment of his two or more assistants. Dealing with the problem of pure staff accumulation, all the researches so far completed point to an average increase of about 5¾ per cent per year. This fact established, it now becomes possible to state Parkinson's Law in mathematical form, thus:

In any public administrative department not actually at war the staff increase may be expected to follow this formula:

$$x = \frac{2k^m + p}{n}$$

Where k is the number of staff seeking promotion through the appointment of subordinates; p represents the difference between the ages of appointment and retirement; m is the number of man-hours devoted to answering minutes within the department; and n is the number of effective units being administered. Then x will be the number of new staff required each year.

Mathematicians will, of course, realise that to find the percentage increase they must multiply x by 100 and divide by the total of the previous year, thus:

$$\frac{100\,(2k^m + p)}{yn}\,\%$$

where y represents the total original staff. And this figure will invariably prove to be between 5·17 per cent and 6·56 per cent, irrespective of any variation in the amount of work (if any) to be done.

The discovery of this formula and of the general principles upon which it is based has, of course, no emotive value. No attempt has been made to inquire whether departments ought to grow in size. Those who hold that this growth is essential to gain full employment are fully entitled to their opinion. Those who doubt the stability of an economy based upon reading each other's minutes are equally entitled to theirs. Parkinson's Law is a purely scientific discovery, inapplicable except in theory to the politics of the day. It is not the business of the botanist to eradicate the weeds. Enough for him if he can tell us just how fast they grow.

8

Aristotle What is the best form of
constitution?

From *The Politics*, trans. T. A. Sinclair, Penguin, 1962, II, I, p. 55; III, I,
pp. 101–2; III, 7, pp. 115–16; IV, 11 and 12, pp. 171–6.

We have undertaken to discuss the form of association or partnership
which we call the state, to ask the question what is the best type of such
partnership—supposing that we are in a position to choose what we
would like. But we must also look at sample constitutions, for example,
those that are in use in cities that have the reputation of being well-
governed, or any others that have been sketched by writers and appear
to be good. Our purpose is partly to see what in them is good and
useful and what is not; but we also wish to make it clear that if we
keep looking for something different from what we find there, we do
not do so out of mere captiousness or a desire to be clever; we have
chosen this method simply because in fact none of the existing constitutions, whether written or actual, is entirely satisfactory. . . .

In considering now *Constitution* in its various kinds and forms, we
must begin by looking at the state and seek a definition of it. There is
no unanimity about this; for example, in regard to its functioning,
some say that action is taken by the state, others that the action is taken
not by the state, but by the oligarchy or by the dictator or whatever it
may be. Obviously the activities of statesman and legislator closely concern the state. The constitution is a way of organising those living in a
state. . . .

Having drawn this distinction we must next consider what constitutions there are and how many. We begin with those that aim at securing the good of all, which we have called 'straight' constitutions, since,
when these have been defined, it will be easy to see the deviation-types.

As we have seen, constitution and *politeuma* are really the same; the citizen body is the sovereign power in states. Sovereignty must reside either in one man, or in a few, or in the many. Whenever the One, the Few, or the Many rule with a view to the common weal, these constitutions must be right; but if they look to the advantage of one section only, be it the One or the Few or the Mass, it is a deviation. For either we must say that those who participate are not citizens or they must share in the common good. The usual names for right constitutions are as follows:

1. One man rule aiming at the common good—Kingship.
2. Rule of more than one man but only a few—Aristocracy.[1]
3. Rule exercised by the bulk of the citizens for the good of the whole community—Polity.[2]

The corresponding deviations are: from kingship, tyranny; from aristocracy, oligarchy; from polity or constitutional government by the many, democracy. For tyranny is sole rule for the benefit of the sole ruler, oligarchy for the benefit of the men of means, democracy for the benefit of the men without means. None of the three aims at the advantage of the whole community. . . .

What is the best constitution and what is the best life for the majority of states and the majority of men? We have in mind men whose standard of virtue does not rise above that of ordinary people, who do not look for an education that demands either great natural ability or a large private fortune, who seek not an ideally perfect constitution, but, first, a way of living in which as many as possible can join and, second, a constitution within the compass of the greatest number of cities. These requirements are not fulfilled by the aristocracies; an aristocratic constitution does not fall within the competence of most cities unless it approximates closely to what we call polity. (The adherence of both to aristocratic principles allows us to use the one name.) Decision on all these points rests on a single set of elementary principles. If we were

---

[1] So-called either because the *best* men rule or because it aims at what is *best* for the state and all its members.

[2] This is the same word as constitution. But it is reasonable to use this term, because, while it is possible for one man or a few to be of outstanding ability, it is difficult for a larger number to reach a high standard in all forms of excellence. But it may be reached in fighting qualities by the general run of people. And that is why in this 'constitutional constitution' the citizen-army is the sovereign body and only those who bear arms are members of it.

right when in our *Ethics* we stated that Virtue is a Mean and that the happy life is life free and unhindered and according to virtue, then the best life must be the middle way, consisting in a mean between two extremes which it is open to those at either end to attain. And the same principle must be applicable to the goodness or badness of cities and states. For the constitution of a city is really the way it lives.

In all states there are three sections of the community—the very well-off, the very badly-off, and those in between. Seeing therefore that it is agreed that moderation and a middle position are best, it is clear that in the matter of possessions to own a middling amount is best of all. This condition is most obedient to reason, and following reason is just what is difficult both for the exceedingly rich, handsome, strong, and well-born, and for the opposite, the extremely poor, the weak, and the downtrodden. The former commit deeds of violence on a large scale, the latter are delinquent and wicked in petty ways. The misdeeds of the one class are due to *hubris*, the misdeeds of the other to rascality. Add the fact that it is among the members of the middle section that you find least reluctance to hold office as well as least eagerness to do so; and both these are detrimental to states. There are other drawbacks about the two extremes. Those who have a super-abundance of all that makes for success, strength, riches, friends, and so forth, neither wish to hold office nor understand the work; and this is ingrained in them from childhood on; even at school they are so full of their superiority that they have never learned to do what they are told. Those on the other hand who are greatly deficient in these qualities are too sub-servient. So they cannot command and can only obey in a servile régime, while the others cannot obey in any régime and can command only in a master-slave relationship. The result is a state not of free men but of slaves and masters, the one full of envy, the other of contempt. Nothing could be farther removed from friendship or from the whole idea of a shared partnership in a state. Sharing is a token of friendship; one does not share even a journey with people one does not like. The state aims to consist as far as possible of those who are like and equal, a condition found chiefly among the middle section. And so the best government is certain to be found in this kind of city, whose com-position is, we maintain, a natural one. The middle class is also the steadiest element, the least eager for change. They neither covet, like the poor, the possessions of others, nor do others covet theirs, as the poor covet those of the rich. So they live less risky lives, not scheming and not being schemed against. Phocylides's wish was therefore justified when he wrote 'Those in the middle have many advantages; that is where I wish to be in society.'

It is clear then both that the political partnership which operates through the middle class is best, and also that those cities have every chance of being well-governed in which the middle class is large, stronger if possible than the other two together, or at any rate stronger than one of them. For the addition of its weight to either side will turn the balance and prevent the extravagances of the opposition. For this reason it is a happy state of affairs when those who take part in the life of the state have a moderate but adequate amount of property; for where one set of people possesses a great deal and the other nothing, the result is either extreme democracy or unmixed oligarchy or a tyranny due to the excesses of the other two. Tyranny often emerges from an over-enthusiastic democracy or from an oligarchy, but much more rarely from middle-class constitutions or from those very near to them. The reason for this we will speak of later when we deal with changes in constitutions.

The superiority of the middle type of constitution is clear also from the fact that it alone is free from fighting among factions. Where the middle element is large, there least of all arise faction and counter-faction among citizens. And for the same reason the larger states are free from danger of splitting; they are strong in the middle. In small states it is easy for the whole body of citizens to become divided into two, leaving no middle at all, and they are nearly all either rich or poor. Democracies too are safer than oligarchies in this respect and longer lasting thanks to their middle class, which is always more numerous and more politically important in democracies than in oligarchies. For when the unpropertied class without the support of a middle class gets on top by weight of numbers, things go badly and they soon come to grief.

An indication of the truth of what we have been saying is to be found in the fact that the best lawgivers have come from the middle class of citizens—Solon, for example, whose middle position is revealed in his poems, and Lycurgus, who was not a king at Sparta, and Charondas and most of the rest. The facts also show why most states have been either democratic or oligarchic; for the middle class being frequently small, whichever of the two extremes, the property-owners or the people, is on top ignores the middle section and conducts the government according to its own notions, and so the result is either democracy or oligarchy. Then again, owing to constant strife and civil war between the people and the wealthier class, neither side, whichever of the two succeeds in gaining the mastery, ever sets up a constitution fair and acceptable all round. Taking political supremacy as a prize of victory they proceed to make a democratic or an oligarchic régime as the case may be. Also, the great cities, when they come to exercise ascendancy over other Greek states, installed democracies or oligarchies in them according to the constitution which each had at home, looking entirely to their own advantage, not to that of the cities themselves. So for these reasons a really 'middle' kind of constitution is seldom or never encountered anywhere. Only one of a long succession of statesmen succeeded with the consent of his fellow citizens in introducing a social order of this kind. And to this day into whatever city you go, you will find that they do not even want a fair settlement; the aim is to get on top, failing which they accept a condition of defeat.

Which constitution is best for the majority, and the reasons for deeming it the best, will be clear from the above. As for all the rest, the different kinds of oligarchy and democracy which we say there are, it is not difficult to arrange them in order of merit, this one better, that one worse; for now that the best is decided upon, proximity to it denotes better, and the farther away one moves from middle-polity, the worse; unless of course one postulates a different standard, for it is possible to discard the preferable in favour of the more expedient.

It is most proper to follow what has been said by a discussion of the question what constitution is advantageous for what states, what kind of society for what kind of people. First we must grasp a principle which is universally applicable to them all: it is essential that that part of the population which desires the maintenance of the constitution should be larger than that which does not. Now every state can be measured either qualitatively or quantitatively, I mean by such qualities as freedom, wealth, education, and good birth, or by quantity, that is by numerical superiority. Look at the parts which make up a state; it is possible that quality may be present in one, quantity in another. The non-noble may be numerically greater than the noble, the poor than the rich; but the quantitative superiority is not enough to outweigh the qualitative inferiority. These must be weighed one against the other. Where the number of the poor is sufficiently large to outweigh any qualitative defeat, there democracy is natural; and the type of democracy will depend on the type of people which has the numerical superiority in each case. Thus, if those who cultivate the soil make up the superior numbers, the democracy will be at the top of the scale; if those engaged in menial work and receiving pay for it predominate, then it will be at the bottom, and the rest in-between. Where, on the other hand, the rich and important people have a greater qualitative superiority than quantitative inferiority, there is oligarchy; and once again its type will depend on the degree of qualitative superiority in those who form the oligarchy.

But at all times a legislator ought to endeavour to attach the middle section of the population firmly to the constitution. If he is framing laws oligarchical in character, he should have the middle class always in view; if democratic, he should again make them attractive to the middle class. Wherever the number of the middle class is larger than a combination of the two extremes, or even than one only, then there is a good chance of permanence for the constitution. There is no danger of rich and poor making common cause against *them*; for neither will want to be subservient to the other, and if they are looking for a compromise, they will not find any better than the middle-class polity which they have already. Their mistrust of each other would make it impossible for them to accept the system of alternation in office. But on all occasions the mediator is well trusted by parties, and the one in the middle is mediator. The better mixed a constitution is, the longer it will last. It is a mistake made by many, even by those seeking to make an aristocratic constitution, not only to give too great preponderance to the rich, but to cheat the people. In the long run mistaken good gives rise to unmistakable evil; for the successful power-grabbing of the rich does more harm to society than lust for power in the people.

9

D. A. Rustow   How does a democracy come into existence?

Excerpts from 'Transitions to democracy: towards a dynamic model', *Comparative Politics*, **2**, 1970, pp. 337–63.

What conditions make democracy possible and what conditions make it thrive? Thinkers from Locke to Tocqueville and A. D. Lindsay have given many answers. Democracy, we are told, is rooted in man's innate capacity for self-government or in the Christian ethical or the Teutonic legal tradition. Its birthplace was the field at Putney where Cromwell's angry young privates debated their officers, or the more sedate House at Westminster, or the rock at Plymouth, or the forest cantons above Lake Lucerne, or the fevered brain of Jean Jacques Rousseau. Its natural champions are sturdy yeomen, or industrious merchants, or a prosperous middle class. It must be combined with strong local government, with a two-party system, with a vigorous tradition of civil rights, or with a multitude of private associations.

Recent writings of American sociologists and political scientists favour three types of explanation. One of these, proposed by Seymour Martin Lipset, Philips Cutright, and others, connects stable democracy with certain economic and social background conditions, such as high per capita income, widespread literacy, and prevalent urban residence. A second type of explanation dwells on the need for certain beliefs or psychological attitudes among the citizens. A long line of authors from Walter Bagehot to Ernest Barker has stressed the need for consensus as the basis of democracy—either in the form of a common belief in certain fundamentals or of procedural consensus on the rules of the game, which Barker (1942, p. 63) calls 'the Agreement to Differ'. Among civic attitudes required for the successful working of a democratic system, Daniel Lerner (1958, pp. 49ff, 60ff) has proposed a capacity for empathy and a willingness to participate. To Gabriel Almond and Sidney Verba (1963), on the other hand, the ideal 'civic culture' of a democracy suggests not only such participant but also other traditional or parochial attitudes.

A third type of explanation looks at certain features of social and political structure. In contrast to the prevailing consensus theory, authors such as Carl J. Friedrich (1942), E. E. Schattschneider (1960), Bernard Crick (1964), Ralf Dahrendorf (1959), and Arend Lijphart (1968) have insisted that conflict and reconciliation are essential to democracy. Starting with a similar assumption, David B. Truman (1951, p. 514) has attributed the vitality of American institutions to the citizens' 'multiple membership in potential groups'—a relationship which Lipset (1960, pp. 88ff) has called one of 'crosscutting politically relevant associations'.[1] Robert A. Dahl (1961) and Herbert McClosky (1964), among others (see Prothro and Grigg, 1960), have argued that democratic stability requires a commitment to democratic values or rules, not among the electorate at large but among the professional politicians—each of these presumably linked to the other through effective ties of political organisation. Harry Eckstein (1961 and 1965), finally, has proposed a rather subtle theory of 'congruence': to make democracy stable, the structures of authority throughout society such as family, church, business, and trade unions, must prove the more democratic the more directly they impinge on processes of government.

Some of these hypotheses are compatible with each other, though they may also be held independently—for example, those about prosperity, literacy, and consensus. Others—such as those about consensus and conflict—are contradictory unless carefully restricted or reconciled. Precisely such a synthesis has been the import of a large body of writing. Dahl (1956) for instance, has proposed that in polyarchy (or 'minorities rule', the closest real-life approximation to democracy) the policies of successive governments tend to fall within a broad range of majority consensus. Indeed, after an intense preoccupation with consensus in the World War II years, it is now widely accepted that democracy is indeed a process of 'accommodation' involving a combination of 'division and cohesion' and of 'conflict and consent'— to quote the key terms from a number of recent book titles (Lijphart; Eckstein; Dahl, 1967).

The scholarly debate thus continues, and answers diverge. Yet

[1] Already A. Lawrence Lowell (1896, vol. 2, pp. 65ff) had spoken of the need for a party alignment where 'the line of division is vertical' cutting across the horizontal division of classes.

there are two notable points of agreement. Nearly all the authors ask the same sort of question and support their answers with the same sort of evidence. The question is not how a democratic system comes into existence. Rather it is how a democracy, assumed to be already in existence, can best preserve or enhance its health and stability. The evidence adduced generally consists of contemporary information, whether in the form of comparative statistics, interviews, surveys, or other types of data. This remains true even of authors who spend considerable time discussing the historical background of the phenomena that concern them—Almond and Verba (1963) of the civic culture, Eckstein (1961 and 1965) of congruence among Norwegian social structures, and Dahl (1961 and 1966) of the ruling minorities of New Haven and of oppositions in Western countries. Their key propositions are couched in the present tense.

There may be a third feature of similarity underlying the current American literature of democracy. All scientific inquiry starts with the conscious or unconscious perception of a puzzle (see Kuhn, 1962). What has puzzled the more influential authors evidently has been the contrast between the relatively smooth functioning of democracy in the English-speaking and Scandinavian countries and the recurrent crises and final collapse of democracy in the French Third and Fourth Republics and in the Weimar Republic of Germany.

This curiosity is of course wholly legitimate. The growing literature and the increasingly subtle theorising on the bases of democracy indicate how fruitful it has been. The initial curiosity leads logically enough to the functional, as opposed to the genetic, question. And that question, in turn, is most readily answered by an examination of contemporary data about functioning democracies—perhaps with badly functioning democracies and nondemocracies thrown in for contrast. The functional curiosity also comes naturally to scholars of a country that took its crucial steps toward democracy as far back as the days of Thomas Jefferson and Andrew Jackson. It accords, moreover, with some of the characteristic trends in American social science in the last generation or two—with the interest in systematic equilibria, in quantitative correlations, and in survey data engendered by the researcher's own questions. Above all, it accords with a deep-seated prejudice against causality. As Herbert A. Simon (1957, p. 65) has strikingly put it,

We are wary, in the social sciences, of asymmetrical relations. They remind us of pre-Humeian and pre-Newtonian notions of causality. By whip and sword we have been converted to the doctrine that there is no causation, only functional interrelation, and that functional relations are perfectly symmetrical. We may even have taken over, as a very persuasive analogy, the proposition 'for every action, there is an equal and opposite reaction'.

Students of developing regions, such as the Middle East, Southern Asia, tropical Africa, or Latin America, naturally enough have a somewhat different curiosity about democracy. The contrast that is likely to puzzle them is that between mature democracies, such as the United States, Britain, or Sweden today, and countries that are struggling on the verge of democracy, such as Ceylon, Lebanon, Turkey, Peru, or Venezuela. This will lead them to the genetic question of how a democracy comes into being in the first place.[2] The question is (or at least was, until the Russian invasion of Czechoslovakia in 1968) of almost equal interest in Eastern Europe. The genesis of democracy, thus, has not only considerable intrinsic interest for most of the world; it has greater pragmatic relevance than further paneygyrics about the virtues of Anglo-American democracy or laments over the fatal illnesses of democracy in Weimar or in several of the French Republics.

In the following section of this article I should like to outline one possible model of the transition to democracy. [...]

The model I should like to sketch in the next few pages is based in large part on my studies of Sweden, a Western country that made the transition to democracy in the period from 1890 to 1920, and of Turkey, a Westernising country where that process began about 1945 and is still underway. The choice of these two is accidental—except in terms of an autobiographical account for which this is not the occasion. I am now in the early stages of a study that will seek to refine the same set of hypotheses in the light of materials from a slightly larger and less arbitrary selection of countries.

A. BACKGROUND CONDITION

The model starts with a single background condition—national unity. This implies nothing mysterious about *Blut und Boden* or daily pledges of allegiance, about personal identity in the psycho-analyst's sense, or about a grand political purpose pursued by the citizenry as a whole. It simply means that the vast majority of citizens in a democracy-to-be must have no doubt or mental reservations as to which

[2] For a general discussion of the question of democracy in the context of recent modernising countries, see Rustow (1967, ch. 7), which states some of the present argument in summary form.

political community they belong to. This excludes situations of latent secession, as in the late Habsburg and Ottoman Empires or in many African states today, and, conversely, situations of serious aspirations for merger as in many Arab states. Democracy is a system of rule by temporary majorities. In order that rulers and policies may freely change, the boundaries must endure, the composition of the citizenry be continuous. As Ivor Jennings (1956, p. 56) phrased it tersely, 'the people cannot decide until somebody decides who are the people'.

National unity is listed as a background condition in the sense that it must precede all the other phases of democratisation but that otherwise its timing is irrelevant. It may have been achieved in prehistoric times, as in Japan or Sweden; or it may have preceded the other phases by centuries, as in France, or by decades, as in Turkey.

Nor does it matter by what means national unity has been established. The geographic situation may be such that no serious alternative has ever arisen—Japan once again being the best example. Or a sense of nationality may be the product of a sudden intensification of social communication in a new idiom developed for the purpose. On the other hand, it may be the legacy of some dynastic or administrative process of unification. The various hypotheses proposed by Deutsch (1953 and 1957) clearly become relevant here.

I have argued elsewhere (1967, pp. 30ff and 1968) that in an age of modernisation men are unlikely to feel a preponderant sense of loyalty except to a political community large enough to achieve some considerable degree of modernity in its social and economic life. This sort of hypotheses must be examined as part of a theory of nationhood, not of one of democratic development. What matters in the present context is only the result.

I hesitate to call this result a consensus, for at least two reasons. First, national unity, as Deutsch argues, is the product less of shared attitudes and opinions than of responsiveness and complementarity. Second, 'consensus' connotes consciously held opinion and deliberate agreement. The background condition, however, is best fulfilled when national unity is accepted unthinkingly, is silently taken for granted. Any vocal consensus about national unity, in fact, should make us wary. Most of the rhetoric of nationalism has poured from the lips of people who felt least secure in their sense of national identity— Germans and Italians in the past century and Arabs and Africans in the present, never Englishmen, Swedes, or Japanese.

To single out national unity as the sole background condition implies that no minimal level of economic development or social differentiation is necessary as a prerequisite to democracy. These social and economic factors enter the model only indirectly as one of several alternative bases for national unity or for entrenched conflict (see B below). Those social and economic indicators that authors are fond of citing as 'background conditions' seem somewhat implausible at any rate. There are always nondemocracies that rank suspiciously high, such as Kuwait, Nazi Germany, Cuba, or Congo-Kinshasa. Conversely, the United States in 1820, France in 1870, and Sweden in 1890 would have been sure to fail one or another of the proposed tests of urbanisation or per capita income—not to speak of newspaper copies in circulation, or doctors, movies, and telephones available to each one thousand inhabitants.

The model thus deliberately leaves open the possibility of democracies (properly so called) in premodern, prenationalist times and at low levels of economic development. To find a meaningful definition of democracy that would cover modern parliamentary systems along with medieval forest cantons, ancient city states (the ones where slavery and metics were absent), and some of the pre-Colombian Indians may prove difficult. It is not a task that forms part of the present project; still, I should not like to foreclose the attempt.

B. PREPARATORY PHASE

I hypothesise that, against this single background condition, the dynamic process of democratisation itself is set off by a prolonged and inconclusive political struggle. To give it those qualities, the protagonists must represent well-entrenched forces (typically social classes), and the issues must have profound meaning to them. Such a struggle is likely to begin as the result of the emergence of a new elite that arouses a depressed and previously leaderless social group into concerted action. Yet the particular social composition of the contending forces, both leaders and followers, and the specific nature of the issues will vary widely from one country to the next and in the same country from period to period.

In Sweden (see Rustow, 1955, chs. 1–3, and Verney, 1957) at the turn of the century, it was a struggle first of farmers and then of an urban lower-middle and working class against a conservative alliance of bureaucrats, large landowners, and industrialists; and the issues were tariffs, taxation, military service, and suffrage. In Turkey (see Ward and Rustow, 1964, and Rustow, 1957, 1965, 1966, and 1967) in the last twenty years it has mainly been a contest of countryside versus city, more precisely of large and middling-size farmers (supported by most

of the peasant electorate) against the heirs of the Kemalist bureau-
cratic-military establishment; the central issue has been industrialisation versus agricultural development. In both these examples, economic
factors have been of prime importance, yet the direction of causality
has varied. In Sweden, it was a period of intense economic development that created new political tensions; at one crucial point, rising
wages enabled the Stockholm workers to overcome the existing tax
barrier for the franchise. In Turkey, conversely, the demand for rural
development was the consequence, not the cause, of beginning democratisation.

There may be situations where economic factors have played a
much lesser role. In India and in the Philippines the prolonged contest between nationalist forces and an imperial bureaucracy over the
issue of self-government may have served the same preparatory function as did class conflict elsewhere. In Lebanon the continuing struggle
is mainly between denominational groups and the stakes are mainly
government offices. Although political struggles of this sort naturally
have their economic dimensions, only a doctrinaire economic determinist would derive colonialism or religious divisions from solely
economic causes.

James Bryce (1921, ii, p. 602) found in his classic comparative study
that, 'One road only has in the past led into democracy, viz., the wish
to be rid of tangible evils'. Democracy was not the original or primary
aim; it was sought as a means to some other end or it came as a
fortuitous by-product of the struggle. But, since the tangible evils
that befall human societies are legion, Bryce's single road dissolves
into many separate paths. No two existing democracies have gone
through a struggle between the very same forces over the same
issues and with the same institutional outcome. Hence, it seems
unlikely that any future democracy will follow in the precise foot-
steps of any of its predecessors. As Albert Hirschman (1963, pp. 6ff)
has warned in his discussion of economic development, the search for
ever more numerous preconditions or prerequisites may end up by
proving conclusively that development always will be impossible—
and always has been.

More positively, Hirschman (1958, 1963 and 1965, pp. 385–93)
and other economists have argued that a country can best launch into
a phase of growth not by slavishly imitating the example of nations
already industrialised, but rather by making the most of its particular
natural and human resources and by fitting these accurately into the
international division of labour. Similarly, a country is likely to attain
democracy not by copying the constitutional laws or parliamentary

practices of some previous democracy, but rather by honestly facing up to its particular conflicts and by devising or adapting effective procedures for their accommodation.

The serious and prolonged nature of the struggle is likely to force the protagonists to rally around two banners. Hence polarisation, rather than pluralism, is the hallmark of this preparatory phase. Yet there are limitations implicit in the requirement of national unity—which, of course, must not only pre-exist but also continue. If the division is on sharply regional lines, secession rather than democracy is likely to result. Even among contestants geographically interspersed there must be some sense of community or some even balance of forces that makes wholesale expulsion or genocide impossible. The Turks are beginning to develop a set of democratic practices among themselves, but fifty years ago they did not deal democratically with Armenians or Greeks. Crosscutting cleavages have their place in this preparatory phase as a possible means of strengthening or preserving that sense of community.

Dahl (1966, p. 397) notes wistfully that 'one perennial problem of opposition is that there is either too much or too little'. The first two elements of the model between them will ensure that there is the right amount. But struggle and national unity cannot simply be averaged out, since they cannot be measured along the same scale. Strong doses of both must be combined, just as it may be possible to combine sharp polarisation with crosscutting cleavages. Furthermore, as Mary Parker Follett (1918 and 1924), Lewis A. Coser (1956, p. 121) and others have insisted, certain types of conflict in themselves constitute creative processes of integration.[3] What infant democracy requires is not a lukewarm struggle but a hot family feud.

This delicate combination implies, of course, that many things can go wrong during the preparatory phase. The fight may go on and on till the protagonists weary and the issues fade away without the emergence of any democratic solution along the way. Or one group may find a way of crushing the opponents after all. In these and other ways an apparent evolution toward democracy may be deflected, and at no time more easily than during the preparatory phase.

[3] A widespread contrary position has recently been restated by Shils (1966, p. 10), who writes in reference to Lebanon: 'Civility will not be strengthened by crisis. It can only grow slowly and in a calm atmosphere. The growth of civility is a necessary condition for Lebanon's development...into a genuinely democratic system.' I find it hard to think of situations where there have been any notable advances in either civility or democracy *except* as the result of crisis.

C. DECISION PHASE

Robert Dahl (1966, p. xi) has written that, 'legal party opposition . . . is a recent and unplanned invention'. This accords with Bryce's emphasis on the redress of specific grievances as democracy's vehicle and with the assumption here that the transition to democracy is a complex process stretching over many decades. But it does not rule out suffrage or freedom of opposition as conscious goals in the preparatory struggle. Nor does it suggest that a country ever becomes a democracy in a fit of absentmindedness. On the contrary, what concludes the preparatory phase is a deliberate decision on the part of political leaders to accept the existence of diversity in unity and, to that end, to institutionalise some crucial aspect of democratic procedure. Such was the decision in 1907, which I have called the 'Great Compromise' of Swedish politics (1955, p. 69), to adopt universal suffrage combined with proportional representation. Instead of a single decision there may be several. In Britain, as is well known, the principle of limited government was laid down in the compromise of 1688, cabinet government evolved in the eighteenth century, and suffrage reform was launched as late as 1832. Even in Sweden, the dramatic change of 1907 was followed by the further suffrage reform of 1918 which also confirmed the principle of cabinet government.

Whether democracy is purchased wholesale as in Sweden in 1907 or on the instalment plan as in Britain, it is acquired by a process of conscious decision at least on the part of the top political leadership. Politicians are specialists in power, and a fundamental power shift such as that from oligarchy to democracy will not escape their notice.

Decision means choice, and while the choice of democracy does not arise until the background and preparatory conditions are in hand, it is a genuine choice and does not flow automatically from those two conditions. The history of Lebanon illustrates the possibilities of benevolent autocracy or of foreign rule as alternative solutions to entrenched struggles within a political community (Binder, 1966). And of course a decision in favour of democracy, or some crucial ingredient of it, may be proposed and rejected—thus leading to a continuation of the preparatory phase or to some sort of abortive outcome.

The decision in favour of democracy results from the interplay of a number of forces. Since precise terms must be negotiated and heavy risks with regard to the future taken, a small circle of leaders is likely to play a disproportionate role. Among the negotiating groups and their leaders may be the protagonists of the preparatory struggle. Other participants may include groups that split off from one or the other side or new arrivals on the political stage. In Sweden these new and intermediate groups played a crucial role. Conservatives and Radicals [led by industrialists on one side and intellectuals on the other] had sharpened and crystallized the issues throughout the 1890s. Then came a period of stalemate when discipline in all the recently formed parliamentary parties broke down—a sort of randomisation process in which many compromises, combinations, and permutations were devised and explored. The formula that carried the day in 1907 included crucial contributions from a moderately conservative bishop and a moderately liberal farmer, neither of whom played a very prominent role in politics before or after this decision phase.

Just as there can be different types of sponsors and different contents of the decision, so the motives from which it is proposed and accepted will vary from case to case. The forces of conservatism may yield from fear that continued resistance may lose them even more ground in the end. (Such thoughts were on the minds of British Whigs in 1832 and of Swedish conservatives in 1907.) Or they may belatedly wish to live up to principles long proclaimed; such was the Turkish transition to a multiparty system announced by President Inönü in 1945. The radicals may accept the compromise as a first instalment, confident that time is on their side and that future instalments are bound to follow. Both conservatives and radicals may feel exhausted from a long struggle or fearful of a civil war. This consideration is likely to loom large if they have been through such a war in recent memory. As Barrington Moore (1966, p. 3) has aptly proposed, the English civil war was a crucial 'contribution of early violence to later gradualism'. In short, democracy, like any collective human action, is likely to stem from a large variety of mixed motives.

The decision phase may well be considered an act of deliberate, explicit consensus. But, once again, this somewhat nebulous term should be carefully considered and perhaps replaced with less ambiguous synonyms. First of all, as Bryce suggests, the democratic content of the decision may be incidental to other substantive issues. Second, in so far as it is a genuine compromise it will seem second-best to all major parties involved—it certainly will not represent any agreement on fundamentals. Third, even on procedures there are likely to be continuing differences of preference. Universal suffrage with proportional representation, the content of the Swedish compromise of 1907, was about equally distasteful to the conservatives (who would rather have continued the old plutocratic voting system) and to the liberals and socialists (who wanted majority rule undiluted by proportional representation). What matters at the decision stage is not what values the leaders hold dear in the abstract, but what concrete steps they are willing to take. Fourth, the agreement worked out by the leaders is far from universal. It must be transmitted to the professional politicians and to the citizenry at large. These are two aspects of the final, or habituation, phase of the model.

D. HABITUATION PHASE

A distasteful decision, once made, is likely to seem more palatable as one is forced to live with it. Everyday experience can supply concrete illustrations of this probability for each of us. Festinger's (1962) theory of 'cognitive dissonance' supplies a technical explanation and experimental support. Democracy, moreover, is by definition a competitive process, and this competition gives an edge to those who can rationalise their commitment to it, and an even greater edge to those who sincerely believe in it. The transformation of the Swedish Conservative Party from 1918 to 1936 vividly illustrates the point. After two decades those leaders who had grudgingly put up with democracy or pragmatically accepted it retired or died and were replaced by others who sincerely believed in it. Similarly, in Turkey there is a remarkable change from the leadership of Ismet Inönü, who promoted democracy out of a sense of duty, and Adnan Menderes, who saw in it an unprecedented vehicle for his ambition, to younger leaders in each of their parties who understand democracy more fully and embrace it more wholeheartedly. In short, the very process of democracy institutes a double process of Darwinian selectivity in favour of convinced democrats: one among parties in general elections and the other among politicians vying for leadership within these parties.

But politics consists not only of competition for office. It is, above all, a process for resolving conflicts within human groups—whether these arise from the clash of interests or from uncertainty about the future. A new political régime is a novel prescription for taking joint chances on the unknown. With its basic practice of multilateral debate, democracy in particular involves a process of trial and error, a joint learning experience. The first grand compromise that establishes democracy, if it proves at all viable, is in itself a proof of the efficacy of the principle of conciliation and accommodation. The first success, therefore, may encourage contending political forces and their leaders to submit other major questions to resolution by democratic procedures.

In Sweden, for instance, there had been a general political stalemate in the last third of the nineteenth century over the prime issues of the day—the taxation and conscription systems inherited from the sixteenth century. But in the two decades after 1918, when democracy was fully adopted by the Swedes, a whole host of thorny questions was wittingly or unwittingly resolved. The Social Democrats surrendered their earlier pacifism, anti-clericalism, and republicanism, as well as the demand for nationalisation of industry (although they found it hard to admit this last point). The conservatives, once staunchly nationalist, endorsed Swedish participation in international organisations. Above all, conservatives and liberals fully accepted government intervention in the economy and the social welfare state.

Of course, the spiral that in Sweden went upward to greater and greater successes for the democratic process may also go downward. A conspicuous failure to resolve some urgent political question will damage the prospects of democracy; if such a failure comes early in the habituation phase, it may prove fatal.

Surveying the evolution of political debate and conflict in the Western democracies over the last century, it is striking to observe the difference between social and economic issues, which democracies handled with comparative ease, and issues of community, which have proved far more troublesome. (The contrast emerges implicitly from the country studies in Dahl, 1966.) With the advantage of a century's hindsight, it is easy to see that Marx's estimate was wrong at crucial points. In nationality he saw a cloak for bourgeois class interests. He denounced religion as the opiate of the masses. In economics, by contrast, he foresaw very real and increasingly bitter struggles that would end by bringing bourgeois democracy crashing down. But in fact democracy has proved most effective in resolving political questions where the major divisions have been social and economic, as in Britain, Australia, New Zealand, and the Scandinavian countries. It has been the fight among religious, national, and racial groups, instead, that has proved most tenacious and has caused recurrent bitterness, as in Belgium, Holland, Canada, and the United States.

The reasons are not hard to find. On the socio-economic front Marxism itself became a sufficient force in Europe to serve to some extent as a self-disconfirming prophecy. But beyond this there is a fundamental difference in the nature of the issues. On matters of economic policy and social expenditures you can always split the difference. In an expanding economy, you can even have it both ways: the contest for higher wages, profits, consumer savings, and social welfare payments can be turned into a positive-sum game. But there is no middle position between Flemish and French as official languages, or between Calvinism, Catholicism, and secularism as principles of education. The best you can get here is an 'inclusive compromise'

(Rustow, 1955, p. 231)—a log-rolling deal whereby some government officers speak French and some Flemish, or some children are taught according to Aquinas, some, Calvin, and some, Voltaire. Such a solution may partly depoliticise the question. Yet it also entrenches the differences instead of removing them, and accordingly it may convert political conflict into a form of trench warfare.

The difficulty that democracy finds in resolving issues of community emphasises the importance of national unity as the background condition of the democratisation process. The hardest struggles in a democracy are those against the birth defects of the political community.

The transition to democracy, it was suggested earlier, may require some common attitudes and some distinct attitudes on the part of the politician and of the common citizen. The distinction is already apparent during the decision phase when the leaders search for compromise while their followers wearily uphold the banners of the old struggle. It becomes even more readily apparent during the habituation phase, when three sorts of process are at work. First, both politicians and citizens learn from the successful resolution of some issues to place their faith in the new rules and to apply them to new issues. Their trust will grow more quickly if, in the early decades of the new régime, a wide variety of political tendencies can participate in the conduct of affairs, either by joining various coalitions or by taking turns as government and opposition. Second, as we just saw, experience with democratic techniques and competitive recruitment will confirm the politicians in their democratic practices and beliefs. Third, the population at large will become firmly fitted into the new structure by the forging of effective links of party organisation that connect the politicians in the capital with the mass electorate throughout the country.

These party organisations may be a direct continuation of those that were active during the preparatory, or conflict, phase of democratisation, and a suffrage extension at the time of the democratic 'decision' may now have given them a free field. It is possible, on the other hand, that no parties with a broad popular base emerged during the conflict phase and that the suffrage extension was very limited. Even under such conditions of partial democratisation of the political structure, a competitive dynamic that completes the process may have been set off. The parliamentary parties will seek support from constituency organisations to insure a steady supply of members for their group in future parliaments. Now this and now that political group may see a chance to steal a march on its opponents by enlarging the electorate or by removing other obstacles to majority control. This, roughly, would seem to have been the nature of British developments between 1832 and 1918. Complete democratisation, of course, is the only logical stopping point for such a dynamic.

The model here presented makes three broad assertions. First, it says that certain ingredients are indispensable to the genesis of democracy. For one thing, there must be a sense of national unity. For another, there must be entrenched and serious conflict. For a third, there must be a conscious adoption of democratic rules. And, finally, both politicians and electorate must be habituated to these rules.

Secondly, the model asserts that these ingredients must be assembled one at a time. Each task has its own logic and each has its natural protagonists—a network of administrators or a group of nationalist literati for the task of unification, a mass movement of the lower class, perhaps led by upper-class dissidents, for the task of preparatory struggle, a small circle of political leaders skilled at negotiation and compromise for the formulation of democratic rules, and a variety of organisation men and their organisations for the task of habituation. The model thus abandons the quest for 'functional requisites' of democracy; for such a quest heaps all these tasks together and thus makes the total job of democratisation quite unmanageable. The argument here is analogous to that which has been made by Hirschman and others against the theory of balanced economic growth. These economists do not deny that the transition from a primitive subsistence economy to a mature industrial society involves changes on all fronts —in working skills, in capital formation, in the distribution system, in consumption habits, in the monetary system, and so forth. But they insist that any country that attempted all these tasks at once would in practice find itself totally paralysed—that the stablest balance is that of stagnation. Hence the economic developer's problem, in their view, becomes one of finding backward and forward 'linkages', that is, of devising a manageable sequence of tasks.

Thirdly, the model does suggest one such sequence from national unity as background, through struggle, compromise, and habituation, to democracy. The cogency of this sequence is brought home by a deviant development in Turkey in the years after 1945. The Turkish commitment to democracy was made in the absence of prior overt conflict between major social groups or their leading elites. In 1950 there was the first change of government as the result of a new electoral majority, but in the next decade there was a drift back into authoritarian practices on the part of this newly elected party, and in 1960–1 the democratic experiment was interrupted by a military coup. These developments are not unconnected: Turkey paid the price in 1960 for having received its first democratic régime as a free gift from the hands of a dictator. But after 1961 there was a further evolution in the more appropriate sequence. The crisis of 1960–1 had made social and political conflict far more acceptable, and a full range of social and economic issues was debated for the first time. The conflict that shaped up was between the military on one side and the spokesmen of the agrarian majority on the other—and the compromise between these two allowed the resumption of the democratic experiment on a more secure basis by 1965.

In the interests of parsimony, the basic ingredients of the model have been kept to four, and the social circumstances or psychological motivations that may furnish each of them have been left wide open. Specifically, the model rejects what are sometimes proposed as preconditions of democracy, e.g. high levels of economic and social development or a prior consensus either on fundamentals or on the rules. Economic growth may be one of the circumstances that produces the tensions essential to the preparatory or conflict phase—but there are other circumstances that might also serve. Mass education and social welfare services are more likely to be the result of democratisation.

Consensus on fundamentals is an implausible precondition. A people who were not in conflict about some rather fundamental matters would have little need to devise democracy's elaborate rules for conflict resolution. And the acceptance of those rules is logically a part of the transition process rather than its prerequisite. The present model transfers various aspects of consensus from the quiescent state of pre-conditions to that of active elements in the process. I here follow the lead of Bernard Crick (1964, p. 24), who has strikingly written:

> It is often thought that for this 'master science' [i.e., democratic politics] to function, there must already be in existence some shared idea of a 'common good', some 'consensus' or *consensus juris*. But this common good is itself the process of practical reconciliation of the interests of the various . . . aggregates, or groups which compose a state; it is not some external and intangible spiritual adhesive. . . . Diverse groups hold together, firstly, because they have a common interest in sheer survival, and, secondly, because they practise politics —not because they agree about 'fundamentals', or some such concept too vague, too personal, or too divine ever to do the job of politics for it. The moral consensus of a free state is not something mysteri-

ously prior to or above politics: it is the activity (the civilising activity) of politics itself.

The basis of democracy is not maximum consensus. It is the tenuous middle ground between imposed uniformity (such as would lead to some sort of tyranny) and implacable hostility (of a kind that would disrupt the community in civil war or secession). In the process of genesis of democracy, an element of what might be termed consensus enters at three points at least. There must be a prior sense of community, preferably a sense of community quietly taken for granted that is above mere opinion and mere agreement. There must be a conscious adoption of democratic rules, but they must not be so much believed in as applied, first perhaps from necessity and gradually from habit. The very operation of these rules will enlarge the area of consensus step-by-step as democracy moves down its crowded agenda.

But new issues will always emerge and new conflicts threaten the newly won agreements. The characteristic procedures of democracy include campaign oratory, the election of candidates, parliamentary divisions, votes of confidence and of censure—a host of devices, in short, for expressing conflict and thereby resolving it. The essence of democracy is the habit of dissension and conciliation over ever-changing issues and amidst ever-changing alignments. Totalitarian rulers must enforce unanimity on fundamentals and on procedures before they can get down to other business. By contrast, democracy is that form of government that derives its just powers from the dissent of up to one half of the governed.

REFERENCES

ALMOND, G. and VERBA, S. (1963) *The Civic Culture*, Princeton University Press.
BARKER, E. (1942) *Reflections on Government*, Oxford University Press.
BINDER, L., ed. (1966) *Politics in Lebanon*, Wiley.
BRYCE, J. (1921) *Modern Democracies*, Macmillan.
COSER, L. A. (1956) *The Function of Social Conflict*, Free Press.
CRICK, B. (1964) *In Defence of Politics*, rev. edn., Penguin.
DAHL, R. A. (1956) *A Preface to Democratic Theory*, University of Chicago Press.
DAHL, R. A. (1961) *Who Governs?*, Yale University Press.
DAHL, R. A., ed. (1966) *Political Oppositions in Western Democracies*, Yale University Press.
DAHL, R. A. (1967) *Pluralist Democracy in the United States: Conflict and Consent*, University of Chicago Press.
DAHRENDORF, R. (1959) *Class and Class Conflict in Industrial Society*, Stanford University Press.
DEUTSCH, K. W. (1953) *Nationalism and Social Communication*, Wiley.

DEUTSCH, K. W. *et al.* (1957) *Political Community and the North Atlantic Area*, Princeton University Press.

ECKSTEIN, H. (1961) *The Theory of Stable Democracy*, Princeton University Press.

ECKSTEIN, H. (1965) *Division and Cohesion in a Democracy*, Princeton University Press.

FESTINGER, L. (1962) *A Theory of Cognitive Dissonance*, Tavistock.

FOLLETT, M. P. (1918) *The New State*, Longmans.

FOLLETT, M. P. (1924) *Creative Experience*, Longmans.

FRIEDRICH, C. J. (1942) *The New Belief in the Common Man*, Little, Brown.

HIRSCHMAN, A. O. (1958) *The Strategy of Economic Development*, Yale University Press.

HIRSCHMAN, A. O. (1963) *Journeys Towards Progress*, New York, Twentieth Century Fund.

HIRSCHMAN, A. O. (1965) 'Obstacles to development: a classification and quasi-vanishing act?' *Economic Development and Cultural Change*, **13**, July.

JENNINGS, W. I. (1956) *The Approach to Self-Government*, Cambridge University Press.

KUHN, T. (1962) *The Structure of Scientific Revolutions*, University of Chicago Press.

LERNER, D. *et al.* (1958) *The Passing of Traditional Society*, New York, Free Press.

LIJPHART, A. (1968) *The Politics of Accommodation*, University of California Press.

LIPSET, S. M. (1960) *Political Man*, Doubleday.

LOWELL, A. L. (1896) *Government and Parties in Continental Europe*, Longmans.

MCCLOSKY, H. (1964) 'Consensus and ideology in American Politics', *American Political Science Review*, **58**, June.

MOORE, B. (1966) *Social Origins of Dictatorship and Democracy*, Beacon Press.

PROTHRO, J. W. and GRIGG, C. M. (1960) 'Fundamental principles of democracy: bases of agreement and disagreement', *Journal of Politics*, **22**, May.

RUSTOW, D. A. (1955) *The Politics of Compromise: a Study of Parties and Cabinet Government in Sweden*, Princeton University Press.

RUSTOW, D. A. (1957) 'Politics and Islam in Turkey' in R. N. Frye, ed. *Islam and the West*, Harvard University Press.

RUSTOW, D. A. (1965) 'Turkey: the tradition of modernity', in L. W. Pye and S. Verba, eds., *Political Culture and Political Development*, Princeton University Press.

RUSTOW, D. A. (1966) 'The development of parties in Turkey', in J. LaPalombara and M. Weiner, eds. *Political Parties and Political Development*, Princeton University Press.

RUSTOW, D. A. (1967) *A World of Nations: Problems of Political Modernization*, Washington Brookings Institution.

RUSTOW, D. A. (1967) 'Politics and development policy', in F. C. Shorter, ed., *Four Studies in the Economic Development of Turkey*, Cass.

RUSTOW, D. A. (1968) 'Nation' in *International Encyclopedia of the Social Sciences*, vol. ii, Macmillan and Free Press.

SCHATTSCHNEIDER, E. E. (1960) *The Semi-Sovereign People*, Holt.

SHILS, E. (1966) 'The prospect for Lebanese civility', in L. Binder, ed., *Politics in Lebanon*, Wiley.

SIMON, H. A. (1957) *Models of Man: Social and Rational*, Wiley.

TRUMAN, D. (1951) *The Governmental Process*, Knopf.

VERNEY, D. A. (1957) *Parliamentary Reform in Sweden, 1866–1921*, Oxford University Press.

WARD, R. E. and RUSTOW, D. A., eds. (1964) *Political Modernization in Japan and Turkey*, Princeton University Press.

10

B. Guy Peters,
John C. Doughtie
and M. Kathleen
McCulloch

Do public policies vary in different types of democratic system?

Adapted from 'Types of democratic systems and types of public policy', *Comparative Politics*, April 1977, pp. 237–55.

With the success of the 'behavioural revolution' in political science have come a number of positive changes in the study of comparative politics. We have long abandoned the strict constitutionalism and institutionalism which had characterised traditional comparative government studies. These have been replaced with a broader conception of politics and the political process. The apparent problem with comparative politics at present is that this revolution has been too successful. Now the study of the input side of the political system—political parties, pressure groups, electoral behaviour, and mass attitudinal configurations—has become so popular that we tend to ignore the 'conversion functions' of the political system—those governmental and institutional configurations so important in traditional comparative politics. Further, we have especially ignored until quite recently the comparative study of the output side of the political system. The reasons for the emphasis on inputs are numerous. One of the most important is the reliance on the Eastonian version of systems theory as an approximation of a paradigm for the discipline.[1] Although some slight attention is given to the processes of decision making, this influential work directs our attention mainly toward political inputs. It further tends to assume a direct correspondence between the inputs and outputs of this political system. Roy Macridis has referred to this focus in comparative politics as 'inputism' and notes that:

[1] See the discussion of this model by Heisler and Kvavik (1974, pp. 34–7). David Easton's model should not bear the entire blame, as several models which have been equally influential in comparative politics have had the same sort of input bias.

The famous 'black box', as graduate students have come to know government, is at best a filter mechanism through which interests express themselves and at its worst a simple transmission mechanism. The role of the state is reduced to the narrow confines of an organisation which channels, reflects, and expresses commands and instructions from 'elsewhere' (Macridis, 1968, p. 85).

Likewise, Martin Heisler and Robert Kvavik in their discussion of the weaknesses of the Eastonian model in studying modern European politics say that

If the [systems] framework is accorded the status of theory, however . . . then some monumental problems are encountered.

First, a casual assumption of behavior indwells the framework qua model: it is difficult to escape the conclusion that 'input-type behavior' (e.g. voting, party and interest-group activity) is the principal source of influences on outputs (i.e. on authoritative decisions, rules and laws). Second, and in part as a corollary of the problem identified in the last sentence, there is a clear assumption of the preeminence of inputs over what Easton has termed 'within-puts' in terms of substantive—i.e. policy-influencing, output-determining—importance and volume. (Heisler and Kvavik, 1974, p. 35).

Another factor leading to an emphasis on input variables is their assumed conceptual clarity.[2] It is (allegedly) clear just what elections mean for the political system. Likewise, the assumption of a relationship between certain attitudinal configurations (e.g., the civic culture) and the political behaviour of mass publics can be readily made, if only in an ex post facto manner.[3] These types of activities not only appear clearly 'political' to the professional political scientist, they also have the appearance of being clearly political to that mythical man in the street.

Some blame for 'inputism' in comparative political analysis must

[2] The categories employed for inputs, however, are often lacking in clarity. For example, the distinction between interest articulation and interest aggregation frequently becomes extremely artificial when analysing political events.

[3] See Almond and Verba (1963). Again, these authors do not bear the blame for the excessive reliance on political culture explanations of system characteristics by themselves. Rather, one of the general tendencies of comparative political studies has been to emphasise the influence of culture while de-emphasising the importance of structures and institutions.

be placed, however, on the existing studies of outputs and public policy. The majority of this literature (to which one of the authors admits adding) tends to be a rather sterile discussion of the relative importance of socioeconomic and political variables in explaining policy outcomes. Not only has there been a relative dearth of theoretical explanations for the patterns of relationship found, but even the usual operationalisation of dependent variables appears weak. Public expenditures are certainly an important aspect of the outputs of the political system, but they cannot be taken to be a sufficient measure of the policies of the political system. There needs to be some concern not only with the conceptual classification of types of expenditures, but also with the less easily quantified, albeit quantifiable aspects of public policy.

Further, the study of public policy as it has been conducted would rather easily lead one to the conclusion that political factors and the nature of regimes are indeed unimportant in determining public policies. Citing the number of studies which conclude that the economic resource base is crucial to the outputs of public policy, Robert Dahl (1971, pp. 26–7) states that 'Because of the powerful impact on governmental policies of such factors as a country's level of socioeconomic development, the characteristics of its social and economic systems, and its traditions, it may well be that the character of the regime has little independent effect upon most governmental policies'. Much of our previous policy research would indeed direct the attention of political scientists away from substantive policy research simply because the independent variables which most political scientists would bring to the analysis had been found to have little impact on policy.

This essay will be an attempt to meet (at least partially) some of these concerns with the literature on comparative public policy. It will relate structural characteristics of political systems to the policy choices made by those systems. This attempt is at a preliminary stage, but we believe that the results are important for our understanding of comparative politics and comparative public policy.

TWO TYPOLOGIES

We will begin this analysis of the relationship of political system types to public policy types by discussing two typologies: one of democratic political systems and the second of public policy. We will be arguing that the variables used by both typologies to classify observations are quite similar, so that there should be some empirical relationship between the political system type and the policies which are adopted by that political system.

A typology of democratic political systems

The first typology, developed by Arend Lijphart (1968a), falls into the traditional domain of comparative politics by seeking to classify different types of political systems. More specifically, it classifies democratic political systems on the basis of two variables: elite behaviour and political culture.

The political elite variable is classified by Lijphart into two categories: competitive and coalescent. The operational definitions of the categories are not made explicit, but for our purposes we will distinguish between elite politics conducted as an adversary proceeding (competitive elite politics) and politics conducted as a co-operative proceeding (coalescent elite politics). The former type of political system operates in the traditional parliamentary fashion of government and opposition, with perhaps compromise but little direct co-operation. In contrast, coalescent politics approximates a 'grand coalition' style of politics, with each major political grouping involved in making decisions.

The political culture variable is classified by Lijphart as being either homogeneous or fragmented. Again, the exact operational definitions of these two classifications are not made clear but we can apply some common-sense categorisations and think of fragmented political cultures as those having significant cleavage along one or more dimensions, such as race, language, religion and region. Further, these cleavages are politicised and relatively intense. In contrast, homogeneous political cultures will lack such intense cleavages. These definitions are obviously little more operational than those supplied by Lijphart, but they do indicate the conceptual space which we believe occupied by the terms employed by Lijphart.

The interaction of the above two variables produces a typology of four cells (see Figure 10.1) which yields four different types of democratic political systems. Two of the cells—centripetal democracy and centrifugal democracy—correspond quite closely to Gabriel Almond's Anglo-American and Continental European types respectively (Almond, 1956, pp. 391–409). They, however, lack any identification with specific geographical cases and therefore hopefully can be applied in a more general fashion. The former of these two types—centripetal democracy—is still best characterised by the United Kingdom and the United States. There is a (relatively) homogeneous political culture but the behaviour of political elites is

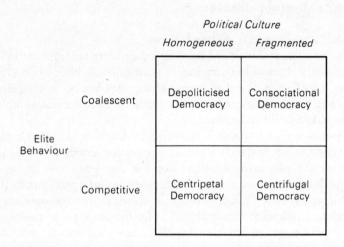

Figure 10.1 The Lijphart typology of democratic systems

characterised by active competition for control of public office and for the shaping of public policy. The scope and intensity of that conflict is, however, restrained by both the relative homogeneity of the cultural values in question as well as a number of institutional and procedural safeguards. Centrifugal democracy, on the other hand is characterised by a lack of agreement and integration at both the elite and the mass level. This tends to produce quite unrestrained political conflict, as well as instability and immobilism. This system can best be typified by France in the Fourth Republic, Weimar Germany and modern Italy.

The other two cells of the typology are somewhat less frequently described system types, occurring as they do primarily in the smaller European democracies. One—consociational democracy—describes the political systems of the Netherlands, Belgium, Switzerland, Austria, and perhaps Canada. In these nations the political culture is at least as fragmented as that found in the centrifugal democracies. The crucial difference is therefore the coalescent or accommodative behaviour of the political elites. Co-operation and bargaining at the elite level tends to prevent the instability and immobilism which would otherwise limit the effectiveness if not the survival of these political systems.

The final cell of the typology—depoliticised democracy—is discussed by Lijphart primarily in terms of a pattern of politics which was emerging at the time (1968) at which he was writing. However, in the real world, the Scandinavian countries most closely approximate this pattern of coalescent elite behaviour with very low levels of politicisation of important national issues. All important elements of the society are included in decision making, with the results approximating those of a grand coalition style of government. One party or coalition does hold the formal positions of governmental authority, but the degree of inclusions of the opposition and the nonparliamentary groups in decision makes the elite politics quite coalescent.

This paper is not intended to be an essay on typologies of political systems, but we would feel somewhat derelict if we did not comment to some degree on this typological formation. This typology attempts to explain political stability through the combination of the variables of elite and mass fragmentation. However, the institutional and motivational linkages appear somewhat unclear at times. Lijphart (1968a, pp. 25–30) does discuss the motivational background of elite behaviour in consociational systems, but does not provide any general explanations for the adoption of coalescent elite behaviour. Some attempts have been made at elaborating such a general motivational device for coalescent behaviour. Heisler and Kvavik (1974, pp. 54–66) for example, have been able to demonstrate that the stability and effectiveness of both Lijphart's 'consociational' and 'depoliticised' democracies can be understood through the mechanism of co-optation of any potential threats to the elite group by a 'continual, regularised access' to the political system. Thus, a more general model describing politics in smaller European democracies may be a more useful approach. However, for the time at hand, we will employ this descriptive typology to determine if it is predictive of types of policy as well as descriptive of types of political system.

A typology of public policies

By this time, several typologies and classifications of public policy have been advanced. At the simplest level, those who work with comparative state and national expenditures have classified expenditures functionally. Lewis Froman (1967, pp. 94–108) has divided policies into 'areal' and 'segmental' categories dependent upon the scope of their impact. Theodore Lowi (1964, pp. 677–715) divided policy into three types: distributive, regulative, and redistributive—dependent upon the impact on society and the manner in which the policy is made. He later adds the category of 'constituent' policies to his former three (Lowi, 1972, pp. 298–310). Finally, building upon the original Lowi typology, Robert Salisbury (1968, pp. 151–75) and later Salisbury and John Heinz (1970, pp. 39–60) have discussed policy as divisible into four classifications: distributive, redistributive, regulative and self-regulative.

	Demand pattern	
	Integrated	Fragmented
Integrated	Redistribution	Regulation
Fragmented	Self-regulation	Distribution

Decisional system

Figure 10.2   The Salisbury typology of public policy

These four types of policy are hypothesised by Salisbury to result from the interaction of two variables: the fragmentation or integration of the demand system, and the fragmentation or integration of decision making (see Figure 10.2). As with the Lijphart typology, the operational measures of fragmentation and integration are not made clear for either level, nor are the exact definitions of policy types. We will therefore again be forced back on a more commonsense definition of these variable, although a number of indicators could be used for each.

The first of the policy types—distribution—is hypothesised to occur when a fragmented demand pattern interacts with a fragmented decisional system. The classic example of this policy type would be the demands from congressional districts for improvements being decided by a legislature. The usual pattern of outputs in such a situation is the 'pork barrel', with each locality receiving some benefits. The most direct contrast to this is a highly integrated decisional system confronted by a limited number of demands from directly conflicting groups. In such a situation, decision making becomes a zero-sum game in which one group cannot be advantaged without another being disadvantaged obviously and directly. This is, then, an obvious case of redistributive politics.

Self-regulative policies are more likely to emerge when a highly integrated set of demands confronts a fragmented decisional system. As with the regulation of the medical and legal professions in the United States—or the management of the availability of petroleum products during the energy crisis—the usual response to such a situation is to allow those pressing demands to regulate themselves. Finally, when fragmented demands confront an integrated decision-making system, we may expect a pattern of regulation. The decision maker is not forced into a zero-sum situation but can instead regulate the differences among groups presenting demands. As Salisbury and Heinz (1970, p. 41) point out, one of the major values of regulative (and self-regulative) policies is their ambiguity regarding winners and losers.

The definition of these policies, as supplied by Lowi and by Salisbury, is again not clearly operationalised, but is generally phrased in terms of the perceptions of the actors involved in the decisions. A more generalisable and more readily operational definition of each can also be supplied. In general, then, we will be looking at these four types of policies in the following manner:

a. *Redistributive policies* take from one group and give to another. In modern societies, policies of this type will be largely economic in their effects, and will tend to redistribute income and wealth from the upper economic classes to the lower. Further, some redistribution of status may also occur, especially through civil-rights legislation conferring benefits upon ethnic groups.

b. *Distributive policies* are also largely economic in their effects but differ in that they tend to provide benefits to all making demands rather than to take from one and give to another. These benefits are generally in terms of goods which can be divided among geographical or functional groupings.

c. *Regulative policies* place constraints on acceptable behaviour and therefore indirectly confer benefits or losses on individuals.

d. *Self-regulative policies* allow groups and individuals affected by regulation to develop and even implement the regulations. On the basis of expertise or of convenience, public officials are willing to provide a stamp of legitimacy for the actions of private groups. These policies will have some of the same effects as regulatory policies—stabilising or controlling one socio-economic sector— but may be substantially different in the direction and type of control exercised.

Lowi and Salisbury have discussed these policy types almost entirely within the American context, and would appear to argue that they are most appropriate for within-system analysis. In such an analysis the difference in policy outputs are a function of the degree of integration of the demands concerning the issue area and the particular institutions within which the policy is to be made. This typology of policy, may, however, be useful in an attempt to analyse policy and policy formation across systems. Although any nation must, of necessity, have some policies of each of these four types, we can still ask the question whether certain internation configurations of decision making and demands produce tendencies toward certain types of policy, just as they do at the level of intranation analysis. There will certainly be variety in each country, but we may still fruitfully inquire whether these differences in regimes may not be as useful in explaining policy differences as the more culturally oriented explanations of Anthony King (1973) and Alexander Groth (1971) or the economic approaches of Thomas Dye. However, given the general similarity of the policy outputs among European and other democratic systems, we have to argue rather slight differences in policy are important as indicators of policy configurations.

Synthesis

The two variables used by Lijphart and by Salisbury to classify political and policy systems have a remarkable degree of similarity. On the input side of the policy system, these variables are both concerned with the level of fragmentation of demands coming from the social and cultural environment. One author refers to this as the fragmentation of the political culture, while the other refers to it as the fragmentation of demands. On the national level, we will argue that the fragmentation of the political culture will generally be related to a fragmentation of the demands placed upon the system. For example, the fragmentation of cultures in France, Belgium, the Netherlands, and a number of the other nations in question is associated with the formation of fragmented and competitive interest-group structures. Likewise, the classification of elites as competitive or coalescent in Lijphart's typology is rather close to

| | Input behaviour | |
	Integrated	Fragmented
Integrated	Depoliticised democracy; Redistribution	Consociational democracy; Regulation
Fragmented	Centripetal democracy; Self-regulation	Centrifugal democracy; Distribution

Decisional system

Figure 10 3   Integration of typologies of political systems
and public policy

classifying decision-making systems as being fragmented or integrated. If a clear distinction between the two can be made, one of the
classifications (Lijphart's) is apparently to be primarily a behavioural
measure, while the second (Salisbury's) is intended to be primarily
structural. However, the effects of the two types of fragmentation-
competition would be logically similar.

From this assumption of the similarity of the two typologies, we
can derive a single typology based on the degree of fragmentation or
integration of the decision-making system (elite) (see Figure 10.3). In
this typology, we hypothesise that the type of political system will
indeed be related to the characteristics of the public policy adopted by
that system. Depoliticised political systems (e.g., Sweden) should
produce more redistributive policies than do other types of political
systems. Centripetal political systems (e.g., the United Kingdom)
should produce more self-regulative policies, and consociational
democracies (e.g., the Netherlands) should produce more regulative
policies than do other systems. Again, we should point out that each
of the four types of political systems will of necessity produce some
of each of the four types of policy. We argue, however, that there
will be tendencies toward certain policy choices as a function of the
political structures of the society.

We will proceed to test these assumptions concerning the relationship of policymaking and the characteristics of the political system in

two ways. The first will be through descriptive accounts of the political system characteristics and the policy outputs of the four countries listed as examples above. Second, we will use a set of measures of the characteristics of public policy, isolate dimensions of policy, and then assess the degree of relationship between system type and policy type.

POLITICAL SYSTEMS AND REDISTRIBUTION: A DESCRIPTIVE ANALYSIS

Due to space limitations, we cannot present the definitive descriptions of each of these political systems and its public policies. Instead, we will attempt to point out briefly why they fit into certain categories and the characteristics of their policy formation.

Redistribution and the depoliticised polity

On the basis of our synthesis of the two typologies, we would clearly expect Sweden to present the characteristics of both a depoliticised political system and a high level of redistribution through the public budget. The term *depoliticised* would appear inappropriate for a nation with such an active political life, but in the term's limited meaning of relatively restrained political discourse and a high level of co-operation and compromise in decision making, it would appear quite fitting. In fact, the standard description of Swedish politics has been that of compromise and the 'depoliticisation' of potentially divisive issues (see Rustow, 1955 and Stjernquist, 1966).

First, Sweden does demonstrate the characteristics of having an integrated elite and an integrated set of demands being placed upon that elite. Thomas Anton makes this point quite clearly:

> . . . on one side there is the governmental structure which, in a small nation, with a long tradition of governmental centralisation, is highly integrated around a strong central government. On the other side stands what may be the best-organised structure of interest groups to be found in the world. Virtually all social interests of any significance—from industrial workers to tennis enthusiasts—are organised into local, regional and national associations—and the most important interests (labour and industry) are further centralised by 'super' organisations that represent the interest of all their associated organisations in national negotiations (Anton, 1969, p. 92).

Sweden then does fit the two defining characteristics of having both an integrated demand pattern and an integrated decision-making system. Does it also display the characteristics of a depoliticised political system and high levels of redistribution? Sweden can perhaps be taken as an archtype of both of these characteristics. The 'politics of compromise' has by now become virtually a cliché in describing Swedish political life. Despite the somewhat trite nature, the characterisation is generally accurate. Again, Anton's description is useful: 'Policy-making is consensual, in that decisions are seldom made without the agreement of virtually all parties to them... Given this emphasis on consensus, and since little is done without prior research anyway, "crises" seldom occur. The result is decision-making which never seems rash, abrupt, irrational or indeed, exciting' (Anton, 1969, p. 94).

On this descriptive basis, the model of depoliticised democracy does fit Sweden. These statements, as well as a number of structural and behavioural mechanisms of politics in Sweden, e.g., the 'spirit of Saltsjöbaden', and 'Harpsund Democracy', indicate that politics has been moved from a plane of conflict to one of compromise.

Finally, we come to the redistributive nature of Swedish public policy. Given the characterisation of Sweden in the popular press, this may not require any justification. However, the comparative data on the four countries being discussed here does clearly indicate the redistributive nature of Swedish policy (see Table 10.1 and

TABLE 10.1 *Values of selected indicators for four countries, 1971*

Indicator	Sweden	France	Netherlands	United Kingdom
Percentage of income tax revenue	44·0	25·1	24·5	37·7
Percentage of spending on welfare	34·1	5·2	26·0	18·0
Percentage of spending on health	5·1	4·0	7·7	10·4
Gini index of income inequality	0·397	0·410	0·390	0·298
Percentage of spending on education	16·1	18·9	16·6	12·6
Percentage of spending on public works	11·8	17·8	12·3	16·9
Percentage of revenue from value-added tax	24·9	43·7	21·8	8·1
Civil servants per 1,000 population	20·8	28·0	28·5	35·5

Appendix A). Interestingly, much of this redistribution—especially the early redistribution of political power—was decided upon by compromise, but during more recent years of majority parliamentarianism, some decisions have been reached without consent of all major parties—especially the Conservative party. In any case, it is fairly clear that the basic history of Swedish public policy has been the successive transfer of political, economic and social power away from the upper classes and downward toward the working classes. This is not to say that there are not elites and 'upper-class' individuals with substantial influence, but only that relative to many other systems a substantial redistribution has occurred.

Centrifugal political systems and distributive policy

Centrifugal political systems have fragmented political cultures and competitive elites. We have hypothesised that such a set of political structures and values should be associated with more distributive public policies than would be found in other types of political systems. As our example of a centrifugal political system we will be using France. Some may argue with this choice, given the recent success of Gaullism and the presence of stable parliamentary majorities. Further, the general modernisation of the economy and society might make even the fragmentation of the mass political culture open to question. We believe that there is a sufficient degree of fragmentation at both levels to justify this classification.

First, at the elite level, the formal decision-making powers in the French political system are fragmented. The division of powers between president, Parliament, and prime minister gives rise to some important questions as to the locus of authority. This division has become important after de Gaulle and Pompidou. Currently, the presence of Gaullists of some stripe in both the Presidency and Parliament tends to diminish the divisiveness of this arrangement. However, the possibility of a severe schism and the lack of integration was quite evident in Pompidou's statements and threats concerning the possibility of a Left majority in the 1973 election.

On a more behavioural level, it is far from clear that Gaullism itself is truly an integrated political movement. The intraparty cleavage is significant, and the majority of Gaullists in Parliament depends upon some groups (RI and CDP) which are only loosely allied with the major Gaullist movement.[4] Beyond this weakness in the majority, there is a long history of non-co-operation between various elite groups (especially the Communists) which clearly distinguishes this competitive situation from the coalescent behaviour of Swedish elites.

[4] The decisions of both Giscard d'Estaing and Chaban-Delmas to run for president in 1974 is a rather good indication of the division within the Gaullist movement.

At the mass level, even with the modernisation of industry and agriculture which has been occurring in France, demands placed upon the political system are still quite fragmented. Whereas we have noted the centralisation of unions and management groups in the bargaining process in Sweden, France has three significant labour organisations and two large management organisations. Even then, the majority of workers and a large proportion of managers are not members of any group. In fact, it has been shown that the traditional sector of the economy is perhaps better organised to make a set of integrated demands than is the more modern sector (see Tarrow, 1971, pp. 354–5). This general lack of organisation, combined with the division of the political system into a number of separate political 'chapels' makes it clear that no set of integrated demands is likely to impinge upon the fragmented decision-making system.

From the above description, albeit brief, we can conclude that the politics of France are characterised by a lack of integration at both the elite and mass levels. It should therefore display the centrifugal characteristics associated with this lack of integration. That the system is still centrifugal is well stated by Philip Williams and Martin Harrison (1972, p. 446):

> Yet although the initial transfer went smoothly, the problem of promoting stable and effective democracy remained one of the least enviable elements in Pompidou's heritage. For, as always, the problem was not simply one of political personnel, but of the nature of wider political attitudes, and of society itself. France today is less stratified and fragmented, her people are less socially and pyschologically isolated than in the past, and social co-operation is greater than it was a generation ago. Yet none of these changes has produced the conditions required for long-term political stability.

Thus, although the centrifugal tendencies of the system have been under control, there is an underlying basis for dissension and immobilism, and for the manifestation of the underlying centrifugal tendencies.

Finally, we come to the question of the nature of public policy in France. Some indication of this policy can be gained by examining Table 10.1, but there is also some descriptive evidence concerning French policy. In discussing French politics of an earlier period, Herbert Lüthy (1955, pp. 323–40) emphasised the importance of *situations acqι ises* and their protection as one of the essential elements of French policy. Policies of this type, defending the existence of personal or local benefits against encroachments of modernisation, are excellent examples of distributive policies. Although the progressive modernisation of French economic life has diminished the importance of these situations, they still do exist:

> In France there are two economies that uneasily coexist: a modern one, most of it implanted since the war by technocrats and a few big State and private firms; and below it, an old, creaking infrastructure, based on artisanship, low turnover with high profits, and the ideal of the small family business. The modern sector has expanded considerably since Lüthy in 1953 described it as 'an isolated enclave inside old France', and today I would say that it predominates, But it has not yet absorbed the old system, which is strongly rooted in the traditional framework of French law and society. This society has been built up of a honeycomb of little sectional interests, each with its clearly defined rights and privileges all mutually suspicious but carefully balancing each other so avoid conflict (Ardagh, 1969, pp. 7–8).

This is an almost perfect description of distributive policy, and the examples are numerous with the most famous being the controversy over the private distillation of alcohol. Here we see a significant vestige of old France in the nature of the policy of the new France.

Consociational political systems and regulative policy
The Netherlands is the nation upon which the model of consociational democracy was based. The presence of a sharply divided mass public, split along religious lines, combined with a highly cooperative elite group, has enabled what might otherwise be an unmanageable political situation to survive and prosper. Lijphart's own work clearly indicates that the Netherlands did fit the characteristics of the consociational democracy (Lijphart 1968b and 1969). We will seek to demonstrate that it can also be characterised as having regulative public policies.

Regulative policies are perhaps the best suited for those nations with severely divided political infrastructures. As Salisbury and Heinz (1970, p. 41) point out, one of the major advantages of regulative policies is that they make it difficult to determine who gains and who loses. Lijphart (1968b, pp. 127–9) points out that once policy decisions are made in the Netherlands, the benefits are usually dispensed in a proportional manner—somewhat similar to what might be expected from a distributive policy system. However, he also points out that many issues are solved by removing them from the political arena, and the 'use of complicated arguments and the juggling of economic facts and figures incomprehensible to most individuals (Lijphart, 1968b, pp. 129–30).

Lijphart's statement is well borne out in the extensive use of economic planning and regulation in the Netherlands. Andrew Shonfield (1965, pp. 211–20), for example, notes the early adoption of indicative planning and an incomes policy by the Netherlands. Although he cites important economic reasons for these policy choices, we can also point out that the use of highly technical economic planning removes one extremely crucial public issue from the political arena and converts it into a depoliticised issue of economic facts and figures. In addition, the numerous regulative actions of boards formed under the 1950 Industrial Organisation Act provide extensive controls over the social and economic systems without direct confrontation between the 'pillars', and further allow for the preservation of proportionality. This whole pattern of policy formation is well summarised by Aber (1969, p. 39) in saying that '... the technical process of economic planning is accorded a position of major influence' due to '... the lack of a political consensus that might resolve economic issues through the electoral process'. Thus the emphasis on regulation in the Netherlands indicates that these types of policy are a convenient means of avoiding many issues which might otherwise severely strain the integration of the nation.

Some of the above discussion of Dutch politics has been purposely written in the past tense. There has been an apparent transformation of the politics of accommodation in the Netherlands into a more depoliticised political system which, paradoxically, may be more unstable than the former consociational system. The cleavages between blocs have lost their sharpness and intensity, and the five major parties so long involved in the politics of accommodation find themselves unable to command either the voters or the deference required to make accommodation work as it had previously. It is perhaps too early to assess the effects of these transformations on policy, but these cases may indeed be instructive if significant changes in policy content and style do follow these significant changes in politics.

Centripetal democracy and self-regulative policies
Centripetal democracy is characterised by a competitive elite and by a homogeneous mass political culture. The most commonly cited examples of this type of democratic system (Almond's Anglo-

American) are the United Kingdom and the United States, although most of the developed members of the Commonwealth would also fit into the classification. In the typology of public policies, the same set of characteristics (integrated demands and fragmented decisional structures) are hypothesised to produce self-regulative policies.

The classification of the political culture and demands of the United Kingdom as being homogeneous or integrated would strike few people as being ill-advised. However, the classification of the elite (decision-making) structures as being fragmented may appear somewhat dubious.[5] This is especially true when we remember that the same structures were classified as coalescent in Sweden and competitive in France. What differentiates the United Kingdom from Sweden and makes it more similar to France? Obviously, the stability of Swedish and British politics, as contrasted to the instability of French politics would appear to make this classification mistaken. However, there is little if any of the 'grand coalition' style of politics, which one tends to associate with coalescent elite behaviour, in British politics. Allen Potter (1966, p. 23) summarises the relationship of mass coalescence and elite competition in British politics when he writes: 'There is virtually no opposition in Britain with a little "o", in the sense of organised activity outside the parliamentary party system aimed at displacing the holders of governmental power. . . . Opposition in Great Britain, as well as in government, is by politicians, offering an alternative government in accordance with the conventions of the parliamentary system—opposition with a capital "O."' While this statement may underestimate the impact of Northern Ireland on British politics, it does point to general mass homogeneity and to the fact that politics is indeed still a competitive enterprise and the parties remain responsible for their actions at the next general election. It is the general responsibility of each government to present a programme, and it is the duty of each opposition to oppose that programme. Ivor Jennings (1968, p. 87) points out that '. . . opposition is regarded as an essential element of the Constitution. The British Constitution not only does not expect conformity, it demands the opposite. The Government has the majority and so can govern; but it must do so under a constant fire of criticism from the opposition.'

While such opposition may be lessened during times of national emergency, and is restrained by a number of institutional norms at

[5] Given the usual conception of the solidarity of the British elite, united by the 'Old School Tie', this characterisation may appear very dubious. The degree of collaboration in policymaking in Britain is documented in Heclo and Wildavsky (1974).

all times, the essential character of politics is competition and is an adversary and not coalescent process. Truth is assumed to emerge from the clash of ideas rather than from coalition—which tends to confirm Disraeli's dictum concerning coalitions.[6]

Finally, we come to the question of the self-regulative nature of the public policy outputs of the United Kingdom. If we were using the United States as our example of this mixture of elite and mass political characteristics, we would have rather less difficulty in justifying such a description of the policy consequences. Within the context of descriptions of American politics, Lowi (1969), Grant McConnell (1966), and others have commented on the tendency toward self-regulation. Likewise, in comparative perspective King (1973), Arnold Heidenheimer (1973, pp. 315-40), Groth (1971), and others have commented on the general preference of the American policy system for self-regulative solutions to questions of potential public action. The traditional stereotype of British policymaking, however, was one of parliamentary decisions produced through an integrated party and elite structure, and then enforced directly through a strong centralised government. In practice, much policy is made in exactly the opposite manner. Shonfield (1965, p. 114) writes that 'In Britain . . . the trouble is that although there is an established tradition of strong unitary central power, there are other potent traditions ingrained in the political system which impede the development of active, interventionist government. There is an abiding prejudice which sees it the natural business of government to react—not to act'. Shonfield (pp. 160–1) in his discussion of the means of conducting business in the modern capitalist world emphasised the place given to industry and labour in the regulation of their own affairs, thus replacing both the dictums of government and the dictums of the marketplace with the agreement of the involved parties. Shonfield (pp. 161–3) further points out that the legal position of associations in British law makes it difficult if not impossible for the government to pass any redistributive legislation severely threatening the continued existence or freedom of any private associations. Michael Brenner (1969, pp. 111–34) points out that such legislation would be politically as well as legally unfeasible for any government.

This quasi-corporate conception of the role of government in relation to private associations has been discussed by a number of authors. Samuel Beer (1965) has dealt extensively with British politics in this

---

[6] Although Disraeli was speaking in somewhat different context, the fact remains that 'England does not love coalitions.' Speech to House of Commons, December 16, 1852.

light. Regarding the consequences for policy. Everett Hagen and Stephanie White (1966, pp. 123–4) provide one of the strongest statements, noting that 'Associations of industrial employers on the one hand and trade unions on the other seem to be regarded in Britain almost coequal in authority with the government, as embodying the public welfare rather than to be regulated in accordance with it, and as entities to be negotiated with rather than regulated . . .' In relation to economic planning, Jack Hayward (1974, p. 405) characterised this as 'toothless tripartism'. He elsewhere notes that British economic policy and economic planning, as compared to the French and other Continental examples, is characterised by an absence of 'strong and positive authority within the executive to overcome the forces of incrementalism and inertia', p. 287. (Hayward, 1975. Potter (1966, p. 33) also comments on this conception of the relative role of government and private associations:

> In governing a modern industrial society, moreover, the administrative structure of the British State is hardly more than a shell, which would break if it were not supported by thousands of organisations—public bodies of all sorts, voluntary services, and affected interests. There are again 'rules of the game', well understood by those who work them which, while recognising that the Government always has the last word, dispose it not to utter it as long as 'there is not yet sufficient agreement among those concerned'. Great Britain is, socially and politically, a pluralistic society, in which the government no more than any other group or institution is outside the interaction of social forces which constitute the society.

This lack of central direction is also noted by Hugh Heclo and Aaron Wildavsky (1974, pp. 366–71) in relation to the spending community, especially the departmentalism of decision making and the linkage of that departmentalism to various affected interests. One final indication of the strength of affected interests in the general area of economic regulation is in the area of agricultural policy, about which J. Roland Pennock (1962, pp. 621–33) notes that British farmers have been even more successful than American farmers in influencing the expansion of agricultural subsidies. All of these studies taken together indicate an apparent preference for self-regulative types of solutions to questions of economic policy, perhaps best stated by the questions during the several strikes of 1973–4 as to who runs Britain—the government or the unions?

This pattern of self-regulation is relatively easy to maintain with respect to economic policy in Britain, but it is substantially more difficult to maintain with respect to social policies. A substantial portion of Britain's annual GNP goes into social services, including the National Health Service—one of the few directly publicly managed health delivery systems in the world. Despite this apparently high degree of public control, there is substantial evidence of influence if indeed not domination of health policies by the health care profession(s). This attitude is rather bluntly stated by the *British Medical Journal*: 'There is complete agreement within the profession that the Health Service should be run by doctors and not by laymen —either social scientist or professional civil servants' (cited by Klein, 1971, p. 365). The planning execution, and policing of health, care then remains largely with the medical profession, and any attempts to alter that—as with the recent attempts to end private hospital practice for consultants—leads to professional outcries and threats to emigrate. We find even here that much of the policy for this system is made by the groups most likely to be affected by the policies.

A number of recent analysts of British government have related these patterns of self-regulation to a number of problems in the structure and processes of cabinet government. Richard Rose (1974, pp. 379–421) provides the most thorough critique, concluding that despite the usual characterisations, British parties have not been capable of providing consistent direction to the policymaking system, and that policymaking has therefore been essentially placed in the hands of the bureaucracy. He further argues that the style, traditions, and structure of the civil service prevent it from providing the needed direction, so that the result is a government of 'directionless consensus' (p. 424). Michael Gordon (1971, p. 55) makes a number of similar points about party government, and notes in reference to government by the civil service that 'This bureaucratic amalgam of caution, policy opportunism, and self-delusion is bad enough. Add to it the two further factors of Whitehall's obsession with secrecy and of the low turnover in the senior ranks of the civil service, and the end product is a potent formula for sluggish and uncreative policy behaviour'. Jeremy Bray (1970, p. 65) refers to this orientation as 'pathological cynicism'. Thus, despite some of the favourable comparisons made of British government to American and other systems, the point remains that there are a number of powerful forces in the policymaking system tending toward indecision, lack of direction and self-regulation.

In three of the four countries discussed—Sweden, the Netherlands and the United Kingdom—private groups have been assigned roles of significant influence over the shape of public policy. How is it then that each of these four countries has been alleged to have different model patterns of policy, especially in the case of the United Kingdom and its characterisation as having self-regulative policies? Here perhaps the most important difference between the United Kingdom and the other two systems is a different conception of the relative position of government vis-à-vis other segments of society. In Britain the government may be a special type of association but it is frequently regarded as just that—simply another of a number of independent groups involved in the policy process. It does not appear to be regarded as the embodiment of the 'general will' or of any other more mystical conception of the state that might place it in a hierarchically superior position to that of private groups. In addition to the differing conceptions of the role of government, the patterns of interaction between government and pressure groups, and among the interest groups themselves, appear to be different in Sweden and the Netherlands from those found in the United Kingdom. In particular, in the Netherlands and Sweden the decision process tends to: (a) involve a wider variety of groups in any one decision; and (b) force direct bargaining among the groups rather than relationships between a single ministry and a particular interest in each issue area. The implications of this vertical integration of ministry and pressure group have apparently not been as deleterious as a similar pattern in the United States, but there remains a lack of direct confrontation of groups and a bargaining out of their demands rather than a bargaining with individual ministries. The latter pattern is more likely to produce patterns taking benefits from one group and giving to another than when each group can develop a clientele relationship with an agency.

Summary

There is some apparent relationship between the characteristics of the mass and elite political cultures and public policies at the national level. There is also some reason to believe that the typology developed for democratic political systems by Lijphart is quite similar in terms of the defining variables to that developed by Salisbury to categorise public policies. Thus, in addition to being a useful means of analysing politics within the United States, the various typologies of public policies which have been developed may also be useful for analysis of policies across nations. Although we have certainly not made a case for this hypothesis, the categorisation of democratic systems developed by Lijphart may be of use in analysing subnational politics.

A QUANTITATIVE ANALYSIS

In addition to the descriptive test presented above, we will also present a quantitative analysis of the hypothesised similarity of the typologies of public policy and of democratic political systems. The analysis will link the four types of political systems with a number of indicators of the types of public policy (see Appendix A). The test to be presented here will be of a rather preliminary nature, but the results should be indicative of the existence of significant differences in public policies between types of political systems.

The data
This analysis is to be conducted for twenty-one developed and democratic political systems. We limited the analysis to developed nations in an attempt to reduce some of the possible confounding effects of levels of economic and social developments on the results. There are still differences in levels of development among the nations included. There are also a number of possible influences of political history and culture which can further confound our results. However, if the fragmentation of the mass political culture and of the political elites is crucial in defining the nature of public policies emanating from a political system, then we should still find significant differences among the groupings of nations.

The data used come from a variety of sources. The major sources were the statistical publications of the individual nations. Also used were the *Europa Yearbook*, the *Yearbook of National Accounts Statistics* issued by the United Nations, and several publications of the OECD. We are cognisant that the collection of data from this variety of sources may present some problems of reliability. However, the classifications of expenditures and revenues used here are frequently used and their definitions are relatively standard across nations and agencies, and great pains were taken to ensure the comparability of the categories across countries.

The first step in developing these data was to classify each of the nations as one of the four types of political systems mentioned by Lijphart. In so far as it was possible, we followed the classification Lijphart himself used. However, several nations included in this analysis were not specifically mentioned by Lijphart and therefore had to be classified on the basis of a reading of the available literature.[7]

[7] Particularly useful in this regard was Gordon Smith (1973). The classification of Canada as consociational rather than centripetal follows the suggestion of Professor Lijphart.

In particular, we have made the assumption that the Scandinavian countries have come to closely approximate depoliticised political systems.[8]

Finally, we come to the indicators of the four types of policy in the Salisbury typology. The measures used are largely taken from the budgetary decisions of the several nations. While the public budget certainly does not contain the entirety of the decisions taken by a nation on policy, it does present a readily quantified picture of the priorities of the nation. The measures chosen for the redistributional policies of the nations are commonly used for such purposes and would seem to require little discussion. The indicators in the other three categories require some justification. Indicators of distributional policies are measures of policies tending to provide private goods highly divisible among individuals, and tending to confer benefits on special groups. Two of the more common expenditures of this type are expenditures for agricultural programmes and for public works—the classic 'pork barrel'. We have used the proportion of total revenues coming from value added and sales taxes as a measure of distributive revenue collection.

The measurement of regulation presents even more difficulties than the measurement of distribution. The measures chosen encompass measures of the activities of the political system in regulating personal behaviour—number of police per capita—as well as activities regulating the social and economic systems—number of civil servants per capita and economic planning activities. These measure some of the more important overt actions of government in attempting to control and regulate its environment.

Self-regulation presents the severest problems of measurement. We are, to some degree, asked to measure the non-decision-making activities of the political system rather than its overt actions, (see Backrach and Baratz, 1962). The measures chosen—all indicator or 'dummy' variables—concern the choices of the political system to regulate important activities within the nation or to leave that area to regulation by the affected parties themselves. The three policy areas chosen—health, the legal system, and industrial disputes—all constitute major areas of concern for any modern society, but there is

[8] The classification of political systems was as follows: Depoliticised: Sweden, Norway, Denmark, Iceland, and Finland. Consociational: Netherlands, Belgium, Switzerland, Austria, Luxembourg, and Canada. Centripetal: United States, United Kingdom, West Germany, Australia, New Zealand, Ireland (Eire), and Israel. Centrifugal: France, Italy, and Japan.

considerable variance in both the existence and degree of direct government intervention. We would have liked to provide more exact measurement of the degree of governmental involvement but the problems of providing this on a cross-national basis proved insuperable.

The indicators chosen for inclusion in this analysis are quite broad measures of the existence of policies of one type or another. We must therefore exercise caution in the interpretation of these findings as definitive indications of the usefulness of the typology in predicting policy. However, if we should find statistically significant differences between categories of political systems, we will have some assurance that this is indeed a fruitful avenue of investigation.

Methods of analysis

The major means of analysis for these data will be to test the significance of differences of means of the various indicators between groups defined on the basis of the four types of political systems. The test of significance used will be the conventional *t*-test. Since we have some indication of the direction of the test, the *t*-test will be one-tailed. In this analysis, we will test each of the four political system types against the combination of the other three categories on the policies which are hypothesised to be most strongly associated with that political system type. For example, the discussion of the typologies indicates that depoliticised political systems should have more redistributional policies than do the other three types of political systems. In addition to examining the relationships with the combination of the three categories, we will also look at the significance of the difference of means with each category of the typology of democratic systems. In this way, we should be able to determine where the major differences lie, and conversely the types of political systems which most closely resemble each other with respect to policies.

The specific hypotheses to be tested in this analysis are:

1. Depoliticised political systems will have significantly higher levels of redistributive policies than will the other three categories of political systems.
2. Centrifugal political systems will have significantly higher levels of distributive policies than will the other three categories of political systems.
3. Consociational political systems will have significantly higher levels of regulative policies than will the other three categories of political systems.

4. Centripetal political systems will have significantly higher levels of self-regulative policies than will the other three categories of political systems.

Thus, in each case, we will hypothesise that each type of political system will tend to make certain types of choices as a product of its structural characteristics.

FINDINGS

Redistributive policies

The findings for our analysis of redistributive policies are presented in Table 10.2. When we look at the differences between depoliticised democracy and the aggregate of the other three categories, there is only one significant difference between groups—on the Gini Index of Income Inequality. This gives us little support for our hypothesis, especially given that this one variable is perhaps a better indicator of the effects of certain policies than of the policies themselves. When we disaggregate the three categories, however, we do receive some more information concerning the differences in policy among these categories. We find that there are no significant differences between the depoliticised and the consociational democracies, while there are significant differences with each of the other two categories. The rather strong similarity in policies of the depoliticised and consociational systems therefore tended to suppress some differences existing between other categories and the depoliticised democracies when the aggregate of three categories was examined. While the evidence here is far from conclusive, these findings do point to the validity of Heisler and Kvavik's assumptions that the smaller European democracies—entirely in the consociational and depoliticised categories—are evolving quite similar patterns of policy and politics (Heisler and Kvavik, 1974, pp. 37–63).

TABLE 10.2 *Difference of means for redistributional policies, 1971**

Depoliticised democracy with:	Income Tax revenue	Welfare spending	Health spending	Gini Index
Centripetal democracy	0·03	0·05	NS	0·03
Centrifugal democracy	NS	0·01	0·03	NS
Consociational democracy	NS	NS	NS	NS
Other three categories	NS	NS	NS	0·05

* Levels of significance of 1 tailed *t*-test.

TABLE 10.3 *Difference of means for distributional policies, 1971**

Centrifugal democracy with:	Value-Added Tax	Agriculture spending	Education spending	Public Works spending
Depoliticised democracy	NS	NS	NS	0·008
Centripetal democracy	0·02	NS	NS	0·004
Consociational democracy	0·002	NS	0·02	NS
Other three categories	0·004	0·05	0·005	0·05

* Levels of significance of 1 tailed *t*-test.

Distributive policies

According to our hypotheses, centrifugal political systems should display higher levels of distributional policies than do the other types of political systems. This hypothesis is supported in Table 10.3. On four of six measures of distributional policy, the centrifugal political systems are significantly higher than the other three categories of political systems. Further, when the total sample is disaggregated, there are significant differences between the centrifugal political systems and each of the other three categories. On this basis, we can say that indeed the policies produced by centrifugal political systems are rather different from those adopted in other democratic political systems.

Regulative policies

We have hypothesised that the consociational democracies should have significantly higher mean scores on regulative measures than do the other three categories of political systems. The data in Table 10.4 provide some support for this hypothesis, although again the pattern is not as strong as we might like. There are two indicators showing

TABLE 10.4 *Difference of means for regulative policies, 1971**

Consociational democracy with:	Civil servants	Police	Indicative Planning	Planning expenditures
Depoliticised democracy	NS	NS	NS	NS
Centripetal democracy	NS	NS	0·05	NS
Centrifugal democracy	0·04	NS	0·03	NS
Other three categories	0·05	NS	0·04	NS

* Levels of significance of 1 tailed *t*-test.

TABLE 10.5 *Difference of means for self-regulative Policies, 1971**

Centripetal democracy with:	Health	Legal system	Industrial disputes	Federalism
Depoliticised democracy	NS	0·01	NS	0·001
Centrifugal democracy	NS	0·01	0·01	0·001
Consociational democracy	NS	NS	0·01	0·05
Other three categories	NS	0·05	NS	0·001

* Levels of significance of 1 tailed *t*-test.

significant differences between the consociational democracies and the aggregate of the other three types of democracy. These two are, however, what we would consider the stronger indicators of the regulative activities and capabilities of the political system.

This set of findings also substantiates our earlier assumption that the policies of the consociational and depoliticised democracies may be quite similar. Again, there are no significant differences between these two categories while there are between consociational democracies and each of the other two categories. Thus, instead of there being four distinct patterns of politics and policy, it appears that there may be only three: one containing both consociational and depoliticised political systems, the centripetal systems, and the centrifugal systems.

Self-regulative policies

Finally, we come to the self-regulative policies. These have been hypothesised to be most prominent in centripetal democracies. The results of the analysis presented in Table 10.5 indicate that indeed there is a strong tendency for centripetal political systems to adopt self-regulative policies. This is true to some degree for each of the three indicators selected for analysis except the control of health services. There was a pronounced pattern for the control of the legal system. The latter finding, however, may be partially influenced by the predominance of Anglo-American legal systems in the centripetal category and is somewhat suspect on that basis. However, in general we can say that centripetal political systems do apparently produce strongly self-regulative patterns of policy. We would therefore expect the same strong pattern to persist were stronger and less culturally dependent measures of self-regulation available.

SUMMARY

This initial effort at the comparative analysis of the Salisbury typology of public policies has shown the general applicability and usefulness of that typology in cross-national research. The categories of policy discussed in that typology appear to have empirical referents which vary significantly across nations. These indicators vary in the manner which would be predicted by the theoretical arguments advanced by Salisbury and Salisbury and Heinz. There is a considerable degree of similarity between this typology of public policy and the Lijphart typology of democratic political systems. These authors embarked upon their efforts at typology formation for different purposes, but have apparently isolated two rather crucial variables in the determination of both the form of the political process and the nature of policy outputs.

A second interesting albeit preliminary conclusion from this analysis is that the consociational and depoliticised democracies are quite similar in their policies. There were no significant differences between these nations with respect to redistributive or regulative policy measures. A further examination revealed that there were no significant differences on any of the policy categories. On this basis, one could argue that the coalescence of political elites and the close contact between those elites and the leadership of interests within the nation has led to one distinguishable pattern of policy rather than two. This pattern would appear to be congruent with that outlined as the 'European Polity'. Of course, this research cannot validate that model, but it does provide some indication of the homogeneity of the outputs.

Although this must still be regarded as a preliminary effort, we have shown some degree of relationship between the type of political system and the outputs of the system. Given the predominant findings of research in American state policy, this finding is rather interesting in itself. Further, there is such a relationship among a group of nations which are (relatively) homogeneous with respect to socio-economic development. Thus, even at this rather crude level of measurement we can discern effects of political system characteristics and would expect even stronger effects with stronger measures.

As with most preliminary efforts, the major conclusion here is that there is a need for further research. The level of measurement and definition of the types of political systems are still not as refined as we would like. Further, various tests for dimensionality can be used to determine more exactly the degree to which the three distinct types of political and policy systems differ, and if in fact there are three distinct types. Finally, there remains a need for a more complete delineation of the relationship between political process and political outcomes. Much of the theoretical discussion of these four types of policies has dealt with processes within a single nation, while we have applied the same sort of terminology to measures of outputs. The relationship between these two different approaches to the same problems needs to be made clear, with the expectation of a more complete comprehension of the relationship of the 'black box' to the outcomes of the policy process.

APPENDIX A

List of Indicators of Public Policy

Redistributional Policy
1. Percentage of total public revenue coming from income tax.
2. Percentage of total public expenditures going to social welfare services.
3. Percentage of total public expenditures going to public health services.
4. Gini Index of Income Inequality.

Distributional Policy
1. Percentage of total public revenue coming from value-added tax.
2. Percentage of total public expenditures going to agricultural support.
3. Percentage of total public expenditures going to public works.
4. Percentage of total public expenditures going to education.

Regulative Policy
1. Number of civil servants per capita.
2. Number of police per capita.
3. Percentage of total public expenditures going to economic planning.
4. Indicator variable on presence or absence of indicative economic planning.

Self-Regulative Policy
1. Indicator variable on presence or absence of nationalised medical service.
2. Indicator variable on presence or absence of public control of the legal profession.

3. Indicator variable on presence or absence of public intervention in labour management disputes.

REFERENCES

ABERT, J. G. (1969) *Economic Policy and Planning in the Netherlands*, Yale University Press.

ALMOND, G. (1956) 'Comparative political systems', *Journal of Politics,* **XVIII**.

ALMOND, G. and VERBA, S. (1963) *The Civic Culture*, Princeton University Press.

ANTON, T. (1969) 'Policy-making and political culture in Sweden', *Scandinavian Political Studies,* **4**.

ARDAGH, J. (1969) *The New French Revolution*, Harper.

BACKRACH, P. and BARATZ, M. (1962) 'The Two Faces of Power', *American Political Science Review,* **LVI**.

BEER, S. (1965) *British Politics in the Collectivist Era,* Knopf.

BRAY, J. (1970) *Decision in Government*, Gollancz.

BRENNER, M. J. (1969) 'Functional representation and interest group theory: some notes on British practice', *Comparative Politics,* **II**.

DAHL, R. A. (1971) *Polyarchy: Participation and Opposition*, Yale University Press.

FROMAN, L. A., Jr. (1967) 'An analysis of public policies in cities', *Journal of Politics,* **XXIX**.

GORDON, M. R. (1971) 'Civil servants, politicians and parties: shortcomings of the British policy process', *Comparative Politics,* **IV**

GROTH, A. J. (1971) *Comparative Politics: A Distributive Approach*, Macmillan.

HAGEN, E. and WHITE, F. (1966) *Great Britain: Quiet Revolution in Planning*, Syracuse University Press.

HAYWARD, J. (1974) 'National aptitudes for planning in Britain, France and Italy', *Government and Opposition,* **IX**.

HAYWARD, J. (1975) 'The politics of planning in France and Britain', *Comparative Politics,* **VII**.

HECLO, H. and WILDAVSKY, A. (1974) *The Private Government of Public Money*, University of California Press.

HEIDENHEIMER, A. J. (1973) 'The politics of public education, health and welfare in the U.S.A. and Western Europe', *British Journal of Political Science,* **III**.

HEISLER, M. and KVAVIK, R. (1974) 'Patterns of European politics: the "European polity" model', in M. Heisler, ed., *Politics in Europe*, David McKay Company.

JENNINGS, I. (1968) *The British Constitution,* Cambridge University Press.

KING, A. (1973) 'Ideas, institutions and the policies of governments: a comparative analysis', *British Journal of Political Science,* **III**.

KLEIN, R. (1971) 'Accountability in the National Health Service', *Political Quarterly,* **XLIII**.

LIJPHART, A. (1968a) 'Typologies of democratic systems', *Comparative Political Studies,* **I**.

LIJPHART, A. (1968b) *The Politics of Accommodation,* University of California Press.

LIJPHART, A. (1969) 'Consociational democracy', *World Politics,* **XXI**.

LOWI, T. J. (1964) 'American business, public policy, case-studies, and political theory', *World Politics,* **XVI**.

LOWI, T. J. (1969) *The End of Liberalism,* W. W. Norton.

LOWI, T. J. (1972) 'Four systems of policy, politics, and choice', *Public Administration Review,* **XXXIII**.

LÜTHY, H. (1955) *France Against Herself,* Praeger.

MCCONNELL, G. (1966) *Private Power of American Democracy,* Vintage.

MACRIDIS, R. (1968) 'Comparative politics and the study of government: the search for focus', *Comparative Politics,* **I**.

PENNOCK, J. R. (1962) 'Responsible government, seperated powers, and special interests: agricultural subsidies in Britain and America', *American Political Science Review,* **LVI**.

POTTER, A. (1966) 'Great Britain: Opposition with a capital "O"', in R. A. Dahl, ed., *Political Opposition in Western Democracies,* Yale University Press.

ROSE, R. (1974) *The Problem of Party Government,* Macmillan.

RUSTOW, D. (1955) *The Politics of Compromise,* Princeton University Press.

SALISBURY, R. H. (1968) 'The analysis of public policy; a search for theories and roles', in A. Ranney, ed., *Political Science and Public Policy* Markham.

SALISBURY, R. H. and HEINZ, J. (1970) 'A theory of policy analysis and some, preliminary applications', in I. Sharkansky, ed., *Policy Analysis in Political Science,* Markham.

SHONFIELD, A. (1965) *Modern Capitalism,* Oxford University Press.

SMITH, G. (1973) *Politics in Western Europe,* Heinemann.

STJERNQUIST, N. (1966) 'Sweden: stability or deadlock', in R. A. Dahl, ed., *Political Opposition in Western Democracies,* Yale University Press.

TARROW, S. (1971) 'The urban–rural cleavage in political involvement: the case of France', *American Political Science Review,* **L V**.

WILLIAMS, P. and HARRISON, M. (1972) *Politics and Society in de Gaulle's Republic,* Longmans.

I I

Anthony King

Why do different governments make different decisions and pursue different policies?

(Adapted from 'Ideas, institutions and the policies of governments: a comparative analysis', *British Journal of Political Science*, 1973, pp. 291–313 and 1974, pp. 409–23).

This paper is about the things governments do and why they do them. It is written in the belief that, while we know quite a lot about decision-making processes in individual countries, we do not know nearly enough about why the governments of different countries make different decisions and pursue different policies. The countries of North America and western Europe are often described as 'welfare states', the implication being that the governments of all of them do broadly similar things in broadly similar ways. As we shall see, however, these broad similarities conceal important, wide divergences. These divergences deserve to be explained.

The paper falls into three parts. The first is concerned with taking a number of countries and a number of policy fields, and with describing—necessarily very briefly—the role played by the State in each. The second consists of brief historical accounts of how the State in each of the countries came to play the role it now does. The third attempts a general explanation of the gross patterns of public policy that will have emerged from Parts I and II.

Two further points by way of apology and self-exculpation. One is that this paper represents the beginning rather than the end of a period of research; it is intended to start trains of thought, not stop them. The other is that the original version of the paper was written while the writer was living at the top of a hill in rural Italy, equipped with only as many books and notes as a small car would carry. For these two reasons, the paper, even as revised, probably bears the same relationship to the truth that one of those imaginative sixteenth-century maps does to the geography of North America—with the coastline and a few large islands picked out correctly, but with the details often wrong and the relationships between some of the parts distorted. Still, political scientists, like cartographers, must start somewhere.

I   THE ROLE PLAYED BY THE STATE

What do modern governments do? In addition to the conduct of defence and foreign relations (the universal 'federative' functions of government, as Locke called them), they do an extraordinary variety of things, ranging from educating the young and operating railways to manufacturing steel and cigarettes. It would be impossible to list all of these activities, but many of the important ones are set out below. In connection with each, the role that the State plays in the United States, Canada, Britain, France and West Germany is described briefly. The choice of countries is fairly arbitrary: clearly more countries could have been chosen, and different ones. But these five will serve for our purposes and, as will appear, the case of the United States is particularly interesting. We begin with communications.

Roads
In all five countries (with the exception of a single privately operated toll road in France) all major roads are built, maintained and operated by the State.

Postal services
Postal services, like roads, are everywhere in the hands of government. In all five countries, the State has a virtual monopoly.

Railways
The State everywhere regulates railway rates, safety standards, and so on; but the pattern of ownership varies considerably. Apart from the 471 miles of the Alaska Railway, all of the railroads in the United States are privately owned (or are in the hands of receivers in bankruptcy); a semi-public corporation (Antrak) operates mainline passenger services on tracks belonging to the privately-owned rail-roads. In Canada, of the two main lines, Canadian Pacific is privately owned, while the other, Canadian National, is the property of the Canadian government. The French railways are operated by a company 51 per cent of whose capital is State-controlled. Britain's railways are wholly State-owned, as are those of West Germany.

Airlines

The five countries' airlines, like their railways, are all closely regulated by the State, but once again the pattern of ownership varies. In only one country, the United States, are the commercial airlines entirely privately owned; and in only one country, West Germany, are they almost entirely publicly owned. In Canada, Britain and France, State-owned airlines coexist with private lines; but in all three countries the State-owned lines—Air Canada, BOAC, BEA, and Air France—are much the larger, accounting for more than 80 per cent of total passenger traffic.

Telephones

Telephone services tend for obvious reasons to be monopolies and in most countries they are State run. The telephone systems of Britain, France, and Germany are all operated as integral parts of the postal system. In the United States, however, the telephones are privately owned, while in Canada the position is mixed, with private ownership in seven of the ten provinces and public in the other three (Alberta, Saskatchewan, and Manitoba).

Radio and television

The relationships of government to radio and television broadcasting are more complicated. The five countries resemble each other in that all have elaborate regulatory machinery (to allocate wavelengths and so on). But there the resemblances end. In the United States, broadcasting is almost entirely in private hands, though a small government-sponsored Public Broadcasting Corporation was created in 1967. In Canada, a publicly-owned network, the CBC, coexists with a private network and a large number of private stations. The position in Britain is roughly similar; radio is only now (1973) ceasing to be a monopoly of the State-owned BBC, but in television the two BBC networks have competed with a private one since the early 1950s. In France, all radio and television broadcasting is in the hands of the government-controlled ORTF. In Germany, all broadcasting is in the hands of public corporations controlled by the *Länder*.

This pattern—of State ownerships being much more common in Europe and even in Canada than in the United States—is repeated, though in a somewhat more complicated form, when we look at the fuel and power industries.

Electricity

In Britain, France, and Germany, electricity generation and transmission are both entirely in the hands of the State. In Canada, government-owned companies and commissions produce and distribute approximately 80 per cent of the country's total consumption, but privately-owned companies are still important, particularly in British Columbia, Alberta, Nova Scotia, and Newfoundland. The position in the United States is roughly the reverse of Canada's, with private generators and distributors accounting for something like 80 per cent of total supply. The United States is one of the few countries where generation and distribution are often under different ownership; the American public sector consists of both transmission facilities, often municipally-owned, and generating plants like those of the Tennessee and Columbia River basins.

Gas

The case of gas is simpler: in Canada and the United States, the facilities for the manufacture, extraction, and distribution of gas are overwhelmingly privately owned; in Britain, France, and Germany, they are publicly owned. The only major exception in Europe is the involvement of private companies in the exploitation of natural gas from under the North Sea.

Coal

The case of coal-mining is also simple: in the United States and Canada, the coal mines are privately owned; in Britain and France, they are publicly owned. In West Germany, whereas the electricity and gas supply industries are entirely state-owned, coal mining is mainly in the hands of a number of private companies.

Oil

In view of the large role played by the State in the other fuel and power industries, at least in western Europe, one might expect a comparable degree of direct State involvement in the oil industry—if not in the field of extraction (there are no major oilfields in Britain, France, or West Germany). at least in the fields of refining and distribution. But this is not so, and in none of the five countries is the oil industry wholly in government hands. France, however, possesses a State-owned company, *Entreprise de Recherches et d' Activités Petrolières*, which competes directly with the major international companies and supplies approximately 40 per cent of France's consumption of raw petroleum. And one of the major international companies itself, British Petroleum (BP), is a mixed public/private concern, in which the British government has a 49 per cent controlling interest.

The role of the State tends to be less direct in sectors of the economy apart from communications and fuel and power; but in at least two of the five countries there are a number of other imporatnt instances of outright public ownership.

Iron and steel
The iron and steel industry is wholly in private hands in four of the five countries; but in Britain 90 per cent of it, in terms of tonnage output, is publicly owned.

Banking
All five countries have State-owned central banks, and in all five the commercial banks are closely regulated by the State. Ordinary commercial banking is, however, in private hands in four of the five. The exception this time is not Britain but France, where the four largest commercial banks, controlling the great bulk of the country's banking business, are government-owned.

Miscellaneous
France indeed is the major exception generally to the general disposition of governments outside the Communist bloc not to get directly involved in manufacturing industry or the service trades. In the United States and Canada, several states and provinces operate retail outlets for alcoholic drinks; and until recently in Britain there were a number of State-owned breweries and public houses. The British government also (somewhat to its own surprise) now owns the aeroengines division of Rolls-Royce. In West Germany, despite the 'privatisation' programme of 1959–65, the government still owns shareholdings in a number of large extractive and manufacturing concerns, notably Volkswagen. The stake of the French State in these sectors is, however, much larger. The biggest single automobile company in France, Renault, is wholly State-owned, and the State has a monopoly of cigarette manufacturing and sales. The French government also owns a large share of the country's airframe and aeroengine industries; Aerospatiale, the makers of the Caravelle and the Concorde, is wholly government-owned.

The State thus plays a more direct role in some economic sectors than in others; it also plays a more direct role in some countries than in others. Indeed, many readers will already have noticed that what is

TABLE 11.1 *Public ownership of various industries and services*

	Roads	Postal services	Electricity	Railways	Telephones
France	S	S	S	S	S
Britain	S	S	S	S	S
West Germany	S	S	S	S	S
Canada	S	S	S/p	S/p	s
United States	S	S	s	—	—

emerging is a large, almost perfect Guttman scale (see Table 11.1) of which it is the vertical axis that matters most here. It indicates that, at least as regards State ownership, the practice of government in America diverges sharply from that in all four of the other countries, especially the three in Europe.

One should not make too much of all this. Whether or not modern governments actually own industries and firms, all of them—as regulators, licensers, subsidisers, standard-setters, rate-setters, taxers, buyers, and sellers—undoubtedly exert a great variety of powerful economic influences. This is as true in the United States and Canada as it is in Europe. Moreover, in some cases it probably matters very little to anybody whether a particular enterprise is publicly owned or not. The commercial banks in France, to take a single example, function exactly now as they did before nationalisation, the French government making something of a virtue of the fact. Nonetheless, the pattern revealed by Table 11.1 is, at the very least, mildly intriguing. It looks even more intriguing, and important, when we move on to look at the State's role in some of the social services.[1]

Old-age pensions

All industrial countries now pay old-age pensions 'as of right' to the majority of their citizens over about 65 years of age. It is hard for the layman to determine how the size of these pensions is related to general earnings and prices in particular countries—whether or not, for example, the State pension enables someone in a particular country to live above whatever is thought to be the 'poverty line' in that country. But a certain amount can be said about who is entitled to pensions and about the relationship between pre- and post-retirement income for those who are.

The United States appears to be the only country in which, although

Airlines	Radio, television	Gas	Coal	Oil	Steel	Banks
S/p	S	S	S	S	—	S/p
S/p	S/p	S	S	s	S	—
S	S	S	s	—	—	—
S/p	S/p	—	—	—	—	—
—	—	—	—	—	—	—

S = predominantly state ownership
s = element of state ownership in predominantly private system
S/p = State and private sectors both substantial

a majority of the aged receive State pensions, a substantial minority do not. As the result of successive extensions to the 1935 social security scheme, about 90 per cent of the United States population is eligible to receive a State pension on retirement; but, because the major extensions are relatively recent, the proportion of those over 65 receiving such pensions as late as 1971 was considerably lower— perhaps in the order of 60–70 per cent. In Canada and Britain, pensions are paid to all residents over the age of 65. The French and German arrangements are less easily described, because in both countries schemes run wholly by the State have been grafted on to (or had grafted on to) them schemes of a quasi-private character. In both countries, however, the proportion of the aged population covered by one scheme or another approaches 100 per cent.

For both State and quasi-State pensioners, the gap between in-work and retirement income appears, on average, to be narrowest in Germany, where post-retirement income is often considerably more than half of immediate pre-retirement income. The gap is substantially greater in all four of the other countries, though it is hard to place them in a neat rank order. In the United States, the maximum social

---

[1] It is extraordinarily difficult to obtain accurate, comparable information on different countries' social services; and, even apart from the problem of information, different countries' social services are exceedingly hard to compare since they differ so widely in their coverage, in|their benefits, in the conditions attached to them, and in their administration. Unless otherwise indicated, most of the information in the following paragraphs is obtained from a survey published by the United States Department of Health, Education, and Welfare (1969).

security pension could only in very unusual circumstances amount to anything approaching 50 per cent of pre-retirement income; it is probably generally a good deal less. In Britain, because old-age pensions are earnings-related only to a very limited extent, the fall in income is precipitous for someone whose previous earnings had been near, at or above average. In Canada, a pensions scheme enacted in 1965 will not reach full maturity until 1976. At that time insured persons (the great bulk of the employed population) will receive roughly 25 per cent of their pre-retirement income plus a flat-rate universal pension; the total will approach 50 per cent, or even 40 per cent, of pre-retirement earnings only for the lower paid. French old-age pensions could until recently be described as 'the worst of any advanced European country' (Ardagh, 1970, p. 438), but recent changes have brought post-retirement incomes to, on average, 40 per cent of pre-retirement.

Unemployment insurance
In addition to the steps that all modern governments take to maintain full employment, or something like it, all of them make provision for unemployment insurance. Almost all workers are covered in our five countries, though there are more exclusions in the United States and Canada than in Europe. The most generous (or, if one prefers, lavish) benefits are payable in Germany, where an unemployed person may receive as much as 90 per cent of his previous earnings for as many as fifty-two weeks; the average benefit is perhaps in the order of 50–60 per cent. The position in France is complicated by the existence of quasi-private schemes alongside the State scheme. Most workers are covered by one of the quasi-private schemes and are entitled to benefits of not less than 40 per cent of wages (and often more) for up to fifty-two weeks. In Britain, a flat-rate benefit of, on average, about 25 per cent of earnings is payable for up to fifty-two weeks; in addition, however, a graduated supplement of one-third of previous earnings is payable for up to thirty-six weeks. In Canada, as elsewhere, the percentage of earnings payable as benefit varies with the size of earnings, the lower the earnings the higher, as a percentage the benefit; the average seems to be about 40 per cent, payable for up to fifty-two weeks. In the United States, although there are considerable variations from state to state, the benefits are fairly consistently the lowest in any of the five countries (on a percentage basis), and the periods during which benefit is payable are the shortest; the average benefit seems to be about 30 per cent of earnings, payable for about twenty-six weeks.

Sickness pay

Less need be said about sickness pay—the benefit paid to those off work through illness—because the differences amongst the five countries are much simpler. In Germany, France, and Britain, generous provision is made. The highest benefits are payable in Germany, where, for instance, an employer must, during the first six weeks of an employee's illness, pay or make up 100 per cent of his salary or wages. By contrast, in Canada and the United States, no State provision is made at all, or virtually none. The only exceptions are four state schemes in the United States—in Rhode Island, New York, New Jersey, and California.

Medical services

The divergencies amongst the five countries in connection with hospital and doctor's services are almost as great, with Britain, Germany, and France at one extreme and the United States at the other. In Britain, all residents (and indeed non-residents if they fall ill while in Britain) are covered by the National Health Service. The NHS is a comprehensive hospital and medical service and, apart from small charges for prescriptions, is 'free' in the sense that no direct charges are made to patients. In France, 98 per cent of the population is covered by State schemes which provide for the reimbursement to the patient of a large proportion of his hospital and medical expenses: 100 per cent in the case of expensive surgery and long illnesses, 75 per cent in the case of routine doctor's visits. The German arrangements are broadly similar to the French save that hospitals, doctors, and chemists are paid directly from State-supervised 'sickness funds' (*Krankenkassen*); a somewhat smaller proportion of the population, about 87 per cent, is covered.

The position in Canada and the United States is complicated by the coexistence of federal and provincial state laws and programmes. The Canadian and American schemes also tend to make a distinction, hardly known in Europe, between hospital services and medical services of other kinds. Otherwise Canada and the United States diverge sharply. In Canada, all ten provinces administer hospital insurance programmes which cover 99 per cent of the Canadian population; the details of the programmes vary, but under federal law they must, if they are to receive federal funds, cover all main in-patient services apart from doctors' fees themselves. Non-hospital medical expenses in Canada are covered by a series of federally-supported provincial schemes; all major medical costs are covered and, to qualify for federal funds, a provincial programme must give entitlement to not less than 90–95 per cent of the province's residents. In the United States, a government insurance scheme ('Medicare') provides hospital insurance for those aged 65 and over, though the coverage is only for stays in hospital of limited duration (90 days during any single spell of illness). Those who are 65 and over may also join a voluntary insurance scheme which covers 80 per cent of non-hospital medical expenses. In addition, the federal government under a plan known as 'Medicaid' assists the states in helping to meet the hospital and medical expenses of the very poor (those in receipt of public assistance). The American arrangements, unlike those in the other countries, are thus restricted to a relatively small proportion of the population, and there are many more 'deductibles', i.e. amounts the patient has to pay himself.

In connection with public ownership, we noticed that the State's role in the United States is much more restricted than in Europe and even in Canada. With the partial exception of old-age pensions, we now find the same pattern reasserting itself in connection with the social services: in Germany, Britain, and France, the State does much; in America it does much less. Table 11.2 makes the point, thought it has to be interpreted somewhat cautiously since the figures for the two countries then in the EEC, France and Germany, are not strictly comparable with those for Britain, Canada, and the United States.

TABLE 11.2 *Social security expenditure as percentage of Gross National Product, 1966*

Germany	France	Britain	Canada	United States
16·0	15·5	12·6	9·6	7·2

Source: Statistical Office of the European Communities (1971, p. 104).

A similar impression is conveyed by Table 11.3. Broadly speaking, a government does more in any social-service field the longer it has been in that field: new programmes tend to be restricted, old ones to be much more elaborate. Table 11.3 therefore sets out the dates at which each of our five countries enacted its initial, major legislation in each of the four fields discussed so far. (In the case of France, some early legislation was not fully implemented: the dates in the Table are dates for legislation that was.) The date for the country last in each field is in bold print. It will be seen that in each case the last country was the United States, twice tied with Canada. Some of the gaps in time separating the United States from other countries are very substantial.

TABLE 11.3 *Year of introduction of various social services*

	Old-age pensions	Unemployment insurance	Sickness pay	Medical services
Germany	1889	1927	1889	1883
Britain	1908	1911	1911	1911
France	1930	1914	**1930**	1930
Canada	1927	(1935)*	—	1947–66
United States	**1935**	**1935**	—	**1965**

* An Act of 1935 was declared unconstitutional, and unemployment insurance was not finally introduced in Canada until 1940.

Again, one should not make too much of these findings. All of these countries supplement their 'as of right' schemes with means-tested provision of one kind or another. And benefits not guaranteed by the State—sickness pay, for example—may nonetheless be available to the bulk of the population as the result of trade-union bargaining or even simple custom. All the same, as we said earlier, the pattern is at least intriguing; and it does persist. Before turning to the problem of explanation, we shall look briefly at just two more social-service fields, one of which (housing) broadly conforms to the pattern, the other of which (education) most emphatically does not.

Housing
To refer to housing as a 'social service' is to classify it as a European would; in Canada and the United States, housing is neither thought of as a social service nor administered as one. As in the case of medical services, the extreme positions are occupied by Britain and the United States. In Britain, slum clearance and housing—especially working-class housing—are regarded as primarily, although not exclusively, the State's responsibility. Of all the dwellings built in Britain each year since the war, the proportion built directly by local authorities has never fallen below 40 per cent and has sometimes risen a good deal higher; in 1969, for example, it was 51 per cent. In the United States, by contrast State activity in the housing market is largely confined to making it easier for private individuals to secure mortgage loans; very few dwellings, proportionately, are provided directly by

government. The figures in Table 11.4, although they relate to the 1950s, are typical of the postwar period. The difference between the two countries is very great.

TABLE 11.4 *Percentage of dwellings provided by Public Authorities*

	1954	*1955*	*1956*	*1957*	*1958*
Britain	73·4	64·2	58·9	58·1	53·3
United States	1·5	1·4	2·1	4·7	5·6

Source: Wendt (1962, p. 236).

Canada, France, and Germany fall somewhere in between (though the peculiarities of German housing policy make it difficult to place Germany on the same dimension as the other four). Canadian policy, is, in its main contours, almost identical to American, except that in Canada more houses would seem to be built directly by public authorities. French policy is a cross between the American and the British, with on the one hand American-style efforts to sponsor a private mortgage market, and on the other British-like efforts to build houses directly. German policy has a strong 'social service' orientation, but by no means all social housing is government-constructed. The main emphasis in Germany has been on the provision of interest-free loans to all sorts of bodies—local authorities, public and private housing associations, and private builders—which in return agree to keep rents low and to house only the relatively low paid. Roughly half of all the housing constructed in West Germany since the war has been of this type.

Education
Our final social-service field, education, stands in complete contrast to all of the others. The State in America, relatively inactive in so many of the other fields, plays in this one as great a role as in the other countries, probably even greater. With regard to primary and secondary education, the policies of all five countries converge on much the same point: the great majority of schools are State schools, and schooling is free and compulsory for all children to age 15 or 16. But in the field of higher education the United States differs strikingly from the others: the proportion of the relevant age group in higher education in the United States is far larger than elsewhere and,

although there is a large private sector in American higher education (which there is not in the three European countries), governments in the United States are nevertheless by far the largest single providers. The number of students in higher education for the decade ending in 1959 are set out in Table 11.5. The absolute magnitudes will have changed considerably since then, and the figures as they stand, for Britain in particular, are probably misleading. All the same, American pre-eminence is clearly established.

TABLE 11.5 *Number of Students in Higher Education per 100,000 of Population*

United States	West Germany	Canada	France	Britain
1,738	1,010	619	409	256

Source: Unesco (1964).

The exceptional case of education apart (and we shall return to it in Part III), we have seen that the State plays a larger direct operating role in our three European countries, and even in Canada, than it does in the United States. We can summarise our findings so far in terms of the proportion of GNP in each of our countries which is accounted for by general government spending, by government spending on the social services, and by spending of public enterprises (see Table 11.6). The figure for West Germany would be higher but for the exclusion of spending by some public enterprises. Once again, the contrast between the United States and the other four countries is marked.

TABLE 11.6 *Expenditure of general Government, Social Security and public enterprises as a percentage of GNP, 1959*

Britain	France	West Germany	Canada	United States
45·3	40·1	38·8	37·4	27·9

Source: Russett *et al.* (1964, p. 63).

II HOW THE STATE CAME TO PLAY THE ROLE IT NOW DOES

So much for description. We could go on almost indefinitely adducing evidence pointing in the same direction, but it would be tedious to, and in any case the point is already made: the part played by the State in the United States is certainly greater than it used to be—hence the talk in America of 'big government'—but, with the major exception of education, it is still, for better or worse, much smaller than elsewhere.

What is the explanation? In a moment we shall turn to face this question directly; but, before we do, we need to set out, if only in summary form, how the State in each of our countries came to play the role it now does. What sorts of administrations have introduced major policy changes? What arguments have been used? What political forces have been brought into play? Outline answers to these questions are given in this part of the paper.[2]

United States

The story of public ownership in the United States is quickly told, because for the most part it is a non-story—of proposals that were not made and of things that did not happen. It was taken for granted from the beginning of the Republic that the State should build roads and run a post office; otherwise it is broadly true to say that public owner-ship—whether in the sense of 'socialism' or in the sense of the govern-ment's setting up or taking over major industrial concerns—has never been on the American political agenda. These are exceptions, to be sure, both in the realm of practice (TVA, many municipal transport undertakings, the Port of New York Authority), and in the realm of ideas (the Populists, Socialists, and Progressives all advo-cated government ownership of the railroads); but a scholar who troubled to write the history of public ownership in America, at least since the Civil War, would be nibbling at the margins of history—and would know it.

With the social services, it is a different matter: as we have seen, although social-service provision (education apart) is on a smaller scale in the United States than elsewhere, it does exist. In America, as elsewhere, State education expanded gradually during the mid- and late nineteenth century. Otherwise almost all of the major innovations in the social services came in a rush during the 1930s: the National Housing Act of 1934, the Social Security Act of 1935, and the Wagner–Seagall Housing Act of 1937. The only exception is

---

[2] Only outline answers can be given, partly for reasons of space, but partly because in many cases the relevant history has not been written: political scientists seldom concern themselves with the pasts of present policies; historians often fail to ask the questions that political scientists would.

Medicare which was adopted in the mid-1960s in the form of an amendment to the original Social Security Act.

Several features of the American experience are worth noting. First, all of the measures were enacted by Congresses and Administrations of a generally reformist character: under Franklin Roosevelt in 1934-7 and Johnson in 1965. Second, with the exception of Medicare, all were introduced during the great depression, i.e. at a time of national crisis. Third, all of the measures, including Medicare, aroused acute controversy at the time they were passed and, more particularly, during the preceding thirty to fifty years. Fourth, all of the measures were opposed by powerful interest groups: the insurance companies, private charities, the doctors, even at times some of the trade unions. The opposition of these groups took the form, not merely of *ad hoc* objections to particular features of the measures, but of principled objections to measures of this type being introduced at all. Fifth, the objections to all of these measures, from whatever quarter, consisted in part of general assertions that it was quite improper for the State to act in spheres that had hitherto been reserved for individuals or voluntary associations. As early as 1898, an official of the Bureau of Labor opposed the introduction of compulsory social insurance into the United States because it rested 'upon principles of state action foreign to American thought' (quoted in Lubove, 1968, pp. 26–7). As late as 1961, the American Medical Association was expressing its opposition to Medicare on identical grounds:

the entire push to make our present system of medical care a federally controlled and operated activity is simply a single battle in a continuing war. Our nation is divided into two camps. At issue is the vital question of the proper role the Federal Government should play in our society.

On one side are those who demand . . . an ever-enlarging role for the Federal Government. On the other side are those, like ourselves, who oppose the efforts now being made to increase the government's direction and control over our way of life (quoted in Feingold, 1966, p. 275).

These features of the American experience—the reformist complexion of the innovating Administrations, the apparent importance of a great national crisis, the presence of acute controversy, the role of interest groups, and the role of general arguments about the State —need to be borne in mind as we look at the other four countries.

Canada

With respect to all of these features, the Canadian experience stands in striking contrast to the American. Not only, as we saw earlier, is public ownership more widely extended in Canada, but it has been extended by governments of different political complexions, under widely varying circumstances, and for the most part in the absence of acute public controversy—whether about the role of the State or anything else.

Ownership by the provinces of telephone and electricity supply systems has been extended piecemeal since about 1900; usually the facilities have been publicly owned more or less from the beginning. Creation of a large State-owned railway system was begun in 1917 by a Conservative Government faced with the possibility of a number of the existing railway companies going bankrupt. The Canadian government already owned several smaller lines and the measure aroused little controversy, except about the valuation of the private companies' stock. Indeed one of the few accounts of the creation of the CNR says simply that the 'Canadian public slid into government ownership' (Currie, 1967, p. 406). If anything, there was even less controversy about public ownership in the field of broadcasting, both main political parties actively supporting the creation in the early 1930s of the Canadian Radio Broadcasting Committee, the immediate precursor of the CBC. Both parties also supported the principle of State ownership when a Liberal Government established Trans-Canada Air Lines (now Air Canada) in 1937.

The case of TCA is worth pausing over, since it vividly points up the Canadian/American contrast without being untypical.[3] The Liberal minister who introduced the bill establishing TCA did not seem at all clear whether he was creating a public or a private enterprise. On the one hand, he hoped that private airline companies would buy into TCA (though only 49 per cent of the stock was to be made available for purchase); on the other, he seemed to doubt whether private buyers would in fact come forward and even whether it was desirable that they should. The Liberal Party espoused private enterprise, yet the minister, C. D. Howe, said of TCA, which was to operate as a semi-autonomous public corporation: 'I think we are getting the best features of government ownership without the obligation of direct government operation, which has proved trouble-some in the past'.

[3] The account in the following two paragraphs and all of the quotations are taken from Corbett (1965, pp. 106–13).

The Conservative opposition, far from contesting the (preponderant) element of public ownership in the bill, criticised the Government for not going further. A former minister, J. Earl Lawson, complained that TCA would be a hybrid:

Personally I cannot claim to be a public ownership man, if by that it is meant one who favours the public ownership of most things in the country, although I have always recognised that there are certain exceptions to my general rule or principle of the greater efficiency of private enterprise. But there is one principle to which I make no exception and of which I am thoroughly convinced, and that is that we should not have ownership or operation which is part public and part private.

The Leader of the Conservative Party and former Conservative Prime Minister, R. B. Bennett, similarly maintained that the trouble with the Government's bill was that it did not create a thoroughgoing State monopoly:

I submit that in the light of the experience we have had in this country, if we are going into this airline business we should own it from the start, and not later.

Tonight we stand in a position to create by Act of this Parliament an enterprise that will have complete control of aerial navigation between the Atlantic and the Pacific . . . If we pass this measure and hand this right over, not to the Crown but to a body of shareholders, and provide that the Crown may buy it back some time in the future if it so desires, we shall be going in the wrong direction.

The writer whose study of airline politics we have been drawing on remarks: 'The establishment of TCA as a public enterprise illustrates vividly the virtual absence in Canadian practical politics of any clear or consistent ideological commitments concerning public ownership. The Liberals professed to be concerned with private enterprise as a value, but ignored it in practice. The Conservative leader contradicted the theories for which his Party was supposed to stand.' It should be added that private airline interests in Canada and the United States lobbied the Government against the bill, but wholly without success: the minister, Mr Howe, told them to 'go back home'.

Given this record with regard to public ownership, it is not surprising to find that the social services in Canada have likewise been extended piecemeal and relatively quietly. As in the United States, the main impetus for change came in the 1930s, during the great depression; but, whereas in the United States the social security and housing acts were passed by a reforming Administration after several decades of fierce controversy, in Canada the chief innovations were proposed by a Conservative Government, had not been preceded by a prolonged period of controversy, and did not provoke a debate on anything like the same scale about the rights and wrongs of State intervention. In the event, much of the Conservative legislation was declared unconstitutional by the Judicial Committee of the Privy Council (mainly on the ground that under the British North America Act it fell outside the purview of the federal government), and it was left to subsequent Liberal Administrations successfully to introduce housing legislation (from 1938) and unemployment insurance (1940), and also to expand greatly (1951, 1965) the provisions of an earlier old-age assistance law. It was also under the Liberals that the hospital and medical insurance programmes already described were introduced—although there already existed a number of provincial schemes that had been established by Governments controlled by a variety of political parties. Only one social-service innovation in Canada has provoked a controversy of American proportions: the introduction by Saskatchewan in 1962 of a compulsory health plan roughly along the lines of the British NHS.

Britain

The British experience resembles the Canadian more than the American, although in Britain a sharp debate on public ownership has gone on for many years between the Labour and Conservative parties. The general terms of the debate are well known. Labour contends that, other things being equal, Britain's basic industries should be publicly owned, the Conservatives that, other things being equal, they should not. The phrase 'other things being equal' is crucial, however. In practice the Labour Party has proposed to nationalise industries only where it has believed that a non-doctrinal, pragmatic case could be made out for doing so. Similarly, the Conservatives have shown themselves willing to expand the public sector where the national interest seemed to demand it or where it seemed essential to avert the consequences of the collapse of an important private company. The Conservatives have also been reluctant—save in the cases of steel and road haulage after 1951—to return to private ownership industries that have been nationalised by Labour.

The extent to which Conservative as well as Labour Governments have been prepared to extend the public sector is indicated by

TABLE 11.7 *Creation of public enterprises in Britain*

Enterprise	Government	Date
Post Office telephones	Conservative	1905
BBC	Conservative	1926
BOAC	Conservative	1939
National Coal Board	Labour	1946
BEA	Labour	1946
British Railways	Labour	1947
Iron and Steel Corp. of Great Britain	Labour	1949
(denationalised by Conservative Government, 1953)		
British Steel Corp.	Labour	1967
Rolls-Royce (aero engine)	Conservative	1971

Table 11.7, which lists most of the main publicly-owned enterprises in Britain and sets out by whom they were created and when. (The electricity and gas supply industries have been omitted because in each case a substantial portion of the industry was already publicly owned—mainly by municipalities—at the time of nationalisation.)

The attitude of the Conservatives is particularly important in the context of our discussion, for reasons that will emerge later. The failure of the Party after 1951 to return to private ownership most of the firms and industries nationalised by Labour (and the list in Table 11.7 is by no means complete) owed something to the circumstances of the time: nationalisation seemed to have been accepted by most of the electorate, and in any case it would have been extremely difficult to find buyers for firms many of which had been on the verge of bankruptcy before being taken over. It also owed a great deal to the unwillingness of most Conservatives to play shuttlecock with important sections of industry. One Tory MP commented at the time: 'I cannot contemplate without horror the nightmare picture of [the] British economy swaying drunkenly between nationalisation and private enterprise according to the turns, now this way and now that, of the electoral pendulum. Rather than this I should prefer to see socialisation a permanency' (Hogg, 1947, p. 294).

But underlying both the Conservatives' slowness to denationalise, and their willingness to create a body like the BBC or to turn Rolls-Royce into a public corporation, was, and is, their conception of the proper role of the State. It has often been pointed out that the British Conservative Party, despite its general commitment to private enterprise, has never been a thoroughgoing anti-statist party and, on the contrary, has historically been 'the party of government'. The following quotations are neither extreme nor untypical:

It is often assumed that Conservatism and Socialism are directly opposed. But this is not completely true. Modern Conservatism inherits the traditions of Toryism which are favourable to the activity and authority of the State (Lord Hugh Cecil quoted in Hogg, 1947, p.44).

Since the days of Bolingbroke our Party has believed in using the power and majesty of the State in order to serve the best interests of our citizens . . . (R. A. Butler quoted in King, 1966, pp. 49–50). In these days, when the main opponent of the Conservative Party is Socialist and not Whig or Liberal, it is important for Conservatives to remember that, traditionally speaking, Conservatives and Tories stood for strong central Government, and their opponents for 'liberty' and 'individualism' . . . The point is . . . that Conservatives do not adhere to any doctrinaire or pedantic belief in private ownership and control (Hogg, 1947, pp. 44, 113).

The continuing battle with Labour over nationalisation has recently made Tories a little more reticent about expressing these sorts of views in public. Nonetheless, this streak of statism in the thinking of British Conservatives is a strong one—as their record with regard to public ownership suggests.

Controversy over the social services in Britain has been nothing like so fierce as over nationalisation. In this field the British experience has been broadly similar to the Canadian and quite unlike the American. Most of the major social-service innovations have been the work of reformist governments in Britain as in the United States, but otherwise the experiences of the two countries have been completely different. None of the major changes in Britain has been the result of a national crisis. The debate between the two parties has almost invariably had more to do with means than ends. The interest groups have been more concerned with specific details than general principles. Almost no one has tried in any connection to deny the propriety of direct State action.

These points could be established with regard to any of the social services in Britain, but perhaps the example of medical care illustrates them best. The story of the National Insurance and National Health Service Acts has often been told in terms of intense interest-group activity and intense partisan conflict. It is true that both Lloyd George (1908–12) and Bevan (1946–8) had to make substantial concessions as the result of pressures from interest groups: the friendly societies, insurance companies, and doctors in Lloyd George's case, mainly the doctors in Bevan's. It is also true that the Conservative

Party actively opposed both measures: in 1911–12 it campaigned in the country against Lloyd George's scheme; in 1946 it voted against the National Health Service Bill in the House of Commons.

But what stands out, especially in contrast to the history of Medicare in the United States, is the relatively narrow basis on which both controversies were conducted. Neither before 1914 nor after 1945 did the interest groups attempt to block the introduction of State-run medical care schemes as such. The friendly societies, for instance, did not try to force Lloyd George to withdraw his insurance scheme entirely—even though the subject of medical insurance was quite new to British politics and even though there was as yet no tangible evidence of public demand for it. Rather, they tried to protect their own interests, strictly construed, by minimizing the amount of competition between themselves and the State and by securing for themselves a large role in the scheme's administration. Similarly, the leaders of the British Medical Association after 1945 did not contend that a national health service should not be set up, but instead confined themselves to such relatively limited issues as the provision of 'private' beds in hospitals and the system of doctors' remuneration.

The opposition of the Conservative Party was just as narrowly based. Its campaign in 1911–12 was partly a purely tactical response to its discovery that the contributions which the Lloyd George scheme required were unpopular in the country, and partly the result of its support for some of the particular claims of the interest groups. Far from contesting the Government's right to introduce a compulsory scheme. the Conservatives in 1911 at first gave the bill a friendly reception in the House of Commons and did not force divisions on the first or second reading. Indeed, on the day Lloyd George introduced his bill, Austen Chamberlain, then a strong contender for the Conservative leadership, wrote in his diary: 'Confound L. G. He has strengthened the Government again. His sickness scheme is a good one, and he is on the right lines this time. I must say I envy him the opportunity, and I must admit that he has made good use of it' (quoted in Bunbury, 1957, p. 56). After 1945 the Conservatives were hardly in a position to oppose in principle the creation of the NHS, since their own election manifesto had committed them to establishing 'a comprehensive health service covering the whole range of medical treatment'. (See Craig, 1970, p. 92). The Party did vote against the second and third reading of Bevan's bill, but only on amendments that permitted them to evade the central issue.

West Germany

In America, Canada, and Britain, State activity can reasonably be said to have 'expanded' over the past sixty years or so. In Germany, by contract, the sphere of the State has always been big. All that has happened recently is that it has got even bigger—and more systematically organised.

The presence of large-scale public ownership in Germany is very little the product of socialist theorising or of British-type acts of nationalisation. It is mainly an inheritance from the end of the nineteenth century, by which time State enterprises were already of great economic importance. Stolper (1967, p. 43) has pointed out that the Wilhelmian Monarchy bequeathed to the Weimar Republic in 1918 a peculiar economic system of mixed ownership in which, in the aggregate, the publicly-owned sector was not much smaller than the private: 'On the eve of the first world war the following services were entirely state owned: the postal, telephone, and telegraph systems . . . and the railroads. Almost fully under municipal or mixed ownership were the gasworks, waterworks, and transport systems. Power production was predominantly under state, municipal, or mixed ownership'. Government-owned banks dominated the Berlin money market and the entire savings bank business; a very considerable proportion of the mines and other industries were State-controlled; State and municipal ownership were preponderant in forestry, and even among large-scale farms State-owned units had some importance. Much of this activity, which had been dispersed amongst the states, was brought under central control in the Weimar period, when the government also acquired a 36 per cent holding in the new national airline, Deutsche Luft Hansa. Since the Second World War, although some State holdings in industry have been 'privatised', the government continues to control substantial proportions of the country's output of ships, aluminium, iron ore, and coal. Moreover the motives for the limited moves towards 'privatisation' have had little to do with antipathy towards public ownership as such, but stem from the federal government's desire to stimulate individual personal savings.

The governments which established or perpetuated State enterprises in the nineteenth century, especially in the 1870s and 1880s, were conservative in orientation and it was an imaginative conservative, Bismarck, who created the German system of social insurance: health insurance in 1883, old-age and invalidity insurance in 1889. Bismarck's motives were mixed, though not necessarily contradictory: on the one hand, he believed strongly that his programme was right in itself (he harked back to Frederick the Great, who wished to be thought of as *le roi des gueux*, 'the king of the beggars'); on the other, he wanted to diminish the appeal of the Social Democrats by securing the loyalty of the workers for the State. Justifying his first social insurance measure before the Reichstag in 1881, Bismarck declared that the policy of the State must be one which

> would cultivate the view . . . among the propertyless classes of the population, those who are the most numerous and the least educated, that the State is not only an institution of necessity but also one of welfare. By recognisable and direct advantages they must be led to look upon the State not as an agency devised solely for the protection of the better-situated classes of society but also as one serving their needs and interests.

This conception was not one calculated to appeal either to the Socialists, who wished to overthrow the State not to live off it, or to the liberals, who, like their fellows elsewhere, wished for reasons of self-interest or ideology (or both) to see the economic role of the State kept to a minimum. What is interesting, however, especially when we compare Germany with other countries, is to note the feebleness of the opposition to Bismarck's proposals. Only a minority of intellectuals, like Treitschke, objected in principle. Most industrialists and business men, already accustomed to a high level of activity on the part of Governments that were in any case sympathetic to their interests, were inclined to see the wisdom of Bismarck's strategy; the Socialists merely complained that he was not going far enough. It was in large part this widespread assumption of the appropriateness of governmental action that made it easy for Bismarck's successors—of all political parties—to extend the social insurance schemes and to commit the State to a large role in the provision of housing.

France

The French experience is harder to characterise than any of the others. There seems to be a fairly sharp discontinuity between the field of direct governmental intervention in the economy, where controversy has often been prolonged and bitter, and the field of the social services, where government activity has been expanded continually, haphazardly, and in the absence of much in the way of public debate. It is difficult to disentangle the role of interest groups from the role of parties because, at least in the Third and Fourth Republics, the parties were so often simply the interest groups in another guise. Perhaps most important, all political tendencies in France seem to be peculiarly ambivalent in their attitude to the State. The Left, or much of it, wishes to use the State to plan the economy and achieve social equality—yet is profoundly suspicious of all governments in the hands of its political opponents. The Right, at least most of it, seeks to defend private property against the encroachments of the State— yet inherits a pre-1789 respect for State institutions and a generalised desire for strong central administration.

In France, as in Germany, there is a long tradition of economic *étatisme*. Factories for the manufacture of tapestries, furniture, and other articles of quality date from the ministry of Colbert, during the reign of Louis XIV. Even during the nineteenth century, when the philosophy of economic liberalism prevailed in France as it did almost everywhere, the State did not surrender any of its existing economic functions and acquired a few new ones. Public monopolies were established, mainly for revenue purposes, in tobacco (1811) and in matches (1872). The country's embryonic telephone system, which had been started under private auspices in the early 1880s, was absorbed into the post office in 1889. But most of the government- owned enterprises in modern France are the result of two more recent waves of nationalisation: the comparatively small one of the mid-1930s, and the veritable deluge of 1944–6. The first came at the time of the Popular Front, the second under the post-resistance governments of de Gaulle. The details are given in Table 11.8.

TABLE 11.8 *Creation of public enterprises in France*

Sud-Aviation	1936	Air France	1945–8
SNCF	1937	Charbonnages de France	1946
Renault	1945	Electricité de France	1946
Crédit Lyonnais	1945	Gaz de France	1946
(and the three other main commercial banks)			

Nationalisation had its opponents in France, as it did in Britain; but, whereas in Britain the Labour Government's postwar pro- gramme of nationalisation encountered strenuous and sustained opposition, in France the opposition, both in 1936–7 and in 1944–6, hardly existed. In the case of the Popular Front, the acts of nationali- sation were carried through more or less by agreement: spokesmen for industry did not dissent from State acquisition of the armaments industry (including airplane manufacture), and French Railways (SNCF) was established as a mixed company with private capital participating. In the case of the far more ambitious 1944–6 programme the opposition was vociferous but was overwhelmed. The commercial banks were nationalised in two days, the coal mines in two hours; the banks were nationalised by 517 votes to 35, the gas and electricity industries by 490 to 60. The reasons for the opposition's isolation undoubtedly had a great deal to do with the peculiar circumstances of the immediate postwar years: the need for rapid national reconstruction, the hostility to private enterprise engendered by the collaborationist record of many leading industrialists. But they undoubtedly had much to do, too, with the fact that most Frenchmen were used to State enterprises and, even if they did not like them much, did not find them alien or outlandish. At any rate, the securities of the new nationalised companies were soon being bid up on the Paris stock exchange.

The history of the social services in France, as in Canada, has had a low political profile—probably partly because, as we noted earlier, State-administered schemes in France have often been added on to, and run in conjunction with, quasi-private schemes which they have not replaced. It was also the case that, long before the introduction of universal, compulsory State insurance, the central government had been administering insurance schemes covering quite large sections of the population, not only State employees. Whether for these or other reasons, none of the major innovations in the social services— in 1910, 1928–30, 1945, and 1967–8—have aroused much controversy or been regarded as important political landmarks. Governments of various complexions have made the changes; some have, some have not, been made at a time of national crisis; interest groups, like the doctors in 1928, have defended their interests but have not apparently though that defending their interests necessitated trying to block the changes entirely; if general questions about the proper role of the State in society were ever raised, history does not record the fact.

III   THE PATTERN EXPLAINED

In part I of this paper we described the gross pattern of public policy in our five countries. In part II we looked at how the pattern developed in each of the countries. We noticed that the countries have pursued policies that diverge widely, at least with respect to the size of the direct operating role of the State in the provision of public services. We also noticed that the United States differs from the four other countries far more than they do from each other. These findings will not have come as a great surprise to anybody, although some readers may have been surprised—in view of the common assumption that all major western countries are 'welfare states'—to discover just how much the countries differ and what different histories they have had.

In any event, it is time now to turn directly to the problem of explanation. Obviously any explanation, were it to account for all of the phenomena we have referred to, would have to be exceedingly elaborate. It would have to encompass a large number of particular events within the five countries as well as the variations amongst them. All we will attempt here is a general explanation of why the United States is so strikingly different. We shall assume that the explanation we need is indeed general: in other words, that the pattern we have observed is not simply the chance outcome of a series of more or less random occurrences. We shall also assume that it is the American pattern, in particular, that needs to be accounted for.

Much of the most important work in the field of public policy in recent years has, of course, been concerned with a very similar problem: accounting for the variations in the expenditure policies of the American states. The writers on this subject have singled out two types of (mainly quantifiable) variable: 'political' (e.g. extent of party competition, relationship between governor and legislature, apportionment of legislative districts), and 'socio-economic' (e.g. *per capita* income, degree of urbanisation, degree of industrialisation). They have then gone on, using correlation techniques, to relate these variables to one another and to the variations in policy to be explained. Unfortunately this approach is denied us here, given the problem we have set ourselves. Quite apart from the fact that we are dealing with five units instead of fifty, there is no reason to suppose that any of the expenditure-in-the-states variables is significantly related to any of the differences between the United States and the other four countries. All five are, or have been during much of their recent history, rich, urban, industrial, and politically competitive; to the extent that there have been variations in, for example, their constitutions, these variations have not had any discernible bearing on their policies. It is, in effect, as though we were trying to account for the differences, not amongst all fifty states, but only amongst (say) New York, New Jersey, Connecticut, Massachusetts, and Pennsylvania.

We must therefore look elsewhere. We shall consider explanations in terms of five possible variables: elites, demands, interest groups, institutions, and ideas.[4] These variables obviously interact with one another, or at least they could. Some examples of such interaction will be noted below, but for simplicity's sake the five variables will mostly be treated separately. As with the other parts of the paper, the discussion will be very brief, with only the main lines of the argument roughed out.

Elites

It could be maintained, first, that government plays a smaller role in the US because *the US, unlike the other four countries, is dominated by an elite which wishes to inhibit the expansion of State activity and succeeds in doing so.* For this proposition to be true, at least one of the following propositions would also have to be true: either America is dominated by an elite whereas the other four countries are not; or the American elite is alone in wishing to limit the sphere of the State; or the American elite is not alone in wishing to limit the sphere of the State but is alone in actually succeeding in doing so. It would also have to be the case that there were in the US factors making for the expansion of State activity, which would have their effect but for the elite's intervention.

Much in this line of argument is not very plausible. America may or may not be dominated by an elite, but, if it is, then so are Canada, Britain, France, and West Germany; there is hardly an industrial country anywhere whose power structure has not been interpreted in the style of C. Wright Mills (1956). There is similarly no reason to suppose—on the assumption that all five countries are dominated by elites—that the American elite is somehow more successful than the others in imposing its will, or in thwarting the wills of others; indeed it would be paradoxical to say of an elite that it was an elite but yet could not get its way in matters that were important to it. Nevertheless there is on element in the elitist explanation—the possiblity that the American elite, if it exists, is alone in wishing to limit the sphere of

[4] It could be claimed that the differences in our five countries' policies should be explained in terms of the countries' different 'needs'. Quite apart from the fact that an explanation in terms of needs would be almost impossible to operationalise, such an explanation, if someone produced one, would almost certainly turn out to be false. It is hard to conceive of any sense in which it would be accurate to say that Germany 'needed' health insurance in the 1880s whereas the United States did not need it until the 1960s, or that France 'needed' a publicly-owned railway system in the 1930s whereas the US still does not need one in the 1970s.

the State—which cannot be dismissed out of hand. We shall come back to it at the end.

Demands

A second possible explanation of the relatively limited role played by government in the US is that, *whereas the mass publics in the other countries have demanded expansions of State activity, the American mass public has not.* In other words, irrespective of whether the United States is dominated by an elite, it may be that little has happened because little has been called for. An alternative rendering of this hypothesis would be that, whereas in any or all of the other countries governments do things whether or not they are demanded, in the US governments act only on demand and, since little has been demanded, little has been done; in other words, public opinion may play a more important part in American political life than elsewhere.[5]

These possibilities raise all sorts of questions, as yet unanswered, in the empirical theory of representation. They also pose a very real problem of evidence: who is to say what the Canadian people wanted in 1917 or the French in the 1920s? All the same, there are a number of points which can be made with some confidence, and, while they should not lead anyone to reject the demands hypothesis outright, they make one wonder whether it can provide more than a very small part of the general explanation we are looking for.

It is hard to think of any act of nationalisation in Canada or Europe that took place as the result of widespread public demand for it. The British case is probably typical. Many historians believe that, if anything, Labour won the 1945 general election despite its commitments to nationalisation not because of them, and that most voters remained pretty indifferent to the Labour Government's subsequent nationalisation measures. Butler and Stokes (1969, pp. 177–8), found in the 1960s that of a panel of electors interviewed twice at an interval of approximately sixteen months, 61 per cent either had no opinion at all on nationalisation or no stable opinion; of the majority with definite opinions, the great majority wanted either no more nationalisation or even the denationalistion of industries already in

[5] We are assuming here that mass demands are in some sense 'given': that politicians and governments do not create demands, only react to them. But of course there is every reason to think that public demands and expectations are as much a consequence as a cause of governmental activity: that politicians frequently respond to demands that they themselves have created: see Murray Edelman (1971). This point does not contradict, but rather reinforces, the argument developed below.

the public sector. Yet in 1967 the Wilson Government nationalised the great bulk of the British iron and steel industry.

The only exception to this pattern of indifference/hostility is probably France in 1944–6, where the overwhelming need for national reconstruction and the anti-patriotic aura that private business had acquired during the Occupation seem to have created a climate of public opinion favourable to State ownership. It has been claimed by a French historian that in 1944 'the great majority of Frenchmen were convinced of the economic, social and political superiority of nationalised industry over private industry'. (Gendarme quoted in Baum, 1958, p. 174.)

The picture is quite different in connection with the social services. Much of the evidence is lacking but, as far as one can make out, popular majorities at most times in all of our five countries have desired—often greatly desired—the extension of existing social services and the establishment of new ones. Even Bismarck and Lloyd George, although they could not be sure whether a demand for social-welfare measures already existed, believed that one soon would exist and that it would be politically expedient to anticipate it. More important for our purposes, the American mass public seems to differ hardly at all in this connection from the mass publics of other countries. The evidence on this point is, for once, abundant. To take only one example, Free and Cantril (1967) report two surveys, taken in 1964 and 1967, which asked samples of the US electorate for their views about government spending in a variety of social-service fields. A summary of the results is set out in Table 11.9. Free and Cantril (p. 13) also found in 1964 that 62 per cent favoured federal aid to education and 63 per cent a hospital insurance scheme for the aged.

TABLE 11.9 *American attitudes towards Social Services, 1964, 1967*

	Present level of spending, or increase %	Reduced level of spending, or none %
Low-rent public housing ('64)	63	22
Urban renewal ('64)	67	21
Community Action ('67)	54	35
Job retraining ('67)	75	21
Head Start ('67)	67	26

Source: Free and Cantril (1967, pp. 11–14).

These findings are not untypical. They suggest rather strongly that the State's comparatively limited provision of social services in the US is not readily attributable to differences in public opinion. They also suggest that, at least in this field, public opinion does not in fact play a larger role in the US than elsewhere—possibly even the reverse.

The explanation in terms of a dominant elite and the explanation in terms of demands are not perhaps very convincing, even on the face of it. Certainly, although much has been written about both elites and demands, neither has often been used for the purpose of explaining variations in policy. The next three lines of argument are, however, frequently advanced, sometimes by different writers, sometimes in combination by the same writer.

Interest groups

The first of these holds that government plays a more limited role in America because, *whereas in other countries interest groups have not prevented the role of government from expanding, in the US they have*. This argument looks straightforward enough, but it could in fact mean one or more of at least three quite different things. It could mean that interest groups are in possession of more politically usable resources in the United States than in other countries; or it could mean that, although interest groups in most countries are almost equally well endowed with resources, interest groups in America, unlike those elsewhere, have used their resources to keep the State within relatively narrow confines; or it could mean that, although American interest groups have no more resources than other interest groups and do not use their resources for different purposes from other interest groups, they do have the good fortune to work within a framework of institutions that affords them the maximum opportunity to use their resources successfully.

The first of these propositions—that interest groups have more resources in the US than elsewhere—would probably at one time have been widely accepted as true; but the work of Beer (1956, pp. 1–23) and others has made it clear that the conditions under which interest groups can be expected to be strong are to be found in most industrial democracies. The interest groups of Britain, West Germany, and Canada have the same sorts of resources at their disposal as those of the United States: leadership skills, knowledge, numbers, access to the media of communication, in some cases, ultimately, the sanction of withdrawing their co-operation. In Britain at least, the major interests are less fragmented organisationally than their American counterparts and succeed in organising a larger proportion of their potential memberships. In Britain and West Germany, groups benefit from being regarded as having a legitimate right to participate actively in governmental decision making. Only in France do interest groups appear to have considerable difficulty in mobilising themselves effectively. Since, France apart, American interest groups are not stronger, in this sense, than interest groups in other countries, it follows that the strength of the American groups cannot be used to explain the idiosyncratic pattern of American policy.

The second of the three propositions mentioned above—that interest groups in the United States are more concerned than those in other countries with keeping the State within narrow confines—is worth saying something about, even though there is no comparative literature on the aims of interest groups—indeed precisely for that reason.

Up till now, academic research on interest groups has tended to take groups' perceptions of their own interests as given: a group's beliefs about its interests *are* its interests. On this interpretation, questions about where a group's true interests lie arise only when they are actually raised within the group, by contending factions or by dissident minorities. Even then, the observer usually merely notes the existence of the differences of opinion and does not adjudicate among them; he does not 'second guess' the group's leadership or take sides in its quarrels.

This approach may be the only one that can be adopted most of the time; but the attempt to comprehend the behaviour of comparable interest groups across national frontiers exposes a latent weakness in it. Suppose that two interest groups, one in one country, one in another, seem, as regards their material interests, to be in very similar situations: both are faced with a piece of new legislation that may reasonably be expected to affect (say) their incomes or hours of work. Suppose further, however, that the group in one country generally accepts the legislation and tries only to modify it in detail, while the group in the other rejects it out of hand and expends enormous resources campaigning against it. One possible explanation for the group's discrepant behaviour may be that they possess different information or are making different predictions about the future. Another may be that they find themselves in different tactical situations such that, if either were in the other's position, it would behave similarly. But another explanation is that the two groups perceive their interests differently. And they may perceive their interests differently because they have absorbed the values, beliefs, and expectations characteristic of the different polities within which they operate. This is too large a theme to be pursued here, but anyone comparing the rhetoric of American interest groups with that of groups in other countries is bound to be struck by what seems to be the American groups' much greater disposition to state their positions in abstract terms and, in particular, to raise, continually, large questions about the role of the State. This tendency probably tells us something about the considerations that American groups have in mind in determining where their interests lie. It undoubtedly tells us a great deal also about the sorts of considerations which the groups believe will appeal to the American mass public and to American decision makers.

The third of the three propositions relating to interest groups suggests that, whatever their resources and their aims, American groups have the great good fortune to work within a framework of institutions that affords them the maximum opportunities for using their resources effectively, especially when what they want to do is prevent things from happening. Since this proposition has more to do with the institutions than with the interest groups themselves, we will consider it in the next section.

Institutions

The classic explanation of the limited role played by the State in the United States as compared with other countries is one having to do with the structure and functioning of American institutions. The contention here is that *the American political system has a number of unusual institutional features, which have the effect of maximising the probability that any given proposal for a change in policy will be rejected or deferred.* These features include: federalism, the separation of powers between executive and legislature, the constitutional position of the Supreme Court, the part played by committees in Congress, the seniority system in Congress, the malapportionment (until quite recently) of congressional districts, and the absence of disciplined political parties.

To do full justice to this explanation would require a paper much longer than this one. It would also require a great deal of imagination, since this explanation, in an even more demanding way than the others, forces us to try to conceive of what the gross pattern of public policy in the United States would be like were American institutions radically other than they are: it is rather like trying to imagine which of two grand masters would win a tournament if they played not chess or even checkers but croquet. This explanation also differs completely from the others discussed so far in that, whereas in the case of elites, demands and interest groups we were arguing that the US does not differ in most material respects from the other four countries, in this case there can be no doubt that political realities as well as constitutional forms in the US are quite unlike those in Canada and western Europe.[6]

The question, then, is not whether America's institutions differ from the other countries' but whether these differences can account for the observed differences in their patterns of policy. There would seem to be three reasons for supposing that they cannot—at least not on their own.

First, as we have already seen, it has never seriously been suggested in the US that certain tasks undertaken by governments in Canada and Europe—for instance, the operation of railways and airlines—should also be undertaken by government in America. Suggestions of this kind have occasionally been made but almost never by major national leaders or parties. And this fact seems hard to attribute to institutional resistances. Of course politicians often refrain from putting forward proposals because they know they have no chance of success; possible courses of action may not even cross their minds for the same reason. But it is very hard to believe that American political leaders have consistently, over a period of nearly a hundred years, failed to advance proposals which they might otherwise have advanced simply or even mainly because they feared defeat as the result of obstruction in the House Rules Committee or an adverse ruling by the Supreme Court. It seems much more probable that politicians in the US have not advanced such proposals either because they did not believe in them themselves, or because they believed that other politicians did not believe in them, i.e. that they could not obtain adequate majorities in the various governmental arenas.

Second, in comparative perspective, even reformist Congresses and Administrations, like those of Franklin Roosevelt and Lyndon Johnson, appear as remarkable for what they have not done as for what they have. Only small excursions have been made into the field of public enterprise; and, among the social service. Medicare is only the most conspicuous instance of State provision having been introduced in the United States on a relatively limited basis although substantially more developed programmes had already been in

[6] Of course the differences may not be so great as they appear on the surface: the absence of a strong system of legislative committees does not necessarily mean the absence of opportunities for delay and obstruction; the presence of disciplined parties does not necessarily mean that leaders can lead their followers anywhere.

existence, sometimes for many years, in other countries. This apparent reluctance on the part of even reformist majorities to expand the role of the State very far cannot be accounted for in institutional terms.

Third, the institutional obstacles, although they undoubtedly exist, can be surmounted. One of the striking things about the American experience is that almost all of the major innovations in the policy fields we have been discussing have been concentrated in a small number of Congresses: Roosevelt's first three, and the 89th elected with Johnson in 1964. And what distinguished these Congresses was not the absence of procedural obstacles (although minor procedural changes were made) but the presence of determined reformist majorities. In 1935 the Social Security Act passed both houses of Congress in under six months; in 1965 Medicare, having been debated in one form or another for nearly twenty years, was enacted in under seven months. The Social Security Act passed the House of Representatives by 371 votes to 33, Medicare by 315 votes to 115. When the will to surmount them is there, the institutional obstacles do not seem so formidable after all.

These points need to be qualified. For one thing, although the obstacles usually referred to—federalism, the separation of powers, and so forth—are not insuperable, it may be that other institutional factors—for example, the structure of American political parties or the expensiveness of political campaigns—result in the election of Congresses and Administrations (especially the former) that are less willing than the electorate to envisage the State's playing an expanded role. For instance, as late as 1961 the congressional liaison staff of the Department of Health, Education, and Welfare reckoned that Medicare still could not command a simple majority in the House of Representatives even though the evidence suggested that public opinion had supported Medicare or something like it for many years. For another, it would be wrong wholly to discount the role played by the Supreme Court prior to 1937. Although not entirely consistent in its judgements, the Court repeatedly struck down legislation that offended against the canons of *laissez-faire*: in 1905, a New York statute regulating working hours in bakeshops; in 1908, a federal law prohibiting 'yellow dog' labour contracts (in which workers bound themselves not to join trade unions); in 1918 and 1922, two federal Child Labor Acts; in 1923, a District of Columbia minimum wage law; and so on. The belief that the Court would strike down other similar pieces of legislation undoubtedly prevented many of them from being considered in the first place.

These qualifications are important. Nevertheless, it seems pretty clear that, for the three reasons given, the institutional explanation by itself is not enough. To the extent that institutional factors operate, they must, it seems, operate in conjunction with others.

Ideas

The time has come to let the cat out of the bag—especially since most readers will have noticed that it has already been squirming for a long time. If the argument so far is correct, it follows that the most satisfactory single solution to our problem is also the simplest: *the State plays a more limited role in America than elsewhere because Americans, more than other people, want it to play a limited role*. In other words, the most satisfactory explanation is one in terms of Americans' beliefs and assumptions, especially their beliefs and assumptions about government.

There is no need to go into detail here about what these beliefs and assumptions are. They can be summarised in a series of catch phrases: free enterprise is more efficient than government; governments should concentrate on encouraging private initiative and free competition; government is wasteful; governments should not provide people with things they can provide for themselves; too much government endangers liberty; and so on.

Obviously many Americans' political beliefs are much more elaborate and subtle than such phrases imply. Obviously, too, not all Americans believe all of these things. The central point is that almost every American takes it for granted that the State has very few—and should have very few—direct operating responsibilities: that the State should opt 'for the role of referee rather than that of manager' (Shonfield, 1965, p. 330). If a proposal is made in the United States that the State should not merely supervise the doing of something by somebody else but should actually do it itself, the onus is on the proposer to demonstrate that the case in favour of State action is simply overwhelming. It has to be overwhelming since Americans, unlike Europeans, are not accustomed to a high level of governmental activity and since it will simply be assumed, probably even by the proposer himself, that the *a priori* objections to State action are exceedingly powerful. It is against this background that organisations like the AMA practically always bring forward highly general anti-State arguments against the most specific proposals entailing an expansion of the government's role.

One example, quoted by Shonfield (p. 330), will give an idea of how pervasive these ideas are. In the early 1960s, during the Kennedy

Administration, the Bureau of the Budget directive to all federal agencies on the use of government-owned production facilities was introduced with a preamble that began: 'Because the private enterprise system is basic to the American economy . . .' It went on to warn any civil servant who proposed to use public enterprise for the 'provision of a product or service' that 'the burden of proof lies on the agency which determines that an exception to the general policy is required'. Nor was the civil servant to imagine, if he came across a piece of public enterprise which was already in operation, that he had no duty to put matters right: 'The existence of government-owned capital assets is not in itself an adequate justification for the government to produce its own goods or services. The need for continued government ownership or operation must be fully substantiated'. Finally, he might be tempted to believe that his obligations had been met once private enterprise had been brought in to take charge of and operate the publicly-owned undertaking. Not so: 'Even the operation of a government-owned facility by a private organisation through the contractual arrangement does not automatically ensure that the government is not competing with private enterprise. This type of arrangement could act as a barrier to the development and growth of competitive commercial sources and procurement through ordinary business channels.' In the United States, in short, the machinery of government is not an accepted piece of institutional apparatus to be made use of as and when required; it is a sort of emergency appliance, to be wheeled out only in the most extreme circumstances and put back in its place, if possible, as soon as the emergency is over.

The contrast between the United States and our other four countries is not complete; most Canadians probably make the same sorts of assumptions as Americans about the role of the State, and the Conservative Party in Britain has a strong bias in favour of the private sector. But the contrast is very great nonetheless. Certainly it is more than great enough to account for the policy divergences we have observed. Not only are social democrats in Canada and Europe committed to making extensive use of the machinery of the State: equally important, conservatives in the other four countries, as we have seen, are also not consistently anti-Statist in attitude; on the contrary, they often express a highly exalted view of the role of the State in economic and social life. It was not a socialist but a British Conservative MP who said: 'In many respects . . . the individual is as much derived from the State as the State is from the individual' (Lord Hugh Cecil quoted in Black, 1950, p. 84). It was not a socialist but de Gaulle who said: 'It is to the State that it falls to build the nation's power, which, henceforth, depends on the economy'.

Before we move on to some final observations and our conclusion, one further question remains to be considered, concerning the chief exception of the American policy pattern: the case of education. Far from government in the United States playing a limited role in this field, it plays a considerably larger role than in any of the other four countries. Why should this be so?

The answer seems to be that education is an issue that lies athwart the predominantly anti-Statist tendency of American thinking. American cultural values contain a latent dilemma. On the one hand, they place great emphasis—much greater than do European values—on equality and on the provision of opportunities for upward social mobility. On the other, they lay equally great emphasis on the sustaining of a highly individualistic social order. The question has been how to provide a degree of equality of opportunity within the existing order. Education has been the answer. Education seems to reconcile equality with individualism. Largely for this reason, in America it became, as Welter has pointed out, a substitute for other forms of social action (Welter, 1962, pp. 189, 241). More to the point, the State could be permitted to be the major supplier of education because, on economic grounds, it was clear that, if the State did not supply education, no one else would. Thus, education was a field—almost the only field—in which the State could expand without competing, except in a very small way, with private institutions. The State's position was also buttressed by the desire of native Americans to 'Americanise' succeeding waves of immigrants. This was not a task that could safely be left to private institutions, since private institutions in practice would have meant (and sometimes did mean) the immigrant communities themselves.

FINAL OBSERVATIONS AND CONCLUSION

At the very beginning of this paper we remarked that its aim was to start trains of thought, not stop them. Since then we have surveyed a vast terrain. Inevitably some matters have been slighted, others not touched on at all. Even if one is disposed to accept the paper's general line of argument, there are a number of areas that still deserve to be explored.

One has to do with the public service and attitudes towards it. In a paper dealing with some of the same questions as this one, Heidenheimer (1973, pp. 325–6) notes that in the United States, especially during the Progressive era, 'mistrust of the probity and efficiency of public officialdom greatly strengthened the position of those who were opposed to public sector expansion on ideological and private-interest grounds'. 'More than that', he adds 'it deterred reformers from even proposing to endow public jurisdictions with more-than regulatory powers.' Clearly this is a contention that cannot be dismissed out of hand; it suggests that, at the least, another variable —perceived quality of the public service—should be considered along with the others we have discussed. What is not clear is how far the late development of the American public service was a cause of the non-expansion of the American State, and how far it was a consequence. It is plausible to argue that the American State was kept within narrow confines because of the poor quality of its servants. It seems equally plausible to argue that, because such a limited view was taken of the State's role, incentives to improve the quality of the public service were lacking. There is probably some truth in both contentions.

Another area worth exploring is implicit in the phrase we have used several times: 'direct operating role of the State'. The emphasis in this paper has been on the things that governments do on their own, not through intermediaries or by means of regulation—in other words, on the State as manager rather than referee. But of course some of the most important things that governments do (by any critieria) fall outside this rubric. Governments not only run things: they also, as we observed earlier, regulate things, license things and subsidise things. All governments pursue such economic objectives as growth, full employment, price stability, and balance-of-payments equilibrium. Comparative research would almost certainly reveal as wide variations in these matters as we have observed in connection with public ownership and the social services. These variations, too, would be worth trying to account for.

If there is variation in policy, there is also variation, as again we have observed, in men's beliefs and attitudes about the role of government and about what the specific objects of government should be. Shonfield's *Modern Capitalism* is largely concerned with such variation as it affects economic policy. Unfortunately this is not a matter that has been gone into systematically, either with regard to individual countries (though there is some work on the United States) or comparatively. This paper, like Hartz's book (1955), has emphasised the anti-Statist, Lockean thrust of most American thought. Closer examination, however, would probably suggest that American Lockeanism was in some sense deformed: that it had for better or worse become largely a pro-business creed. If ideas are as important as this paper has suggested, it follows that if we are to understand public policy we must know much more about the ideas of those who make policy.

This point leads directly to another. We talked in Part 3 of the beliefs and assumptions of 'Americans', and it probably is true that the level of consensus about the desirability of government's playing a limited role is high in the US. But how high? And is this belief in the limited role of government consistent with other things that Americans also believe? If not, do Americans value the limited role of government more or less highly than other things they value? Are preferences and preference orderings about these matters distributed randomly through the American population, or is the distribution skewed in some way?

The literature relevant to these questions is suggestive. It suggests that, while the belief in limited government is widespread, it is by no means universal; that the belief in limited government is not consistent with other things that Americans believe; and that, where the belief in limited government comes into conflict with other things Americans believe, the other beliefs are often likely to be preferred.

The simple point that Americans are by no means unanimous in their hostility towards 'big government' emerges from a number of studies, including the one by Free and Cantril cited earlier (p. 129). Free and Cantril's findings also indicate that, to the extent that Americans are hostile towards big government, their hostility is in many cases not consistent with their views on more concrete questions, especially those connected with income maintenance and social welfare. Free and Cantril asked their sample in 1964, for example, whether or not they agreed with the following statement: 'Social problems here in this country could be solved more effectively if the government would only keep its hands off and let people in local communities handle their own problems in their own ways.' Nearly half of the sample, 49 per cent, said they did agree, but despite the wording of the statement, fully 38 per cent said they did not. And, since this was the same sample which produced substantial majorities in favour of new government programmes in the fields of education and health insurance, at least some respondents must have given replies which, on the face of it, seem inconsistent. The Free and Cantril data do not by themselves show that, forced to choose between their preference for hands-off government and their preference for (say) Medicare, the respondents would have chosen Medicare; but.

on the basis of other survey findings, there is every reason to suppose that they would.

Evidence of this sort raises in one's mind the possibility that the role of the State in America is limited, not because all Americans believe it should be and are prepared to act on that belief, but because those who make policy in America—ultimately the politicians— believe is should be. It is at least possible that the policy makers could, if they wanted to, greatly expand government's role in the social services and might even, for good or ill, be able to extend the sphere of State management and ownership. Perhaps there is something in the elitist explanation after all. Be that as it may, an emphasis on ideas, as in this paper, leads directly to the question: whose ideas? Crucial though this question is, it is, alas, too large a question to be pursued here.

If one had to sum up the argument of this paper in a phrase, it would be that Louis Hartz in *The Liberal Tradition in America* was right, perhaps even righter than he knew. There is nothing new, of course, in our assertion that a limited conception of the role of government is a central element in American political thinking: every textbook has a paragraph on the subject. There is nothing new either in our saying that Europeans and even Canadians do not share this conception to anything like the same degree—if they share it at all. What probably is new in this paper is the contention that these differences in beliefs and assumptions are crucial to an understanding of the distinctive pattern of American policy. It is our contention that the pattern of American policy is what it is, not because America is dominated by an elite (though it may be); not because the demands made on government are different from those made on governments in other countries; not because American interest groups have greater resources than those in other countries; not because American institutions are more resistant to change than those in other countries (though they probably are); but rather because Americans believe things that other people do not believe and make assumptions that other people do not make. More precisely, elites, demands, interest groups, and institutions constitute neither necessary nor sufficient conditions of the American policy pattern; ideas, we contend, constitute both a necessary condition and a sufficient one.

REFERENCES

ARDAGH, J. (1970) *The New France: De Gaulle and After,* Penguin Books.
BAUM, W. C. (1958) *The French Economy and the State,* Princeton Univesrity Press.

BEER, S. H. (1956) 'Pressure groups and parties in Britain', *American Political Science Review,* **L.**

BLACK, R. J., ed. (1950) *The Conservative Tradition,* Adam and Charles Black.

BUTLER, D. and STOKES, D. (1969) *Political Change in Britain,* Macmillan.

BUNBURY, H. N. (1957) *Lloyd George's Ambulance Wagon,* Methuen.

CRAIG, F., ed. (1970) *British General Election Manifestos 1918–1966,* Political Reference Publications.

CURRIE, A. W. (1967) *Canadian Transportation Economics,* University of Toronto Press.

EDELMAN, M. (1971) *Politics as Symbolic Action: Mass Arousal and Quiescence,* Markham.

FEINGOLD, E., ed. (1966) *Medicare: Policy and Politics,* Chandler.

FREE, L. A. and CANTRIL, H. (1967) *The Political Beliefs of Americans,* Rutgers University Press.

HARTZ, L. (1955) *The Liberal Tradition in America,* Harcourt, Brace.

HEIDENHEIMER, A. J. (1973) 'The politics of public education, health and welfare in the U.S.A. and Western Europe: how growth and reform potentials have differed', *British Journal of Political Science,* **III.**

HOGG, Q. (1947) *The Case for Conservatism,* Penguin Books.

KING, A., ed. (1966) *British Politics: People, Parties and Parliament,* D. C. Heath.

LUBOVE, R. (1968) *The Struggle for Social Security 1900–1935,* Harvard University Press.

MILLS, C. W. (1956) *The Power Elite,* Oxford University Press.

PINSON, K. S. (1954) *Modern Germany,* Macmillan.

RUSSETT, B. M. *et al.* (1964) *World Handbook of Social and Political Indicators,* Yale University Press.

SHONFIELD, M. (1965) *Modern Capitalism,* Oxford University Press.

STATISTICAL OFFICE OF THE EUROPEAN COMMUNITIES (1971) *Basic Statistics of the Community.*

STOLPER, G. (1967) *The German Economy 1870 to the Present,* Weidenfeld and Nicolson.

UNESCO (1964) *World Survey of Education,* **4**

UNITED STATES DEPARTMENT OF HEALTH, EDUCATION AND WELFARE (1969) *Social Security Programs Throughout the World.*

WELTER, R. (1962) *Popular Education and Democratic Thought in America,* Columbia University Press.

WENDT, P. F. (1962) *Housing Policy—The Search for Solutions,* University of California Press.

I 2

J. C. Davies   Why do revolutions occur?

Excerpts from 'Toward a theory of revolution', *American Sociological Review*, **27**, no. **1**, 1962 pp. 5-19.

In exhorting proletarians of all nations to unite in revolution, because they had nothing to lose but their chains, Marx and Engels most succinctly presented that theory of revolution which is recognised as their brain child. But this most famed thesis, that progressive degradation of the industrial working class would finally reach the point of despair and inevitable revolt, is not the only one that Marx fathered. In at least one essay he gave life to a quite antithetical idea. He described, as a precondition of widespread unrest, not progressive degradation of the proletariat but rather an improvement in workers' economic condition which did not keep pace with the growing welfare of capitalists and therefore produced social tension.

A noticeable increase in wages presupposes a rapid growth of productive capital. The rapid growth of productive capital brings about an equally rapid growth of wealth, luxury, social wants, social enjoyments. Thus, although the enjoyments of the workers have risen, the social satisfaction that they give has fallen in comparison with the increased enjoyments of the capitalist, which are inaccessible to the worker, in comparison with the state of development of society in general. Our desires and pleasures spring from society; we measure them, therefore, by society and not by the objects which serve for their satisfaction. Because they are of a social nature, they are of a relative nature.[1]

Marx's qualification here of his more frequent belief that degradation produces revolution is expressed as the main thesis by de Tocqueville in

[1] The *Communist Manifesto* of 1848 evidently antedates the opposing idea by about a year. See Wilson (1940, p. 157); Feuer (1959, p. 1). The above quotation is from Marx and Engels (1955, i, 94).

his study of the French Revolution. After a long review of economic and social decline in the seventeenth century and dynamic growth in the eighteenth, de Tocqueville concludes:

> So it would appear that the French found their condition the more unsupportable in proportion to its improvement. . . . Revolutions are not always brought about by a gradual decline from bad to worse. Nations that have endured patiently and almost unconsciously the most overwhelming oppression often burst into rebellion against the yoke the moment it begins to grow lighter. The régime which is destroyed by a revolution is almost always an improvement on its immediate predecessor. . . . Evils which are patiently endured when they seem inevitable become intolerable when once the idea of escape from them is suggested.[2]

On the basis of de Tocqueville and Marx, we can choose one of these ideas or the other, which makes it hard to decide just when revolutions are more likely to occur—when there has been social and economic progress or when there has been regress. It appears that both ideas have explanatory and possibly predictive value, if they are juxtaposed and put in the proper time sequence.

Revolutions are most likely to occur when a prolonged period of objective economic and social development is followed by a short period of sharp reversal.[3] The all-important effect on the minds of people in a particular society is to produce, during the former period, an expectation of continued ability to satisfy needs—which continue to rise—and, during the latter, a mental state of anxiety and frustration when manifest reality breaks away from anticipated reality. The actual state of socio-economic development is less significant than the expectation that past progress, now blocked, can and must continue in the future.

Political stability and instability are ultimately dependent on a state of mind, a mood, in a society. Satisfied or apathetic people who are poor in goods, status, and power can remain politically quiet and their opposites can revolt, just as, correlatively and more probably, dissatisfied poor can revolt and satisfied rich oppose revolution. It is the dissatisfied state of mind rather than the tangible provision of 'adequate' or 'inadequate' supplies of food, equality, or liberty which produces the

---

[2] de Tocqueville (1856, p. 214). The Stuart Gilbert translation (1955, pp. 176–7), gives a somewhat less pungent version of the same comment. *L'Ancien régime* was first published in 1856.

[3] Revolutions are here defined as violent civil disturbances that cause the displacement of one ruling group by another that has a broader popular basis for support.

revolution. In actuality, there must be a joining of forces between dissatisfied, frustrated people who differ in their degree of objective, tangible welfare and status. Well-fed, well-educated, high-status individuals who rebel in the face of apathy among the objectively deprived can accomplish at most a *coup d'état*. The objectively deprived, when faced with solid opposition of people of wealth, status, and power, will be smashed in their rebellion as were peasants and Anabaptists by German noblemen in 1525 and East Germans by the Communist elite in 1953.

Before appraising this general notion in light of a series of revolutions a word is in order as to why revolutions ordinarily do not occur when a society is generally impoverished—when, as de Tocqueville put it, evils that seem inevitable are patiently endured. They are endured in the extreme case because the physical and mental energies of people are totally employed in the process of merely staying alive. The

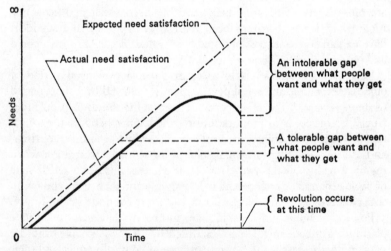

Figure 12.1 Need Satisfaction and Revolution

Minnesota starvation studies conducted during World War II[4] indicate clearly the constant preoccupation of very hungry individuals with fantasies and thoughts of food. In extremis, as the Minnesota research poignantly demonstrates, the individual withdraws into a life of his own, withdraws from society, withdraws from any significant kind of activity unrelated to staying alive. Reports of behaviour in Nazi con-

---

[4] The full report is Keys *et al.* (1950). See Brozek (1953), pp. 107–18 for a brief analysis.

centration camps indicate the same preoccupation (Cohen, 1963, pp. 123, 125, 131–40). In less extreme and barbarous circumstances, where minimal survival is possible but little more, the preoccupation of individuals with staying alive is only mitigated. Social action takes place for the most part on a local, face-to-face basis. In such circumstances the family is a—perhaps the major—solidary unit[5] and even the local community exists primarily to the extent families need to act together to secure their separate survival. Such was life on the American frontier in the sixteenth through nineteenth centuries. In very much attenuated form, but with a substantial degree of social isolation persisting, such evidently is rural life even today. This is clearly related to a relatively low level of political participation in elections (see Campbell, 1960, ch. 15). As Zawadzki and Lazarsfeld have indicated (1935, pp. 224–51), preoccupation with physical survival, even in industrial areas, is a force strongly militating against the establishment of the community-sense and consensus on joint political action which are necessary to induce a revolutionary state of mind. Far from making people into revolutionaries, enduring poverty makes for concern with one's solitary self or solitary family at best and resignation or mute despair at worst. When it is a choice between losing their chains or their lives, people will mostly choose to keep their chains, a fact which Marx seems to have overlooked.[6]

It is when the chains have been loosened somewhat, so that they can be cast off without a high probability of losing life, that people are put in a condition of proto-rebelliousness. I use the term proto-rebelliousness because the mood of discontent may be dissipated before a violent outbreak occurs. The causes for such dissipation may be natural or social (including economic and political). A bad crop year that threatens a return to chronic hunger may be succeeded by a year of natural abundance. Recovery from sharp economic dislocation may take the steam from the boiler of rebellion.[7] The slow, grudging grant of re-

---

[5] For community life in such poverty, in Mezzogiorno Italy, see Banfield (1958). The author emphasises that the nuclear family is a solidary, consensual, moral unit (see p. 85) but even within it, consensus appears to break down, in outbreaks of pure, individual amorality—notably between parents and children (see p. 117).

[6] A remarkable and awesome exception to this phenomenon occurred occasionally in some Nazi concentration camps, e.g. in a Buchenwald revolt against capricious rule by criminal prisoners. During this revolt, one hundred criminal prisoners were killed by political prisoners. See Cohen (1953, p. 200).

[7] See Rostow (1941, pp. 206–21) for the relation between economic fluctuation and the activities of the Chartists in the 1830s and 1840s.

forms, which has been the political history of England since at least the Industrial Revolution, may effectively and continuously prevent the degree of frustration that produces revolt.

A revolutionary state of mind requires the continued, even habitual but dynamic expectation of greater opportunity to satisfy basic needs, which may range from merely physical (food, clothing, shelter, health, and safety from bodily harm) to social (the affectional ties of family and friends) to the need for equal dignity and justice. But the necessary additional ingredient is a persistent, unrelenting threat to the satisfaction of these needs: not a threat which actually returns people to a state of sheer survival but which puts them in the mental state where they believe they will not be able to satisfy one or more basic needs. Although physical deprivation in some degree may be threatened on the eve of all revolutions, it need not be the prime factor, as it surely was not in the American Revolution of 1775. The crucial factor is the vague or specific fear that ground gained over a long period of time will be quickly lost. This fear does not generate if there is continued opportunity to satisfy continually emerging needs; it generates when the existing government suppresses or is blamed for suppressing such opportunity.

Three rebellions or revolutions are given considerable attention in the sections that follow: Dorr's Rebellion of 1842, the Russian Revolution of 1917, and the Egyptian Revolution of 1952. Brief mention is then made of several other major civil disturbances, all of which appear to fit the J-curve pattern (Fig. 12.1).[8] After considering these specific disturbances, some general theoretical and research problems are discussed.

No claim is made that all rebellions follow the pattern, but just that the ones here presented do. All of these are 'progressive' revolutions on behalf of greater equality and liberty. The question is open whether the pattern occurs in such markedly retrogressive revolutions as Nazism in Germany or the 1861 Southern rebellion in the United States. It will surely be necessary to examine other progressive revolutions before one can judge how universal the J-curve is. And it will be necessary, in the interests of scientific validation, to examine cases of serious civil disturbance that fell short of producing profound revolution—such as the Sepoy Rebellion of 1857 in India, the Pullman Strike of 1894 in America, the Boxer Rebellion of 1900 in China, and the Great Depression of the 1920s and 1930s as it was experienced in

---

[8] This curve is of course not to be confused with its prior and altogether different use by Floyd Allport in his study of social conformity. See Allport (1947, pp. 55–67).

Austria, France, Great Britain, and the United States. The explanation for such still-born rebellions—for revolutions that might have occurred —is inevitably more complicated than for those that come to term in the 'normal' course of political gestation.

[Eds.: Davies' discussion of Dorr's Rebellion in Rhode Island has been omitted.]

TABLE 12.1 *Population of European Russia (1480–1895)*

	Population in Millions	Increase in Millions	Average Annual Rate of Increase*
1480	2·1	—	—
1580	4·3	2·2	1·05%
1680	12·6	8·3	1·93%
1780	26·8	14·2	1·13%
1880	84·5	57·7	2·15%
1895	110·0	25·5	2·02%

* Computed as follows: dividing the increase by the number of years and then dividing this hypothetical annual increase by the population at the end of the preceding 100-year period.
Source for gross population data: *Entsiklopedicheskii Slovar*, St. Petersburg, 1897, vol. 40, p. 631. Russia's population was about 97% rural in 1784, 91% in 1878, and 87% in 1897. See Masaryk (1919, p. 162n.)

THE RUSSIAN REVOLUTION OF 1917

In Russia's tangled history it is hard to decide when began the final upsurge of expectations that, when frustrated, produced the cataclysmic events of 1917. One can truly say that the real beginning was the slow modernisation process begun by Peter the Great over two hundred years before the revolution. And surely the rationalist currents from France that slowly penetrated Russian intellectual life during the reign of Catherine the Great a hundred years before the revolution were necessary, lineal antecedents of the 1917 revolution.

Without denying that there was an accumulation of forces over at least a 200-year period,[9] we may nonetheless date the final upsurge as beginning with the 1861 emancipation of serfs and reaching a crest in the 1905 revolution.

The chronic and growing unrest of serfs before their emancipation in 1861 is an ironic commentary on the Marxian notion that human beings are what social institutions make them. Although serfdom had been shaping their personality since 1647, peasants became

[9] There is an excellent summary in Brutzkus (1953, pp. 517–40).

increasingly restive in the second quarter of the nineteenth century.[10]
The continued discontent of peasants after emancipation is an equally
ironic commentary on the belief that relieving one profound frustration
produces enduring contentment. Peasants rather quickly got over their
joy at being untied from the soil after two hundred years. Instead of
declining, rural violence increased.[11] Having gained freedom but not
much free land, peasants now had to rent or buy land to survive:
virtual personal slavery was exchanged for financial servitude. Land
pressure grew, reflected in a doubling of land prices between 1868 and
1897.

It is hard thus to tell whether the economic plight of peasants was
much lessened after emancipation. A 1903 government study indicated that even with a normal harvest, average food intake per peasant
was 30 per cent below the minimum for health. The only sure contrary item of evidence is that the peasant population grew, indicating
at least increased ability of the land to support life, as Table 12.1 shows.

The land-population pressure pushed people into towns and cities,
where the rapid growth of industry truly afforded the chance for
economic betterment. One estimate of net annual income for a peasant
family of five in the rich blackearth area in the late nineteenth century
was 82 roubles. In contrast, a 'good' wage for a male factory worker
was about 168 roubles per year. It was this difference in the degree of
poverty that produced almost a doubling of the urban population
between 1878 and 1897. The number of industrial workers increased
almost as rapidly. The city and the factory gave new hope. Strikes in
the 1880s were met with brutal suppression but also with the beginning of factory legislation, including the requirement that wages be
paid regularly and the abolition of child labour. The burgeoning proletariat remained comparatively contented until the eve of the 1905
revolution.[12]

---

[10] Jacqueries rose from an average of 8 per year in 1826–30 to 34 per year in
1845–9. Masaryk (1919, vol. 1, p. 130). This long, careful, and rather
neglected analysis was first published in German in 1913 under the title *Zur
Russischen Geschichts-und Religionsphilosophic.*

[11] Jacqueries averaged 350 per year for the first three years after emancipation. Masaryk (1919, pp. 140–1).

[12] The proportion of workers who struck from 1895 through 1902 varied
between 1·7 per cent and 4·0 per cent per year. In 1903 the proportion rose
to 5·1 per cent but dropped a year later to 1·5 per cent. In 1905 the proportion
rose to 163·8 per cent, indicating that the total working force struck, on the
average, closer to twice than to once during that portentous year. In 1906
the proportion dropped to 65·8 per cent; in 1907 to 41·9 per cent; and by
1909 was down to a 'normal' 3·5 per cent. Masaryk (1919, p. 175n).

There is additional, non-economic evidence to support the view that 1861 to 1905 was the period of rising expectations that preceded the 1917 revolution. The administration of justice before the emancipation had largely been carried out by noblemen and landowners who embodied the law for their peasants. In 1864 justice was in principle no longer delegated to such private individuals. Trials became public, the jury system was introduced, and judges got tenure. Corporal punishment was alleviated by the elimination of running the gauntlet, lashing, and branding; caning persisted until 1904. Public joy at these reforms was widespread. For the intelligentsia, there was increased opportunity to think and write and to criticize established institutions, even sacrosanct absolutism itself.

But Tsarist autocracy had not quite abandoned the scene. Having inclined but not bowed, in granting the inevitable emancipation as an act not of justice but grace, it sought to maintain its absolutist principle by conceding reform without accepting anything like democratic authority. Radical political and economic criticism surged higher. Some strong efforts to raise the somewhat lowered floodgates began as early as 1866, after an unsuccessful attempt was made on the life of Alexander II, in whose name serfs had just gained emancipation. When the attempt succeeded fifteen years later, there was increasing state action under Alexander III to limit constantly rising expectations. By suppression and concession, the last Alexander succeeded in dying naturally in 1894.

When it became apparent that Nicholas II shared his father's ideas but not his forcefulness, opposition of the intelligentsia to absolutism joined with the demands of peasants and workers, who remained loyal to the Tsar but demanded economic reforms. Starting in 1904, there developed a 'League of Deliverance' that co-ordinated efforts of at least seventeen other revolutionary, proletarian, or nationalist groups within the empire. Consensus on the need for drastic reform, both political and economic, established a many-ringed circus of groups sharing the same tent. These groups were geographically distributed from Finland to Armenia and ideologically from liberal constitutionalists to revolutionaries made prudent by the contrast between their own small forces and the power of Tsardom.

Events of 1904–5 mark the general downward turning point of expectations, which people increasingly saw as frustrated by the continuation of Tsardom. Two major and related occurrences made 1905 the point of no return. The first took place on the Bloody Sunday of 22 January 1905, when peaceful proletarian petitioners marched on the St Petersburg palace and were killed by the hundreds. The myth that the Tsar was the gracious protector of his subjects, however surrounded he might be by malicious advisers, was quite shattered. The reaction was immediate, bitter, and prolonged and was not at all confined to the working class. Employers, merchants, and white-collar officials joined in the burgeoning of strikes which brought the economy to a virtual standstill in October. Some employers even continued to pay wages to strikers. University students and faculties joined the revolution. After the great October strike, the peasants ominously sided with the workers and engaged in riots and assaults on landowners. Until peasants became involved, even some landowners had sided with the revolution.

The other major occurrence was the disastrous defeat of the Russian army and navy in the 1904–5 war with Japan. Fundamentally an imperialist venture aspiring to hegemony over the people of Asia, the war was not regarded as a people's but as a Tsar's war, to save and spread absolutism. The military defeat itself probably had less portent than the return of shattered soldiers from a fight that was not for them. Hundreds of thousands, wounded or not, returned from the war as a visible, vocal, and ugly reminder to the entire populace of the weakness and selfishness of Tsarist absolutism.

The years from 1905 to 1917 formed an almost relentless procession of increasing misery and despair. Promising at last a constitutional government, the Tsar, in October, 1905, issued from on high a proclamation renouncing absolutism, granting law-making power to a duma, and guaranteeing freedom of speech, assembly, and association. The first two dumas, of 1906 and 1907, were dissolved for recalcitrance. The third was made pliant by reduced representation of workers and peasants and by the prosecution and conviction of protestants in the first two. The brief period of a free press was succeeded in 1907 by a reinstatement of censorship and confiscation of prohibited publications. Trial of offenders against the Tsar was now conducted by courts martial. Whereas there had been only 26 executions of the death sentence, in the 13 years of Alexander II's firm rule (1881–94), there were 4,449 in the years 1905–10, in six years of Nicholas II's soft regimen.[13]

But this 'white terror', which caused despair among the workers and intelligentsia in the cities, was not the only face of misery. For the peasants, there was a bad harvest in 1906 followed by continued crop failures in several areas in 1907. To forestall action by the dumas, Stolypin decreed a series of agrarian reforms designed to break up the

[13] Masaryk (1919, p. 189n).

power of the rural communes by individualising land ownership. Between these acts of God and government, peasants were so preoccupied with hunger or self-aggrandisement as to be dulled in their sensitivity to the revolutionary appeals of radical organisers.

After more than five years of degrading terror and misery, in 1910 the country appeared to have reached a condition of exhaustion. Political strikes had fallen off to a new low. As the economy recovered, the insouciance of hopelessness set in. Amongst the intelligentsia the mood was hedonism, or despair that often ended in suicide. Industrialists aligned themselves with the government. Workers worked. But an upturn of expectations, inadequately quashed by the police, was evidenced by a recrudescence of political strikes which, in the first half of 1914—on the eve of war—approached the peak of 1905. They sharply diminished during 1915 but grew again in 1916 and became a general strike in February 1917.[14]

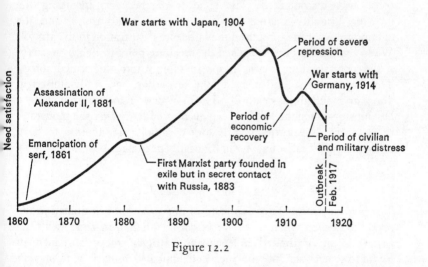

Figure 12.2

Fig. 12.2 indicates the lesser waves in the tidal wave whose first trough is at the end of serfdom in 1861 and whose second is at the end of Tsardom in 1917. This fifty-six-year period appears to constitute a

[14] In his *History of the Russian Revolution*, Leon Trotsky presents data on political strikes from 1903 to 1917. In his *Spirit of Russia*, Masaryk presents comparable data from 1905 through 1912. The figures are not identical but the reported yearly trends are consistent. Masaryk's figures are somewhat lower, except for 1912. Cf. Trotsky (1959, p. 32) and Masaryk (1919, p. 197n).

single long phase in which popular gratification at the termination of one institution (serfdom) rather quickly was replaced with rising expectations which resulted from intensified industrialisation and which were incompatible with the continuation of the inequitable and capricious power structure of Tsarist society. The small trough of frustration during the regression that followed the assassination of Alexander II seems to have only briefly interrupted the rise in popular demand for more goods and more power. The trough in 1904 indicates the consequences of war with Japan. The 1905–6 trough reflects the repression of 22 January and after, and is followed by economic recovery. The final downturn, after the first year of war, was a consequence of the dislocations of the German attack on all kinds of concerted activities other than production for the prosecution of the war. Patriotism and governmental repression for a time smothered discontent. The inflation that developed in 1916 when goods, including food, became severely scarce began to make workers self-consciously discontented. The conduct of the war, including the growing brutality against reluctant, ill-provisioned troops, and the enormous loss of life, produced the same bitter frustration in the army.[15] When civilian discontent reached the breaking point in February 1917, it did not take long for it to spread rapidly into the armed forces. Thus began the second phase of the revolution that really started in 1905 and ended in death to the Tsar and Tsardom—but not to absolutism—when the Bolsheviks gained ascendancy over the moderates in October. A centuries-long history of absolutism appears to have made this post-Tsarist phase of it tragically inevitable.

THE EGYPTIAN REVOLUTION OF 1952

The final slow upsurge of expectations in Egypt that culminated in the revolution began when that society became a nation in 1922, with the British grant of limited independence. British troops remained in Egypt to protect not only the Suez Canal but also, ostensibly, to prevent foreign aggression. The presence of foreign troops served only to heighten nationalist expectations, which were excited by the Wafd, the political organisation that formed public opinion on national rather than religious grounds and helped establish a fairly unified community —in striking contrast to late-nineteenth-century Russia.

But nationalist aspirations were not the only rising expectations in Egypt of the 1920s and 1930s. World War I had spurred industrialisa-

[15] See Trotsky (1959, pp. 18–21) for a vivid picture of rising discontent in the army.

tion, which opened opportunities for peasants to improve, somewhat, their way of life by working for wages in the cities and also opened great opportunities for entrepreneurs to get rich. The moderately wealthy got immoderately so in commodity market speculation, finance, and manufacture, and the uprooted peasants who were now employed, or at any rate living, in cities were relieved of at least the notion that poverty and boredom must be the will of Allah. But the incongruity of a money-based modern semi-feudality that was like a chariot with a gasoline engine evidently escaped the attention of ordinary people. The generation of the 1930s could see more rapid progress, even for themselves, than their parents had even envisioned. If conditions remained poor, they could always be blamed on the British, whose economic and military power remained visible and strong.

Economic progress continued, though unevenly, during World War II. Conventional exports, mostly cotton, actually declined, not even reaching depression levels until 1945, but direct employment by Allied military forces reached a peak of over 200,000 during the most intense part of the African war. Exports after the war rose sharply until 1948, dipped, and then rose sharply to a peak in 1951 as a consequence of the Korean war. But in 1945 over 250,000 wage earners[16]—probably over a third of the working force—became jobless. The cost of living by 1945 had risen to three times the index of 1937 (see *International Financial Statistics*, 1950–3). Manual labourers were hit by unemployment; white-collar workers and professionals probably more by inflation than unemployment. Meanwhile the number of millionaires in pounds sterling had increased eight times during the war (La Couture, 1958, p. 99).

Frustrations, exacerbated during the war by Germany and thereafter by Soviet propaganda, were at first deflected against the British[17] but gradually shifted closer to home. Egyptian agitators began quoting the Koran in favour of a just, equalitarian society and against great differences in individual wealth. There was an ominous series of strikes, mostly in the textile mills, from 1946–8.

At least two factors stand out in the postponement of revolution.

[16] Issawi (1954, p. 262). J. & S. Lacouture (1958, p. 100), give a figure of over 300,000. Bullard (1958, p. 221) estimates total employment in industry, transport, and commerce in 1957 to have been about 750,000.

[17] England threatened to depose Farouk in February 1942, by force if necessary, if Egypt did not support the Allies. Capitulation by the government and the Wafd caused widespread popular disaffection. When Egypt finally declared war on the Axis in 1945, the prime minister was assassinated. See J. & S. Lacouture (1958, pp. 97–8) and Issawi (1954, p. 268).

The first was the insatiable post-war world demand for cotton and textiles and the second was the surge of solidarity with king and country that followed the 1948 invasion of the new state of Israel. Israel now supplemented England as an object of deflected frustration. The disastrous defeat a year later, by a new nation with but a fifteenth of Egypt's population, was the beginning of the end. This little war had struck the peasant at his hearth, when a shortage of wheat and of oil for stoves provided a daily reminder of a weak and corrupt government. The defeat frustrated popular hopes for national glory and—with even more portent—humiliated the army and solidified it against the bureaucracy and the palace which had profiteered at the expense of national honour. In 1950 began for the first time a direct and open propaganda attack against the king himself. A series of peasant uprisings, even on the lands of the king, took place in 1951 along with

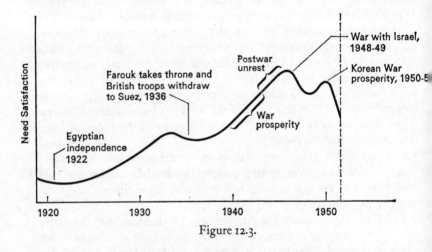

Figure 12.3.

some 49 strikes in the cities. The skyrocketing demand for cotton after the start of the Korean war in June, 1950 was followed by a collapse in June, 1952. The uncontrollable or uncontrolled riots in Cairo, on 26 January 1952, marked the fiery start of the revolution. The officers' coup in the early morning of 23 July only made it official.

OTHER CIVIL DISTURBANCES

The J-curve of rising expectations followed by their effective frustration is applicable to other revolutions and rebellions than just the two already considered. Leisler's Rebellion in the royal colony of New York in 1689 was a brief dress-rehearsal for the American Revolution eighty-six years later. In an effort to make the colony serve the crown better, duties had been raised and were being vigorously collected. The tanning of hides in the colony was forbidden, as was the distillation of liquor. An embargo was placed on unmilled grain, which hurt the farmers. After a long period of economic growth and substantial political autonomy, these new and burdensome regulations produced a popular rebellion that for a year displaced British sovereignty. (See Reich, 1953.)

The American Revolution itself fits the J-curve and deserves more than the brief mention here given. Again prolonged economic growth and political autonomy produced continually rising expectations. They became acutely frustrated when, following the French and Indian War (which had cost England so much and the colonies so little), England began a series of largely economic regulations having the same purpose as those directed against New York in the preceding century. From the 1763 Proclamation (closing to settlement land west of the Appalachians) to the Coercive Acts of April, 1774 (which among other things, in response to the December, 1773 Boston Tea Party, closed tight the port of Boston), Americans were beset with unaccustomed manifestations of British power and began to resist forcibly in 1775, on the Lexington–Concord road. A significant decline in trade with England in 1772 may have hastened the maturation of colonial rebelliousness.

The curve also fits the French Revolution, which again merits more mention than space here permits. Growing rural prosperity, marked by steadily rising land values in the eighteenth century, had progressed to the point where a third of French land was owned by peasant-proprietors. There were the beginnings of large-scale manufacture in the factory system. Constant pressure by the bourgeoisie against the state for returns was met with considerable hospitality by a government already shifting from its old landed-aristocratic and clerical base to the growing middle class. Counter to these trends, which would *per se* avoid revolution, was the feudal reaction of the mid-eighteenth century, in which the dying nobility sought in numerous nagging ways to retain and reactivate its perquisites against a resentful peasantry and importunate bourgeoisie.

But expectations apparently continued rising until the growing opportunities and prosperity rather abruptly halted, about 1787. The fiscal crisis of the government is well known, much of it a consequence of a 1·5 billion livre deficit following intervention against Britain in the American war of independence. The threat to tax the nobility severely—after its virtual tax immunity—and the bourgeoisie more severely may indeed be said to have precipitated the revolution. But less well-known is the fact that 1787 was a bad harvest year and 1788 even worse; that by July, 1789 bread prices were higher than they had been in over seventy years; that an ill-timed trade treaty with England depressed the prices of French textiles; that a concurrent bumper grape crop depressed wine prices—all with the result of making desperate the plight of the large segment of the population now dependent on other producers for food. They had little money to buy even less bread. Nobles and bourgeoisie were alienated from the government by the threat of taxation; workers and some peasants by the threat of starvation. A long period of halting but real progress for virtually all segments of the population was now abruptly ended in consequence of the government's efforts to meet its deficit and of economic crisis resulting from poor crops and poor tariff policy (see Lefebvre, 1947, pp. 101–9, 145–8, 196; and Le Bon, 1913, p. 143).

The draft riots that turned the city of New York upside down for five days in July 1863 also follow the J-curve. This severe local disturbance began when conscription threatened the lives and fortunes of working men whose enjoyment of wartime prosperity was now frustrated not only by military service (which could be avoided by paying $300 or furnishing a substitute—neither means being available to poor people) but also by inflation.

Even the riots in Nyasaland, in February and March 1959, appear to follow the pattern of a period of frustration after expectations and satisfactions have risen. Nyasaland workers who had enjoyed the high wages they were paid during the construction of the Kariba dam in Rhodesia returned to their homes and to unemployment, or to jobs paying $5 per month at a time when $15 was considered a bare minimum wage.

One negative case—of a revolution that did not occur—is the depression of the 1930s in the United States. It was severe enough, at least on economic grounds, to have produced a revolution. Total national private production income in 1932 reverted to what it had been in 1916. Farm income in the same year was as low as in 1900; manufacturing as low as in 1913. Construction had not been as low since 1908. Mining and quarrying was back at the 1909 level. For much of the population, two decades of economic progress had been wiped out. There were more than sporadic demonstrations of unemployed, hunger marchers, and veterans. In New York City, at least twenty-nine people died of starvation. Poor people could vividly contrast their own past condition with the present—and their own present condition with that of those who were not seriously suffering.

There were clearly audible rumbles of revolt. Why, then, no revolution?

Several forces worked strongly against it. Among the most depressed, the mood was one of apathy and despair, like that observed in Austria by Zawadzki and Lazarsfeld. It was not until the 1936 election that there was an increased turnout in the national election. The great majority of the public shared a set of values which since 1776 had been official dogma—not the dissident programme of an alienated intelligentsia. People by and large were in agreement, whether or not they had succeeded economically, in a belief in individual hard work, self-reliance, and the promise of success. (Among workers, this non-class orientation had greatly impeded the establishment of trade unions, for example.) Those least hit by the depression—the upper middle-class businessmen, clergymen, lawyers, and intellectuals—remained rather solidly committed not only to equalitarian values and to the established economic system but also to constitutional processes. There was no such widespread or profound alienation as that which had cracked the loyalty of the nobility, clergy, bourgeoisie, armed forces, and intelligentsia in Russia. And the national political leadership that emerged had constitutionalism almost bred in its bones. The major threat to constitutionalism came in Louisiana; this leadership was unable to capture a national party organisation, in part because Huey Long's arbitrariness and demagogy were mistrusted.

The major reason that revolution did not nonetheless develop probably remains the vigour with which the national government attacked the depression in 1933, when it became no longer possible to blame the government. The ambivalent popular hostility to the business community was contained by both the action of government against the depression and the government's practice of publicly and successfully eliciting the co-operation of businessmen during the crucial months of 1933. A failure then of co-operation could have intensified rather than lessened popular hostility to business. There was no longer an economic or a political class that could be the object of widespread intense hatred because of its indifference or hostility to the downtrodden. Had Roosevelt adopted a demagogic stance in the 1932 campaign and gained the loyalty to himself personally of the Army and the FBI, there might have been a Nazi-type 'revolution', with a potpourri of equalitarian reform, nationalism, imperialism, and domestic scapegoats. Because of a conservatism in America stemming from strong and long attachment to a value system shared by all classes, an anti-capitalist, leftist revolution in the 1930s is very difficult to imagine.

SOME CONCLUSIONS

The notion that revolutions need both a period of rising expectations and a succeeding period in which they are frustrated qualifies substantially the main Marxian notion that revolutions occur after progressive degradation and the de Tocqueville notion that they occur when conditions are improving. By putting de Tocqueville before Marx but without abandoning either theory, we are better able to plot the antecedents of at least the disturbances here described.

Half of the general, if not common, sense of this revised notion lies in the utter improbability of a revolution occurring in a society where there is the continued, unimpeded opportunity to satisfy new needs, new hopes, new expectations. Would the Russian Revolution have taken place if the Tsarist autocracy had, quite out of character, truly granted the popular demands for constitutional democracy in 1905? Would the Cairo riots of January, 1952 and the subsequent coup actually have occurred if Britain had departed from Egypt and if the Egyptian monarchy had established an equitable tax system and in other ways alleviated the poverty of urban masses and the shame of the military?

The other half of the sense of the notion has to do with the improbability of revolution taking place where there has been no hope, no period in which expectations have risen. Such a stability of expectations presupposes a static state of human aspirations that sometimes exists but is rare. Stability of expectations is not a stable social condition. Such was the case of American Indians (at least from our perspective) and perhaps Africans before white men with Bibles, guns, and other goods interrupted the stability of African society. Egypt was in such a condition, *vis-à-vis* modern aspirations, before Europe became interested in building a canal. Such stasis was the case in Nazi concentration camps, where conformism reached the point of inmates co-operating with guards even when the inmates were told to lie down so that they could be shot (Kogon, 1950, pp. 284–6). But in the latter case there was a society with externally induced complete despair, and even in these camps there were occasional rebellions of sheer desperation. It is of course true that in a society less regimented than concentration camps, the rise of expectations can be frustrated successfully, thereby defeating rebellion just as the satisfaction of expectations does. This, however, requires the uninhibited exercise of brute force as it was used in suppressing the Hungarian rebellion of 1956. Failing the continued ability and persistent will of a ruling power to use such force, there appears to be no sure way to avoid revolution short of an effective,

affirmative, and continuous response to the almost continuously emerging needs of the governed.

To be predictive, my notion requires the assessment of the state of
mind—or more precisely, the mood—of a people. This is always
difficult, even by techniques of systematic public opinion analysis.
Respondents interviewed in a country with a repressive government
are not likely to be responsive. But there has been considerable progress
in gathering first-hand data about the state of mind of peoples in
politically unstable circumstances. One instance of this involved interviewing in West Berlin, during and after the 1948 blockade, as reported by Buchanan and Cantril. They were able to ascertain, however
crudely, the sense of security that people in Berlin felt. There was a
significant increase in security after the blockade.[18]

Another instance comes out of the Middle Eastern study conducted
by the Columbia University Bureau of Applied Social Research and
reported by Lerner (1958). By directly asking respondents whether
they were happy or unhappy with the way things had turned out in
their life, the interviewers turned up data indicating marked differences
in the frequency of a sense of unhappiness between countries and
between 'traditional', 'transitional', and 'modern' individuals in
these countries (pp. 101–3. See also Kilpatrick and Cantril, 1910, pp.
158–73). There is no technical reason why such comparisons could
not be made chronologically as well as they have been geographically.

Other than interview data are available with which we can, from
past experience, make reasonable inferences about the mood of a
people. It was surely the sense for the relevance of such data that
led Thomas Masaryk before World War I to gather facts about
peasant uprisings and industrial strikes and about the writings and
actions of the intelligentsia in nineteenth-century Russia. In the
present report, I have used not only such data—in the collection of
which other social scientists have been less assiduous than Masaryk—
but also such indexes as comparative size of vote as between Rhode
Island and the United States, employment, exports, and cost of living.
Some such indexes, like strikes and cost of living, may be rather closely
related to the mood of a people; others, like value of exports, are much
cruder indications. Lest we shy away from the gathering of crude data,
we should bear in mind that Durkheim developed his remarkable
insights into modern society in large part by his analysis of suicide rates.
He was unable to rely on the interviewing technique. We need not

---

[18] Buchanan (1953, pp. 577–83, at p. 578). The full study is Buchanan and
Cantril (1953, esp. pp. 85–90).

always ask people whether they are grievously frustrated by their government; their actions can tell us as well and sometimes better.

In his *Anatomy of Revolution*, Crane Brinton describes 'some tentative uniformities' that he discovered in the Puritan, American, French, and Russian revolutions. The uniformities were: an economically advancing society, class antagonism, desertion of intellectuals, inefficient government, a ruling class that has lost self-confidence, financial failure of government, and the inept use of force against rebels. All but the last two of these are long-range phenomena that lead themselves to studies over extended time periods. The first two lend themselves to statistical analysis. If they serve the purpose, techniques of content analysis could be used to ascertain trends in alienation of intellectuals. Less rigorous methods would perhaps serve better to ascertain the effectiveness of government and the self-confidence of rulers. Because tensions and frustrations are present at all times in every society, what is most seriously needed are data that cover an extended time period in a particular society, so that one can say there is evidence that tension is greater or less than it was N years or months previously.

We need also to know how long is a long cycle of rising expectations and how long is a brief cycle of frustration. We noted a brief period of frustration in Russia after the 1881 assassination of Alexander II and a longer period after the 1904 beginning of the Russo-Japanese War. Why did not the revolution occur at either of these times rather than in 1917? Had expectations before these two times not risen high enough? Had the subsequent decline not been sufficiently sharp and deep? Measuring techniques have not yet been devised to answer these questions. But their unavailability now does not forecast their eternal inaccessibility. Physicists devised useful temperature scales long before they came as close to absolute zero as they have recently in laboratory conditions. The far more complex problems of scaling in social science inescapably are harder to solve.

We therefore are still not at the point of being able to predict revolution, but the closer we can get to data indicating by inference the prevailing mood in a society, the closer we will be to understanding the change from gratification to frustration in people's minds. That is the part of the anatomy, we are forever being told with truth and futility, in which wars and revolutions always start. We should eventually be able to escape the embarrassment that may have come to Lenin six weeks after he made the statement in Switzerland, in January, 1917, that he doubted whether 'we, the old [will] live to see the decisive battles of the coming revolution' (Quoted in Carr, 1950, p. 69).

REFERENCES

ALLPORT, F. H. (1947) 'The J-Curve Hypothesis of Conforming Behaviour' in
T. H. Newcomb and E. L. Hartley, eds., *Reading in Social Psychology*,
Holt, first published in *Journal of Social Psychology*, 5, May, 1934.
BANFIELD, E. C. (1958) *The Moral Basis of a Backward Society*, Free Press.
BROZEK, J. (1953) 'Semi-starvation and Nutritional Rehabilitation', *Journal
of Clinical Nutrition*, 1, January.
BRUTZKUS, B. (1953) 'The Historical Peculiarities of the Social and Economic
Development of Russia' in R. Bendix and S. M. Lipset, eds., *Class, Status
and Power*, Free Press.
BUCHANAN, W. (1953) 'Mass Communication in Reverse', *International Social
Science Bulletin*, 5.
BUCHANAN, W. and CANTRIL, H. (1953) *How Nations See Each Other*, Univer-
sity of Illinois Press.
BULLARD, R., ed. (1958) *The Middle East: A Political and Economic Survey*,
Oxford University Press.
CAMPBELL, A. *et al.* (1960) *The American Voter*, John Wiley.
CARR, E. H. (1950) *A History of Soviet Russia, Vol. 1, The Bolshevik Revolu-
tion: 1917–1923*, Macmillan.
COHEN, E. A. (1953) *Human Behaviour in the Concentration Camp*, Norton.
FEUER, L. S. (1959) *Karl Marx and Friedrich Engels: Basic Writings on
Politics and Philosophy*, Doubleday.
International Financial Statistics: monthly report of the International
Monetary Fund, Washington.
ISSAWI, C. (1954) *Egypt at Mid-Century*, Oxford University Press.
KEYS, A. *et al.* (1950) *The Biology of Human Starvation*, University of
Minnesota.
KILPATRICK, F. P. and CANTRILL, H. (1960) 'Self-Anchoring Scaling, a Measure
of Individual's Unique Reality Words', *Journal of Individual Psychology*,
16.
KOGON, E. (1950) *The Theory and Practice of Hell*, Farrar, Strauss.
LACOUTURE, J. and S. (1958) *Egypt in Transition*, Criterion Books.
LEFEBVRE, G. (1947) *The Coming of the French Revolution*, Princeton Univer-
sity Press.
LERNER, D. (1958) *The Passing of Traditional Society*, Free Press.
MASARYK, T. G. (1919) *The Spirit of Russia*, Allen and Unwin.
MARX, K. and ENGELS, F. (1955) *Selected Works in Two Volumes*, Foreign
Languages Publishing House, Moscow.
REICH, J. R. (1953) *Leisler's Rebellion*, University of Chicago Press.
ROSTOW, W. W. (1941) 'Business Cycles, Harvests and Politics: 1790–1850',
Journal of Economic History, 1, November.
TOCQUEVILLE, A. DE (1856) *The Old Regime and the French Revolution*, trans.
John Bonner, Harper.
TOCQUEVILL, A. DE (1955) *The Old Regime and the French Revolution*, trans.
Stuart Gilbert, Doubleday.
TROTSKY, L. (1959) *History of the Russian Revolution*, Doubleday.
WILSON, E. (1940) *To the Finland Station*, Doubleday.
ZAWADZKI, B. and LAZARSFELD, P. F. (1935) 'The Psychological Consequences
of Unemployment', *Journal of Social Psychology*, 6, May.

13

Theda Skocpol Why have the outcomes
of the Russian and
Chinese revolutions been
different?

From 'Old regime legacies and communist revolutions in Russia and China', *Social Forces,* December 1976, pp. 284-315.

From a broad comparative and historical perspective the Russian and Chinese revolutionary transformations—two of the most momentous happenings of the tumultuous twentieth century—seem very similar indeed (Moore, 1966; Skocpol, 1976; Wolf, 1969). Both revolutions broke out in huge agrarian empires that had become subject to intense pressures from more industrialised nations abroad. Massive peasant rebellions contributed indispensably to each revolutionary drama. Aristocratic, semi-bureaucratic, and autocratic old regimes gave way to centralised, bureaucratic and mass-mobilising collectivist regimes, as the revolutionary conflicts led to the expropriation of the traditional state officials and landed upper classes, as well as foreign and domestic capitalists, and brought to the fore in their stead the Bolshevik and Chinese Communist parties. Certainly these similarities in the causes and outcomes of their revolutions are sufficient to mark the national trajectories of 'modernising' Russia and China as examples of one distinctive developmental pattern in contrast to the diverse alternative paths that have been followed by other countries—routes such as liberal or authoritarian capitalist industrialisation or neo-colonial dependent development. Nevertheless, as the Chinese Revolution has progressed into its third decade since the consolidation of national political power by the Communists, important contrasts to the Soviet outcomes have become strikingly apparent—differences both of official ideologies and policies and of actual patterns of socio-economic and political organisation. This essay will attempt to show how differences in the Chinese versus Soviet revolutionary outcomes can be attributed in part to effects of differences in the pre-revolutionary socio-political and economic structures of Romanov Russia and late Imperial China. But before I proceed with this explanatory argument, let me survey some of the important differences between Soviet Russia and Communist China.

DIFFERENCES BETWEEN SOVIET AND CHINESE COMMUNIST SOCIETIES

Even though both the Russian and the Chinese Communists are dedicated to state-directed economic development as a means of advancement toward the goal of socialist society, significant differences show up clearly in their ideologies and programmes for economic growth. In Soviet Russia, from the inception of planned economic development in the 1920s, the greatest emphasis has always been placed on the rapid expansion of heavy industry. The tactics for accomplishing this have included the direct importation or imitation of the technologies, large-scale organisational forms, and methods of labour discipline employed by the currently most advanced Western capitalist enterprises (Gerschenkron, 1960). Soviet economic development has entailed rapid urbanisation, often outrunning the provision of consumer goods and public services, and the coercive exploitation or neglect of a stagnant collectivised agriculture and rural society (Nove, 1969). Industrialisation, moreover, was, at least until the 1960s, accompanied by the maintenance or widening of wage and salary, rank, and educational differentials among the strata of Soviet citizens (Black, 1960; Inkeles, 1968; Matthews, 1972). For in Soviet Russia, progress toward socialism has been equated with the steady expansion of a planned metropolitan-industrial economy with disciplined factory workers labouring under the guidance of professional administrators and Party co-ordinators. The role of peasants has been merely to provide a surplus of agricultural produce and manpower to fuel the expansion of the progressive socialist industrial sector.

For a few years after coming to national power in 1949, the Chinese Communists unabashedly imitated the Soviet strategy and tactics for socialist economic development, but between 1958 and 1970 there emerged the clear outlines of a distinctively Chinese strategy for economic development. In sharp contrast to any Soviet-style, one-sided emphasis on heavy industrial development, the Chinese are also channelling investment and leadership resources into the development of collectivised peasant farming and into the development of both agriculture- and consumer-oriented light industries (Perkins, 1975; Yeh, 1967). A concerted effort is being made to retard urbanisation (Perkins, 1975, pp. 136–7) and to hold steady or reduce income, rank, and social status differentials both between urban and rural workers, and between leaders and led (Riskin, 1974). There is official encouragement for the launching of small-scale industrial enterprises based on 'intermediate technologies' by local and provincial authorities and collectives in areas outside the present regions of greatest industrial advancement (Riskin, 1971; Sigurdson, 1973). Peasants and the rural economy in general are not dismissed as mere passive auxiliaries in the march toward socialism. Rather the realisation of that very goal is held to depend on the degree to which urban–rural differences are overridden, and the extent to which the peasants, as the majority of the people, become conscious makers of their own future (Gray, 1973; Gurley, 1971; Meisner, 1974).

These policy departures by the Chinese from Soviet strategies also imply the fostering of alternative organisational forms. To be sure, the socio-political institutions of Communist China resemble those of Soviet Russia in many ways, for in both countries centralised parties and state bureaucracies, backed by disciplined armies, set the framework of political, economic, and social life for all citizens (Barnett, 1967; Moore, 1950; Schapiro, 1967; Schurmann, 1968). Yet, whereas Soviet developmental policies naturally led to the hegemony of centralised planning bureaucracies empowered both to direct and to initiate all programmes considered nationally significant, Chinese developmental policies have encouraged the devolution of considerable powers to plan, and especially to initiate, economic and social programmes to provincial, prefectural, and local levels, leaving national authorities freer to concentrate on co-ordination and facilitation of the diversified and situationally adapted regional and local efforts (Bastid, 1973; Nove, 1969; Schurmann, 1967). Moreover, Soviet policies encouraged leadership in society to concentrate in the hands of cliques of managers of large enterprises, professional bureaucrats, and national and regional Party leaders, and favoured the institutionalisation of styles of leadership based on 'one-man' managerial authority and the manipulation of differentials in individual material rewards (Cliff, 1955; Granick, 1960; Schurmann, 1968, ch. 4). In contrast, Chinese Communist development policies seem to encourage a wider diffusion of leadership opportunities and capacities, and sanction a continuing role for the 'mass-line' style of leadership, which calls for basic-level Party cadres recurrently to organise and mobilise groups of rank-and-file peasants and workers on the basis of collective incentives (Gray, 1973; Lewis, 1963; Riskin, 1974; Schurmann, 1966; Selden, 1969).

Nowhere do these differences between Russia and China reveal themselves more clearly than in the establishment, forms, and functions of collectivised peasant agriculture within the two Communist systems. The original collectivisation of peasant holdings in Russia between 1929 and 1933 was aptly described by Stalin as a 'revolution from above' (Carr, 1971, p. 106). Party members and urban workers descended suddenly on bewildered peasant communities, forced them to surrender supplies for the cities and industry, and finally corralled them into production collectives that could be used by non-local Party authorities and government administrators to supervise and manage the future planting, reaping, and surrender of surpluses to the state (Bernstein, 1967; Lewin, 1966; Nove, 1969, chs 6–7; Volin, 1970, ch. 10). When 'socialist' agriculture, originated and managed in this fashion, proved inefficient and unproductive, the Soviet authorities allowed the impoverished peasants to devote 'extra' time and energy to the cultivation on private plots of food crops that could be sold for market prices above state procurement levels. Only the expansion of the individualist agricultural sector alongside the bureaucratic-collective one allowed Russian agriculture successfully to supply the burgeoning urban–industrial sector (Karcz, 1971, pp. 54–6; Nove, 1969, pp. 184–5, 238–44); but at the cost of draining rural socialist forms of any positive significance for the rural population.

In China, collective agriculture has developed very differently. Collectivisation originally occurred in the 1950s as a multi-stage movement based on the mobilisation within the localities of 'poor' and 'middle' peasants. Leadership was provided by Party cadres of peasant background and often native origin—people who frequently had already played leadership roles during the War with Japan or in the revolutionary struggles to expropriate the landlords (Bernstein, 1967). The Chinese Communists have not instituted or used collectivisation simply as a means of expropriating agricultural surpluses. Their efforts have also been directed at using group organisations and incentives, urban advice and expertise, and peasant mobilisation for agricultural work or local industrial projects to allow rural people to improve steadily their own livelihood even as they generate surplus resources, part of which they are encouraged to retain and reinvest locally in social services or production projects (Gray, 1969, 1973; Sigurdson, 1973). In contrast to what happened in the Soviet Union, collectivised agriculture in China is and promises to remain a vital institution for peasants and for Chinese society as a whole.

In sum, then, there are significant differences—of ideology, policy, and socio-economic and political organisation—between the Communist Chinese and Soviet Russian revolutionary outcomes—differences that are as much worth attempting to explain as are the common patterns of cause and outcome shared by the two revolutions.

How then may we explain the variations in the revolutionary outcomes? Naturally this question invites attention to antecedent differences in Russia and China. But which ones?

Already it is becoming quite commonplace for students of Russia and/or China to argue that the post-revolutionary divergences are rooted in the contrasting ways in which the two Communist parties came to national political power during the revolutionary struggles in 1917–21 in Russia and before 1949 in China. This explanatory approach links the Bolsheviks' ascendancy through an urban insurrection and conventional defensive warfare to their subsequent preference for an urban–industrial strategy of socialist development, and links the Chinese Communists' ascendancy through rural guerilla warfare to their ultimate commitment to a more peasant and rural-oriented strategy of socialist development. Such links and correspondences are of course very real and important, and constitute a valid proximate explanation of the divergent outcomes. The only difficulty is that the explanation does not go far enough. For one is left wondering *why* the Bolsheviks used one approach to gain national political power, while the Chinese Communists employed a very different one. Unless this question is answered sociologically, all that remains is the (frequently encountered) implication that the Bolsheviks were expedient people who 'chose' a quick and easy path to power, while the Chinese Communists made 'choices' with more democratic promise—or if one's silent preferences are different, that the Bolsheviks and later the Stalinists were hard-nosed and efficient, while the Maoists, at least since 1949, are impractical romantics!

But in practice, explanations that implicitly or explicitly stress elite choices as the root of the Chinese versus Russian contrasts do not work at all. For in each revolution there were revolutionary elites willing to try strategies akin to the ones that ultimately paid off in the *other* country. This is patently obvious for China. There the Chinese Communist party was established under direct Soviet tutelage in 1921, and set out deliberately to recapitulate the Bolshevik strategy of organising the industrial proletariat and seizing power away from moderate revolutionaries in an urban insurrection (Chesneaux, 1962; Kau, 1974). Moreover, once the Chinese Communists consolidated national power they stressed for almost a decade Soviet-style policies and practices, and recurrently since the late 1950s there have been leadership factions desirous of reverting to those models (Gray, 1973). In Russia, proto-Chinese alternatives appear less obviously on the historical record, but nevertheless they were there. Before 1917 the Socialist Revolutionary party advocated and organised for a peasant-based and peasant-oriented socialist revolution (Radkey, 1958). During 1918 the Left Socialist Revolutionaries, and some leftist Bolshevik leaders, advocated peasant-based guerilla warfare to preserve the revolution from invading Germans as well as native counterrevolutionaries (Cohen, 1971, ch. 3; Radkey, 1963, ch. 9). And during the 'Industrialisation Debate' of the 1920s, the Bukharinists advocated gradual rural-oriented economic development, with the peasants to be coaxed into socialism through rural co-operatives (Cohen, 1971; Erlich, 1960). All of these were, considered in the Russian context, alternatives which in certain respects resembled the Maoist strategies that later proved so successful in China.

If leadership choices are not enough to explain the divergent courses of the Russian and Chinese Revolutions, then a more basic place to look is at social structural legacies from the old regimes. Perhaps certain inheritances from the past helped to shape specific variations in the revolutionary outcomes, not simply by 'surviving', of course, but rather because they set different limits for successful revolutionary strategies. Initially they set limits for gaining state power within the context of popular and elite struggles against the institutions and classes of the old regimes, and then for using that state power, once consolidated, to promote 'socialist' economic development. Let me, in the remainder of this essay, develop this explanatory possibility, first by drawing some comparisons between the socio-political and economic structures of Late Imperial China versus pre-1917 Romanov Russia, and then by suggesting how the contrasting old-regime structural patterns directly and indirectly conditioned the possibilities for Communist political leaderships to consolidate and then use revolutionary state power.

Before I proceed, let the reader take careful note of the explanatory logic that I propose to employ. The focus will be on linking differences in old-regime structural patterns to differences in Communist revolutionary outcomes. In the process, the sheer fact of the occurrence of the revolutionary transformations themselves will be taken for granted, and no attempt will be made to explain why these Communist revolutions occurred in Russia and China, either as opposed to non-revolutions or to non-Communist revolutions. In fact, for the purposes at hand, the overall causes and actual occurrence of the revolutions not only can, but logically must be taken as given—for these constitute the very background against which it is possible to formulate the problem of explaining variations in outcomes. Moreover, it is important that the Chinese and Russian old regimes and revolutions were broadly similar in many ways, for comparative-historical analysis can fruitfully identify concomitant variations only against the background of similarities shared by the cases being examined. Finally, it should be noted that the approach I shall be using to relate prerevolutionary patterns to revolutionary outcomes is social-structural analysis—which is, of course, not the only possible explanatory approach. Cultural–determinist arguments (e.g., Eisenstadt and Azmon, 1975) might be developed as an alternative or a supplement. With these provisos in mind, let us proceed next to comparisons of the old-regime socio-political structures and economies of Russia and China.

CONTRASTS BETWEEN PRE-REVOLUTIONARY RUSSIA AND CHINA

Socio-political structures

Russia and China under the old regimes were both massive agrarian empires held together by partially bureaucratised administrative and military state organisations headed by autocratic hereditary monarchs. Nevertheless, the two agrarian autocracies differed significantly in the ways landlords related to the state organisations, to socio-political leadership functions generally, and in the ways localised groups of peasants related to the extra-locally powerful dominant elites and classes. I shall discuss each of these matters in turn, commencing with the structural position of the peasantry, which, after all, constituted the vast majority of the population and the chief source of politically exploitable economic and human resources in both Romanov Russia and Ch'ing China.

The position of the peasantry   In most of late traditional China, and in the most populous core agricultural regions of eighteenth- and nineteenth-century Russia as well, peasants lived in villages consisting of stem or joint families, each of which cultivated, largely with its own labour, portions of the surrounding land (Matossian, 1968; Tawney, 1932, ch. 2). But as soon as we proceed from this common ground to ask how the peasant villages fit into the broader structural designs of their respective societies, we immediately notice that while corporately organised peasant villages typically functioned as basic community units in Russia, in China the basic local units were the larger and more inclusive 'standard marketing communities', in which peasants as a distinctive class or social stratum lacked any exclusive corporate (or associational) existence.

In Russia, until after the Emancipation of 1861, most peasants were serfs, tied to the land they cultivated and forced to pay tribute: taxes to the state, and in the case of the private serfs also rent, in the forms of labour services or payments in cash or kind, to noble landlords (Robinson, 1932). After the Emancipation, redemption payments were substituted for the traditional noncommercial rents to landlords, with the effect that proportionately more of the overall tribute was channelled through the state (Volin, 1970, pp. 49–56). Yet both before and after the Emancipation, the peasants were legally tied to *obshchinas*, corporate units typically corresponding to (or encompassing) villages, in which were vested the common possession of land and other economic resources, as well as collective responsibility for the enforcement of payments of rents and or taxes by members (Robinson, 1932, ch. 7; Watters, 1968).

One of the most important and distinctive functions of the *obshchina* was the periodic repartitioning of its cultivable land, that is, its division among the taxable 'souls' of the village in a manner calculated to ensure rough equality of access for all to the main resources needed to produce for external obligations and subsistence needs. Apparently this particular practice was historically originated by the autocracy and the serf owners as a device to facilitate the squeezing of maximum tribute from the serfs (Blum, 1961, pp. 508–23; Watters, 1968, pp. 137–8). But once instituted, repartition became a powerful support for peasant community solidarity, and it continued to be practised by many ex-serf communities even after the state ceased to enforce or encourage it (Robinson, 1932, ch. 7; Watters, 1968, pp. 144–5).

The immediate government of the *obshchina* rested in the hands of the assembly of the heads of the families of the village. Naturally the peasants were never free from the supervision and arbitrary interference of either the landlords (for private serfs before 1861) or the bureaucratic agents of the state (for all peasants after 1861). Still, on an everyday basis, peasants were allowed to handle their own affairs as long as taxes, army recruits, and rents were forthcoming. Thus, either the entire assembly or else its elected part-time leaders took the responsibility for matters ranging from the distribution of repartitioned lands and the allocation of seigneurial and/or tax obligations and military draft calls, to the all-important planning of the many agricultural tasks that had to be co-ordinated by the *obshchina* members because their individual holdings were dispersed and inter-mixed and because they (typically) practised the three-field system of cultivation (Blum, 1961, pp. 523–7; Robinson, 1932; Vucinich, 1960). In sum, because the *obshchina* was a self-governing collective association that performed many functions that directly involved each family, it enforced solidarity among Russian peasants and afforded them considerable autonomy vis-à-vis landlords and the state.

The situation was quite different in China. A clear picture of the structure and functioning of local communities in late traditional China emerges from the empirical and theoretical investigations of G. William Skinner, who argues that

> the landscape of rural China was occupied by cellular systems of roughly hexagonal shape. The nucleus of each cell was one of approximately 45,000 market towns (as of the mid-nineteenth century), and its cytoplasm may be seen in the first instance as the trading area of the town's market. The body of the cell—which is to say the immediately dependent area of the town—typically included fifteen to twenty-five villages. . . . (1971, p. 272).

The 'standard' or basic level market town was the site of a periodic market visited regularly by the peasants of the surrounding villages; in turn, standard market towns were arrayed geographically around 'intermediate' markets, and so on up the urban hierarchy. For the peasants, the standard market town was the relevant centre—but not only because the peasants regularly attended the periodic markets to make purchases from artisans and peddlars and to sell their own produce. This much was certainly also true of Russian peasants, who similarly visited local towns to buy and sell on periodic market days and to attend church services and religious celebrations (Matossian, 1968, p. 30; Rozman, 1976, ch. 3). More than this, the Chinese market town/area was the arena of virtually every function and organisation that involved the peasants beyond the family and the neighbourhood:

> It delimited an important system of informal administration and a crucial arena of local politics. It constituted the social world of peasants, whose brides normally came from another village within the marketing system and whose extended kin groups, voluntary associations, and clientage relationships were typically contained within it. Major temples in the market town took the whole

complex of villages in the marketing system as their parish (Skinner, 1971, p. 272).

The standard market town was not, however, simply a bigger, more complex analogue to the Russian village peasant community. Although there were a variety of types of organisations or associations—e.g., lineages, temples, secret societies, self-defence militias, irrigation or water control projects—that brought peasants within the marketing community together for social events or common purposes, nevertheless the decisive fact about such bodies was that they were not strictly peasant groupings. Instead such bodies were normally promoted and led, either openly or informally, by leisured and literate members of the local gentry, a landlord class (Freedman, 1958; Fried, 1953; Skinner, 1971). What is more, the gentry leaders of the locally organised associations frequently had ties to analogous leaders in other standard marketing communities; consequently they were able to co-ordinate on a broader local–regional scale many activities which depended on peasant participation in the localities. For example, gentry managers might mobilise contributions and co-ordinate peasant labour from several communities to undertake water-control projects which could benefit agricultural productivity in many villages; similarly, in times of political instability, gentry leaders might unofficially tax 'middle' and 'rich' peasants in order to pay the upkeep of the local militia recruited from the ranks of impoverished local peasants (who might otherwise turn to banditry or rebellion) (Kuhn, 1970; Myers, 1975; Skinner, 1964, pp. 32–43).

With the gentry landlords so actively involved in local associations, there was little basis remaining for the peasants to organise 'on their own' at the level of the marketing community (Fei, 1946). Nor did the peasant village *per se* possess land in common, or co-ordinate agricultural work as did the Russian communes, for Chinese agriculture was based on individual families owning or renting their own lands, each faring as it could amidst the vagaries of weather, politics, markets, and demographic fortune (Buck, 1930; Perkins, 1969, chs 5–9). Families could become indebted (to merchants or gentry) and lose their land and local residence altogether; or they could accumulate land and liquid resources over perhaps several generations until they possessed enough to hire labourers, rent out land, and invest in credit operations, and thereby generate dependable income sufficient to provide leisure to study the Confucian classics and adopt the 'status manner' of the gentry. Existing gentry families, in turn, could dissipate their wealth, or subdivide it through inheritance, and thus fall back down into the ranks of the peasantry. In short, there was no officially enforced and frozen distinction between landlords and peasants as in Russia. And the considerable economic and status mobility that the Chinese system allowed can be seen as congruent with patterns of association in the local communities which ran vertically across the landlord and peasant strata, not horizontally within them.

Landed upper classes and the state   In addition to the situation of the peasantry, the other important socio-political contrast between Russia and China which we will survey is the relation of the landlords to the Imperial state organisations. It should be emphasized at the outset that in *neither* Russia nor China (until after 1900) were the landed upper classes able to exert formal, collective political leverage against the authority of Tsar or Emperor. In contrast, for example, to European landed aristocracies such as the French, or even the Prussian, neither the Chinese gentry nor the Russian nobility possessed corporate organisations with traditionally legitimate rights to share in the governing process of the old regime (Feldmesser, 1960; Wakeman, 1970). Nevertheless, the embeddedness of the Chinese gentry in the localities and its ramified functional links to the peasantry and the local economies provided it as a class with a much stronger basis to counterbalance and limit the reach of the Imperial power than did the weak local roots and antagonistic opposition to the serf/peasant communities of the Russian landed nobility.

Why were the local roots of the Russian nobility so weak? After all, many nobles owned serfs and estates worked by serf labour, and these characteristics might appear to make them a stronger class than the Chinese gentry whose agricultural fortunes depended on rents from tenants. But the very same historical tendencies that created serf agriculture in Russia also shaped the nobility into an internally fragmented class nearly totally dependent on autocracy for its status and livelihood.

Serfdom in Russia was consolidated not by commercialising landlords (as in much of Eastern Europe after 1400), but rather under the impetus of centralising Tsars determined to extract from the Russian people sufficient resources to support military forces for defence and expansion in threatening geopolitical environments (Blum, 1961, chs 8–14; Hellie, 1971; Pipes, 1974, Pt 1). Traditionally footloose Russian peasants had to be tied to the land if they were to be kept at work producing taxable surpluses. Concomitantly the Tsars needed military officers and officials to man the state organisations required for external warfare and internal social control. Over a period of centuries the lands of independent nobles and princes were expropriated and passed out as rewards for official careers to a new class of service nobles. As this happened, the Tsars took pains to ensure that no new groupings of independent landed aristocrats could arise (Pipes, 1974, ch. 7; Raeff, 1971). Service nobles were given rights to serf 'souls' and to landed estates, yet typically their possessions were not concentrated in one locality or even one province, but were scattered over different regions of the empire. Moreover, until the eighteenth century, adult male nobles were forced to pursue service careers from youth until old age, with the Tsar reserving the right to shunt individuals from post to post, province to province, at will. Under these conditions, local and regional solidarity among nobles could not develop, agriculture was naturally regarded only as a source of income, not as an object of managerial concern, and 'local government', such as it was, was the affair of serf communities and estate agents operating under bureaucratic scrutiny, not a sphere in which local landowners exerted important leadership.

During the eighteenth century Russian nobles were finally released from life-long state service and their private property rights were fully officially confirmed. Moreover, the Russian economy experienced comparatively rapid commercial development. Nevertheless, the situation of the nobles did not change much (Raeff, 1966). Now increasingly oriented to Western European upper-class life styles, the Russian nobles still gravitated toward state employment as the one sure site of opportunities to reside in the cities and to earn salaries to supplement the very meagre incomes (if any) that most obtained from the serf-estates, the inheritance of which was subdivided in each generation. Nor did the vast majority of landlords possess either the capital or the knowledge or inclination to turn to commercial agriculture (and indeed the conditions for it were poor in most regions of Russia). By the mid-nineteenth century a large majority of Russian nobles were either impoverished or heavily indebted to the state and the minority of well-to-do were mostly prospering through official careers (Blum, 1961, chs 19–20).

The reforms after 1860, including the Emancipation of the serfs, did not reverse the powerlessness and economic decline of the landed nobility. Most used their redemption payments (compensation for the loss of serf ownership) to pay off debts to the state or for education or consumption, not for economic investments (Robinson, 1932, ch. 8). Even the formation of the *zemstvos*—local and provincial representative bodies to which nobles had privileged electoral access

—could not alter the long-established pattern of noble 'function-lessness' vis-à-vis the bureaucratic state on the one hand and the peasant communities on the other. For the Imperial authorities retained a monopoly of administration and coercion and continued to tax away most of the agricultural surplus, while the *obshchinas* continued to manage agriculture along traditional lines. At best the *zemstvos* established a foothold through the provision, on a very restricted fiscal basis, of educational, welfare and advisory-economic services in the localities, but this service sector grew up alongside, not within, the hierarchy of societal political power. The *zemstvos* were tolerated by the Imperial bureaucracy only to the extent that they did not challenge central controls and policy making prero-gatives (Vucinich, 1960).

In Imperial China the gentry evolved quite differently from the Russian nobility. Like the Russian service class, the Chinese gentry were substantially dependent on state employment for their status (and even livelihoods, in the sense that the largest fortunes seem to have been accumulated during successful official careers) (Michael, 1955). Moreover, Chinese landlords depended to a considerable extent on Imperial backing to defend them against peasant rebellions and banditry and to enforce their rights to collect rents from tenants. Nevertheless, Chinese dynasties and their centrally deployed official-doms traditionally coexisted politically with locally rooted landed notables. Indeed the Imperial bureaucracy never penetrated as exten-sively into the localities as did the Russian autocratic state (Rozman, 1976), and the lowest-level Chinese officials (who were always out-siders to the areas they administered) had to co-operate with local landlords and literati in order to ensure smooth tax collections and the maintenance of order (Ch'u., 1962, ch. 10).

In traditional China local communities and elites could prosper without complete dependence on Imperial initiatives or employ-ments. Especially in significantly commercialised areas of agrarian China, landlords could make profits by renting out lands and tendering usurious loans to peasants, and local people could afford to create associations (e.g., clans, religious sodalities, militias, and irrigation projects) and pay fees to support gentry directors to manage them (Chang, 1962). Besides, flourishing local and regional trading networks made it possible for merchants rapidly to accumu-late fortunes—which they typically subsequently invested in land and in Confucian educations for their sons, thus transforming their heirs into gentry. By this process the gentry could be continually reju-venated from outside agriculture, where only modest fortunes could accumulate given the practice of equal inheritance and the low rate of return to investments in land (Perkins, 1969, pp. 93–6).

Another condition facilitating mobility into and out of the gentry lay in the fact that Imperial authorities in China never established any juridically closed hereditary nobility. This helped to prevent locally rooted upper classes from consolidating into corporate aristocracies, and the resulting mobility complemented the unique competitive process by which the Chinese state recruited its officials.

Indeed the reason why Chinese rulers were *able* to coexist with a partially autonomous landed upper class lies in the workings of the Confucian examination system for recruiting state officials, for this system, operating normally, helped to extend the Imperial reach informally into the heart of every local community (Chang, 1955; Michael, 1955; Skinner, 1971). Under this system, Imperial authorities periodically convened examinations at graduated levels of difficulty to test candidates' mastery of the Confucian classics. There were strict quotas (adjustable according to Imperial needs and policies, such as the policy of maintaining regional balances) for what proportions could pass, and the Imperial authorities followed relatively consistent patterns of recruiting Imperial officials from among individuals who successfully passed the exams. In the local communities, meanwhile, wealthy families paid Confucian scholars to educate their sons or protégés in what was essentially an entire style of life, or status manner, as well as a set of difficult skills requisite for obtaining the highly desired official posts. Invariably, there were in any locality always more Confucian-tutored aspirants to state service than ever either passed all of the requisite exams or obtained official appointments. Because such local literati shared the class interests and status-manner of the Imperial officials, they were normally inclined to co-operate with the magistrates to maintain order. And their co-operation was quite valuable because, as local leaders, they were familiar with local conditions and played strategic roles in the various types of peasant-based associations which (as we have seen) flourished in the local communities.

Moreover, even successful career officials in traditional China did not become cut off from their home localities (Michael, 1955; Skinner, 1971). For obvious reasons, officials were required to serve in administrative posts away from their home provinces and towns. But they were also forbidden to move their families with them, and were encouraged to return home periodically for ritually prescribed family occasions (e.g., several years of mourning at a parent's death), and for other periods of retirement interspersed within the typical official career. In addition, nothing prevented officials from investing the proceeds earned during years of official service (from salaries, but even more from informally sanctioned graft) in land or commercial enterprises left to the management of kin who remained behind in their home communities. Finally, when ex-officials themselves came home temporarily or permanently, they often played very influential roles in local politics, not the least because their old official ties could help their home communities to obtain favours or lenient treatment from Imperial officials (Kuhn, 1970).

In sum, the systems of official recruitment and deployment in Imperial China, operating in symbiosis with the socio-economic dynamics of local communities, ensured that there were always in any community Confucian gentry involved in local leadership roles and available for informal co-operation with similarly educated Imperial officials, who, in turn, needed the help of local leaders in order to govern.

The Chinese gentry were, therefore, the indispensable support for Imperial rule. Particular dynasties lost their ability to rule effectively only when major sectors of the gentry went over to rebellions, and new dynasties, whether founded by rebellion or invasion, consolidated their rule only with gentry co-operation. And the co-operation of local gentry leaders was just as important as that of active officials. During the mid-nineteenth century, in fact, the waning Ch'ing dynasty was saved from defeat at the hands of the Taiping rebels not by its own armies and officials alone, but through the efforts of locally based and regionally co-ordinated armies organised by retired officials working in co-operation with local elites in their home communities (Kuhn, 1970). This was possible only because those elites led associations that could readily mobilise peasant manpower and local economic resources. Thus, especially during the final decades of its existence (from 1860 to 1911), the Chinese Imperial system was a regime in which power was balanced between the dynasty and its bureaucrats on the one hand, and a locally and regionally powerful landed upper class on the other.

Modern industrial developments under the old regimes

Having surveyed the agrarian-based socio-political structures of the old regimes, it yet remains for me to discuss how and to what extent modern industry had developed in Russia and China prior to the outbreak of the revolutionary crises and the rise to power of the Communist revolutionaries. Neither Russia nor China commenced industrialisation in the relatively autonomous and spontaneous manner of England, with indigenous agricultural commercialisation and consumer demand as the predominant stimuli. Rather both responded to pressures and examples from more industrially advanced foreign military competitors. Yet both the timing and nature of the foreign pressures and the kinds and extent of the responses to foreign examples differed greatly between the two old regimes.

Long before they had to contend with military competition from mechanised European nations. Russian rulers were accustomed to borrowing techniques from the West and imposing them on Russian society. During the seventeenth century Muscovy came into sustained military conflict with European monarchical absolutisms. In adaptive response there came a remarkable effort, explosively initiated under Peter the Great (1682–1725), to rework the Russian state and economy by amalgamating the most efficient patterns of bureaucratic state service, manufacturing, and military technology and organisation then existing in Western Europe with the inherited Russian forms of serfdom and patrimonal despotism (Raeff, 1971). In fact, the reforms 'from above' of Peter and his immediate successors succeeded in making Russia a formidable European military power, not to be eclipsed until the mid-nineteenth century, when the technologies and infrastructural advances associated with industrialisation again gave the Western powers a qualitative military advantage (Esper, 1969).

Once the Crimean War of 1854 to 1856 revealed Russia's renewed backwardness and vulnerability within the European states system (of which Russia was now irrevocably a member), the Tsars and their officials responded in what was really a very traditional fashion. They instituted a progression of reforms from above, all designed in one way or another to help Russia to catch up militarily with her potential enemies (Seton-Watson, 1967, ch. 10; Von Laue, 1963). First serfdom was abolished and the military and judicial systems reformed; then a programme of railroad construction through state and foreign investments was instituted; finally, from the late 1880s a crash programme of government-subsidised heavy industrialisation was launched. All such policies could be pursued even against resistance from social classes—in the face of landlord opposition to freeing the selfs; despite merchants' reluctance to compete with foreign capitalists or to modernise business practices; against peasant unrest and riots protesting crushing tax burdens—because the Russian autocratic state was, as always, the monopole of power in the society. Especially in the final decades before its collapse in war, the Tsarist state alone took the effective intitiative in launching changes within Russia.

In absolute terms, moreover, the changes wrought at state initiative were very great (Carson, 1959; Gerschenkron, 1960). Of course when the grim reckoning of World War came in 1914, Russia still had by no means caught up with the West economically (Goldsmith, 1961). Judged in terms of their avowed purposes, therefore, the post-Crimean Tsarist reforms were failures – largely because the vast agricultural sector of the Russian economy remained for the most part untransformed in structure and technique. Yet, especially after 1890, Russia experienced remarkably rapid industrial growth. Mining, petroleum refining, metallurgical and chemical industries, and textiles all developed rapidly. Overall industrial expansion averaged about 5 per cent per annum between 1888 and 1913, a rate higher on a per capita basis than industrial growth in either the United States or Germany during that period (Nove, 1969, p. 12). Heavy industrial expansion in particular occurred through importation from the West of the very latest manufacturing technologies, which in turn were designed into the most large-scale and modern of factory organisations. Nor was the industry concentrated in merely one region, or only on the margins of the empire; there were several important areas of industrial concentration, including the regions around the capitals (St. Petersburg and Moscow), as well as the Ukraine, Polish Russia, the Donets Basin, and the Urals (Nove, 1969, p. 16; Seton-Watson, 1967, p. 782, map 13). Moreover, although the advent of World War I found Russia with a much less dense and redundant railroad network than her neighbouring enemy, Imperial Germany, nevertheless there had been built up a primary grid of links connecting all of the administrative and industrial cities to one another, and these in turn to the ports and military frontiers of both European and Asian Russia (Seton-Watson, 1967, p. p780–1, map 12). One student of Russian development, Alec Nove, has neatly summed up the economic situation of the Tsarist regime at the end: 'Russia was the least developed European power, but a European power none the less' (1969, p. 16).

China, on the other hand, had not traditionally experienced compelling military pressure from pre-industrial European states. Traders and missionaries were the Westerners who, from as early as the thirteenth century, had initiated intermittent and limited contacts with a China ever reluctant to take serious account of Western ways (Franke, 1967). It was not until the nineteenth-century industrialisation of Western Europe provided gunboats to back up the demands of Western merchants and soul-seekers that they were able to attain sustained access to the Chinese economy and society. But from the

Opium War of 1839–42 through a series of imperialist incursions and military victories culminating after 1895 in the carving of (still nominally sovereign) China into spheres of foreign influence, Chinese authorities were increasingly compelled to respond to the evident economic and military superiority of the European nations (and ultimately Japan as well).

Nevertheless, the Chinese Imperial government's response to the Western industrial advantage could not resemble that of the Tsarist government after 1854. China lacked a history of cultural adaptation from above, but even more important, the Chinese central government could not wield significant leverage over the Chinese society and economy as a whole. This was true not only because Chinese emperors had never been as strong against the gentry as the Russian Tsars had always been over their service nobility, but also because by the mid-nineteenth century, at exactly the time when Western intrusions on Chinese sovereignty became militarily compelling, the Chinese Manchu (Ch'ing) dynasty was at the nadir of its influence and control over events within Chinese society. For during the middle decades of the century, the dynasty was saved from overthrow by massive peasant-based rebellions only through the military intervention of regional gentry-led armies and administrations—which, in the aftermath of the rebellions (from the 1860s on), retained de facto control of large sectors of the Imperial bureaucracy and of over 50 per cent of the tax revenues officially collected within the empire (Kuhn, 1970; Wang, 1973, ch. 4). Unofficially, local gentry collected and controlled still more of the surpluses generated by the agrarian–commercial economy. Consequently, even as Imperial authorities came increasingly to recognise the need to promote industrial development, railroad building, and the technological modernisation and professionalisation of Chinese military forces, they found themselves without access to the financial revenues that might have allowed the central government to invest heavily in these things and thus to promote national development in a co-ordinated way calculated to reinforce Chinese political power vis-à-vis foreign enemies (Feuerwerker, 1969, ch. 5).

In turn, the weakness of the Chinese government encouraged foreign interests to encroach more and more on Chinese sovereignty. The obvious effect of this was to undermine the authority and power of the Manchus still further. Another consequence was that most of the little modern industrialisation that did occur in China right up through 1949 happened within or near foreign-controlled Treaty Ports or spheres of influence. Industrial enterprises, established either by foreign investors or by Chinese capitalists seeking the legal advantages of operating in the foreign administrated areas or the economic advantages of trading with foreigners, grew up to process a limited range of Chinese raw materials or agricultural products for export or for sale within the treaty ports or their immediate hinterlands. These were primarily light industries and most enterprises were small or medium in scale. The total output of all modern industries never (before 1949, let alone 1911) exceeded 3·5 per cent of the national income of China, and industrial workers remained substantially fewer than 1 per cent of the labour force (Chesneaux, 1962, ch. 2; Feuerwerker, 1962, chs 3–5 ch. 3). (Roughly comparable figures for late Tsarist Russia were 16 per cent and 5 per cent respectively [Goldsmith, 1961, pp. 442, 468–9; Uldricks, 1974, pp. 402].) In short, even the direct and indirect effects of capitalist imperialism did not produce any major structural change in the workings of the Chinese economy before 1949 (Murphey, 1974).

Instead, the traditional Chinese agrarian/commercial economy continued to function, its operations modified mainly at the margins. G. William Skinner (1965, pp. 211–28) has estimated that about 90 per cent of China's traditional marketing system remained intact through 1949. Most trade remained focused within the traditional regional and local-periodic markets, served by traditional merchants and peddlers supplying goods still produced primarily by local peasants and artisans or non-mechanised workshops, rather than the products of modern industries. Only a far more extensively developed system of modern transportation, especially railroad and highway, could have allowed the treaty port industries and enterprises, centred mainly along the coasts and major rivers, to transform the structure and marketing flows of the resilient traditional system. Yet by 1912 China had only less than 10,000 kilometres of railroads, and even by 1945 there were still less than 25,000 kilometres (Feuerwerker, 1968, pp. 42). (By 1904, Russia already had 60,000 kilometres and by 1916, more than 64,000 kilometres [Goldsmith, 1961, p. 442; Seton-Watson, 1967, p. 520].) The lines were few and poorly distributed, and did not reach far into the interior of the country, while nearly half of the track was located in Manchuria, which fell under Japanese control after 1930 (Chesneaux, 1962, p. 423; Feuerwerker, 1968, ch. 7).

In sum, modern industrial development in China before 1911 (or 1949) was very limited and marginal. Certainly it was much less extensive and transformative in its impact than Russian industrialisation before 1917.

The preceding discussion has established some important differences between pre-revolutionary China and Russia. Now it is time to assess how the differences of socio-political structure and modern economic development of the old regimes can help us to account for the later variations between the revolutionary regimes in Russia and China. I shall argue that the old-regime legacies helped to shape the revolutionary futures in three main ways, with the effects cumulating and thus reinforcing one another. First, differences between the socio-political structures of old-regime Russia and China guaranteed that revolutionary crises would develop differently, causing Communist revolutionaries in the two societies to be faced with different revolutionary tasks and different possibilities for mobilising popular rebellious forces. Second, the contrasting levels, extensiveness, and internal geopolitical relevance of modern economic development within Russia versus China meant that post-autocratic state power could be consolidated with modern urban resources in post-1917 Russia but not in post-1911 China. And third, even once Communist revolutionaries in the two countries had consolidated national political power, the different economic conditions inherited from the old regimes favoured different development strategies—which, moreover, were congruent with the contrasting political capacities that had been acquired by the two revolutionary parties during their struggles for power. Let me elaborate on each of these very general assertions in turn.

Pre-revolutionary socio-political structures and the development of the revolutionary crises

In neither Russia nor China did revolutionary crises emerge directly as a result of mass discontent or the activities of ideological radicals. In both cases, rather, the political, administrative, and military institutions of the autocracy were suddenly weakened and disorganised due to the direct or indirect effects of foreign pressures (Skocpol, 1976). In China, ineffective attempts by the Manchus to cope with imperialist pressures induced politically organised gentry groups, along with their provincial military allies, to depose the dynasty in 1911 (Fairbank *et al.,* 1973, ch. 24; Wright, 1968). In Russia, the autocracy was too autonomous and strong vis-à-vis class forces to be deposed by any internal force, even after suffering international humiliations as in the Crimean War of 1854–6 and the

Russo-Japanese War of 1905–6. Instead, the Russian state finally dissolved only under the impact of defeat in prolonged, total modern warfare in World War I. Still, in both instances, China from 1911, and Russia from March 1917, the result of the sudden collapse of the autocracy was to open the way for spreading and deepening political and social conflicts. The traditional focus of order disintegrated and a revolutionary situation emerged.

Nevertheless the significance of the collapse of autocracy was quite different in Russia and China, because the old-regime structures that came apart from the top down had been put together differently in the first place.

In Russia the autocracy collapsed only when the Tsarist administration and armies were so overwhelmed by the burdens of unsuccessful total warfare as to be on the verge of complete disintegration (Golovino, 1931; Gronsky and Astrov, 1929; Kennan, 1969). The 'February' Revolution was itself occasioned by the war-induced insubordination of the Petrograd Garrison, traditionally a mainstay of Tsarist authority (Rabinowitch, 1972, pp. 172–3). Within days and weeks after the fall of the monarchy, the police and administrative organisations of the old regime dissolved, and by midsummer (as the war continued without success) even the front-line armies were beginning to disintegrate through desertions or rank-and-file revolts against officers (Anweiler, 1958, ch. 3; Ferro, 1971; Pethybridge, 1972).

In turn, once the Tsarist state collapsed, the single strong point of the old regime, the keystone of the entire edifice, was gone. Having been completely dependent on the autocracy, the nobility (officials and landlords) and the bourgeoisie (domestic and foreign) were suddenly left vulnerable to popular rebellions from below. The remnant landed gentry were supremely vulnerable, for they were functionally irrelevant to the processes of agricultural production and village level government, and yet still enjoyed property rights in lands coveted by the neighbouring peasant communities. The mass of the peasants in turn (especially those of central Russia) possessed in the institution of the *obshchina* a collective organisation through which they could spontaneously rebel against landlords on their own, without inducement or leadership from urban radical elites, given only the opportunity offered by the disintegration of Tsarist administrative and military power upon which the gentry depended for defence of their privileges (Volin, 1970, ch. 6; Wolf, 1969, pp. 89–92). Not surprisingly, therefore, within a few months after March 1917, the Russian landed nobility as a class was swept away by snowballing peasant revolts (Chamberlain, 1935, ch. 11). Meanwhile in the urban centres, administrators, army officers, professionals, and capitalists were attacked by striking industrial workers and mutinous soldiers (Anweiler, 1958, ch. 3; Avrich, 1963; Uldricks, 1974). In short, all of the dominant classes and elites of the old regime were suddenly and thoroughly rendered quite powerless.

As a consequence, the revolutionary socialist parties, would-be consolidators of alternative regimes, were left to contend in a virtual power vacuum. Not until after one of the revolutionary parties—the Bolsheviks—had triumphed in the intra-revolutionary competition, did serious counter-revolutionary threats begin to emerge (1918–20), in part because scattered elements of the old regime formed uneasy alliances with defeated revolutionary contenders. Yet these counter-revolutionary movements had administrative or military bases only at the peripheries of European Russia. Consequently, the various counter-revolutionary forces were always divided from one another and suffered from political contradictions within their own ranks (Chamberlin, 1935). These movements presented a challenge to the Bolsheviks' attempts to consolidate revolutionary state power, but perhaps a less serious challenge than the conditions of spreading disintegration and popular anarchy within which the Bolsheviks (like all of the elite contenders after 1917) had to manoeuvre. For the Bolsheviks did not so much ever face the task of making the Revolution—in the sense of combating and defeating the dominant institutions of the old regime—as they faced the imperatives of rebuilding political order out of virtual chaos. This was because the old regime had necessarily come apart in a manner suited to its structure. It took no less a crisis than the strains of defeat and prolonged participation in World War I to overwhelm the Tsarist army and bureaucracy, the central supports of the old regime, yet once these supports gave way, no significant remnants of the old regime remained intact for long.

But the bases on which a new national order could be built were quite limited, and this, too, was a legacy of the structure of the old regime. The very success of the revolt by the independent peasant communities ruled them out as a possible basis for national reintegration. Having seized the opportunity to attack the landlords and take their lands virtually unaided, the peasant communities wanted only to turn inward and to be left alone to carry on their self-governing and subsistence-oriented existence (Male, 1971; Shanin, 1972). Whatever progress towards political reintegration the Bolsheviks (or any other revolutionary elite) could make would thus have to be based upon the social and infrastructural resources of the urban centres.

Turning now to China, we can see that the revolutionary crisis developed after 1911 in quite a different manner from Russia after March 1917, and again the explanation lies in the structural patterns of the old regime that was disintegrating. Whereas the revolutionary crisis in Russia was occasioned and characterised by the collapse of the entire framework of the old regime, in China in 1911 only the co-ordinating centre was removed, while the local and regional administrative and military power of the gentry and the warlords remained intact—indeed were initially enhanced by the removal of the meagre restraints that the Manchus had been able to impose in the name of national unity (Ichiko, 1968; Wilbur, 1968; Young, 1970). Nor were the Chinese peasants able to rebel spontaneously and autonomously, in the manner of the Russian peasants, against the landlords. For the Chinese gentry retained their local economic and political predominance, as they either directly usurped former Imperial administrative positions in the districts and provinces, or else came to terms with the regional warlord organisations that claimed administrative power (Kuhn, 1968; Muramatsu, 1966; Selden, 1971 ch. 1).

Thus when modern-style revolutionary elites and parties emerged in the urban centres of China after 1919, they faced a very different situation from the one which suddenly confronted Russian revolutionaries in 1917. The dominant classes and elites of the old regime were still very much in place. The removal of the autocracy had not resulted directly in social revolution but only in deepening national political disintegration, leaving China more vulnerable than ever to foreign powers. But the gentry and the warlords remained potent internal opponents of any revolutionary movements aiming to reunite and reorient the nation (Wilbur, 1968). Both the peasantry and the urban workers were potential supporters for such a revolutionary movement, for these classes had interests opposed to the gentry and bourgeoisie (both domestic and foreign) (Bianco, 1968; Chesneaux, 1962). Yet given the continued administrative-military power of the gentry and the warlords, neither the peasants nor the workers were able to carry out a successful revolution from below without leadership and protection by organised revolutionary forces. Thus, virtually all possibilities for popular alliances remained open, but only if revolutionaries could build administrative and military apparatuses to gain direct access to territories and populations over which warlords or gentry retained control. Still, the disunity and competition of the provincially and regionally based warlord–gentry connections at least provided possibilities for alliance and manoeuvre for would-be revolutionary movements (Wilbur, 1968).

Modern urban resources and the consolidation of revolutionary state power

A second way in which old-regime legacies affected the course of revolutionary struggles in China and Russia had to do with whether or not the modern urban industrial sectors that had developed prior to the revolutions provided adeqate resources for a revolutionary party to consolidate state power.

In revolutionary Russia this question of urban resources was posed quite compellingly because, once the peasants had carried through their inward- and backward-looking revolts against the landlords and all other locally present remnants of the Tsarist system, only urban resources were easily available to any would-be consolidators of state power. Hence it was of great significance that European Russia possessed at its core and around its edges a series of major industrial and administrative cities, linked together by a network of railroad and telegraph lines.

Among the contending revolutionary parties, the tightly knit and internally disciplined Bolsheviks were in the best position to exploit these urban resources, since, especially after August 1917 , they had the closest and most plentiful ties to the organised industrial workers and military garrisons within and near the most industrialised and administratively strategic northeastern urban centres. None of the other revolutionary parties was in a good position to outmanoeuvre the Bolsheviks, not only because the other parties were less unified and disciplined, but also because their strongest popular bases were not so centrally located. The Mensheviks had their greatest relative strength in the peripheral areas of the Caucasus and Georgia, while the Socialist Revolutionaries were strongest in the provincial cities and towns of the most heavily agricultural provinces and along the western and southwestern fronts (Anweiler, 1958, pp. 76–85; Radkey, 1963).

With great tactical skill, the Bolsheviks, from the summer of 1917 through their Petrograd coup in 'October' and on until the competing parties had been manoeuvred out of all strategic positions, used their political links to workers and soldiers to consolidate and extend Party control of the cities, fronts, and railroad links within northeastern Russia (Anweiler, 1958; Pethybridge, 1972). Then they were in a position to attempt to consolidate and extend urban-based administrative and police controls over the entire country during the Civil War (1918–21) (Chamberlin, 1935).

That the Bolsheviks (or any party) could succeed at all in consolidating national power on this basis, no matter how clever and ruthless their tactics, certainly depended on the degree of modern industrial and transportation development that had been accomplished under the old regime. Most of the existing Russian war industries, and the stockpiles of arms and munitions produced by them during 1917, fell into the hands of the Bolsheviks (Garder, 1959, p. 39). Industrial workers, many of them Party members, were available and widely distributed in sufficient numbers to staff such indispensable units as the food collection teams sent out to seize grain from the peasants and the Red Vanguard units interspersed among the peasant conscripts to give fighting spirit to the revolutionary armies (Ellis, 1974). Besides, no strategy of consolidating the revolution by seizing and then defending the capitals and other important administrative cities could have won without the European Russian railroad network, which made it possible to move loyal troops and political cadres quickly from place to place along the interior defensive lines that the Bolsheviks enjoyed during the Civil War. It is no accident that one of the most vivid and frequently encountered images of the Bolshevik revolutionary leadership is that of the Commander-in-Chief of the Red Army, Leon Trotsky, whisking from front line to front line in his command headquarters—a railroad car.

In China, modern urban resources played a far more complicated role in the revolutionary process. As in Russia, the leaderships of the principal revolutionary parties were recruited from an intelligentsia committed by educational experience and political principle to the furthering of 'modern, urban' ways (North and Pool, 1966; Wilbur, 1970). Moreover, the initial mass political bases of both the Kuomintang Nationalists and the Chinese Communist party were recruited from among the people of the Westernised Treaty Port cities, and between 1922 and 1926 the two parties were allied in an attempt to reunite and revolutionise China through mass-supported military campaigns to capture control from warlords of the principal urban centres of coastal China (Wilbur, 1968). On their own, the Chinese Communists were attempting simultaneously to build an exclusive organised base among the industrial proletariat which would allow them to capture control of the urban-centred revolution from the Kuomintang (Chesneaux, 1962).

But the Chinese Communists' feeble attempts in 1926–7 to seize power through Bolshevik-style urban coups and guided mass uprisings only led to disaster. Unlike the Bolsheviks in 1917, they did not benefit from the war-induced disintegration of standing armies potentially loyal to counter-revolution. The Communists were pushed out of the cities (and most administrative towns) of China altogether, forced to pursue a do-or-die strategy of rural guerilla warfare, while the now rightist re-oriented Kuomintang was left in control of the most modernised urban centres.

During over twenty years in the countryside of China, between 1927 and 1949, the Chinese Communists gradually developed tactics to drive the warlords and gentry from regional and local political–military and economic power (Schurmann, 1968, pp. 412-37). They finally forged direct links to the peasants within the local communities—links which enabled them to mobilise peasant manpower and rural economic resources more directly and efficiently than any previous political movement in (at least recent) Chinese history (Selden, 1971). That the Communists were eventually able to do this depended, at least in a negative sense, on the fact that the Chinese peasants had not been able to rebel effectively against the gentry on their own. The peasantry 'needed' direct protection by the Red Army and local leadership tied to the Communist party in order to gain collective organisational leverage to attack the gentry (Hinton, 1966). In the very process of providing these factors, the Chinese Communists both displaced, and in a sense, replaced the warlord–gentry nexus of provincial–local power left over from the collapsing old regime: the peasants still remained oriented to non-parochial leaders with a foothold in the localities; only the Party and Red Army hierarchies replaced the landed and official gentry (Barnett, 1967, Pt. 4).

Yet the CCP's ultimate success with its peasant-mobilisation strategy depended not only on its ability to displace the gentry and directly mobilise the peasantry, but also on the *inability* of the Kuomintang Nationalists to consolidate nation-wide centralised administrative and military control over China between 1928 (by which time the Nationalists had defeated most overt warlord military opposition) and 1937 (when the Japanese invaded China with full force). This was something that the Nationalists made every attempt to do, drawing to the fullest degree possible on the resources of the most modernised cities of coastal and central China, especially Shanghai and Nanking. True, the Nationalists did not follow a policy of mobilising human resources, for in their attempt to call a halt to the social revolutionary process after 1927, they eschewed direct political mobilisation of workers and students (Cavendish,

1965). Yet the Nationalists milked the industrial wealth of the cities, taxed their national and international commercial flows, and manipulated to maximum political advantage the processes of modern finance institutionalised in the urban banks (Fairbank *et al.,* 1973, pp. 792–3; Feuerwerker, 1968; Paauw, 1957, ch. 8). But all of the urban-generated revenues the Nationalist government could lay its hands on were not enough to pay the costs of a truly national army that could supplant the military organisations of warlords (who remained in place as nominal allies in all but a few core provinces) or to pay for an administrative apparatus sufficiently extensive, loyal, and efficient to penetrate into the rural localities and divert agrarian revenues from the gentry and provincial potentates to the Nationalist centre (Fairbank *et al.,* 1973, pp. 791–3; Gillin, 1967; Tien, 1972). Nor did the KMT leaders have access to any extensive and centralised primary railroad network which could be used, in the manner of the Bolsheviks, to deploy and redeploy small but loyal bodies of military, police, and administrative personnel, Instead National 'authority' in the interior and in the North and South of China depended on the maintenance, through periodic payoffs, of cross-cutting alliances with locally and provincially based authorities.

As a result, Nanking was in no position to mobilise or co-ordinate Chinese national efforts to defend the country against Japanese invasion. Once that invasion came in earnest in 1937, the Nationalist government was driven completely out of the modernised cities of eastern China. After being feebly re-established in the western hinterland cut off from its accustomed revenue sources, the regime was in an even less favourable position either to expel the Japanese or to counter the rising power of the Communists (Fairbank *et al.,* 1973, pp. 797–807). Meanwhile, the wartime situation of superficial foreign occupation and exacerbated military divisions among its enemies provided the Chinese Communists with especially favourable conditions to pursue and deepen their rural mobilisation approach to generating the resources necessary to consolidate revolutionary state power in China (Meisner, 1970)—something they accomplished very rapidly once the United States defeated Japan in World War II.

But the point is that the Chinese Communists could never have survived as an organised political and rebellious military force after 1927 if the Kuomintang had been able to impose, from its modern urban base, as tight administrative–military controls on China as the Bolsheviks were able to impose on Russia from their urban base after 1918. And surely the difference between the Bolsheviks' success and the Kuomintang's failure cannot be explained only by differences in party characteristics and policies—for the Kuomintang had advantages not available to the Bolsheviks after November 1917 (e.g., an intact military organisation) to counterbalance the Bolshevik-style qualities that it lacked (e.g., centralised discipline and an orientation toward mass mobilisation). But the Bolsheviks could operate within an urban network where modern industries and transportation facilities were thoroughly integrated with the urban–administrative hierarchy through which the autocratic regime had formerly exerted its monopolistic powers, while the Kuomintang had to contend with an economy and urban network thoroughly bifurcated between a quantitatively and geographically marginal modern urban sector on the one hand, and a vast, traditional, agrarian-commercial sector on the other, In the post-1917 Russia, nationwide state power could probably be reconsolidated *only* on the basis of modern urban resources; in post-1911 China, modern urban resources were hopelessly inadequate to this task. Instead, revolutionaries had to work around and destroy the remnants of the old regime in the hinterland and countryside. The way from Canton, the birthplace of modern Chinese nationalism, to Peking, the traditional administrative capital of China, lay not in a brief, smooth trip through the upstart Treaty Ports of Nanking and Shanghai, but in a long, arduous trek through the rural backlands of Shensi.

Revolutionary outcomes: building on inherited economic and accumulated political strengths

Once Communists consolidated revolutionary state power in Russia in the early 1920s and in China in the early 1950s, they had at their disposal new and powerful means to formulate and implement development policies for their entire societies. Immediately after consolidating power, both the Bolsheviks and the Chinese Communists found it relatively easy to rebuild their countries' economies to pre–World War I and pre–World war II levels, respectively, by straightforwardly restoring old enterprises and economic linkages within a context of national order and administrative planning. That the Chinese Communists were so readily able and willing to pursue a Soviet-style strategy of placing emphasis on heavy industries can in large part be attributed to the fact that Chinese national authorities had suddenly regained, albeit in war-damaged condition, modern industrial plants that had been built up in formerly occupied areas such as Manchuria (Schurmann, 1968, ch. 4). With relatively modest investments of capital and administrative expertise, such industries could be quickly rebuilt up to and somewhat beyond pre-War levels (Perkins, 1969, ch. 4). The Bolsheviks had faced a similar situation with their inherited industrial economy in 1921 (Nove, 1969). But both parties came face to face with real dilemmas once restorative industrial growth had played itself out (in Russia by 1925 and in China by 1956). At that point the question arose whether future economic development could continue to be based on absolute national political priority for investments in heavy industry. Russia under Stalinist direction answered yes, while China, especially insofar as Maoist policies have taken hold, has answered no.

Why the difference? The answer requires and allows us to tie together the separate strands of the overall argument developed in this paper. In brief, the Soviets and the Chinese Communists each found that future development for their country could best build on the inherited strengths of the existing economy—with those strengths to be dynamically harnessed, of course, by the vast new powers of the revolutionary state as a mobiliser of investment capital and mass human energies. Equally important, the respective political capacities accumulated by each party in the course of struggling to consolidate state power were well suited to the implementation of economic development strategies based on the different inherited economic strengths.

Soviet Russia, by 1926, was in crisis. Industrial growth was halting in the absence of major new investments, while the burgeoning peasant population was refusing to market crops in amounts sufficient to feed the cities and supply industries (Lewin, 1966; Nove, 1969, chs 4–7; Volin, 1970, ch. 9). Within the Communist party, policy struggles raged over how to proceed. On the 'Right', Bukharin and his allies advocated increasing the production of, and lowering the prices for, manufactured consumer goods in order to induce the peasantry to raise and sell more agricultural products in exchange. On the other hand, adopting policies advocated by the defeated Trotskyist 'Left', Stalin gradually forged an alternative strategy that called for huge, sustained investments in heavy industries, coupled with administrative mechanisms (collectivisation from above) to force the peasantry to grow crops, surrender surpluses, and release manpower for the sudden urban-industrial expansion.

Stalin's approach was the one that triumphed—in large part because it came to be seen by most of the Soviet political elite as the better way to bring their capacities to bear upon solving Russia's economic dilemma. Bukharin's approach would necessarily have condemned the country to a very gradual economic growth, with the party and state administration called on to sit back and let market forces dictate much of the direction and pace of development. Stalin, in contrast, called (in speeches full of martial metaphors) for a reversion to Civil War-style activism. The party and state organisations, having been originally built up during the Civil War, and still being led primarily by men whose most vivid and rewarding revolutionary experiences had been during that period of intense struggle, were well suited and naturally inclined towards exactly the activist stance proposed by Stalin in 1928–9 (Cohen, 1971, pp. 312–36). Mobilising urban-based party and worker teams to go out into the politically hostile country-side to seize grain from and reorganise the peasant communities was exactly the kind of activity that had led to victories for the same leaders and organisations in the recent heroic past. Not surprisingly, they were predisposed to turn to the old Civil War expedients in order to cope with still another crisis for the revolution.

But, of course, this time the task at hand was not winning a Civil War but propelling national industrial development. The Stalinist strategy, consonant though it was with Bolshevik revolutionary experiences and organisational capacities, could work at all only because the Soviets could build upon economic conditions continuing from the pre-revolutionary era. Stalin's successful programme of crash heavy industrialisation (see Nove, 1969), obviously bene-fited from being able to build on the substantial existing heavy-industrial base. Bukharin's strategy would have been more promising if Soviet Russia had inherited well-developed consumer industries or a rural sector sufficiently commercially oriented to provide strong demand for light industries. In addition, the Soviet agricultural sector *could* be squeezed as brutally and wastefully as Stalinist policies demanded only because that sector was (and traditionally had been) 'slack' relative to its potential capacity for per capita production, and because the 'scissors crisis' of the 1920s was essentially occasioned not by failure of agricultural production, but by the reluctance of the peasants, newly liberated from Tsarist and landlord exactions, to market their produce (Volin, 1970, ch. 9). Essentially Stalin's approach called for the Communists to replace old-regime mechanisms for squeezing agriculture with more direct bureaucratic controls by the Soviet state. Once this was done, heavy industriali-sation could continue in Russia, even though the human cost, especially to the peasantry, was terrible.

In China, once the Communists had restored the industries of Manchuria and the coastal centres to their pre-War levels, they began to come up against the limits of an economy very different from that which the Russians had to deal with from the 1920s (Magdoff, 1975; Perkins, 1975). For one thing, there was a well-developed heavy industrial base only in Manchuria. In other centres, overall industrial development was much less, and light industries and commercial enterprises were often more predominant. Even more decisive, the rural economy of China had problems and possibilities diametrically opposite to those of Russian agriculture. Chinese agriculture became, between 1400 and 1900, maximally productive within the limits of the traditional technology, social structure, and available land area, and the Chinese population expanded steadily from 1700, until it virtually saturated the expansive capacity of the agrarian sector (from roughly 1850 on) (Elvin, 1973; Ho, 1959; Perkins, 1969). Moreover, much of Chinese economic life remained, right through 1949, oriented to and dependent upon well-developed intra-regional- and intra-local-marketing-area networks of trade and preindustrial commodity production (Skinner, 1965). Thus the Chinese Communists faced a situation in which even the most brutal Stalin-style methods of appropriating agricultural surpluses and channelling them into heavy industry could not have worked as they did in post-1928 Russia, for the inherited industrial base on which the Chinese would have to build was far more restricted than that available to the Soviets, while the objective barriers to forcing sudden increases in agricultural production and marketing were much more formidable than they had been in Russia.

On the positive side, moreover, the Chinese Communists enjoyed some advantages that the Bolsheviks had lacked, for the economic and political orientations of the Chinese peasantry were far more suited to furthering peasant participation in national development efforts than had been those of the Russian peasantry after 1917. The Chinese peasantry was not strictly subsistence-oriented, nor was it unaccustomed to following extra-village leadership in projects to improve conditions for agricultural production. Even under the old regime, recall, Chinese peasants had been closely linked within market areas to gentry, merchants, and artisans. In addition, the Chinese Communists themselves had, during the Yenan period of the Chinese Civil War, acquired extensive experience and developed grassroots political organisations and techniques for directly mobilising peasants to take part in efforts to increase agricultural and small-scale industrial production (Schran, 1975; Selden, 1971). Such efforts, along with peasant mobilisation for military activities and anti-landlord struggles, had been necessary ingredients in the Maoist recipe for successful revolutionary guerilla warfare before 1949.

Immediately after 1949, the Yenan economic projects seemed to Chinese leaders somewhat irrelevant to the overriding task of promoting national economic development—although mass mobilisation continued to be relied on for completing land reform and accomplishing agricultural collectivisation during the 1950s. But once Soviet-styled industrialisation efforts began to run up against the limits imposed by the Chinese agricultural economy, some party leaders took inspiration from the Yenan projects and the collectivisation experiences. They began to formulate an approach to national development that would supplement continuing moderate industrial investments with local and regional party-led and mass-mobilising projects designed to increase agricutural productivity. They would meet peasant needs on the basis of small investments in labour-intensive enterprises and basic social services. A first trial for such an approach was badly botched during the Great Leap Forward of 1958-9. In consequence, there emerged, during the 1960s, a fierce struggle between 'Maoists' who wanted to push forward with rural-oriented and mass-mobilising development strategies (extending them to urban industries and higher educational institutions as well), and 'Liuists' who wanted to retrench toward a Soviet-style, bureaucratically administered development strategy, modified only slightly to spur agricultural growth through added capital investments and privileges for more efficient peasant producers. Only after intra-party struggles had culminated in the Maoist-encouraged mass uprisings (and temporary Peoples' Liberation Army take-over) of the 'Great Proletarian Cultural Revolution' of 1965-8, was the policy struggle decided primarily in favour of the Maoist line (Schram, 1973).

Significantly, nothing like the Cultural Revolution *could* have happened in Soviet Russia during the 1920s—for no Bolshevik leadership faction was willing so much as to contemplate appealing outside the party, even to resolve a policy issue believed to be of fundamental importance for the future of the nation (Cohen, 1971). The Bolsheviks' revolutionary experiences had understandably encouraged in them an overriding obsession with party discipline, for the crises of 1917–21 had presented the Bolsheviks primarily with tasks of consolidating the revolution through assserting and holding *control over* non-party forces—including not only anarchic peasants and reluctant (former old-regime) functionaries (Ellis, 1974), but even rebellious workers and soldiers (Avrich, 1970). In contrast, the revolutionary experiences of the Chinese Communists had taught them to encourage and rely upon non-party mass forces, and had therefore left at least some Chinese leaders open to the possibility of appealing to 'the people' to help resolve intra-party policy struggles.

Since the Cultural Revolution, the Maoist development strategy has apparently worked rather well, and had gained widespread support within a Chinese leadership that includes many rehabilitated 'Liuists' (for there has been nothing like the Stalinist Great Purge of the 1930s) (Schram, 1973, pp. 106–7). Nor should it seem surprising that this has happened, for the Maoist approach to Chinese development is not romantic or irrational. Just as the Stalinist strategy in Russia represented a practical way to bring to bear the political capacities of the Bolsheviks, as they had been forged in the Russian revolutionary struggles, on the economic situation inherited from the old regime and the revolution, so does the Maoist development strategy in China represent the logical way for the Chinese Communists to apply their accumulated revolutionary experiences and organisational capacities to propel the Chinese economy along a distinctive path to industrialisation. This path takes into account the fact that this economy has always been strongest and most vital in its agrarian regions and localities.

CONCLUSIONS

This essay began by posing the problem of how to explain differences between Soviet Russia and Communist China—differences that are particularly related to their contrasting patterns of state-guided economic development. In this final section I have suggested that the different strategies for economic development chosen through intra-leadership struggles in the Bolshevik party after 1921 and the Chinese Communist party after 1949 can be explained as responses to the different economic structural conditions existing in the post-revolutionary situations, responses that at the same time allowed each party-state to bring into active play the distinctive political capacities it had acquired during the revolutionary struggles for state power. Thus old-regime legacies have shaped the post-revolutionary divergences both directly and indirectly. For the economic conditions faced by the Soviets after 1921 and the Chinese Communists after 1949 were directly determined in their overall pattern by the developments that had, or had not, occurred under the Tsarist and Imperial systems. And the political capacities accumulated by the revolutionary parties were forged in the fires of struggles to consolidate state power—struggles shaped, in turn, by the contrasting structural patterns and modern industrial 'accomplishments' of the disintegrating old regimes. As Marx once said (to rearrange a bit): Even when men 'seem engaged·in revolutionising themselves, and things in creating something that has never existed . . . [m]en make their own history, but they do not make it under circumstances chosen by themselves, but under circumstances given and transmitted from the past' (1852, p. 97).

Does this then suggest that revolutions change nothing? Not at all. Never have societies experienced such sudden and thoroughgoing transformations—of political institutions, socio-economic structures, and legitimating formulas—as Russia and China through their twentieth-century social revolutions. The point is not that no fundamental changes occurred, but that those which did occur recapitulated certain structural patterns of the old regime—patterns which are more fundamental than the presence or absence of particular classes or particular state forms. Thus, just as Romanov Russia and Manchu China, despite very great overall resemblances, differed (a) in the ways that power was distributed within the dominant strata, (b) with respect to how peasant communities fit into the larger societal wholes, and (c) in the degrees and kinds of state-guided industrialisation, so, too, do Soviet Russia and Communist China differ in parallel ways despite their many similarities as Communist revolutionary regimes.

Yet this essay has attempted not only to establish the existence of such structural continuities between old and new regimes, but also to say something about *how* the continuities came about. Communist revolutionaries in Russia and China helped overthrow, or benefited from the overthrowing of traditional landed upper classes, capitalist bourgeoisies, and semi-bureaucratic monarchical states. But they did not do away with states or with economic surplus-controlling functions altogether. Instead they re-established state power and societal economic controls on new bases. In the struggles to do precisely these things, *the revolutionaries had to meet strength with strength and build future strengths on past accomplishments*. Either way, they ended up, to a significant extent, replacing the old dominant classes and elites, thus ensuring that the new regime would recapitulate certain underlying structural themes of the old.

Nevertheless, it made an important difference whether revolutionaries were prompted to forge the new regime primarily by building upon the strengths of the old—as in Russia—or mainly by combatting the strengths of the old in a prolonged struggle—as in China. In Russia, the crisis of the old regime presented revolutionaries with the opportunities and dilemmas of chaos, along with the temptations to rebuild quickly on inherited infrastructural foundations. In China, the crisis of the old regime offered both revolutionary opportunities and surviving obstacles to be overcome, and made the possibility for consolidating victory dependent on an unprecedented mobilisation of peasant participation into organised revolutionary efforts. In achieving revolutionary victory by countering old strengths with new ones, the Chinese Communists not only displaced and replaced the gentry and Imperial bureaucracy, but also consolidated a revolution with greater inherent dynamism—greater potential for generating further socio-political and cultural transformations beyond sheer industrialisation—than the Russian Revolution, which was consolidated by the Bolsheviks primarily through superimposing new political strengths upon inherited administrative and economic foundations. Thus old-regime patterns shape revolutionary futures most decisively by determining the forms of revolutionary crises and the tasks and opportunities for organised revolutionary forces.

Nor should this be an unwelcome truth. For, since old regimes vary in their structures, the implication is that all revolutions will not turn out the same, even if they are similarly caused and politically consolidated under like auspices. Even if, as in Russia, the 'tradition of all the dead generations weighs like a nightmare on the brain of the living', quite possibly other old-regime legacies will contribute to more helpful developments in other revolutionary societies.

REFERENCES

ANWEILER, O. (1958) *The Soviets*, Pantheon, 1974.
AVRICH, P. H. (1963) 'Russian factory committees in 1917', *Jahrbücher für Geschichte Osteuropas* 11 (June).
AVRICH, P. H. (1970) *Kronstadt 1921*, Norton, 1974.
BARNETT, A. D. (1967) *Cadres, Bureaucracy, and Political Power in Communist China*, Columbia University Press.
BASTID, M. (1973) 'Levels of economic decision-making', in Schram (1973), below.
BERNSTEIN, T. P. (1967) 'Leadership and mass mobilisation in the Soviet and Chinese collectivisation campaigns of 1929–30 and 1955–56: a comparison', *The China Quarterly* 31 (July–September).
BIANCO, L. (1968) 'Les paysans et la révolution Chine, 1919–1949', *Politique Etrangère*.
BLACK, C. E., ed. (1960) *The Transformation of Russian Society*, Harvard University Press.
BLUM, J. (1961) *Lord and Peasant in Russia: From the Ninth to the Nineteenth Century*, Princeton University Press.
BUCK, J. L. (1930) *Chinese Farm Economy*, University of Chicago Press.

CARR, E. H. (1971) *The October Revolution: Before and After*, Vintage Books,

CARSON, G. B., Jr. (1959) 'The state and economic development: Russia, 1890–1939', in H. G. J. Aitken, ed. *The State and Economic Growth.* Social Science Research Council.

CAVENDISH, P. (1969) 'The "New China" of the Kuomintang', in J. Gray, ed. *Modern China's Search for a Political Form*, Oxford University Press.

CHAMBERLIN, W. H. (1935) *The Russian Revolution, 1917–1921* (2 vols.), Grosset & Dunlap, 1965.

CHANG, C. (1955) *The Chinese Gentry: Studies on their Role in Nineteenth Century Chinese Society,* University of Washington Press.

CHANG, C. (1962) *The Income of the Chinese Gentry*, University of Washington Press.

CHESNEAUX, J. (1962) *The Chinese Labor Movement, 1919–1927*, Stanford University Press, 1968.

CH'Ü, T'-UNG-TSU (1962) *Local Government in China Under the Ch'ing*, Harvard University Press.

CLIFF, T. (1955) *State Capitalism in Russia*, Pluto Press, 1974.

COHEN, S. F. (1971) *Bukharin and the Bolshevik Revolution*, Knopf.

CROWLEY, J. B., ed. (1970) *Modern East Asia: Essays in Interpretation*, Harcourt, Brace and World.

EISENSTADT, S. N. and YAEL AZMON, eds. (1975) *Socialism and Tradition*, Humanities Press.

ELLIS, J. (1974) 'The Russian Civil War 1917–1920', in *Armies in Revolution,* Oxford University Press.

ELVIN, M. (1973) *The Pattern of the Chinese Past,* Stanford University Press.

ERLICH, A. (1960) *The Soviet Industrialization Debate, 1924–1928*, Harvard University Press.

ESPER, T. (1969) 'Military self-sufficiency and weapons technology in Muscovite Russia', *Slavic Review* 28 (June).

FAIRBANK, J. K., REISCHAUER, E. O. and CRAIG, A. M. (1973) *East Asia. Tradition and Transformation*, Houghton Mifflin.

FEI, HSIAO-TUNG (1946) 'Peasantry and gentry: an interpretation of Chinese social structure and its changes', *American Journal of Sociology 52*, July.

FELDMESSER, R A (1960) 'Social classes and political structure', in Black 1960), above.

FERRO, M (1971) 'The Russian Soldier in 1917: Undisciplined, Patriotic, and Revolutionary', *Slavic Review, 30*, September.

FEUERWERKER, A (1968) *The Chinese Economy, 1912–1949*, Center for Chinese Studies, University of Michigan.

FEUERWERKER, A (1969) *The Chinese Economy, ca 1870–1911*, Center for Chinese Studies, University of Michigan.

FRANKE, W (1967) *China and the West: The Cultural Encounter, 13th to 20th Centuries,* Harper & Row.

FREEDMAN, M. (1958) *Lineage Organization in Southeastern China*, Athlone Press.

FRIED, M. H. (1953) *Fabric of Chinese Society*, Praeger.

GARDER, M. (1959) *A History of the Soviet Army*, Praeger, 1966.

GERSCHENKRON, A. (1960) 'Problems and patterns of Russian economic development', in Black (1960), above.

GILLIN, D. G. (1967) *Warlord: Yen Hsi-shan in Shansi Province, 1911–1949*, Princeton University Press.

GOLDSMITH, R. W. (1961) 'The economic growth of Tsarist Russia, 1860–1913', *Economic Development and Cultural Change, 9*, April.

GOLOVINE, N. N. (1931) *The Russian Army in the World War*, Yale University Press.

GRANICK, D. (1960) *The Red Executive*, Doubleday.

GRAY, J. (1969) 'The economics of Maoism', *Bulletin of the Atomic Scientists, 25*, February.

GRAY, J. (1973) 'The two roads: alternative strategies of social change and economic growth in China', in Schram (1973), below.

GRONSKY, P. P. and ASTROV, N. J. (1929) *The War and the Russian Government*, Yale University Press.

GURLEY, J. (1971) 'Capitalist and Maoist economic development', in E. Friedman and M. Selden, eds., *America's Asia*, Vintage Books.

HELLIE, R. (1971) *Enserfment and Military Change in Muscovy*, University of Chicago Press.

HINTON, W. (1966) *Fanshen: A Documentary of Revolution in a Chinese Village*, Vintage Books.

HO, PING-TI (1959) *Studies on the Population of China, 1368–1953*, Harvard University Press.

HO, PING-TI and TSOU, TANG, eds. (1968) *China in Crisis*, Vol. 1, Book 1, University of Chicago Press.

ICHIKO, C. (1968) 'The role of the gentry: an hypothesis', in Wright (1968), below.

INKELES, A. (1968) *Social Change in Soviet Russia*, Harvard University Press.

KARCZ, J. (1971) 'From Stalin to Brezhnev: Soviet agricultural policy in historical perspective', in J. R. Millar, ed., *The Soviet Rural Community*, University of Illinois Press.

KAU, YING-MAO (1974) 'Urban and rural strategies in the Chinese Communist Revolution', in Lewis (1974), below.

KENNAN, G. F. (1969) 'The breakdown of the Tsarist autocracy', in R. Pipes, ed., *Revolutionary Russia*, Doubleday Anchor.

KUHN, P. (1968) 'Comments', in Ho and Tsou (1968), above.

KUHN, P. (1970) *Rebellion and Its Enemies in Late Imperial China*, Harvard University Press.

LEWIN, M. (1966) *Russian Peasants and Soviet Power: A Study of Collectivization*, Northwestern University Press, 1968.

LEWIS, J. W. (1963) *Leadership in Communist China*, Cornell University Press.

LEWIS, J. W., ed. (1974) *Peasant Rebellion and Communist Revolution in Asia*, Stanford University Press.

MAGDOFF, H. (1975) 'China: contrasts with the U.S.S.R.', *Monthly Review, 27*, July–August.

MALE, D. J. (1971) *Russian Peasant Organisation Before Collectivisation*, Cambridge University Press.

MARX, K. (1852) 'The eighteenth brumaire of Louis Bonaparte', in *Karl Marx and Frederick Engels: Selected Works*, International Publishers.

MATOSSIAN, M. (1968) 'The peasant way of life', in Vucinich (1968), below.

MATTHEWS, M. (1972) *Class and Society in Soviet Russia*, Walker.

MEISNER, M. (1970) 'Yenan communism and the rise of the Chinese People's Republic', in Crowley (1970), above.

MEISNER, M. (1974) 'Utopian socialist themes in Maoism', in Lewis (1974), above.

MICHAEL, F. (1955) 'State and society in nineteenth century China', *World Politics, 7,* April.

MOORE, B., Jr. (1950) *Soviet Politics—The Dilemma of Power,* Harper and Row, 1965.

MOORE, B. (1966) *Social Origins of Dictatorship and Democracy,* Beacon Press.

MURAMATSU, Y. (1966) 'A documentary study of Chinese landlordism in late Ch'ing and early Republican Kiangnan', *Bulletin of the School of Oriental and African Studies, 29.*

MURPHEY, R. (1974) 'The treaty ports and China's modernization', in M. Elvin and G. W. Skinner, eds., *The Chinese City Between Two Worlds,* Stanford University Press.

MYERS, R. H. (1975) 'Cooperation in traditional agriculture and its implications for team farming in the People's Republic of China', in Perkins (1975), below.

NORTH, R. C. and POOL, I. DE SOLA (1966) 'Kuomintang and Chinese Communist Elites', in H. D. Lasswell and D. Lerner, eds., *World Revolutionary Elites,* M.I.T. Press.

NOVE, A. (1969) *An Economic History of the U.S.S.R.,* Penguin Books.

PAAUW, D. S. (1957) 'The Kuomintang and economic stagnation, 1928–1937', *Journal of Asian Studies, 16,* February.

PERKINS, D. H. (1969) *Agricultural Development in China, 1368–1968,* Aldine.

PERKINS, D. H. (1975) 'Growth and changing structure of China's twentieth-century economy" in Perkins, ed., *China's Modern Economy in Historical Perspective,* Stanford University Press.

PETHYBRIDGE, R. (1972) *The Spread of the Russian Revolution: Essays on 1917,* Macmillan.

PIPES, R. (1974) *Russia Under the Old Regime,* Scribner's.

RABINOWITCH, A. (1972) 'The Petrograd garrison and the Bolshevik seizure of power', in A. and J. Rabinowitch, eds., *Revolution and Politics in Russia,* University of Indiana Press.

RADKEY, O. H. (1958) *The Agrarian Foes of Bolshevism: Promise and Default of the Russian Socialist Revolutionaries, February to October 1917,* Columbia University Press.

RADKEY, O. H. (1963) *The Sickle Under the Hammer: The Russian Socialist Revolutionaries in the Early Months of Soviet Rule,* Oxford University Press.

RAEFF, M. (1966) *Origins of the Russian Intelligentsia: The Eighteenth-Century Nobility,* Harcourt, Brace & World.

RAEFF, M. (1971) *Imperial Russia 1682–1825,* Knopf.

RISKIN, C. (1971) 'Small industry and the Chinese model of development', *The China Quarterly, 46,* April–June.

RISKIN, C. (1974) 'Incentive systems and work motivations: the experience of China', *Working Papers for a New Society, 1,* Winter.

ROBINSON, G. T. (1932) *Rural Russia Under the Old Regime,* University of California Press, 1969.

ROZMAN, G. (1976) *Urban Networks in Russia, 1750–1800, and Premodern Periodization,* Princeton University Press.

SCHAPIRO, L. (1967) *The Government and Politics of the Soviet Union,* rev. edn., Vintage Books.

SCHRAM, S. R. (1973) *Authority, Participation, and Cultural Change in China,* Cambridge University Press.

SCHRAN, P. (1975) 'On the Yenan origins of current economic policies', in Perkins (1975), above.

SCHURMANN, F. (1966) 'Organisational principles of the Chinese Communists', in R. MacFarquhar, ed., *China Under Mao: Politics Takes Command,* The M.I.T. Press.

SCHURMANN, F. (1967) 'Politics and economics in Russia and China', in Treadgold (1967), below.

SCHURMANN, F. (1968) *Ideology and Organization in Communist China,* 2nd edn., University of California Press.

SELDEN, M. (1969) 'The Yenan legacy: the mass line', in A. D. Barnett, ed., *Chinese Communist Politics in Action,* University of Washington Press.

SELDEN, M. (1971) *The Yenan Way in Revolutionary China,* Harvard University Press.

SETON-WATSON, H. (1967) *The Russian Empire, 1801-1917,* Oxford University Press.

SHANIN, T. (1972) *The Awkward Class: Political Sociology of Peasantry in a Developing Society: Russia 1910-1925,* Oxford University Press.

SIGURDSON, J. (1973) 'Rural industry and the internal transfer of technology', in Schram (1973), above.

SKINNER, G. W. (1964) 'Marketing and social structure in rural China (Part I)', *Journal of Asian Studies, 24,* November.

SKINNER, G. W. (1965) 'Marketing and social structure in rural China (Part II)', *Journal of Asian Studies, 24,* February.

SKINNER, G. W. (1971) 'Chinese peasants and the closed community: an open and shut case', *Comparative Studies in Society and History, 13,* July.

SKOCPOL, T. (1976) 'France, Russia, China: a structural analysis of social revolutions', *Comparative Studies in Society and History, 18,* April.

TAWNEY, R. H. (1932) *Land and Labour in China,* Beacon, 1966.

TIEN, HUNG-MAO (1972) *Government and Politics in Kuomintang China, 1927-1937,* Stanford University Press.

TREADGOLD, D. W., ed. (1967) *Soviet and Chinese Communism: Differences and Similarities,* University of Washington Press.

ULDRICKS, T. J. (1974) 'The "crowd" in the Russian revolution: towards reassessing the nature of revolutionary leadership', *Politics and Society, 4.*

VOLIN, L. (1970) *A Century of Russian Agriculture,* Harvard University Press.

VON LAUE, T. H. (1963) *Sergei Witte and the Industrialization of Russia,* Atheneum, 1974.

VUCINICH, A. (1960) 'The state and the local community', in Black (1960), above.

VUCINICH, W. S., ed. (1968) *The Peasant in Nineteenth-Century Russia,* Stanford University Press.

WAKEMAN, F. (1970) 'High Ch'ing: 1683-1839', in Crowley (1970), above.

WANG, YEH-CHIEN (1973) *Land Taxation in Imperial China, 1750-1911,* Harvard University Press.

WATTERS, F. M. (1968) 'The peasant and the village commune', in Vucinich (1968), above.

WILBUR, M. C. (1968) 'Military separatism and the process of reunification under the nationalist regime, 1922–1937', in Ho and Tsou (1968), above.

WILBUR, M. C. (1970) 'The influence of the past: how the early years helped to shape the future of the Chinese Communist Party', in J. W. Lewis, ed., *Party Leadership and Revolutionary Power in China,* Cambridge University Press.

WOLF, E. R. (1969) *Peasant Wars of the Twentieth Century,* Harper & Row.

WRIGHT, M. C. (1968) *China in Revolution: The First Phase, 1900–1911,* Yale University Press.

YEH, C. K. (1967) 'Soviet and Communist Chinese industrialization strategies', in Treadgold (1967), above.

YOUNG, E. P. (1970) 'Nationalism, reform, and republican revolution: China in the early twentieth century', in Crowley (1970), above.

SECTION 3

Some problems

The problems with which Section 3 is concerned are, in the main, not technical. They are not to do with the practical difficulties of digging out facts or of organising surveys. They are concerned with why such things should be done at all. In Sartori's words, we shall be examining problems of methodology and doing some thinking about thinking. One of the first things to think about is the business of comparison itself. It is rare for a political scientist to attempt comparison of countries or their political systems as such. Normally he will compare certain kinds of political behaviour or particular segments of political life in their different contexts. But here we are faced with one of the central problems in comparative politics. What often seems to be 'the same thing' (for example, the cohesion of a political party in the excerpt from Holt and Turner) has an unfortunate habit of becoming something significantly different once we study and attempt to compare it. Instead of comparing Cheddar and Camembert as kinds of cheese we find ourselves trying to do something like comparing Cheddar cheese and blue chalk. But unlike the comparer of cheeses, the practitioner of comparative politics cannot eat his mistakes (however palatable or unpalatable). He is more likely to get them published in a learned book or journal. Holt and Turner thus criticise the grounds on which political parties in Britain and North America are compared in one recent work. This central problem recurs in other readings in Section 3.

The next problems stem from the part played by bias and subjectivity in political inquiry. Bias, the selective perception of political reality, is, contends Jenkins, built into the structure of the political world. The problem for the comparative political analyst is how to overcome this everyday bias in his own work. But does this imply a total rejection of all that is subjective? Not so, says Hacker, for whom objectivity is 'not only fiction but a harmful one'. Partly this argument rests on the case that we cannot anyway hope to be fully objective. This case Hacker buttresses by showing how even the most scientific-looking examples of political science involve subjective judgments. But subjectivity has, too, a positive value. What political science needs is individuals who are not afraid to hold their own opinions and who are sufficiently industrious and talented to produce works of scholarship that are capable of persuading others to their view. This is surely an unexceptionable plea. But is it sufficient to solve the problems of political science?

The other readings of Section 3 relate to problems of concept formation and the scientific value-neutrality of comparative politics. In Sartori's view the problem is less the absence of academic initiative and originality than the lack of a sufficiently precise language by the aid of which works of originality can be conceived and conveyed to fellow workers in the field. The demands that have been made of contemporary comparative political science have been largely ducked by its practitioners. Instead of confronting its problems directly and with a sense of logic, the concepts of comparative politics—the units used to construct theoretical systems, which are used also to make sense of the political world and with the aid of which data are collected—have been 'stretched' to the extent that they often now have no precise meaning. Sartori, too, is concerned to point out that the resort to measurement and the language of quantification is not sufficient to satisfy the ambitions of a number of political scientists to be more 'scientific'. Methods borrowed from the natural sciences are, it seems, unlikely to provide solutions to the specific problems of political science. Sartori sees more hope in the application of carefully worked out concepts within the comparative method rather than in a greater reliance on such methods as the statistical.

Macintyre is also interested in the scientific status of political science.

He makes a critical examination of the rigour with which the comparative method has been used in political science and finds it wanting. But there are other problems to be faced in deciding whether the study of politics can be considered to be a science. They involve the kind of generalisations political science is capable of producing. These generalisations are likely to be very different from those of other sciences for a number of reasons. But, from the point of view of establishing key problems in the practice of comparative politics, it is worth noting that Macintyre, too, concludes with an emphasis on the role of values and of subjectivity both in the world of practical politics and in that of its academic study.

In reading Section 3 it should be borne in mind that not only is the practice of comparative politics coloured by the personality and views of its practitioner, but so also is the view of his work taken by those who attempt to evaluate it.

14

R. *Holt and*   Non-comparable data
J. *Turner*

Excerpt from 'The methodology of comparative research', in R. T. Holt and J. E. Turner, eds., *The Methodology of Comparative Research*, Free Press, ch. 1, pp. 16–18.

The hazards can be subtle but serious when one is using indices that require cross-cultural validity. To illustrate one of these hazards, let us examine briefly Professor Samuel Beer's discussion of 'party cohesion' in his excellent, perceptive study of the British political system. He looks at this phenomenon at several places throughout the book, and he seems to reach the following conclusion (Beer, 1965, p. 350):

> ...these mass parties had managed in a remarkable degree to 'speak with one voice'. To an Attlee harassed by Bevanite rebels on the backbenches, in the constituencies, and among the unions, or to a Macmillan assaulted by Suez rebels under the leadership of a Cecil, this assertion may seem painfully laughable. It is when we look at the situation in the light of what once prevailed—or what prevails in other parties such as those of the United States—that we properly appreciate the degree of cohesion achieved. The rise of party unity in parliamentary divisions is the most striking exhibit. From the mid-nineteenth century, when it had fallen to American levels, party cohesion in Britain had steadily risen until in recent decades *it was so close to 100 per cent that there was no longer any point in measuring it.*

Note at the outset that, even without the reference to 'American levels', this statement loses some of its thrust unless it is viewed comparatively. But how we view it comparatively depends largely on the way in which the variable 'party cohesion' has been measured. Professor Beer measures it by examining the frequency of votes against the party leadership. In seeking to illustrate the unity of the Parliamentary Labour Party in quantitative terms, he drew a sample of division lists (about which we shall have something to say shortly) during the first parliamentary session of the Attlee régime, 1945–6. From this sample, he detected only one division in which members of the Labour Party voted against the Government, and on that vote only four MPs from the majority party walked into the opposition lobby. This is certainly close to 100 per cent cohesion when compared with the frequency of votes against the party leadership in the American Congress. Or is it? To answer this question we need to look at the setting in which votes against party leaders occur in the House of Commons and in the American Congress to see whether the index is a cross-culturally valid one.

Three points should be made about votes against party leadership as an index of party cohesion in the British system:

1. The sanctions that the party leaders can impose upon those who jump the whip are extremely severe, and are certainly of a different order of magnitude from those that operate in the American Congress. For this reason, negative votes against the leadership constitute a far more serious act.

2. In addition to the normal sanctions that support the maintenance of party discipline, a special sanction can be employed against members of the Ministry who vote against their government; they will almost automatically lose their jobs, an outcome that very few of them are willing to risk. Since about 25 per cent of the MPs in the government party (including the whips) are in this category, the government is, in effect, guaranteed a large bloc of votes on any issue. To include these people in the analysis tends to distort the index; some measure of the voting patterns of just the backbenchers, who have a wider range of options, would probably be a more sensitive indicator of party cohesion.

3. An index that takes account only of those who actually vote against the government necessarily treats abstainers as government supporters for the purpose of measuring party cohesion. Because negative votes against the government may have serious consequences for an individual MP, some dissidents express their disagreements with the leadership by wilfully abstaining. In the House of Commons, a three-line whip issued by a party usually requires that its members be in the division lobbies except under out-of-the-ordinary circumstances. This means that many abstentions are likely to be wilful, and it would be more appropriate to treat them as indicators of diminished cohesion.

To see how abstentions might be taken into consideration, let us examine the situation at the time of the vote on the Bretton Woods Agreement—the one division in the 1945-6 parliament in which Professor Beer noted four votes against the Attlee Government. This vote was taken on the evening of 13 December 1945. Just a few minutes before this vote, the House was divided on the issue of the American Loan. On this division, which was conducted under a three-line whip, twenty-three Labour backbenchers voted against the Government, and at least three others were known to have wilfully abstained. Then, within a matter of minutes, the Labour backbenchers, again under three-line discipline, were called on to support the Bretton Woods Agreement, which was closely related to the issue of the American Loan. On this vote only four backbenchers marched into the opposition lobby. But these four rebels did not represent all of the dissidence by any means. Twenty-three Labour MPs who were in the lobbies to vote in favour of the American Loan (some of them reluctantly) did *not* record their votes on Bretton Woods a few moments later. In addition, eighteen rebels who were in the House to register their opposition to the American Loan did *not* vote on the Bretton Woods measure. It is highly probable that these forty-one people wilfully abstained on this second vote, which was on an unpopular measure. The patterns of *backbencher* voting of the two issues were as follows:

	American loan	Bretton Woods
Number of backbenchers*	311	311
Yes votes	(258) 83·0%	(238) 76·5%
No votes	(23) 7·4%	(4) 1·3%
Probable and known abstainers	(3) 1·0%	(42) 13·5%
Unknown	(27) 8·7%	(27) 8·7%

* Five backbenchers were known to have been sick or abroad and hence unable to participate in the voting.

These are not included among the number of backbenchers in this listing. Some commentators have indicated that approximately 44 backbenchers abstained on the American Loan. This, however, is hardly a plausible figure. The total number of backbenchers voting 'yes' and 'no' was 281, leaving only a total of 36 remaining backbench members—a number that includes those who were sick or abroad.

The importance of these points becomes even clearer if we look briefly at the meanings that are attached to voting against the leadership in the American Congress. In the undisciplined Congressional party, the individual legislator is relatively freer to vote against his leaders. His opposing votes may be prompted by one or more of several factors: ideological outlook, personal frustration, antagonism toward the political style of the leadership, constituency interests, and national pressure groups to which he is vulnerable. On a given issue, he may have told his party chieftains that he is willing to vote 'Yes' if it will 'make a difference', and then vote 'No' with the acquiescence of the party leaders because his support was not needed or because the cause was already lost.[1] In this freewheeling system, negative votes may be used as measures of ideological position, personal loyalties, blocs influencing each other, and the impact of national pressure groups and/or constituency pressures. With relatively few sanctions at the disposal of the party leaders to keep their members in line, the researcher has a rich data base when he uses negative votes as an indication of any or several of these factors.

The British MP, by contrast, is much more constrained by party discipline, and a vote against his leaders is a much more serious matter and is more likely to be used upon fundamental differences with his party leaders. For him, constituency interests are less influential in his voting decisions, and pressure groups are less operative upon him as an individual.

It is apparent, then, that votes against the leadership mean quite different things in the British and American legislative chambers. For this reason they cannot be used as an index of the same thing. Professor Beer's analysis may indicate that there is more party discipline in Britain than in the United States. But whether, on the face of it, it indicates greater party cohesion is another matter.

---

[1] Obviously, an abstention on important votes has different nuances in Congress, when contrasted with the House of Commons. Congressmen may refuse to record their votes because of conflict between their personal views and those of their constituents, and occasionally they may abstain so that the other side can win—a concession that will enable them to get something they want on another issue. But most abstainers in Congressional voting are simply absent from the House or Senate when the roll-calls are taken.

REFERENCE

BEER, S. (1965) *British Politics in the Collectivist Age*, Knopf.

15

R. *Jenkins*   Biased data

Excerpt from 'National profiles', in *Exploitation*, Paladin, 1971, ch. 2, pp. 63–7.

There is a complex relationship between objective social structures and man's subjective perception of those structures. In the short term it is the subjective image that determines decisions and choices though the consequences of these actions are determined in the long run by the objective structure. When the subjective image is derived from practical experience it is closely related to the objective structure; when the subjective image is the result of propaganda or conjecture, it frequently departs from the objective structure and results in actions with consequences opposite to the intentions behind the actions.[1]

It is inherent in the structure of the international system that beliefs held by the population of one nation about the intentions of another nation be more a matter of subjective conjecture than objective fact. Social truths have a tendency to become relativised and nationalised. In addition, some beliefs are self-fulfilling or self-negating while the physical power behind the beliefs of some national élites is so great that the élite is able to change the world to fit the subjective belief. This is known as hyperstatisation: the United States State Department acts in such a way that its subjective theories of world politics (like the zero-sum theory where the USSR gains what the USA loses and vice versa) become objective theories. That is, United States foreign policy is handled in such a way that its relations with other states *become* zero-sum.

[1] For a phenomenological approach to this problem, see Berger and Luckman (1966). For a Marxist view, see Jenkins (1969).

In the relations between states there is a greater potential, because of the physical power behind rich states, for subjective theories to become objective facts than in any other area of human behaviour. The USA has the military hardware necessary to make the world fit the subjective theory of the world structure that the United States élite believes in. For this reason, subjective images are of immense importance to international relations.

There are several factors working towards the nationalisation of reality; some, like propaganda and censorship, are obvious, and others, like the structural factors influencing the flow of news, are perhaps even more important. In the end it becomes difficult, if not impossible, to distinguish between the deliberate nationalisation of reality and the unconscious factors that also work in this direction: censorship and propaganda are often unconscious processes simply because human beings (including news editors) tend to notice items of information that support their own particular (national) concept of reality and ignore items that contradict this reality. Selective perception of other nations emphasises the image that has already been constructed of these other nations. At the best of times, the process by which news is gathered and sent leaves the news itself open to many different interpretations and even plain falsifications. Thus the western image of China as aggressive leads to the assumption that border trouble between India and China is provoked by China (when in fact, Indian troops invaded Chinese territory first). Because our own nationalised image of the world divides it into friendly and hostile nations we have a ready-made structure for interpreting events and those events which do not fit the structure tend to be ignored. Because of this ready-made structure, we are rarely confronted with contradictory news stories —we know who to believe and who not to believe. However, the world of nations is not made into a perfect nationalised reality without internal contradictions. To use the old Arab proverb, it is *not* true of states that

> the friend of my friend is my friend
> and the friend of my enemy is my enemy.

Because our nationalised image of the world is not completely polarised into a group of friendly states that are all friendly with each other, and a group of hostile states which are also all friendly with each other, contradictions and conflicting interpretations arise. These contradictions arise most clearly when two states like Pakistan and India, which Britain regards as both friendly, go to war. British correspondents in India and Pakistan then mail home reports in which the reality is so nationalised that their stories are not simply contradictory but mirror images of one another.

However, it is not necessary to cite the contradictory reports from two sides of a war in order to illustrate the distortions that structure foreign news. Even the mass circulation papers in rich nations have only a few correspondents abroad. The London *Times* has correspondents in Washington, New York, Moscow, three or four assigned to the other European capitals, one to Latin America, one to Africa, one to Asia and one to South-East Asia.

This list alone indicates something about the image of the world that *The Times* has. Only since 1967 has there been a correspondent in Latin America. Previously, *The Times* was entirely dependent on the big press agencies and, in special cases, on the correspondents of USA newspapers. The five big press agencies (AFP, AP, Reuter, TASS, and UPI) all belong to rich nations: France, Britain, the USSR and the USA. Furthermore, the smaller a nation the more dependent is its press on the five big agencies. Now the first function of each of these agencies is to select news that is of relevance to their own nation. Thus, the image of the world that TASS sends back to Moscow is very different from the image that UPI sends back to New York. Although the flow of news is controlled by four rich nations, there is, of course, nothing to stop a paper in Sweden from taking reports from all five agencies and deriving an independent image by 'reading between the lines' and taking into account the nationality of the news agency. This is in fact done: Scandinavian papers frequently quote all five agencies in their foreign news reports.[2] The same is true of any other rich nation that does not have correspondents abroad—they can produce a 'mix' of images from the USA through Britain and France to the USSR. The same is not true of poor nations. Take the flow of news from Argentina to Mexico; it goes through UPI via New York. Consequently, all Mexico's information about Argentina is filtered through the USA image and vice versa. There is only a flow of news between Mexico and Argentina to the extent that the news is of interest to the United States. Another example indicates the way in which news and images are controlled by the rich nations. Take Cuba and Venezuela; TASS is the only credited agency in Cuba and UPI the only credited agency in Venezuela. Cuba does not trust UPI as a source of information because it is owned by the United States and Venezuela does not trust TASS because it is run by the USSR. In the event, the information that Venezuela receives from Cuba comes via Cuban exiles

[2] Though in Sweden at least, United States agencies account for around 60 per cent of foreign news and TASS for only 3 per cent.

and Cuba depends on guerrillas in Venezuela for its news stories. In the end, these are the main sources of news that get printed in Cuba and Venezuela.

These are some of the international factors that limit the free flow of news and nationalise reality. Reality is relative within nations too. If the Venezuelan correspondent of the *New York Times* has personal contact with President Betancourt then he will not have any contact with the Communists or the Nationalist guerrillas. As one correspondent put it: 'Today I can pick up the phone and get right through to Frondizi, Prado, Betancourt or almost any other Latin American President. If I write the truth, I'll never even get to their barbers. Back home, that means I'm not doing so good! Besides, my paper wouldn't print it anyway' (Gerassi, 1966, p. 45).

There is, then, no such thing as objective news. Right from the start there is a choice of perspective and an imposed filter that goes with it. If the foreign correspondent wants to report what the President of a nation is doing and thinking then he has to play the President's game—which means that he cannot contact those who are trying to overthrow him. But it means more than this, it means that the foreign correspondent ends up seeing the nation he is in through the eyes of its President—not exactly the best way of finding out what is going on.

Besides these inevitable distortions that occur on the spot, the correspondent carries in his head an image of what his readers want to hear, what is relevant to them. This image biases the reporting of events and the choice of events; it also biases the sub-editing that goes on in the offices of the paper back home. At its most trivial, this bias leads to headlines like this: 'No Britons on Crashed Plane'. The short article below it mentions briefly that the aircraft hit a moutain and all 137 people aboard were killed. Had there been Britons on the plane, the enormity of the disaster would have been padded out to several columns, giving names and addresses of the dead, etc., etc.

It is not so trivial when events in Argentina or South Africa are only reported if they affect British financial interests and, needless to say, it is not simply the *Financial Times* that takes British business interests as the yardstick of relevance in the selection of news.

There are facts and there is news; generally the facts are not printed, just the news. 'It is news, for example, that a United States oil company, given the right to exploit 1,000,000 Argentine acres, is investing $200 million. It is fact that the money is deposited in New York and is taken out as a loan on local currency in Argentina, resulting in no benefit to the local economy' (Gerassi, 1966, p. 42).

Yet this difference between news and facts is not necessarily part of a conscious conspiracy. To the people of Latin America, AP and UPI are United States agencies and the whole process becomes a vicious circle. People only tell UPI and AP what they think the State Department in Washington wants to know. In turn, UPI and AP only ask questions that they think Americans will be interested in—and that usually means questions about Latin-American élites, and so on. No doubt the same is true of TASS in Cuba, or Reuters in Tanzania. In the end, the only news that reaches the rich nations from the poor nations is news about the interests of rich nations. Because poor nations find out about each other through the news agencies of the rich nations, the only information that flows between them is that which is also of interest to rich nations.

This is the case with a 'free' press. However, no press is free to print what it likes; in the west the press prints what is compatible with its advertising revenue and, to a lesser extent, what is compatible with the State. In the east, the State alone decides what news is compatible with its own interests.

REFERENCES

BERGER, P. and LUCKMAN, T. (1966) *The Social Construction of Reality*, Doubleday.

GERASSI, J. (1966) *The Great Fear in Latin America*, Collier-Macmillan.

JENKINS, R. (1969) 'Some notes on the social functions of conflict theory', in *Studies in Progress*, no. 1, Institute for Peace and Conflict Research, Copenhagen.

16

A. *Hacker*   Inescapable subjective
                              judgments

Excerpts from 'The utility of quantitative methods in political science', in
J. C. Charlesworth, ed., *Contemporary Political Analysis*, Collier-Macmillan,
1967, pp. 134–9.

Several years ago there appeared an article entitled 'Measurement
concepts in the theory of influence'.[1] The author's intention was to
construct a mathematical model capable of measuring the relative influence of two actors in a political setting. Terms were defined and
delimited with care and precision: in place of ambiguous prose,
rigorous symbols were used throughout. The basic model was a four-
cell table (Fig. 16.1), but, as the article proceeded, it was shown
that many variations could be played on the fundamental theme.

		R_1	
		B_1	B_2
R_2	B_1	O_{11}	O_{12}
	B_2	O_{21}	O_{22}

Figure 16.1

[1] March (1957, pp. 202–26). This article and the ones to be cited subsequently are simply used as illustrations and are not intended to be a
systematic review of the literature. For such a review, see Fagen (1961, pp.
888–900). This bibliographical essay cites 18 books and 66 articles and papers
by 64 authors.

Quite clearly, the author felt that only if such techniques of analysis were used would discourse on a subject like political influence become meaningful.

THE PRESIDENT AND THE SPEAKER

Those who are preoccupied with model-building are usually quick to acknowledge that formalised constructs must ultimately be put to an operational test. In other words, the empty boxes must sooner or later be filled with empirical contents. Therefore, readers were told that the influence model could easily be applied to a real and important aspect of political life. It could measure 'the influence relationship between the President of the United States and the Speaker of the House of Representatives, with respect to outcomes defined in terms of a bill passing the House' (March 1957, p. 217). This is an excellent example, one allowing full scope for comparing the legislative influence of two key individuals. Thoughts come to mind of such Speakers as Henry Clay, 'Uncle Joe' Cannon, and Sam Rayburn—congressional titans prepared to do battle with successive occupants of the White House. The reader's appetite was further whetted as the author proceeded to fill in his original matrix. For he was not unwilling to provide numerical indices signifying the outcomes when the President and the Speaker alternatively announce that they support or oppose a particular piece of legislation (Fig. 16.2).

		President	
		For	*Against*
Speaker	For	0·9	0·4
	Against	0·6	0·1

Figure 16.2

Which President, which Speaker, and what bill are involved here? The answer, one learns, is none at all. This is, we are told, a 'hypothetical matrix'. It is not a description of anything that has ever happened in real political life. The numerical indices—0·9, 0·4, 0·6, 0·1 —do look as precise as one might hope for. But they are a Potemkin's Village covering the fact that the framework has yet to be used to study legislative influence.

The author, however, persists in his desire to be helpful. He is willing to tell us just what kind of data are needed if the boxes are to be filled properly (March 1957, p. 223). We have to know:

1. The political party of the President.
2. The political party of the Speaker.
3. The substantive area of the bill considered.
4. The President's position on the bill.
5. The Speaker's position on the bill.
6. The outcome of the bill in the House.

The comment that follows is, beyond a doubt, the most illuminating of all: 'There is no need to go into the details of securing information on these values. The techniques are the standard ones of historical and field research.' 'No need'? There may be no need to tell us how to obtain these six straightforward facts. We all know where to find the *New York Times* and the *Congressional Quarterly*. And it is not impossible to corner the Speaker and find out his position on a bill. But what we do need to be told is how these pieces of information are to be transformed into numerical 'values'. Here the need for enlightenment is overpowering.

The year is 1947. The President is a Democrat. The Speaker is a Republican. The bill, sponsored by Robert A. Taft and Fred Hartley, is in the area of labour relations. The President has announced that he opposes passage of the bill. The Speaker has said he favours passage. The Taft-Hartley bill passes the House by a large majority. There is the information in a nutshell. But it defies comprehension to see how these data can be translated into 'values' such as 0·9, 0·4, 0·6, and 0·1 so as to fit the cells of the matrix. What, it may be asked, are the 'standard' techniques of 'historical and field research' that will permit us to quantify the comparative influences of Harry Truman and Joe Martin over the fortunes of the Taft-Hartley bill? The author does not go into this question at all. 'There is no need to', he has said. The suspicion arises that those who build models have little knowledge of or interest in empirical research. Perhaps they feel that their mathematical contributions are the truly creative work, that the drudgery of fact-grubbing can be relegated to lesser scribes.

SENATORIAL POWER

Yet such an accusation may be unwarranted, or at least premature. An attempt to link model-building and empirical research is to be found in a study entitled 'The concept of power'.[2] The article opens with a straightforward attempt to define power and to express that definition symbolically. Power is viewed as a relationship between individuals, not as a substance or a property that a person may happen to have. The strength or weakness of a power relation can, for example, be stated in terms of relative probabilities (Dahl, 1957, p. 204).

> The probability that the Senate will vote to increase taxes if the President makes a nationwide television appeal for a tax increase is 0·4. The probability that the Senate will vote to increase taxes if the President does not make such an appeal is 0·1.

Such probabilities, it is suggested, might be worked out if the following formulas were employed:

$$P(a, x|A, w) = p_1 = 0\cdot4,$$
$$P(a, \bar{x}|A, \bar{w}) = p_2 = 0\cdot1,$$

where

(A, w) = A does w. For example, the President makes a nationwide television appeal for tax increases.

$(A, \bar{w})$ = A does not do w.

(a, x) = a, the respondent, does x. For example, the Senates votes to increase taxes.

$(a, \bar{x})$ = a does not do x.

$P(u|v)$ = Probability that u happens when v happens.

Of course, the indices 0·4 and 0·1 are again hypothetical. For no specific President, Senate, tax bill, or television appeal has been studied here. Nor is it suggested how data for a problem such as this might be secured or translated into quantitative terms. The figures 0·4 and 0·1 are apparently introduced to imply that it is possible to transform power relations into numerical indices.

If this were the end of the exercise, it would be of small interest. What is significant is that the author proceeds from his symbolic rendering of power to rank not hypothetical actors or role-players but actual members of the United States Senate. He takes thirty-four senators, sitting between 1946 and 1954, and ranks them in order of the power each has been shown to possess when it comes to determining the course of foreign policy and tax legislation. Put very briefly, a senator's power is measured by how frequently a majority of his col-

[2] Dahl (1957, pp. 201–15). In the opening footnote, the author acknowledges 'a particularly heavy debt to March'.

leagues line up with him on a side of an issue.[3] Using sixty-five foreign-policy roll-call votes in this nine-year period, for example, it is possible to rank the senators on their relative power. Thus, Carl Hayden of Arizona and Warren Magnuson of Washington are tied for first place, Wayne Morse of Oregon ranks sixteenth, and Harry Byrd of Virginia is twenty-ninth.

This is an interesting and informative exercise. There is one troublesome question that tends to arise, however, whenever a transition from model-building to empirical research is attempted. In this case, it is not at all clear just how far the symbolic rendering of power at the outset of the study in any way aided the ranking exercise that came later. By all appearances, it seems quite possible to have analysed the roll-call votes of the thirty-four senators without first formulating mathematical equations on probability. Doubtless the author would reply that his mathematical model helped him to introduce a rigour into his thinking that he would not otherwise have had. He might even say that his formal conceptualisation of power opened his eyes to new insights concerning legislative behaviour and that, aided by these new perceptions, he was stimulated to rank the power of senators in the way that he did. It is, of course, impossible to explore either motives or motivations in instances like these. Mathematical reasoning, like all efforts at clear thinking, can sharpen the mind. But whether such exercises lead to a heightened sensitivity to the realities of political behaviour cannot be either proved or disproved.

What will be raised at this point is a seemingly simple-minded query but one with important ramifications. If sixty-five foreign-policy roll calls are used as a basis for ascertaining the relative power of senators, can it be said that all sixty-five of these votes are of equal significance? In the method that was employed, each of the roll-call votes was given identical weight. That is, no effort was made to distinguish 'significant' bills from those which might be considered comparatively inconsequential. Presumably, it takes more power to rally the majority over to your side on an important foreign-aid appropriation than it does to recruit votes for an uncontroversial amendment. If power is to be scaled in a meaningful way, then weights must be assigned to the items comprising the scale. The problem, treated rather casually up to now, is how to devise weights that reflect the actual emphasis which operate in political life.

[3] There are, of course, all sorts of common-sense objections to such a definition of senatorial power, and they are anticipated by Dahl. See also MacRae and Price (1959, pp. 212–18).

JUDICIAL OPINIONS

At least one attempt has been made at a solution. In an article on 'Predicting Supreme Court decisions mathematically', an effort was made to analyse the factors that led the judges to decide cases one way or another (Kort, 1957, pp. 1–12). In studying a group of right-to-counsel cases, the author concluded that there were twenty-four 'pivotal factors', any one or combination of which might guide the Court in making up its mind. These factors are apparently quite standard ones in right-to-counsel cases, and the record will show which ones were present in any given case. Thus, a plaintiff may have had his request for an assigned counsel denied or he may have had no assistance of counsel at time of sentencing or he may have been especially young or immature. It is possible to categorise these factors because the Supreme Court, unlike the Congress, hands down official opinions giving the reasons why it acted as it did. Close reading of these opinions should show which factors guided the judges and to which they assigned greatest weight.

The assumption of the study was that the weighting was actually in the data themselves. In some cases, many factors will be cited in the opinion as leading to the Court's determination. In other cases, one or only a few factors will be mentioned. The presumption is thus drawn that the more important a factor is the less it will have to be supported by additional factors. Conversely, the presence of few supporting factors in a decision indicates that the one or two that are cited carry significant weight. This is an imaginative approach, and the author has created a formula that assigns a numerical weight to each of the twenty-six factors noted in right-to-counsel cases. The formula is a technical one, involving square roots, and there is no need to reproduce it here. Thus, for example, 'request for assigned counsel denied' receives a weight of 43·7; 'no assistance of counsel at time of sentencing' is weighted at 38·0; and 'youth and concomitant immaturity of defendant' has 33·7. The twenty-six weights range from a low of 5·2 to a high of 68·3. Thus, the weights assigned to the factors mentioned in any case can be summed, and this gives an indication of the strength of a plaintiff's plea in the eyes of the Court. The author shows that, if the weights total 389·1 or more, the petitioner will win; if they are less than 370·4, he will lose.

But can it be said that the weights are 'in' the opinions and need only be extracted and inserted in the formula? Unfortunately for the readers of this study, the author did not make public which of the twenty-six factors he found in the cases he read. This is a serious omission, for it is not at all clear that his reading of the cases is the last word in interpretation. A Supreme Court opinion is not presented in tabular form. It is a work of prose, often quite disorganised prose. Content analysis of an opinion is far from being a simple or unambiguous matter. Because this is so, one colleague took it upon himself to obtain privately from the author a list of the factors presumed to be present in each of the right-to-counsel cases. This colleague (Fisher, 1958, p. 334 and n. 24) then read the cases for himself and, not surprisingly, discovered that his assessment of which factors were present in a given opinion differed from the one originally made. The point, of course, is that, in political science as in medicine, diagnosticians can differ. And here, it should be noted, the difference of opinion between scholars was not on an issue like which of two foreign-policy bills is 'more important'. On the contrary, the weights given to the factors were supposed to have been derived from the judges' own behaviour, from what they said in their written opinions. One would think at least that scholars could agree on the content of a Supreme Court opinion, but apparently even this is impossible. Yet if this cannot be done, it is hard to visualise a scholarly consensus on systems of weighing for the far more complex behaviour to be found among legislatures and electorates. All in all, it is necessary to conclude that weights cannot be thought of as lying dormant in the data.[4] For weighting is ultimately a question of interpretation, and it requires the scholar to impose his personal judgment on the facts he has before him. . . .

THE UNBRIDGED CHASM

We have arrived at a great divide, a yawning chasm than can only be crossed if someone undertakes to build a bridge. But the bridge is not being built, and there is some reason to suspect that it never will be. Therefore, the explorers who have reached the canyon's rim have

[4] Guttman Scaling is frequently used to measure intensity, but the operation it performs should not be regarded as weighting. A Scale will contain a number of items, e.g., eight roll-call votes on foreign aid or six survey questions on civil rights. But the 'distances' between all of the items on the Scale are equidistant. In consequence, the Scale itself is unweighted even though the persons whose behaviour is analysed by it will be shown to act or feel with varying intensities. There is, of course, nothing to prevent anyone from setting up the Scale items any way he wishes. Thus instead of 100-80-60-40-20, he might take note of the differences in importance of the 'space' separating items and have the Scale read 100-70-60-35-15. However, such an adjustment is usually frowned upon for fear of introducing a subjective evaluation of the data into the Scale.

pitched their tents and are apparently settling in for good. They occupy their time designing models that will be useful once the chasm is spanned. But they make no serious effort to build the bridge, even though they know it is needed. For one thing, it is a dangerous operation and there may be heavy casualties. Anyway, bridge-building is for engineers, and these explorers pride themselves on being scientists and mathematicians.

The problem has two parts to it. The first is securing the facts, and the second is evaluating the facts once they have been obtained. Game theory, for example, is currently one of the more fashionable mathematical approaches. Much has been said and written about its potentialities for increasing our political understanding. Yet one of its most enthusiastic proponents admits that 'as matters now stand, the application of game theory is limited by the absence of needed data' (Snyder, 1955, p. 73). What is perhaps most interesting is that the kind of information needed if game theory is to be made operational is called 'data' at all. For facts are only transformed into data if they are obtained and ordered in a systematic way. The problem for political research, it hardly needs saying, is that there are too many of the wrong kind of facts and too few of the right kind. Most of the facts we have are either not facts at all, being rather opinions, or they refuse to fit into a systematic order. The facts we do not have are unavailable not for lack of digging but because the human mind is simply not capable of understanding some aspects of individual and social behaviour. It is, for instance, impossible to 'synthesise' the psychological and sociological aspects of a problem. The question remains unresolved not because work is not being done but because there are limits to man's comprehension of himself and his environment. The 'data' needed to apply game theory to the Supreme Court or the Cold War are of such an order that they will never be secured. Whether it is worth refining the mathematics of the model, given the futility of the whole enterprise, is a serious question.

But suppose that the 'data' could be obtained. We have, to use another illustration, all sorts of information on the social influences that form political attitudes. Survey research, for the most part unassisted and unhampered by mathematical models, has been able to turn up all manner of facts about the ways in which environment shapes the outlook of individuals. However, almost everyone has had parents, has a job or is supported by someone with a job, has gone to school, and has aspirations concerning his role in society. We may be able to secure data on a wide range of social influences working on a person, but these facts must be assessed for their significance compared with the other facts we have. What, say, is the role played by formal education (Key, 1961, pp. 341–2).

> While it is plain that education significantly shapes politically relevant attitudes, it must be conceded that isolation of the effects of the school system from other influences forming political man is not readily accomplished. Intensive studies in life histories of individuals would permit more confident assignment of weights to the factors of family, education, occupational interests, social status, and other such influences.

We might, indeed, study the life histories of a sample of adult citizens. In each case, we would doubtless come up with some kind of factual information on the influence of family, education, occupation, and social status on the formation of politically relevant attitudes. But, if past experience is any guide, the information in these biographies will be so difficult to interpret that assigning weights to the several influential factors will never be realised.[5] Nor is there much likelihood that a 'general theory' of attitude formation will emerge from such a research exercise.

MEASURING 'GOODNESS'

Does this mean that the weighting of variables is entirely futile? The answer, on the contrary, is that it is a necessary enterprise which has been done in the past and which should be continued in the future. Over twenty years ago, when research was conducted in a far more simple-minded way, there was a scholar who thought it would be a good idea to rate various American cities on the 'goodness of life' enjoyed by their inhabitants (Thorndike, 1939 and 1940). There is no point in claiming that life in Dallas is preferable to life in Seattle unless one has a way of measuring the quality of existence in those two cities. So a 'G-Score' was constructed. The 'goodness' of a city was determined by summing its ratings on twenty-four statistical items. The scale contained items like the infant death rate, the average salary paid to teachers, the per capita number of automobiles, and so forth. If an item was negative—that is, signified a diminution of the quality of life—then the reverse ratio of that factor was used in the scale. The decision that there would be only twenty-four items on the G-Score

---

[5] Riesman's *Faces in the Crowd* (1952) is a collection of twenty-one such life histories. It would be a challenging exercise for someone to go through these biographies and try to assign weights to the factors that influenced the political outlooks of the individuals who were studied.

and the selection of the particular items to be included were made, unilaterally and unblushingly, by the scholar who conceived of the project in the first place.

To be sure, some factors contribute more to the 'goodness of life' of a city than do others. Modern agnosticism might protest that there is no objective way of knowing if one factor is more significant than another. In contemporary research, all factors would be weighted equally, for this would at least avoid controversy. Alternatively, residents of cities might be asked what they felt were the most significant factors making for civic virtue, and, in this way, the judgments of the citizens themselves would be accepted as an index. But the man who invented the G-Score was neither an agnostic nor a democrat. He assigned a weight to each of the twenty-four items on the scale. And, moreover, they were his, presumably more competent, evaluations and not those of the man in the street. Thus, the frequency of home ownership was

TABLE 16.1. *G-Score weights*

High per capita or percentage	ELT	HS	DA	DR	JS	RS
Expenditure on teachers' salaries	4·0	4·0	5·0	7·0	3·0	7·5
Expenditure on textbooks and supplies	5·0	5·0	5·0	7·0	5·0	3·0
Persons 16 to 17 attending school	3·0	6·0	4·0	5·0	5·0	6·0
Persons 18 to 20 attending college	5·0	6·0	4·0	5·0	5·0	6·0
Average high school teacher's salary	3·0	5·0	6·0	7·0	5·0	7·5
Average grade school teacher's salary	2·5	4·0	6·0	7·0	3·0	7·5
Average factory worker's wage	3·0	5·0	4·0	5·0	5·0	4·5
Home ownership	4·0	4·0	2·0	1·0	3·0	4·5
Electricity installations	3·5	4·0	3·0	2·0	7·0	4·5
Gas installations	5·0	4·0	1·0	2·0	1·0	1·5
Automobile ownership	3·0	2·0	1·0	2·0	7·0	—
Telephone installations	7·5	0·5	1·0	2·0	3·0	3·0
Television sets	4·5	2·0	1·0	2·0	3·0	—
Literacy	2·5	6·5	7·0	5·0	7·0	6·0
'Quality' magazine circulation	3·5	4·5	1·0	5·0	3·0	3·0
Reversed indices						
Infant death rate	8·5	4·0	6·0	5·0	7·0	4·5
General death rate	6·5	6·0	4·0	1·0	7·0	1·5
Typhoid death rate	3·5	4·0	5·0	3·0	3·0	3·0
Appendicitis death rate	3·0	4·0	4·0	1·0	1·0	3·0
Mothers' childbirth death rate	3·0	4·0	6·0	5·0	5·0	6·0
Syphilis death rate	3·0	4·0	5·0	5·0	1·0	3·0
Homicide death rate	2·5	4·0	7·0	10·0	3·0	4·5
Automobile accident death rate	3·0	0·5	5·0	1·0	1·0	4·5
Incidence of poverty	8·5	7·0	7·0	5·0	7·0	6·0

weighted at four points, standing higher than the literacy rate (which got 2·5) and lower than the per capita expenditure on textbooks and school supplies (which got 5·0).

The selection of items and the distribution of weights, then, was the reasoned judgment of a single scholar. Although doubtless he could have given justifications for the choices he made, he did not bother to do so, probably knowing in advance that his explanations would be unsatisfactory to anyone inclined to be critical of the project. Put another way, some decisions simply cannot be justified—although that is not the same as saying that the making of such decisions is unjustifiable. Table 17.1 lists the twenty-four items in the G-Score, and the first column gives the weights assigned to these items. The next five columns contain the weights that five other persons, working independently and without knowing the original weights, gave to the items.[6]

The result is a series of comparative judgments on G-Score weights, all made by individuals who may be presumed to be competent in the field under consideration. It is not surprising that their weights differ from those originally assigned, and this is not simply because the criteria of 'goodness' have changed since 1939. Nor is it any less surprising that they do not agree with each other, for quite clearly there cannot be a consensus on what makes for the quality of life in 1963. It would be silly to ask these five persons to confer around a table, compromise their differences, and concur on a weighting system. The judgment of a committee is hardly what is wanted on a question like this. It may be suggested that the G-Score is in fact a 'moral' evaluation, providing more area for disagreement than might a 'factual' problem. But is this so? A twenty-four-item scale might be drawn up listing factors influencing the passage of the Taft-Hartley bill. A group of scholars might similarly be asked to weight each item as was done for the G-Score. All indications are that they would fail to agree no less on this than on a 'moral' question. Perceptions of reality vary as between observers, and, so long as they do, 'objectivity' will remain not only a fiction but a harmful one. For the vain pursuit of 'objective' knowledge deflects attention and energy from more worthwhile avenues of approach to political understanding.

[6] The original G-Score summed to 144 points, but for present purposes it has been adjusted to 100 points. Only one change was made in the items in asking for new assignments of weights: the original items on radios were changed to television sets. The following graduate students in the Department of Government at Cornell University were kind enough to participate in this exercise: Harvey Simmons, Dean Alfange, Donald Robinson, John Stanley, and Roger Smith.

IN PRAISE OF SUBJECTIVITY

Scholars always have differed and always will differ in their descriptions and explanations of the political world they see. If it has been reiterated here that there is a need for weighting—for determining the significance of operative factors—the conclusion must be that this is a highly sub-jective endeavour. The G-Score is not a mathematical model, but it can serve as a fine model for contemporary model-builders. What must be abandoned is the hope that political analysis can be either objective or scientific. The underlying method of the natural and physical sciences is inapplicable to political study: 'Objectivity is closely bound up with the social aspect of scientific method, with the fact that science and scientific objectivity do not and cannot result from the attempts of an individual scientist to be "objective", but from the co-operation of many scientists' (Popper, 1945, ii, 205). There may be co-operation among political scientists in the sense that they share and criticise each other's research. However, this communication does not produce an agreed-upon body of knowledge. Indeed, controversy rather than con-sensus is the rule on all questions of method and content transcending the commonplace. At this time, it is hard to point to any 'findings' that have been accepted by the scholarly community. As matters now stand, there are cliques, coteries, and lone wolves talking past one another or to themselves.

'At this time. . . .' 'As matters now stand. . . .' Phrases such as these have become all too familiar in recent years. The pleas for more *time* assume that mathematical methods are but babes in arms, creatures with unlimited potentialities if only they may be nurtured to adulthood. The assumption is that the passage of time will somehow bring not only more refined techniques but ultimately an enhanced understanding of the political process. Yet those who ask for time never really examine just what it is their request implies. Will there be a greater consensus among scholars on perceived realities in 1977 than there is now? The evidence, if such it can be called, is that, so long as scholars are affected by differing interests and spring from differing backgrounds, disagree-ments over political facts will persist. There is little reason to believe that mathematical approaches will lead to changed perceptions within a discipline or produce a consensus among its members. The demand for more time carries with it a theory concerning the progress of human knowledge that is highly tenuous. It assumes that, somehow, contrary to all past experience, students of politics will begin to agree on some major propositions about the world they are studying. Just what breed of men these scholars of the future will be, devoid of opinions and obstinacy, is difficult to imagine.

We must make do with and make the best of the materials at hand. What is wanted is more subjective analysis, more individual scholarship, and more research that is highly personal in conclusion and design. Each student of politics must describe the world as he sees it, holding onto the faith that his perceptions and evaluations are valid. There must be a certain display of arrogance here, a sense that everyone is out of step except one's self. There is also involved the courage to weather the scorn of more conventional colleagues. For this agreement will only be obtained if controversial elements are stripped away, leaving ideas and approaches that are unexceptionable. If the great theorists of the past —from Plato through Freud—made some contribution to our understanding of politics, it is not simply because they were men of surpassing intellect. It is also because they had the audacity to select those factors they felt were important and to emphasise them to the neglect or even exclusion of others. This is what Thomas Hobbes and Edmund Burke did. It was also the method of Karl Marx and Sigmund Freud. It is easy enough to say that any of these theories overweights a single factor, that what emerges is a caricature rather than a rounded depiction. These men knew they were drawing caricatures, but they had the courage to omit the qualifications and reservations that would detract from the major points they sought to make. If the traditional writers were wrong —and all of them were—their errors were brilliant in conception and imaginative in design. Their wrongheadedness, in short, has aided our political understanding more than all the level-headed models of those who manage to avoid criticism by confining their generalisations to the unobjectionable.

At the same time, there is little profit in exhorting scholars to surpass their native talents. The man who is now sitting in a cubicle at some university drawing up a computer programme is not an unborn Rousseau or a stifled John Stuart Mill. It may seem unkind to say so, but the typical mathematical political scientist is no more an extraordinary person than the rest of us. His perception of reality is as conventional or as distorted as those of others, and his powers of analysis are apt to be as muddled as the next person's. Access to an electronic computer or knowledge of the calculus does not transform a mediocre mind into a superior intellect. For this reason, then, it is idle to tell the model-builder that he should turn to old-fashioned political philosophy in the hope that his redirected efforts will take us farther toward attaining the good life or the just polity. Even if he abandoned mathematics for moral philosophy, it is doubtful if his contribution to political knowledge would be much more memorable.

If these comments have been critical of so much of the pretentiousness that surrounds the mathematical approaches, it is only because most of us are rather unpretentious individuals. At the risk of sounding patronising, it may be noted that the expansion of higher education will require more professors of political science, and the quality of the persons entering this expanded profession will not be very high. Yet the customs of academe require that all do research, at least to obtain the doctorate. If the researcher is a rather ordinary individual, and most will be, then it does not really matter whether he spends his time building models or if he mulls over the minor works of Montesquieu. Unlike medicine, where there is the problem of allocating scarce resources, political science can permit each scholar to labour in whatever vineyard he thinks is important. Although the suggestion may have been made here that model-building is a waste of time, it should also be noted that no alternative activity is being proposed for those lured by the siren call of mathematics. Political knowledge will only grow as each of us does the kind of research he wants to do. Throughout history, most of what has passed as scholarship has been profitless and is soon forgotten. But the atmosphere in which most of us are allowed to engage in fads and fantasies is also the atmosphere that will nourish a serious thinker who, probably unappreciated by his contemporaries, will eventually be acknowledged as someone who made a significant contribution to our understanding of political life.

REFERENCES

DAHL, R. A. (1957) 'The concept of power', *Behavioural Science*, 2, July.
FAGEN, R. P. (1961) 'Some contributions of mathematical reasoning to the study of politics', *American Political Science Review*, 55, December.
FISHER, F. M. (1958) 'The mathematical analysis of Supreme Court decisions', *American Political Science Review*, 52, June.
KEY, V. O. (1961) *Public Opinion and American Democracy*, Knopf.
KORT, F. (1957) 'Predicting Supreme Court decisions mathematically', *American Political Science Review*, 51, March.
MACRAE, D. and PRICE, H. D. (1959) 'Scale positions and "power" in the Senate', *Behavioural Science*, 4, July.
MARCH, J. G. (1957) 'Measurement concepts in the theory of influence', *The Journal of Politics*, 19, May.
POPPER, K. (1945) *The Open Society and its Enemies*, Routledge.
RIESMAN, D. (1952) *Faces in the Crowd*, Yale University Press.
SNYDER, R. C. (1955) 'Game theory and the analysis of political behaviour', *Research Frontiers in Politics and Government*, Washington, Brookings Institution.
THORNDIKE, E. L. (1939) *Your City*, Harcourt.
THORNDIKE, E. L. (1940) *144 Smaller Cities*, Harcourt.

17

G. Sartori   Faulty concepts

Reprinted from 'Concept misformation in comparative politics', *American Political Science Review*, Vol. 54, 1970, pp. 1033-53.

'To have mastered "theory" and "method" is to have become a *conscious thinker*, a man at work and aware of the assumptions and implications of whatever he is about. To be mastered by "method" or "theory" is simply to be kept from working' (Mills, 1959, p. 27; italics added by Sartori). The sentence applies nicely to the present plight of political science. The profession as a whole oscillates between two unsound extremes. At the one end a large majority of political scientists qualify as pure and simple unconscious thinkers. At the other end a sophisticated minority qualify as overconscious thinkers, in the sense that their standards of method and theory are drawn from the physical, 'paradigmatic' sciences.

The wide gap between the unconscious and the overconscious thinker is concealed by the growing sophistication of statistical and research techniques. Most of the literature introduced by the title 'Methods' (in the social, behavioural or political sciences) actually deals with survey techniques and social statistics, and has little if anything to share with the crucial concern of 'methodology', which is a concern with the logical structure and procedure of scientific inquiry. In a very crucial sense there is no methodology without *logos*, without thinking about thinking. And if a firm distinction is drawn—as it should be—between methodology and technique, the latter is no substitute for the former. One may be a wonderful researcher and manipulator of data, and yet remain an unconscious thinker. The view presented in this article is, then, that the profession as a whole is grievously impaired by methodological unawareness. The more we advance technically, the more we leave a vast, uncharted territory behind our backs. And my underlying complaint is that political scientists eminently lack (with exceptions) a training in logic—indeed in elementary logic.

I stress 'elementary' because I do not wish to encourage in the least the overconscious thinker, the man who refuses to discuss heat unless he is given a thermometer. My sympathy goes, instead, to the 'conscious thinker', the man who realises the limitations of not having a thermometer and still manages to say a great deal simply by saying hot and cold, warmer and cooler. Indeed I call upon the conscious thinker to steer a middle course between crude logical mishandling on the one hand, and logical perfectionism (and paralysis) on the other hand. Whether we realise it or not, we are still swimming in a sea of naivete. And the study of comparative politics is particularly vulnerable to, and illustrative of, this unfelicitous state of affairs.

I. THE TRAVELLING PROBLEM

Traditional, or the more traditional type of, political science inherited a vast array of concepts which had been previously defined and refined —for better and for worse—by generations of philosophers and political theorists. To some extent, therefore, the traditional political scientist could afford to be an 'unconscious thinker'—the thinking had already been done for him. This is even more the case with the country-by-country legalistic institutional approach, which does not particularly require hard thinking.[1] However, the new political science engages in re-conceptualisation. And this is even more the case, necessarily, with the new comparative expansion of the discipline.[2] There are many reasons for this *renovatio ab imis*.

One is the very 'expansion of politics'. To some extent politics is *objectively* bigger on account of the fact that the world is becoming more and more politicised (more participation, more mobilisation, and in any case more state intervention in formerly non-governmental spheres). In no small measure, however, politics is *subjectively* bigger in that we have shifted the focus of attention both toward the periphery of politics (*vis-à-vis* the governmental process), and toward its input side. By now—as Macridis (1968, p. 81) puts it—we study everything that is 'potentially political'. While this latter aspect of the expansion of politics is disturbing—it ultimately leads to the disappearance of politics —it is not a peculiar concern for comparative politics, in the sense that

[1] This is by no means a criticism of a comparative item by item analysis, and even less of the 'institutional-functional remarks' approach. On the latter see the judicious remarks of Braibanti (1968, 44–9).
[2] For the various phases of the comparative approach see Eckstein (1963).

other segments of political science are equally and even more deeply affected.[3]

Aside from the expansion of politics, a more specific source of conceptual and methodological challenge for comparative politics is what Braibanti calls the 'lengthening spectrum of political systems' (1968, pp. 36–7). We are now engaged in world-wide, cross-area comparisons. And while there is an end to geographical size, there is apparently no end to the proliferation of political units. There were about 80 States in 1946; it is no wild guess that we may shortly arrive at 150. Still more important, the lengthening spectrum of political systems includes a variety of primitive, diffuse polities at very different stages of differentiation and consolidation.

Now, the wider the world under investigation, the more we need conceptual tools that are able to travel. It is equally clear that the pre-1950 vocabulary of politics was not devised for world-wide, cross-area travelling. On the other hand, and in spite of bold attempts at drastic terminological innovation,[4] it is hard to see how Western scholars could radically depart from the political experience of the West, i.e. from the vocabulary of politics which has been developed over millennia on the basis of such experience. Therefore, the first question is: how far, and how, can we travel with the help of the available vocabulary of politics?

By and large, so far we have followed (more or less unwittingly) the line of least resistance: broaden the meaning—and thereby the range of application—of the conceptualisations at hand. That is to say, the larger the world, the more we have resorted to *conceptual stretching*, or conceptual straining, i.e. to vague, amorphous conceptualisations. To be sure, there is more to it. One may add, for instance, that conceptual stretching also represents a deliberate attempt to make our conceptualisations value free. Another concurrent explication is that conceptual straining is largely a 'boomerang effect' of the developing areas, i.e. a feedback on the Western categories of the diffuse polities of the Third World.[5] These considerations notwithstanding, conceptual stretching

[3] On the 'fallacy of inputism' see again the remarks of Macridis (1968, pp. 84–7). In his words, 'The state of the discipline can be summed up in one phrase: the gradual disappearance of the political' (p. 86). A cogent statement of the issue is Paige (1966, p. 49ff). My essay (1969, pp. 65–100) is also largely concerned with the fallacy of inputism viewed as a sociological reduction of politics.

[4] The works of Riggs are perhaps the best instance of such bold attempts. For a recent presentation see Riggs (1970), esp. pp. 95–115. While Riggs's innovative strategy has undeniable practical drawbacks, the criticism of Landau (1969, pp. 325–34) appears somewhat unfair.

[5] On the boomerang effect of the developing areas more in the final section.

does represent, in comparative politics, the line of least resistance. And the net result of conceptual straining is that our gains in extensional coverage tend to be matched by losses in connotative precision. It appears that we can cover more—in travelling terms—only by saying less, and by saying less in a far less precise manner.

A major drawback of the comparative expansion of the discipline is, then, that it has been conducive to indefiniteness, to undelimited and largely undefined conceptualisations. We do need, ultimately, 'universal' categories—concepts which are applicable to any time and place. But nothing is gained if our universals turn out to be 'no difference' categories leading to pseudo-equivalences. And even though we need universals, they must be *empirical* universals, that is, categories which somehow are amenable, in spite of their all-embracing very abstract nature, to empirical testing. Instead we seem to verge on the edge of *philosophical* universals, understood—as Croce defines them—as concepts which are by definition supra-empirical.[6]

That the comparative expansion of the discipline would encounter the aforementioned stumbling block was only to be expected. It was easy to infer, that is, that conceptual stretching would produce indefiniteness and elusiveness, and that the more we climb toward high-flown universals, the more tenuous the link with the empirical evidence. It is pertinent to wonder, therefore, why the problem has seldom been squarely confronted.

Taking a step back, let us begin by asking whether it is really necessary to embark on hazardous world-wide comparisons. This question hinges, in turn, on the prior question, Why compare? The unconscious thinker does not ask himself why he is comparing; and this neglect goes to explain why so much comparative work provides extensions of knowledge, but hardly a strategy for acquiring and validating new knowledge. It is not intuitively evident that to compare is to control, and that the novelty, distinctiveness and importance of comparative politics consists of a systematic testing, against as many cases as possible, of sets of hypotheses, generalisations and laws of the 'if.... then' type.[7] But if comparative politics is conceived as a method of

[6] More precisely in Croce (1942, pp. 13–17), universals are defined *ultra-rappresentativi*, as being above and beyond any conceivable empirical representability.

[7] For the comparative method as a 'method of control' see especially Lijphart (1969). According to Lijphart the comparative method is a 'method of discovering empirical relationships among variables' (p. 2); and I fully concur, except that this definition can be entered only at a later stage of the argument.

control, then its generalisations have to be checked against 'all cases', and therefore the enterprise must be—in principle—a global enterprise. So the reason for world-wide comparisons is not simply that we live in a wider world; it is also a methodological reason.

If two or more items are identical, we do not have a problem of comparability. On the other hand, if two or more items have nothing, or not enough in common, we rightly say that stones and rabbits cannot be compared. By and large, then, we obtain comparability when two or more items appear 'similar enough', that is, neither identical nor utterly different. But this assessment offers little positive guidance. The problem is often outflanked by saying that we make things comparable. In this perspective to compare is 'to assimilate', i.e. to discover deeper or fundamental similarities below the surface of secondary diversities. But this argument equally affords little mileage and conveys, moreover, the misleading suggestion that the trick resides in making the unlike look alike. Surely, then, we have here a major problem which cannot be disposed of with the argument that political theorists have performed decently with comparing since the time of Aristotle, and therefore that we should not get bogged by the question 'What is comparable?' any more than our predecessors. This argument will not do on account of three differences.

In the first place if our predecessors were culture bound this implied that they travelled only as far as their personal knowledge allowed them to travel. In the second place, our predecessors hardly disposed of quantitive data and were not quantitatively oriented. Under both of these limitations they enjoyed the distinct advantage of having a substantive understanding of the things they were comparing. This is hardly possible on a world-wide scale, and surely becomes impossible with the computer revolution. A few years ago Karl Deutsch (1966, p. 156), predicted that by 1975 the informational requirements of political science would be satisfied by some 'fifty million card-equivalents [of IBM standard cards] . . . and a total annual growth rate of perhaps as much as five million'. I find the estimate frightening, for computer technology and facilities are bound to flood us with masses of data for which no human mind can have any substantive grasp. But even if one shares the enthusiasm of Deutsch, it cannot be denied that we have here a gigantic, unprecedented problem.

In the third place, our predecessors were far from being as unguided as we are. They did not leave the decision about what was homogenous —i.e., comparable—and what was heterogenous—i.e., non-comparable —to each man's genial insights. As indicated by the terminology, their comparisons applied to things belonging to 'the same genus'.

That is to say, the background of comparability was established by the *per genus et differentiam* mode of analysis, i.e., by a taxonomical treatment. In this context, comparable means something which belongs to the same class. Hence the class provides the 'similarity element' of comparability, while the 'differences' enter as the species of a genus, or the sub-species of a species—and so forth, depending on how fine the analysis needs to be. However, and here is the rub, the taxonomical requisites of comparability are currently neglected, if not disowned.

We are now better equipped for a discussion of our initial query, namely, why the travelling problem of comparative politics has been met with the poor remedy of 'conceptual stretching' instead of being squarely confronted. While there are many reasons for our neglect to attack the problem frontally, a major reason is that we have been swayed by the suggestion that our difficulties can be overcome by switching from 'what is' questions to 'how much' questions. The argument runs, roughly, as follows. As long as concepts point to differences of *kind*, i.e., as long as we pursue the either-or mode of analysis, we are in trouble; but if concepts are understood as a matter of more-or-less, i.e., as pointing to differences in *degree*, then our difficulties can be solved by measurement, and the real problem is precisely how to measure. Meanwhile—waiting for the measures—class concepts and taxonomies should be looked upon with suspicion (if not rejected), since they represent 'an old fashioned logic of properties and attributes not well adapted to study quantities and relations'.[8]

According to my previous analysis, a taxonomic unfolding represents a requisite condition for comparability, and indeed a background which becomes all the more important the less we can rely on a substantive familiarity with what is being compared. According to the foregoing argument, instead, quantification has no ills of its own; rather, it provides a remedy for the ills and inadequacies of the *per genus et differentiam* mode of analysis. My own view is that when we dismiss the so-called 'old fashioned logic' we are plain wrong, and indeed the victims of poor logic—a view that I must now attempt to warrant.

II. QUANTIFICATION AND CLASSIFICATION

What is very confusing in this matter is the abuse of a quantitative idiom which is nothing but an idiom. All too often, that is, we speak of

[8] Hempel, quoted in Martindale (1959, p. 87). Martindale aptly comments that 'Hempel's judgments are made from the standpoint of the natural sciences'. But the vein is not dissimilar when the statistically trained scholar argues that 'whereas it is admittedly technically possible to think always in terms of attributes and dichotomies, one wonders how practical that is': Blalock (1964, p. 32).

degrees and of measurement 'not only without any actual measurements having been performed, but without any being projected, and even without any apparent awareness of what must be done before such measurements can be carried out' (Kaplan, 1964, p. 213). For instance, in most standard textbooks one finds that nominal scales are spoken of as 'scales of measurement' (e.g. Festinger and Katz, 1953; and Selltiz, 1959). But a nominal scale is nothing else than a qualitative classification, and I fail to understand what it is that a nominal scale does, or can, measure. To be sure classes can be given numbers; but this is simply a coding device for identifying items and has nothing to do with quantification. Likewise the incessant use of 'it is a matter of degree' phraseology and of the 'continuum' image leave us with qualitative-impressionistic statements which do not advance us by a hair's breadth toward quantification. In a similar vein we speak more and more of 'variables' which are not variables in any proper sense, for they are not attributes permitting graduations and implying measurability. No harm necessarily follows if it pleases us to use the word variable as a synonym for the word concept; but we are only deluding ourselves if we really believe that by *saying* variable we *have* a variable.

All in all, coquetting (if not cheating) with a quantitative idiom grossly exaggerates the extent to which political science is currently amenable to quantification, and, still worse, obfuscates the very notion of quantification. The dividing line between the jargon and the substance of quantification can be drawn very simply: quantification begins with numbers, and when numbers are used in relation to their arithmetical properties. To understand, however, the multifaceted complexities of the notion beyond this dividing line is a far less simple matter. Nevertheless one may usefully distinguish—in spite of the close interconnections—among three broad areas of meaning and application, that is, between quantification as (i) measurement, (ii) statistical manipulation and, (iii) formal mathematical treatment.

In political science we generally refer to the first meaning. That is to say, far more often than not the quantification of political science consists of (*a*) attaching numerical values to items (pure and simple measurement), (*b*) using numbers to indicate the rank order of items (ordinal scales) and (*c*) measuring differences or distances among items (interval scales).[9]

[9] There is some question as to whether it can really be held that ordinal scales are scales of measurement: most of our rank ordering occurs without having recourse to numerical values, and whenever we do assign to our ordered categories, these numbers are arbitrary. However, there are good reasons for drawing the threshold of quantification between nominal and

Beyond the stage of measurement we do own, in addition, powerful statistical techniques not only for protecting ourselves against sampling and measurement errors, but also for establishing significant relationships among variables. However, statistical processing enters the scene only when sufficient numbers have been pinned on sufficient items, and becomes central to the discipline only when we dispose of variables which measure things that are worth measuring. Both conditions—and especially the latter—are hard to meet.[10] Indeed, a cross-examination of our statistical findings in terms of their theoretical significance—and/or of a 'more relevant' political science—shows an impressive disproportion between bravura and relevance. Unfortunately, what makes a statistical treatment theoretically significant has nothing to do with statistics.

As for the ultimate stage of quantification—formal mathematical treatment—it is a fact that, so far, political science and mathematics have engaged only 'in a sporadic conversation'.[11] It is equally a fact that we seldom, if ever, obtain isomorphic correspondences between empirical relations among things and formal relations among numbers.[12] We may well disagree about future prospects,[13] or as to whether it

---

ordinal scales rather than between ordinal and interval scales. (See Tufte, 1969, esp. p. 645). On the other hand, even if the gap between ordinal scales and interval measurement is not as wide in practice as it is in theory, nonetheless from a mathematical point of view the interesting scales are the interval and even more, of course, the cardinal scales.

[10] Otherwise the comparative method would largely consist of the statistical method, for the latter surely is a stronger technique of control than the former. The difference and the connections are cogently discussed by Lijphart (1969).

[11] Benson (1967, p. 132). The chapter usefully reviews the literature. For an introductory treatment see Alker (1965). An illuminating discussion on how quantification enters the various social sciences is in Lerner (1961, *passim*).

[12] A classic example is the (partial) mathematical translation of the theoretical system of *The Human Group* of George C. Holmans by Simon (1967, chap. 7). No similar achievement exists in the political science field. To cite three significant instances, political science issues are eminently lacking in Arrow (1951, chap. 8); in the contributions collected in Lazarsfeld (1954); in Kemeny and Snell (1962).

[13] Perhaps the mathematical leap of the discipline is just around the corner waiting for non-quantitative developments. If one is to judge, however, from the 'mathematics of man' issue of the *International Social Science Bulletin* introduced by Claude Levi-Strauss (IV, 1954), this literature is very deceiving. More interesting is Kemeny (1961, pp. 35–51); and the modal logic developed by the Bourbaki group, *Eléments de Mathématique*, appearing periodically (Paris: Hermann). For a general treatment see Kemeny, Snell, Thompson (1957).

makes sense to construct formalised systems of quantitatively well defined relationships (mathematical models) so long as we wander in a mist of qualitatively ill-defined concepts. If we are to learn, however, from the mathematical development of economics, the evidence is that it 'always lagged behind its qualitative and conceptual improvement'.[14] And my point is, precisely, that this is not a casual sequence. It is for a very good reason that the progress of quantification should lag—in whatever discipline—behind its qualitative and conceptual progress.

In this messy controversy about quantification and its bearing on standard logical rules we simply tend to forget that *concept formation stands prior to quantification*. The process of thinking inevitably begins with a qualitative (natural) language, no matter at which shore we shall subsequently land. Correlatively, there is no ultimate way of by-passing the fact that human understanding—the way in which our mind works—requires cut-off points which basically correspond (in spite of all subsequent refinements) to the slices into which a natural or qualitative language happens to be divided.

There is a fantastic lack of perspective in the argument that these cut-off points can be obtained via statistical processing, i.e., by letting the data themselves tell us where to draw them. For this argument applies only *within* the frame of conceptual mappings which have to tell us first of what reality is composed. Let it be stressed, therefore, that long before having data which can speak for themselves the fundamental articulation of language and of thinking is obtained logically —by cumulative conceptual refinement and chains of co-ordinated definitions—not by measurement. Measurement of what? We cannot measure unless we know first what it is that we are measuring. Nor can the degrees of something tell us what a thing is. As Lazarsfeld and Barton (1965, p. 155, Sartori's italics) neatly phrase it, 'before we can investigate the presence or absence of some attribute ... or before we can rank objects or measure them in terms of some variable, *we must form the concept of that variable*'.

The major premise is, then, that quantification enters the scene after, and only after, having formed the concept. The minor premise is that the 'stuff' of quantification—the things underpinned by the numbers—cannot be provided by quantification itself. Hence the rules of concept

---

[14] Spengler (1961, p. 176). Spengler equally points out that 'the introduction of quantitative methods in economics did not result in striking discoveries' (*ibid.*). While formal economic theory is by now highly isomorphic with algebra, mathematical economics has added little to the predictive power of the discipline and one often has the impression that we are employing guns to kill mosquitos.

formation are independent of, and cannot be derived from, the rules which govern the treatment of quantities and quantitative relations. Let us elaborate on this conclusion.

In the first place, if we never really have 'how much' findings—in the sense that the prior question always is how much *in what*, in what conceptual container—it follows from this that how much quantitative findings are an internal element of 'what is' qualitative questions: the claim that the latter should give way to the former cannot be sustained. It really follows, in the second place, that 'categoric concepts' of the either-or type cannot give way to 'gradation concepts' of the more-than-less-than type.

What is usually lost sight of is that the either-or type of logic is the very logic of classification building. Classes are required to be mutually exclusive, i.e., class concepts represent characteristics which the object under consideration must either have or lack. Two items being compared must belong first to the same class, and either have or not have an attribute; and only if they have it, the two items can be matched in terms of which has it *more* or *less*. Hence the logic of gradation belongs to the logic of classification. More precisely put, the switch from classification to gradation basically consists of replacing the signs 'same-different' with the signs 'same-greater-lesser', i.e., consists of introducing a quantitative differentiation within a qualitative sameness (of attributes). Clearly, then, the sign 'same', established by the logic of classification is the requisite condition of introducing the signs 'plus-minus'.

The retort tends to be that this is true only as long as we persist in thinking in terms of attributes and dichotomies. But this rejoinder misses the point that—aside from classifying—we dispose of no other unfolding technique. Indeed, the taxonomical exercise 'unpacks' concepts, and plays a non-replaceable role in the process of thinking in that it decomposes mental compounds into orderly and manageable sets of component units. Let it be added that at no stage of the methodological argument does the taxonomical unpacking lose weight and importance. As a matter of fact, the more we enter the stage of quantification, the more we need uni-dimensional scales and continua; and dichotomous categorisations serve precisely the purpose of establishing the ends, and thereby the uni-dimensionality, of each continuum.

Having disposed of the fuzziness brought about by the abuse of a quantitative idiom, attention should immediately be called to the fact-finding side of the coin. For my emphasis on concept formation should not be misunderstood to imply that my concern is more theoretical than empirical. This is not so, because the concepts of any social science are not only the elements of a theoretical system; they are equally, and just as much, data containers. Indeed data is information which is distributed in, and processed by, 'conceptual containers'. And since the non-experimental sciences basically depend on fact-finding, i.e., on reports about external (not laboratory) observables, the empirical question becomes what turns a concept into a valuable, indeed a valid, fact-finding container.

The reply need not be far-fatched: the lower the discriminating power of a conceptual container, the more the facts are misgathered, i.e., the greater the misinformation. Conversely, the higher the discriminating power of a category, the better the information. Admittedly, in and by itself this reply is not very illuminating, for it only conveys the suggestion that for fact-finding purposes it is more profitable to exaggerate in over-differentiation than in over-assimilation. The point is, however, that what establishes, or helps establish, the discriminating power of a category is the taxonomical infolding. Since the logical requirement of a classification is that its classes should be mutually exclusive and jointly exhaustive, it follows from this that the taxonomical exercise supplies an orderly series of well sharpened categories, and thereby the basis for collecting adequately precise information. And this is indeed how we know whether, and to what extent, a concept has a fact-gathering validity.

Once again, then, it appears that we have started to run before having learned how to walk. Numbers must be attached—for our purposes—to 'things', to facts. How are these things, or facts, identified and collected? Our ultimate ambition may well be to pass from a science 'of species' to a science of 'functional co-relations' (Lasswell and Kaplan, 1950, pp. xvi–xvii). The question is whether we are not repudiating a science of species in exchange for nothing. And it seems to me that premature haste combined with the abuse of a quantitative idiom is largely responsible not only for the fact that much of our theorising is muddled, but also for the fact that much of our research is trivial and wasteful.

Graduate students are being sent all over the world—as LaPalombara (1968, p. 66) vividly puts it—on 'indiscriminate fishing expeditions for data'. These fishing expeditions are 'indiscriminate' in that they lack taxonomical backing; which is the same as saying that they are fishing expeditions without adequate nets. The researcher sets out with a 'check-list' which is, at best, an imperfect net of his own. This may be an expedient way of handling his private research problems, but remains a very inconvenient strategy from the angle of the additivity and the comparability of his findings. As a result, the joint enterprise of comparative politics is menaced by a growing potpourri of disparate, non-cumulative and—in the aggregate—misleading morass of information.

All in all, and regardless of whether we rely on quantitative data or on more qualitative information, in any case the problem is the same, namely, to construct fact-building categories that own sufficient discriminating power.[15] If our data containers are blurred, we never know to what extent and on what grounds the 'unlike' is made 'alike'. If so, quantitative analysis may well provide more misinformation than qualitative analysis, especially on account of the aggregating circumstance that quantitative misinformation can be used without any substantive knowledge of the phenomena under consideration.

To recapitulate and conclude, I have argued that the logic of either-or cannot be replaced by the logic of more-and-less. Actually the two logics are complementary, and each has a legitimate field of application. Correlatively, polar opositions and dichotomous confrontations cannot be dismissed: they are a necessary step in the process of concept formation. Equally, impatience with classification is totally unjustified. Rather, we often confuse a mere enumeration (or check-list) with a classification, and many so-called classifications fail to meet the minimal requirements for what they claim to be.

The overconscious thinker takes the view that if the study of politics has to be a 'science', then it has to be Newton (or from Newton all the way up to Hempel). But the experimental method is hardly within the reach of political science (beyond the format of small group experimentation) and the very extent to which we are systematically turning to the comparative method of verification points to the extent to which no stronger method—including the statistical method—is available. If so, our distinctive and major problems begin where the lesson of the more exact sciences leaves off. This is tantamount to saying that a wholesale acceptance of the logic and methodology of physics may well be self-defeating, and is surely of little use for our distinctive needs. In particular, and whatever their limits, classifications remain the requisite, if preliminary, condition for any scientific discourse. As Hempel (1952, p. 54) himself concedes, classificatory concepts do lend themselves to

[15] It hardly needs to be emphasised that census data—and for that matter most of the data provided by external agencies—are gathered by conceptual containers which hopelessly lack discrimination. The question with our standard variables on literacy, urbanisation, occupation, industrialisation, and the like, is whether they really measure common underlying phenomena. It is pretty obvious that, across the world, they do not; and this quite aside from the reliability of the data gathering agencies.

the description of observational findings and to the formulation of initial, if crude, empirical generalisations. Moreover, a classificatory activity remains the basic instrument for introducing analytical clarity in whatever we are discussing, and leads us to discuss one thing at a time and different things at different times. Finally, and especially, we need taxonomical networks for solving our fact-finding and fact-storing problems. No comparative science of politics is plausible—on a global scale—unless we can draw on extensive *information* which is sufficiently *precise* to be meaningfully *compared*. The requisite condition for this is an adequate, relatively stable and, thereby, *additive filing system*. Such a filing system no longer is a wild dream, thanks to computer technology and facilities—except for the paradoxical fact that the more we enter the computer age, the less our fact-finding and fact-storing methods abide by any logically standardised criterion. Therefore, my concern with taxonomies is also a concern with (1) the data side of the question, and (2) our failure to provide a filing system for computer exploitation. We *have* entered the computer age—but with feet of clay.

III. THE LADDER OF ABSTRACTION

If quantification cannot solve our problems, in that we cannot measure before conceptualising, and if, on the other hand, 'conceptual stretching' is dangerously conducive to the Hegelian night in which all the cows look black (and eventually the milkman is taken for a cow), then the issue must be joined from its very beginning, that is, on the grounds of concept formation.

A few preliminary cautions should be entered. Things conceived or meaningfully perceived, i.e., concepts, are the central elements of propositions, and—depending on how they are named—provide in and by themselves guidelines of interpretation and observation. It should be understood, therefore, that I shall implicitly refer to the conceptual element problems which in a more extended treatment actually and properly belong to the rubric 'propositions'. By saying concept formation I implicitly point to a proposition-forming and problem-solving activity. It should also be understood, in the second place, that my focus will be on those concepts which Bendix (1963, p. 533) describes as 'generalisations in disguise'. In the third place, I propose to concentrate on the vertical members of a conceptual structure, that is, on (1) *observational terms*, and (2) the vertical disposition of such terms along a *ladder of abstraction*.

While the notion of abstraction ladder is related to the problem of the levels of analysis, the two things do not coincide. A highly abstract level of analysis may not result from 'ladder climbing'. Indeed a number of universal conceptualisations are not abstracted from observables: they are 'theoretical terms' defined by their systemic meaning.[16] For instance the meaning of isomorphism, homeostasis, feedback, entropy, etc., is basically defined by the part that each concept plays in the whole theory. In other instances, however, we deal with 'observational terms', that is, we arrive at highly abstract levels of conceptualisation via ladder climbing, via abstractive inferences from observables. For instance, terms such as group, communication, conflict, and decision can either be used in a very abstract or in a very concrete meaning, either in some very distant relation to observables or with reference to direct observations. In this case we have, then, 'empirical concepts' which can be located at, and moved along, very different points of a ladder of abstraction. If so, we have the problem of assessing the level of abstraction at which observational or (in this sense) empirical concepts are located, and the rules of transformation thus resulting. And this seems to be the pertinent focus for the issue under consideration, for our fundamental problem is how to make extensional gains (by climbing the abstraction ladder) without having to suffer unnecessary losses in precision and empirical testability.

The problem can be neatly underprinted with reference to the distinction, and relation, between the *extension* (denotation) and *intension* (connotation) of a term. A standard definition is as follows: 'The extension of a word is the class of *things* to which the word applies; the intension of a word is the collection of *properties* which determine the things to which the word applies.[17] Likewise, the denotation of a word is the totality of objects indicated by that word; and the connotation is the totality of characteristics anything must possess to be in the denotation of that word.[18]

Now, there are apparently two ways of climbing a ladder of abstraction. One is to broaden the extension of a concept by diminishing its

[16] See Kaplan (1964, pp. 56–7, 63–5). According to Hempel theoretical terms 'usually purport to not directly observable entities and their characteristics.... They function ... in scientific theories intended to explain generalizations' (1958, ii, 42). While it is admittedly difficult to draw a neat division between theoretical and observational terms, it is widely recognised that the former cannot be reduced to, nor derived from, the latter. For a recent assessment of the controversy, see Meotti (1969, pp. 118–34).

[17] I quote from Salmon (1963, pp. 90–1). The distinction is more or less the same in any textbook of logic.

[18] 'Connotation' is also applied, more broadly, to the associations, or associated conceptions brought to mind by the use of a word. As indicated by the text, I intend here the narrower meaning.

attributes or properties, i.e., by reducing its connotation. In this case a more 'general', or more inclusive, concept can be obtained without any loss of precision. The larger the class, the lesser its differentiae; but those differentiae that remain, remain precise. Moreover, following this procedure we obtain conceptualisations which no matter how all-embracing, still bear a traceable relation to a collection of specifics, and —out of being amenable to identifiable sets of specifics—lend themselves to empirical testing.

On the other hand, this is hardly the procedure implied by 'conceptual stretching', which adds up to being an attempt to augment the extension without diminishing the intension: *the denotation is extended by obfuscating the connotation*. As a result we do not obtain a more general concept, but its counterfeit, a mere generality (where the pejorative 'mere' is meant to restore the distinction between correct and incorrect ways of subsuming a term under a broader genus). While a general concept can be said to represent a collection of specifics, a mere generality cannot be underpinned, out of its indefiniteness, by specifics. And while a general concept is conducive to scientific 'generalisations', mere generalities are conducive only to vagueness and conceptual obscurity.

The rules for climbing and descending along a ladder of abstraction are thus very simple rules—in principle. We make a concept more abstract and more general by lessening its properties or attributes. Conversely, a concept is specified by the addition (or unfolding) of qualifications, i.e., by augmenting its attributes or properties. If so, let us pass on to consider a ladder of abstraction as such. It is self-evident that along the abstraction ladder one obtains very different degrees of inclusiveness and, conversely, specificity. These differences can be usefully underpinned—for the purposes of comparative politics—by distinguishing three levels of abstraction, labelled, in shorthand, HL (high level), ML (medium level), and LL (low level).

High level categorisations obtain universal conceptualisations: whatever connotation is sacrificed to the requirement of global denotation —either in space, time, or even both.[19] HL concepts can also be visualised as the ultimate genus which cancels all its species. Descending a step, medium level categorisations fall short of universality and thus can be said to obtain general classes: at this level not all differentiae are sacrificed to extensional requirements. Nonetheless, ML concepts are

---

[19] The space and time dimensions of concepts are often associated with the geography versus history debate. I would rather see it as the 'when goes with when?' question, that is, as a calendar time versus historical time dilemma. But this line of development cannot be pursued here.

intended to stress similarities at the expense of uniqueness, for at this level of abstraction we are typically dealing with generalisations. Finally, low level categories obtain specific, indeed configurative conceptualisations: here denotation is sacrificed to accuracy of connotation. One may equally say that with LL categories the differentiae of individual settings are stressed above their similarities: so much so that at this level definitions are often contextual.

A couple of examples may be usefully entered. In a perceptive essay which runs parallel to my line of thinking Neil J. Smelser (1967, p. 103) makes the point that, for purposes of comparability, 'staff is more satisfactory than administration . . . , and administration is more satisfactory than civil service'. This is so, according to Smelser, because the concept of civil service 'is literally useless in connection with societies without a formal state or governmental apparatus'. In this respect 'the concept of administration is somewhat superior . . . but even this term is quite culture-bound'. Hence the more helpful term is 'Weber's concept of staff . . . since it can encompass without embarassment various political arrangements . . .' In my own terms the argument would be rephrased as follows. In the field of so-called comparative public administration, 'staff' is the high level universal category. 'Administration' is still a good travelling category, but falls short of universal applicability in that it retains some of the attributes associated with the more specific notion of 'bureaucracy'. Descending the ladder of abstraction further we then find 'civil service', which is qualified by its associations with the modern State. Finally, and to pursue the argument all the way down to the low level of abstraction, a comparative study of, say, French and English state employees will discover their unique and distinguishing traits and would thus provide contextual definitions.

The example suggested by Smelser is fortunate in that we are offered a choice of terms, so that (whatever the choice) a different level of abstraction can be identified by a different denomination. The next example is illustrative, instead, of the far less fortunate situation in which we may have to perform across the whole ladder of abstraction with one and the same term. In illustrating his caution that many concepts are 'generalisations in disguise', Bendix (1963, p. 536) comes across such a simple concept as 'village'. Yet he notes that the term village may be misleading when applied to Indian society, where 'the minimum degree of cohesion commonly associated with this term is absent'. Even in such a simple case, then, a scholar is required to place the various associations of 'village' along an abstraction ladder in accord with the travelling extension afforded by each connotation.

Clearly, there is no hard and fast dividing line between levels of abstraction. Borders can only be drawn very loosely; and the number of slices into which the ladder is divided largely depends on how fine one's analysis needs to be. Three slices are sufficient, however, for the purposes of logical analysis. And my major concern is, in this connection, with what goes on at the upper end of the ladder, at the crucial juncture at which we cross the border between medium level general concepts and high level universals. The issue may be formulated as follows: how far up can an observational term be pushed without self-denying results?

In principle the extension of a concept should not be broadened beyond the point at which at least one relatively precise connotation (property or attribute) is retained. In practice, however, the requirement of positive identification may be too exacting. But even if no minimal positive identification can be afforded, I do not see how we can renounce the requirement of negative identification. The crucial distinction would thus be between (1) concepts defined by negation or *ex adverso*, i.e., by saying what they are *not*, and (2) concepts *without negation*, i.e., no-opposite concepts, conceptions without specified termination or boundaries. The logical principle involved in this distinction is *omnis determinatio est negatio*, that is, any determination involves a negation. According to this principle the former concepts are, no matter how broad, *determinate*; whereas the latter are indeterminate, literally *without termination*.

If this principle is applied to the climbing process along a ladder of abstraction, and precisely to the point at which ML categories are turned into HL universals, in the first instance we obtain *empirical universals*, whereas in the second instance we obtain universals which lack empirical value—*pseudo-universals* for an empirical science. The reason for this is that a concept qualified by a negation may, or may not, be found to apply to the real world; whereas a non-bounded concept always applies by definition: having no specified termination, there is no way of ascertaining whether it applies to the real world or not. An empirical universal is such because it still points to *something*; whereas a non-empirical universal indiscriminately points to *everything* (as any researcher on the field soon discovers).

The group concept lends itself nicely as an illustration of the foregoing (other examples will be discussed in greater detail later), and is very much to the point in that it represents the first large-scale attempt to meet the travelling problem of comparative politics. In the group theory of politics (Bentley, David Truman, and Earl Lathan being the obvious references) it is clear enough that 'group' becomes an all-embracing category: not only an analytical construct (as the queer and unclear terminology of the discipline would have it), but definitely a universal construct. However, we are never really told what group *is not*. Not only 'group' applies *everywhere*, as any universal should; it equally applies to *everything*, that is, never and nowhere shall we encounter non-groups.[20] If so, how is it that the group theory of politics has been followed—in the fifties—by a great deal of empirical research? The reply is that the research was not guided by the universal construct but by intuitive concrete conceptualisations. Hence the 'indefinite group' of the theory, and the 'concrete groups' of the research, fall wide apart. The unfortunate consequences are not only that the research lacks theoretical backing (for want of medium level categories, and especially of a taxonomic framework), but that the vagueness of the theory has no fit for the specificity of the findings. We are thus left with a body of literature that gives the frustrating feeling of dismantling theoretically whatever it discovers empirically.

There is, then, a break-off point in the search for universal inclusiveness beyond which we have, theoretically, a 'nullification of the problem' and, empirically, what may be called an 'empirical vaporisation'. This is the point at which a concept is not even determined *ex adverso*. By saying that no-opposite universals are of no empirical use I do not imply that they are utterly useless. But I do wish to say that whenever notions such as groups or—as in my subsequent examples— pluralism, integration, participation, and mobilisation, obtain no termination, i.e., remain indeterminate, they provide only tags, chapter headings, i.e., the main entries of a filing system. From an empirical point of view pseudo-universals are only funnels of approach and can only perform, so to speak, an allusive function.

Turning to the middle slice—the fat slice of the medium level categories—it will suffice to note that at this level we are required to perform the whole set of operations that some authors call 'definition by analysis', that is, the process of defining a term by finding the genus to which the object designated by the word belongs, and then specifying the attributes which distinguish such object from all the other species of the same genus. When Apter (1971) complains that our 'analytical categories are too general when they are theoretical, and too descriptive where they are not', I understand this complaint to apply to our disorderly leaps from observational findings all the way up to universal

---

[20] This criticism is perhaps unfair to Truman (1951). However, in spite of its penetrating anatomy the pace of the inquiry is set by the sentence that 'an excessive preoccupation with definition will only prove a handicap' (p. 23). For a development of this line of criticism see Sartori (1959, pp. 7–42).

categories—and vice versa—by-passing as it were the stage of definition by analysis. Apter is quite right in pleading for 'better intermediate analytical categories'. But these intermediate categories cannot be constructed, I fear, as long as our contempt for the taxonomical exercise leaves us with an atrophied medium level of abstraction.

The low level of abstraction may appear uninteresting to the comparative scholar. He would be wrong, however, on two counts. First, when the comparative scholar is engaged in field work, the more his fact-finding categories are brought down to this level, the better his research. Second, it is the evidence obtained nation-by-nation, or region-by-region (or whatever the unit of analysis may be) that helps us decide which classification works, or which new criterion of classification should be developed.

While classifying must abide by logical rules, logic has nothing to do with the usefulness of a classificatory system. Botanists, mineralogists and zoologists have not created their taxonomical trees as a matter of mere logical unfolding; that is, they have not imposed their 'classes' upon their animals, any more than their animals (flowers or minerals) have imposed themselves upon their classifiers. Let it be added that the information requirements of such an unsettled science as a science of politics can hardly be satisfied by single-purpose classifications (not to mention single-purpose checklists). As I have stressed, we desperately need standard fact-finding and fact-storing containers (concepts). But this standardisation is only possible and fruitful on the basis of 'multi-purpose' and, at the limit, all-purpose classifications. Now, whether a

TABLE 17.1. *Ladder of Abstraction*

Levels of abstraction	Major comparative scope and purpose	Logical and empirical properties of concepts
HL: *High level categories* Universal conceptualisations	Cross-area comparisons among heterogeneous contexts (global theory)	Maximal extension Minimal intension Definition by negation
ML: *Medium level categories* General conceptualisations and taxonomies	Intra-area comparisons among relatively homogeneous contexts (middle range theory)	Balance of denotation with connotation Definition by analysis, i.e. *per genus et differentiam*
LL: *Low level categories* Configurative conceptualisations	Country by country analysis (narrow-gauge theory)	Maximal intension Minimal extension Contextual definition

classification may serve multiple purposes, and which classification fits this requirement best, this is something we discover inductively, that is, starting from the bottom of the ladder of abstraction.

The over-all discussion is recapitulated in Table 17.1 with respect to its bearing on the problems of comparative politics. A few additional comments are in order. In the first place, reference to three levels of abstraction brings out the inadequacy of merely distinguishing between 'broad' and 'narrow' meanings of a term.[21] For this does not clarify, whenever this is necessary, whether we distinguish, (1) between HL universal and ML general conceptualisations, or (2) between ML genuses and species or, (3) between ML and LL categories, or even (4) between HL universal and LL configurative conceptualisations.

In the second place, and more important, reference to the ladder of abstraction forcibly highlights the drastic loss of logical articulation, indeed the gigantic leap, implied by the argument that *all* differences are 'a matter of degree'. This cannot be conceded, to begin with, at the level of universal categories. But all differences cannot be considered a matter of more-or-less at the medium level either. At the top we inevitably begin with opposite pairs, with polar opposites, and this is tantamount to saying that the top ML categories definitely and only establish differences in *kind*. From here downwards definitions are obtained via the logic of classification, and this implies that a logic of gradation cannot be applied as long as we establish differences between species. Differences in degree obtain only after having established that two or more objects have the same attributes or properties, i.e., belong to the same species. Indeed, it is only *within* the same class that we are entitled—and indeed required—to ask which object has more or less of an attribute or property.

In principle, then, it is a fallacy to apply the logic of gradation whenever ladder climbing (or descending) is involved. If we are reminded that along the ladder we augment the extension by diminishing the denotation (and vice versa), what is at stake here is the presence or absence of a given property; and this is not a matter of degree, but a matter of establishing the level of abstraction. Hence it is only after having settled at a given level of abstraction that considerations of more-and-less correctly apply. And the rule of thumb seems to be that the higher the level of abstraction, the less a degree language applies (as anything but a metaphor); whereas the lower level of abstraction, the

[21] The same caution applies to the distinctions between micro and macro, or between molecular and molar. These distinctions are insufficient for the purpose of underpinning the level of analysis.

more a degree optics correctly and necessarily applies, and the more we profit from gradation concepts.

In the third place, and equally important, reference to the ladder of abstraction casts many doubts on the optimistic view—largely shared by the methodological literature—that 'The more universal a proposition, i.e., the greater the number of events a proposition accounts for, the more potential falsifiers can be found, and the more informative is the proposition.'[22] The sentence suggests a simultaneous and somewhat natural progression of universality, falsifiers and informative content. It seems to me, instead, that reference to the correct technique of ladder climbing (and descending) confronts us at all points with choosing between range of explanation (thereby including the explanation of the relationships among the items under investigation), and accuracy of description (or informative accuracy). By saying that the 'informative content' of a proposition grows by climbing the abstraction ladder, we should not be misled into understanding that we are supplying more descriptive information. Hence it is dubious whether we are really supplying more potential falsifiers (let alone the danger of 'overly universal' propositions of no informative value for which falsifiers cannot be found).

Before concluding it should not pass unnoticed that in this section I have never used the word 'variable', nor mentioned operational definitions, nor invoked indicators. Equally, my reference to gradation concepts and to considerations of more-or-less has been, so far, entirely pre-quantitative. What is noteworthy, then, is the length that has been travelled before entering the problems which seem to monopolise our methodological awareness. There is nothing wrong, to be sure, in taking up an argument at whichever point we feel that we have something to say—except that the tail of the methodological argument should not be mistaken for its beginning. Since I have taken up the issue at an early stage, I cannot possibly carry it through to its end. It behoves me, nonetheless, to indicate how I would plug what I have said into what shall have to remain unsaid.[23]

For one thing, it should be understood that by considering concepts —the genus—I have not excluded the consideration of variables, which are a species. That is, a variable is still a concept; but a concept is not necessarily a variable. If all concepts could be turned into variables, the

---

[22] I quote Allardt (1968, p. 165). But the sentence is illustrative of a current mood.

[23] In this latter connection an excellent reader still is Lazarsfeld and Rosenberg (1955). See also its largely revised and updated revision, Boudon and Lazarsfeld (1965–66).

difference could be considered provisional. Unfortunately, as a scholar well versed in quantitative analysis puts it, 'all the most interesting variables are nominal' (Rose, n.d., p. 8). Which is the same as saying that all the most interesting concepts are not variables in the proper, strict sense of implying 'the possibility of measurement in the most exact sense of the word'.[24]

A closely linked and similar argument applies to the operationist requirement. Just as concepts are not necessarily variables, definitions are not necessarily operational. The definitional requirement for a concept is that its *meaning* is declared, while operational definitions are required to state the conditions, indeed the operations, by means of which a concept can be *verified* and, ultimately, measured. Accordingly we may usefully distinguish between definition of meaning and operational definition. And while it is obvious that an operational definition still is a declaration of meaning, the reverse is not true.

The contention often is that definition of meaning represents a pre-scientific age of definition, which should be superseded in scientific discourse by operational definitions. However, this contention can hardly meet the problems of concept formation, and indeed appears to ignore them. As the ladder of abstraction scheme helps to underline, among the many possible ways and procedures of defining the *ex adverso* definitions and taxonomic unfoldings (or definition by analysis) some correspond to different levels of analysis and play, at each level, a non-replaceable role. Moreover operational definitions generally entail a drastic curtailment of meaning for they can only maintain those meanings that comply with the operationist requirement. Now, we are surely required to reduce ambiguity by cutting down the range of meanings of concepts. But the operational criterion of reducing ambiguity entails drastic losses in conceptual richness and in explanatory power. Take, for instance, the suggestion that 'social class' should be dismissed and replaced by a set of operational statements relating to income, occupation, educational level, etc. If the suggestion were adopted wholesale, the loss of conceptual substance would be not only considerable, but unjustified. The same applies, to cite another instance, to 'power'. To be concerned with the measurement of power does not imply that the meaning of the concept should be reduced to what can be measured about power—the latter view would make human behaviour in whatever collective sphere almost inexplicable.

It should be understood, therefore, that operational definitions imple-

[24] Lazarsfeld and Barton (1965, p. 170). This notably excludes, for the authors, the application of 'variable' to items that can be ranked but not measured.

ment, but do not replace, definitions of meaning. Indeed there must be
a conceptualisation before we engage in operationalisation. As Hempel
recommends, operational definitions should not be 'emphasised to the
neglect of the requirement of systematic import'.[25] This is also to say
that definitions of meaning of theoretical import, hardly operational
definitions, account for the dynamics of intellectual discovery and stimu-
lation. Finally, it should be understood that empirical testing occurs
before, and also without, operational definitions. Testing is any method
of checking correspondence with reality by the use of pertinent observations; hence the decisive difference brought about by operationalisation
is verification, or falsification, by measurement.[26]

Speaking of testing, indicators are indeed precious 'testing helpers'.
As a matter of fact it is difficult to see how theoretical terms could be
empiricised and tested otherwise, that is, without having recourse to
indicators. Indicators are also expedient shortcuts for the empirical
checking of observational terms. Yet the question remains: Indicators
of what? If we have fuzzy concepts, the fuzziness will remain as it is.
That is to say that indicators cannot, in and by themselves, sharpen our
concepts and relieve us from composing and decomposing them along
a ladder of abstraction.

IV. COMPARATIVE FALLACIES: AN ILLUSTRATION

We may now confront in more detail how the ladder of abstraction
scheme brings out the snares and the faults of our current way of
handling the travelling problem of comparative politics. For we may
now settle at a less rarified level of discussion and proceed on the basis
of examples. It is pretty obvious that my line of analysis largely cuts
across the various theories and schools that propose themselves for
adoption in comparative politics, for my basic preoccupation is with the
ongoing work of the 'normal science', i.e., with the common conceptual problems of the discipline. Nonetheless it will be useful to
enter here a somewhat self-contained illustration which bears not only
on discrete concepts, but equally on a theoretical framework. I have

[25] (1952, p. 60). At p. 47 Hempel writes: 'it is precisely the discovery of
concepts with theoretical import which advances scientific understanding;
and such discovery requires scientific inventiveness and cannot be replaced
by the—certainly indispensable, but also definitely insufficient—operationist
or empiricist requirement of empirical import alone.'

[26] This is not to say that operationalisation allows *eo ipso* for quantitative
measurements, but to suggest that either operational definitions are ultimately conducive to measurement, or may not be worthwhile.

thus selected for my first detailed discussion the categories of 'structure' and 'function', and this precisely on account of their crucial role in establishing the structural-functional approach in the political science setting.[27]

In introducing his pioneering comparative volume, Almond [and Coleman] (1960, p. 59) boldly asserts: 'What we have done is to separate political function from political structure.' This separation is indeed crucial. But ten years have gone by and the assignment remains largely unfulfilled. Indeed the structural-functional school of thought is still grappling—with clear symptoms of frustration—with the preliminary difficulty of defining 'function'—both taken by itself and in its relation to 'structure'.[28]

Whether function can be simply conceived as an 'activity' performed by structures; or whether it is more proper to construe function as an 'effect';[29] or whether function should be conceived only as a 'relation' among structures[30]—this controversy turns out to be largely immaterial in the light of our substantive performance. That is to say, if our attention turns to the functional vocabulary in actual use, a perusal of the literature quickly reveals two things: a tantalising anarchy (on this more later), and, second, that the functional terminology employed most of the time by most practitioners definitely carries a purposive or teleological connotation. Skilful verbal camouflage may well push the teleological implication in the background. Yet it is hard to find a functional argumentation which really escapes, in the final analysis, *Zweck-*

[27] I specify political science setting to avoid the unnecessary regression to Malinowski and Radcliff-Brown. This is also to explain why I set aside the contributions of Talcott Parsons and of Marion J. Levy. Flanigan and Fogelman (1967, pp. 72–9) distinguish between three major streams, labelled (1) eclectic functionalism, (2) empirical functionalism (Merton), and (3) structural-functional analysis. My discussion exclusively applies to part of the latter.

[28] It should be understood that by now the structural-functional label applies to a widely scattered group operating on premises which are largely at variance.

[29] This focus was suggested by R. K. Merton (1957), whose concern was to separate function—defined as an 'observable objective consequence'—from 'subjective disposition', i.e., aims, motives and purposes (p. 24 and *passim*, pp. 19–84). In attempting to meet the difficulties raised by the Mertonian focus, Robert T. Holt (1967, pp. 88–90) construes functions as 'sub-types' of effects, and precisely as the 'system-relevant effect of structures'; understanding system-relevance as the 'system-requiredness' which is determined, in turn, by the 'functional requisites' of a given system. My own position is that Merton overstated his case thereby creating for his followers unnecessary and unsettled complications.

[30] This is the mathematical meaning of function.

rationalität, what Max Weber called rationality of ends.[31] We may well quarrel about the definition;[32] yet the substance of the matter remains that the definitional controversy has little bearing on our subsequent proceedings. If so, it suits my purposes to settle for the ways in which most people use 'function' in practice (regardless of how they theorise about it), and thereby to settle for the common sense, unsophisticated meaning.

When we say, somewhat naively, that structures 'have functions', we are interested in the reason for being of structures: we are implying, that is, that structures exist *for* some end, purpose, destination or assignment.[33] This is tantamount to saying that 'function' points to a means-end relationship (which becomes, from a systematic viewpoint, also a part-whole relationship), i.e., that function is the activity performed by a structure—the means—*vis-à-vis* its ascribed or actually served purpose.[34] Conversely, dis-function, non-functionality, and the like, indicate—from different angles—that the assigned purpose is not served by a given structure. And this current usage of function goes a long way to explain, in turn, our difficulties with structure.

The major problem with 'structure' is, in fact, that political bodies and institutions largely bear, if not a functional denomination, a functional definition. Either under the sheer force of names—which is in itself a tremendous force—or for the sake of brevity, political structures are seldom adequately defined on their own terms—*qua structures*. That is to say, on the one hand, that we dispose of a functional

---

[31] Rationality of ends should not be confused with *Wertrationalität*, value rationality, among other reasons because in the former perspective all conceivable ends can be hypothesised as being equally valid. Hence in the *Zweckrationalität* perspective there is little point in unmasking functions as 'eu-functions' or, conversely, as 'caco-functions'. Whether the good goals of one man are the bad goals of the next man becomes relevant only if we enter a normative, *Wertrationalität* discussion.

[32] For the many additional intricacies of the subject that I must neglect, a recent, interesting reader largely focused on the 'debate over functionalism' is Demerath and Peterson (1967). For a critical statement of the inherent limitations of functionalism see Runciman (1963, pp. 109–23). Hempel (1959, pp. 271–307) equally takes a critical view of 'the logic of functional analysis' but his standpoint is often far removed from our problems.

[33] This is not to fall prey to the subjectivistic fallacy on which Merton (1957) builds his case. Purpose may be a 'motivation' of the actor, but may equally be—as it is in teleological analysis—an 'imputation' of the observer.

[34] 'Unintended functions'—the fact that structures may serve ends and obtain results which were neither foreseen nor desired by the structure builders—can be entered, for the economy of my argument, into the list of the purposes actually served. Likewise 'latent functions' are immaterial to my point.

(purposive) vocabulary, whereas we badly lack a structural (descriptive) vocabulary; and that, on the other hand, even when we deliberately ask 'what is', we are invariably prompted to reply in terms of 'what for'. What is an election? A means (a structure) *for* electing office holders. What is a legislature? An arrangement *for* producing legislation. What is a government? A set-up *for* governing. The structure is almost invariably perceived and qualified by its salient function.[35] This makes a great deal of sense in practical politics, but represents a serious handicap for the understanding of politics.

The plain fact is, then, that the structural-functional analyst is a lame scholar. He claims to walk on two feet, but actually stands on one foot —and a bad foot at that. He cannot really visualise the interplay between 'structure' and 'function' because the two terms are seldom, if ever, neatly disjointed: the structure remains throughout a twin brother of its imputed functional purposes. And here we enter a somewhat vicious whirl which leads the approach to conclusions which, if true, would be self-denying.

Whatever else the structural-functional scholar may have failed to discover, he feels pretty sure about three points: first, no structure is unifunctional, i.e., performs only one function; second, the same structure can be multifunctional, i.e., can perform across different countries widely different functions; third, and therefore, the same function has structural alternatives, i.e., can be performed by very different structures. Now, to some extent these points are undeniable—but only to the extent sensed at any time by any perceptive comparative scholar. My quarrel is with the emphasis, which is unwarranted and positively misleading.

Is it really the *same* structure that functions differently? Or is the functional performance different because the structure is not the same? The thesis generally lacks adequate evidence on the structural side. For instance, 'elections' are multifunctional (they may well serve the purpose of legitimising a despot), but 'free elections' are not.[36] That is

[35] Riggs makes the same point, namely, that 'current terminology quite confusingly links structural and functional meanings' from the opposite angle that expressions such as 'legislature and public administrator... are normally defined structurally, the first as an elected assembly, the second as a bureaucratic office'; but then goes on to say that 'the words ... also imply functions' Riggs, n.d., (p. 23). It should be understood, therefore, that my 'structural definition' calls for a thorough structural description. If the argument were left at defining a legislature as an elected assembly, then it can be made either way, as Riggs does.

[36] I cite the title of MacKenzie's book *Free Elections* (1958) to imply that a real structural underpinning may well presuppose a hundred-page description.

to say, as soon as the electoral process obtains a structural underpinning —the minute and multiple structural conditions that make for free voting—electoral multifunctionality rapidly comes to an end. If the voter *is* offered alternatives, if the candidates *are* free to compete, if fraudulent counting *is* impossible, then free elections do serve—everywhere—the purpose of allowing an electorate to select and dismiss office holders. In view of this primary, fundamental purpose the *same* electoral structure (same in providing all the necessary safeties) either approaches unifunctionality, or leaves us with non-functionality, e.g., with the finding that illiterate voters are unable to use electoral mechanisms which presuppose literacy.

While the most serious problem and default is that the structures are inadequately pinpointed and described, let me hasten to add that we are not performing much better from the functional end of the argument. For our functional categories also generally lack adequate underpinning. Surprisingly enough—if one considers the far greater ease with which the functional side of the problem can be attacked—our functions tend to be as unhelpful as our structures.

For instance, if one asks, 'Why a party system?' the least challengeable and most inclusive reply might be that parties perform a communication function. And if the problem is left at that, it easily follows that the authorities and the citizens 'communicate', in some sense, in any polity, i.e., even when no party system exists. Hence party systems have structural alternatives—*quod erat demonstrandum*. But the problem cannot be left at that, i.e., with an unbounded, no-difference notion of communication which nullifies the problem. And the underpinning of communication brings out, first, that there is an essential difference between up-going and descending communication, and, second, that it is equally important to distinguish between 'communication-information' and 'communication-pressure'. If so, to define a party system as an instrument for 'communicating' demands and conveying 'information' to the authorities, is to miss the point. A party system is, in reality, a mechanism for *sustaining* demands—and *pressing* demands—all the way through to policy implementation. What is at stake, then, is the passage from a two-way (reversible) communication-information to a prevalence of up-going communication-pressure. And for this latter purpose we have not devised, so far, any structural alternative. A party system turns out to be, therefore, a non-replaceable, *unique structure* as soon as we spell out its distinctive, crucial reason for being.

A more careful scrutiny goes to show, then, that the multifunctional, multistructural argument has been pushed far too far, indeed to the point of becoming erroneous. Aside from the error, the irony of the situation is that, as it stands, the thesis appears self-defeating. If the same structure performs utterly different functions in different countries, and if we can always find structural alternatives for whatever function, what is the use of structural-functional analysis?

Pulling the threads together, I need not spend much time in arguing that the stalemate and the mishandlings of the structural-functional approach have a lot to do with the ladder of abstraction.

On the functional side of the coin we are encumbered by a wealth of haphazard functional categories which are merely enumerated (hardly classified according to some criterion, and even less according to the logical requirements of a taxonomical tree-type unfolding), and definitely provide no clues as to the level and type of analysis (e.g., total versus partial systems analysis) to which they apply.[37] As a result the global functional argument developed by a number of structural-functionalists remains suspended in mid-air—for lack of a co-ordinated medium level taxonomic support—and is left to play with overstretched, if not contentless, functional universals.

On the structural side of the coin we are confronted, instead, with little more than nothing. Structures qualified on their own right hardly exist—at least in the Almond line of thinking.[38] This is all the more regrettable in view of the fact that while functions are meant to be (at least in global comparative politics) broad explanatory categories which do not require a low level specification, structures bear, instead, a closer relation to observables, and definitely need underpinning all the way down the ladder. With structures understood as organisational structures we are required, in fact, to descend the ladder all the way down to low level configurative-descriptive accounts.

Starting from the top, one can identify—with the help of minor

[37] A sheer list of the functional denominations, roles or attributions scattered throughout the literature on political parties suffices to illustrate the point, and would be as follows: participation, electioneering, mobilisation, extraction, regulation, control, integration, cohesive function, moderating function, consensus maintenance, simplification of alternatives, reconciliation, adaptation, aggregation, mediation, conflict resolution, brokerage, recruitment, policy making, expression, communication, linkage, channelment, conversion, legitimising function, democratisation, labelling function.

[38] I make specific reference to Almond because I believe that his very conception of structure is largely responsible for this outcome. For instance, 'By structure we mean the observable activities which make up the political system. To refer to these activities as having a structure simply implies that there is a certain regularity to them' (1966, p. 21). In the subsequent paragraph one reads: 'We refer to particular sets of roles which are related to one another as *structures*.' Under such porous and excessively sociological criteria, 'structure' becomes evanescent.

terminological devices—at least four different levels of analysis: (1) structural principles (e.g., pluralism), (2) structural conditions (e.g., the class or the economic structure), (3) organisational patterns (with relation to membership systems), (4) specific organisational structures (e.g., constitutions). By saying 'structural principles' I mean that as an HL category the notion of structure can only point to the principles according to which the component part of politics, or of societies, are related to each other. With reference, instead, to the low level of abstraction it should be clear that constitutions and statutes are not the 'real' structure. Nonetheless behaviour under written rules is easier to pin down than behaviour under diffuse roles, and excessive anti-formalism leads us to neglect organisational theory and the extent to which legally enforced regulations do mould behaviour.

In summing up, not only has the structural-functional scholar ignored the ladder of abstraction, but he has inadvertently destroyed, during his reckless climbing, his own ladder.[39] So much so that the approach encounters exactly the same perplexity as, say, general systems theory, namely, 'Why has no scholar succeeded in presenting a structural-functional formulation which meets the requirements of empirical analysis' (Flanigan and Fogelman, 1967, pp. 82–3). Now, it is hardly surprising that the general systems theorist should encounter great difficulties in deriving testable propositions about politics, since he is required to proceed deductively on the basis of theoretical primitives.[40] But this is not the case with the structural-functional approach, which is not necessarily committed to whole systems analysis and enjoys the distinctive empirical advantage of leaning extensively—especially with segmented systems analysis—on observational terms.[41] So, why should the structural-functional scholar remain tied to 'a level of analysis which [does] not permit empirical testing?' (Flanigan and Fogelman, 1967). According to my diagnosis there is no intrinsic reason for this. Quite to the contrary, we may expect very rewarding returns, and the empirical

[39] This complaint is *ad hoc*, but could be expanded at length. On the general lack of logical and methodological status of the approach two strong critical statements are: Dowse (1966, pp. 607–22); and Kalleberg (1966, pp. 69–82). While the two authors are overconscious thinkers, I would certainly agree with Dowse's concluding sentence, namely, that 'to ignore trivial logical points is to risk being not even trivially true' (p. 622).

[40] On general systems theory one may usefully consult Young (1968, ch. 2). See also Urbani (1968, pp. 795–819).

[41] While there is some controversy on the respective merits and shortcomings of the two strategies, the structural-functional approach is not inherently tied to either one. For the partial versus whole systems controversy the two stances are well represented by J. LaPalombara (1970), who favours the segmented approach.

promise (and distinctiveness) of the approach may well near fulfilment, if we only learn how to manoeuvre along a ladder of abstraction.

Let us now pass on to a more loose discussion—the second part of this illustration—for which I have selected a somewhat different family of categories: pluralism, integration, participation and mobilisation.[42] While one may think of many other examples that would suit my purposes just as well, the four categories in question are representative in that they are used for significant theoretical developments not only under a variety of different frameworks, but also by the non-affiliated scholar, thereby including—in the case of participation and mobilisation—the scholar who happens to be interested only in statistical manipulations.

Given the fact that pluralism, integration, participation and mobilisation are culture-bound concepts which may reflect—as far as we know at the outset—a distinctive Western experience, the methodological caveat here is that the reference area should make for the starting point of the investigation. So to speak, we are required to elaborate our culture-bound concepts in a 'we–they' clockwise direction. It is proper, therefore, to start with the question: How do we understand pluralism, integration, participation and mobilisation in their domestic, original context?

At home 'pluralism' does not apply to societal and/or political structure, nor to interplay between a plurality of actors. Pluralism came to be used, in the Western literature, to convey the idea that a pluralistic society is a society whose structural configuration is shaped by pluralistic beliefs, namely, that all kinds of autonomous sub-units should develop at all levels, that interests are recognised in their legitimate diversity, and that dissent, not unanimity, represents the basis of civility. Pluralism is indeed—as already noted—a highly abstract structural *principle*. Yet the term points to a *particular* societal structure—not merely to a developed stage of differentiation and specialisation—and does retain a wealth of characterising connotations whenever we discuss, in the Western democracies, our internal policies and problems.

'Integration' can be conceived as an end-state, as a process, or as a function performed by integrating agencies (parties, interest groups, etc.). In any case, in the Western politics integration is not applied to

[42] The relevant 'family difference' is that structure and function are not culture-bound concepts, while the four other categories are. This is also to note that the travelling problem of comparative politics cannot be reduced to the construction of 'non-culture bound' conceptualisations. How to use those conceptualisations which cannot help being culture bound is equally a problem.

whatever kind of 'putting together', to *whatever* state of amalgamation. For instance, when American scholars discuss their own domestic problems, they have definite ideas of what is, and what is not, integration. They would deny that integration has anything to do with 'enforcing uniformity'. They are likely to assume, instead, that integration both presupposes and generates a pluralistic society (as qualified above). And, surely, an integrative agency is required to obtain a maximum of coalescence and solidarity with a minimum of coercion.[43]

Similar points can be made with regard to participation and mobilisation. Regardless of whether 'participation' is used normatively (as pointing to a basic tenet of the democratic ideal) or descriptively (as reflecting a democratic experience), in either case in our domestic discussions participation is not any such kind of 'taking part'. Thus the advocates of a participatory democracy are hardly satisfied by any kind of involvement in politics. To them participation means *self-motion*; it does not mean being manipulated or coerced into motion. And surely the original definite meaning of the term conveys the idea of a free citizen who acts and intervenes—if he so wishes—according to *his* best judgment. So conceived, participation is the very opposite, or the very reverse, of mobilisation. Mobilisation does not convey the idea of individual self-motion, but the idea of a malleable, passive collectivity which is being *put into motion* at the whim of persuasive—and more than persuasive—authorities. We say that individuals 'participate' but we cannot say about the same individuals that they 'mobilise'—they *are mobilised*.

It is quite clear, then, that pluralism, integration, participation and mobilisation all have specific connotations which can be pinned down, and are in fact retained—no matter how implicitly—in our Western inquiries and controversies. However, in the context of global comparative politics the specificity of these notions gets lost: there is no end to pluralism; integration is applied indifferently to pluralistic and non-pluralistic settings; and participation and mobilisation are turned into largely overlapping notions. There is no end to pluralism, for we are never told what is non-pluralism. Since pluralism exists somewhere, the assumption appears to be that 'to a different degree' pluralism will be

[43] Since we are discussing here macro-problems and macro-theory I need not follow the concepts under investigation all the way down the ladder of abstraction. I should not let pass unnoticed, however, that 'integration' also belongs to the vocabulary of sociology and psychology, thereby lending itself to very fine lower level distinctions. See e.g., W. S. Landecker (1955, pp. 19–27).

found to exist everywhere. However, a different degree *of what?* This is indeed the irony of using a degree language—intended when used appropriately to convey precision—for conveying elusiveness. Likewise the meaning of integration changes, and eventually evaporates, en route. Finally, and similarly, the distinction between participation and mobilisation only holds at home. With most comparative oriented scholars mobilisation comes to mean whatever process of social activation; and participation is currently applied by the discipline at large both to democratic and mobilisational techniques of political activation.

At this stage of the argument I need not labour at explaining why and how we obtain these drastic losses of specifity. They result, as we know, from conceptual stretching, which results, in turn, from incorrect ladder climbing: the clumsy attempt to arrive at 'travelling universals' at the expense of precision, instead of at the expense of connotation (i.e., by reducing the number of qualifying attributes). What remains to be highlighted are the consequences of this state of affairs.

Take, for instance, the formidable errors in interpretation and prediction which are suggested by the universal, unspecified application of 'pluralism' and 'integration'. If we say that African societies are not pluralistic but 'tribalistic', the argument is likely to be that a situation of tribalistic fragmentation hardly provides the structural basis not only for integrative processes to occur, but also for bringing integrative agencies to the fore. Indeed my argument would be that the functional needs, or feedbacks, of a fragmented society are at odds with the functional feedbacks, or needs, of a pluralistic society. In Europe, for instance, medieval fragmentation generated monarchial absolutism. However, if pluralism is vapourised into an empty generality, then we are authorised to call African societies pluralistic, and the unfortunate implication may well be that we expect Africans to solve their problems as if they had to deal with Western-type societies.[44]

'Mobilisation' is also a worthwhile example in that it confronts us with a problem that has only been mentioned, so far, in passing. While pluralism, integration and participation are derived from our experience with democracy—i.e., from the context of the democratic polities—we also dispose of a limited set of terms which originate from a totalitarian context. This is the case of the term mobilisation, which derives from military terminology—especially the German total mobilisation of

[44] The point could be extended at great length; e.g., I would assume that only in a truly pluralistic society (i.e., qualified by the characteristics conveyed by the Western use of term) may differentiation result in, and join forces with, integration. But much of the literature on political development seems to miss this essential condition.

World War I—and enters the vocabulary of politics via the militia type of party (as Duverger calls it), and specifically via the experience of fascism and of nazism.[45] Nonetheless the term is currently applied also to the democratic polities—and this means that we have drawn a 'reversed extrapolation' (i.e., a counter-clockwise extrapolation). And since we often complain that our terminology is democracy-centred, my first complaint is that we fail to take advantage of the fact that we do have terms which escape the democratic bias. However, the inconvenience resulting from reversed extrapolations are seen best on a broader scale, and with particular reference to what I call the 'boomerang effect' of the developing areas.[46]

Western scholars travelling across Africa or South-East Asia discover that our categories hardly apply, which is hardly surprising. From this they conclude—and this is the boomerang effect—that the Western categories also should not be applied to the West. But this is a strange inference. Granted that global comparative polities requires minimal common denominators, it does not follow that we should escape Western parochialism by masquerading in non-Western clothes. For one thing, it may well be that a number of ancient civilisations appear diffuse and amorphous to the Western observer precisely because he lacks the categories for coping with devious, overly sedimented, 'non-rational' structural patterns. On the other hand, and assuming that underdeveloped political societies may be far less structured than others, this is no reason for feeding back shapelessness where structural differentiation does exist. Hence, reversed extrapolations are a fallacy, and the problem of establishing a minimal common denominator does not authorise us to feed primitivism and formlessness into non-primitive settings.

If I may generalise from the foregoing, it appears that much of the ongoing work of the discipline is plagued by 'meaningless together-ness', and thereby by dangerous equivocations and distortions. In particular, and especially important, under these conditions we are dangerously exposed to 'begging the question', i.e., to assuming what we should be proving: the *petitio principii* fallacy. For instance, if 'mobilisation' is applied to a democratic polity the suggestion is that

[45] Shils and Deutsch relate the notion also to Mannheim's 'fundamental democratisation' (see esp. Deutsch, 1961, p. 494). But while Mannheim may well have provided the bridge across which 'mobilisation' entered the vocabulary of democracy, the fact remains that the term was commonly used in the early thirties, in Italy and in Germany, as reflecting a distinctly totalitarian experience.

[46] The boomerang effect is also responsible, in part, for the disappearance of politics (*supra*, note 3).

democracies mobilise more or less as totalitarian régimes do. Conversely, if 'participation' is applied to a totalitarian system the suggestion is that democratic participation also occurs, to some extent at least, in non-democratic settings. Now this may well be the case. But the case cannot be proven by *transferring the same denomination* from one context to another. For this amounts to pure and simple terminological camouflage: things are declared alike by making them *verbally* identical.

All in all, then, it can hardly be held that our 'losses of specificity' are compensated by gains in inclusiveness. I would rather say that our gains in travelling capacity, or in universal inclusiveness, are verbal (and deceptive) while our 'gains in obfuscation' are very substantial.

I cannot discuss this further. As LaPalombara (1968, p. 72) vividly puts it, 'so many of our generalisations about the political process move with apparent randomness from the micro to the macroanalytic levels' —the result being 'messiness caused by confusion as to the level of analysis'. Following this line of complaint I have argued that confusion as to the level of analysis brings about these unfortunate results: (1) at the higher levels, macroscopic errors of interpretation, explanation and prediction; (2) at the lower levels, a great deal of wasteful data mis-gathering; (3) at all levels, confusion of meaning and destruction of the sharpness of our concepts. We do lack words. But conceptual stretching and poor logic have largely impoverished the analytical articulation and the discriminating power of the words that we do have. And my feeling is that only too often major differences are being cancelled on the thin basis of secondary, trivial similarities. It would hardly make sense to say that men and fishes are alike in that both classes share a 'swimming capability'. Yet much of what we are saying in global comparative polities may not make much more sense.

Let me stress, to conclude, that according to my scheme of analysis all of this is unnecessary. Awareness of the ladder of abstraction shows that the need for highly abstract, all-embracing categories does not require us to inflate, indeed to evaporate, the observational, empirically-linkable, categories that we do have. Moreover, if we know how to climb and descend along a ladder of abstraction—and thereby know where we stand in relation to the 'property space' of the analysis that we are pursuing—not only conceptual stretching is ruled out, but also faulty analogies and the begging-the-question fallacy can be disposed of.

V. SUMMARY

Especially during the last decade comparative politics as a substantive field has been rapidly expanding. The scale, if not the scope, of this expansion raises thorny and unprecedented problems of method. But we seem to embark more and more in comparative endeavours without *comparative method*, i.e., with inadequate methodological awareness and less than adequate logical skills. That is to say, we seem to be particularly naïve *vis-à-vis* the logical requirements of a world-wide comparative treatment of political science issues.

My focus is conceptual—about concepts—under the assumption that concepts are not only elements of a theoretical system, but equally tools for fact-gathering, data containers. The empirical problem is that we badly need information which is sufficiently precise to be meaningfully comparable. Hence we need a filing system provided by discriminating, i.e., taxonomic, conceptual containers. If these are not provided, data misgathering is inevitable; and statistical, computerised sophistication is no remedy for misinformation. The theoretical problem can be stated, in turn, as follows: we grievously lack a disciplined use of terms and procedures of comparison. This discipline can be provided, I suggest, by awareness of the ladder of abstraction, of the logical properties that are implied, and of the rules of composition and decomposition thus resulting. If no such discipline is obtained, conceptual mishandling and, ultimately, conceptual misformation is inevitable (and joins forces with data misgathering).

Thus far the discipline has largely followed the line of least resistance, namely, 'conceptual stretching'. In order to obtain a world-wide applicability the extension of our concepts has been broadened by obfuscating their connotation. As a result the very purpose of comparing—control— is defeated, and we are left to swim in a sea of empirical and theoretical messiness. Intolerably blunted conceptual tools are conducive, on the one hand, to wasteful if not misleading research, and, on the other hand, to a meaningless togetherness based on pesudo-equivalences.

The remedy resides—I submit—in our combined ability (1) to develop the discipline along a medium level of abstraction with better intermediate categories, and (2) to manoeuvre, both upwards and downwards, along a ladder of abstraction in such a way as to bring together assimilation and differentiation, a relatively high explanatory power and a relatively precise descriptive content, macro-theory and empirical testing. To be sure, no level of analysis can be exactly translated and converted into the next level. In this sense, something is always lost (and gained) along the ladder. But a disciplined use of terms and procedures of comparison generates, at each level, sets of propositions which either reinforce or contradict the propositions of the neighbouring levels.

The suggestion has recently been put forward that 'political scientists turn to mathematics for [the] rules of logic' required 'to introduce the necessary deductive power into a paradigm'.[47] I have taken the more sober, and indeed counter-perfectionistic view that we should not encourage the 'overconscious thinker' paralysed by overly ambitious standards. But surely we cannot expect an unconscious thinker lacking elementary logical training and discipline to meet the intricate new problems arising from global comparisons.

[47] Holt and Richardson (1970, p. 70). The chapter is perhaps perfectionistic, but surely a very intelligent and stimulating 'stock taking' overview.

REFERENCES

ALKER, H. R. (1965) 'Mathematics and politics', in Lerner and Lasswell (1965), below.
ALLARDT, E. (1968) 'The merger of American and European traditions of sociological research: contextual analysis', *Social Science Information*, 1.
ALMOND, G. A. and COLEMAN, J. S. (1960) *The Politics of the Developing Areas*, Princeton University Press.
ALMOND, G. A. and POWELL, G. B. (1966) *Comparative Politics: a Developmental Approach*, Little, Brown.
APTER, D. E. (1971) 'Political studies and the search for a framework', in C. Allen and W. Johnson, eds., *African Perpsectives*, Cambridge University Press.
ARROW, K. J. (1951) 'Mathematical models in the social sciences', in Lerner and Lasswell (1965) below.
BENDIX, R. (1963) 'Concepts and generalizations in comparative sociological studies', *American Sociological Review*, 28.
BENSON, O. (1967) 'The mathematical approach to political science', in J. C. Charlesworth, ed. (1969) below.
BLALOCK, H. M. (1964) *Causal Inferences in Non-experimental Research*, University of North Carolina Press.
BOUDON, R. and LAZARSFELD, P. F. (1965–66) *Méthodes de la Sociologie*, 2 vols. Mouton, The Hague.
BRAIBANTI, R. (1968) 'Comparative political analytics reconsidered', *Journal of Politics*, 30, February.
CHARLESWORTH, J. C., ed. (1967) *Contemporary Political Analysis*, New York, Free Press.
CROCE, B. (1942) *Logica come Scienza del Concetto Puro*, Laterza.
DEMERATH, N. J. and PETERSON, R. A., eds. (1967) *System, Change and Conflict*, New York, Free Press.
DEUTSCH, K. W. (1961) 'Social mobilization and political development', *American Political Science Review*, 55, September.
DEUTSCH, K. W. (1966) 'Recent trends in research methods', in J. C. Charlesworth, ed., *A Design for Political Science: Scope, Objectives and Methods*, American Academy of Political and Social Science.
DOWSE, R. E. (1966) 'A functionalist's logic', *World Politics*, 18, July.
ECKSTEIN, H. (1963) 'Introduction', H. Eckstein and D. E. Apter, eds., *Comparative Politics*, New York, Free Press.

FESTINGER, L. and KATZ, D., eds. (1953) *Research Methods in the Behavioural Sciences*, New York, Dryden.

FLANIGAN, W. and FOGELMAN, E. (1967) 'Functional analysis', in Charlesworth (1967) above.

GROSS, L., ed. (1959) *Symposium on Sociological Theory*, Harper and Row.

HEMPEL, C. F. (1952) *Fundamentals of Concept Formation in Empirical Science*, University of Chicago Press.

HEMPEL, C. F. (1958) 'The theoretician's dilemma', in H. Fiegl, M. Scriver and G. Maxwell, eds., *Minnesota Studies in the Philosophy of Science*, University of Minnesota Press.

HEMPEL, C. F. (1959) 'The logic of functional analysis', in Gross (1959) above.

HOLT, R. T. (1967) 'A proposed structural-functional framework', in Charlesworth (1967).

HOLT, R. T. and RICHARDSON, J. M. (1970) 'Competing paradigms in comparative politics', in Holt and Turner (1970).

HOLT, R. T. and TURNER, J. E., eds. (1970) *The Methodology of Comparative Research*, New York, Free Press.

KALLEBERG, A. L. (1966) 'The logic of comparison', *World Politics*, **18**.

KAPLAN, A. (1964) *The Conduct of Inquiry*, Chandler.

KEMENY, J. G. (1961) 'Mathematics without numbers' in Lerner (1961) below.

KEMENY, J. G., SNELL, J. L. and THOMPSON, G. L. (1957) *Introduction to Finite Mathematics*, Prentice-Hall.

KEMENY, J. G. and SNELL, J. L. (1962) *Mathematical Models in the Social Sciences*, Ginn.

LANDAU, M. (1969) 'A general commentary', in R. Braibanti, ed., *Political and Administrative Development*, Duke University Press.

LANDECKER, W. S. (1955) 'Types of integration and their measurements', in Lazarsfeld and Rosenberg (1955) below.

LAPALOMBARA, J. (1968) 'Macrotheories and microapplications in comparative politics', *Comparative Politics*, **1**, October. (See also pp. 299–313 of this Reader.)

LAPALOMBARA, J. (1970) 'Parsimony and empiricism in comparative politics: an anti-scholastic view', in Holt and Turner (1970) above.

LASSWELL, H. D. and KAPLAN, A. (1950) *Power and Society*, Yale University Press.

LAZARSFELD, P. F. and BARTON (1965) 'Qualitative measurement in the social sciences: classifications, typologies and indices', in Lerner and Lasswell (1965).

LAZARSFELD, P. F., ed. (1954) *Mathematical Thinking in the Social Sciences*, New York, Free Press.

LAZARSFELD, P. F. and ROSENBERG, M., ed. (1955) *The Language of Social Research*, New York, Free Press.

LERNER, D., ed. (1961) *Quantity and Quality*, New York Free Press.

LERNER, D. and LASSWELL, H. D., eds. (1965) *The Policy Sciences*, Stanford University Press.

LIJPHART, A. (1969) *Comparative Politics and the Comparative Method*, paper presented at the Torino IPSA Round Table.

MACRIDIS, R. (1968) 'Comparative politics and the study of government: the search for focus', *Comparative Politics*, **1**, October.

MACKENZIE, W. J. M. (1958) *Free Elections*, Allen & Unwin.

MARTINDALE, D. (1959) 'Sociological theory and the ideal type', in Gross (1959) above.

MEOTTI, A. (1969) 'L'eliminazione dei Termini Teorici', *Rivista di Filosofia*, 2.

MERTON, R. K. (1957) *Social Theory and Social Structure*, rev. edn., New York, Free Press.

MILLS, C. W. (1959) 'On intellectual craftsmanship', in Gross (1959) above.

PAIGE, G. D. (1966) 'The rediscovery of politics', in J. D. Montgomery and W. I. Siffin, eds. (1966) *Approaches to Development*, McGraw-Hill. (See also pp. 361–371 of this Reader.)

RIGGS, F. W. (1970 'The comparison of whole political systems', in Holt and Turner (1970) above.

ROSE, R. (manuscript, no date) 'Social measure and public policy in Britain —the empiricizing process.'

RUNCIMAN, W. C. (1963) *Social and Political Theory*, Cambridge University Press.

SALMON, W. C. (1963) *Logic*, Prentice-Hall.

SARTORI, G. (1959) 'Gruppi di pressione o gruppi di interessi?' *Il Mulino*.

SARTORI, G. (1969) 'From the sociology of politics to political sociology', in S. M. Lipset, ed. (1969) *Politics and the Social Sciences*, Oxford University Press.

SELLTIZ, *et al.* (1959) *Research Methods in Social Relations*, rev. edn., Holt, Rhinehart & Winston.

SIMON, H. A. (1967) *Models of Man*, Wiley.

SMELSER, N. J. (1967) 'Notes on the methodology of comparative analysis of economic activity', *Transactions of the Sixth World Congress of Sociology*, vol. ii. International Sociological Association.

SPENGLER, J. J. (1961) 'Quantification in economics: its history', in Lerner (1961) above.

TRUMAN, D. (1951) *The Governmental Process*, Knopf.

TUFTE, E. R. (1969) 'Improving data analysis in political science', *World Politics*, 21, July.

URBANI, G. (1968) 'General systems theory: un nuovo strumento per l'analisi dei sistemi politici?', *Il Politico*, 4.

YOUNG, O. R. (1968) *Systems of Political Science*, Prentice-Hall.

18

A. C. MacIntyre   Is a science of comparative politics possible?

Reprinted from 'Is a science of comparative politics possible?' in *Against the Self-Images of the Age: Essays on Ideology and Philosophy*, Duckworth, 1971, pp. 260–79.

There was once a man who aspired to be the author of the general theory of holes. When asked 'What kind of hole—holes dug by children in the sand for amusement, holes dug by gardeners to plant lettuce seedlings, tank traps, holes made by roadmakers?' he would reply indignantly that he wished for a *general* theory that would explain all of these. He rejected *ab initio* the—as he saw it—pathetically common-sense view that of the digging of different kinds of holes there are quite different kinds of explanations to be given; why then he would ask do we have the concept of a hole? Lacking the explanations to which he originally aspired, he then fell to discovering statistically significant correlations; he found for example that there is a correlation between the aggregate hole-digging achievement of a society as measured, or at least one day to be measured, by econometric techniques, and its degree of technological development. The United States surpasses both Paraguay and Upper Volta in hole-digging. He also discovered that war accelerates hole-digging; there are more holes in Vietnam than there were. These observations, he would always insist, were neutral and value-free. This man's achievement has passed totally unnoticed except by me. Had he however turned his talents to political science, had he concerned himself not with holes, but with modernisation, urbanisation or violence, I find it difficult to believe that he might not have achieved high office in the American Political Science Association.

I

The ultimate aim of this paper is constructive; the scepticism which infects so much of my argument is a means and not an end. I do not want to show that there *cannot* be a general science of political action, but only to indicate certain obstacles that stand in the way of the founding of such a science and to suggest that the present practice of so-called political science is unlikely to overcome these obstacles. In writing more specifically of *comparative* political science I do not wish to suggest that there could be any other sort of political science; this the APSA recognised when it merged what was its section devoted to comparative politics into the general body. It is with the claim to be using legitimate *comparative* methods which could enable us to advance and to test genuine law-like *cross-cultural* generalisations that I shall initially be concerned. I shall not be concerned to question the possibility of genuine and relevant comparison and even of cross-cultural comparison for other purposes: to exhibit the march of the *Weltgeist* through history, for instance, or to draw moral lessons about the respective benefits of barbarism and civilisation. These may or may not be reputable activities; I shall not argue for or against them here. I shall be solely interested in the project of a political *science*, of the formulation of cross-cultural, law-like causal generalisations which may in turn be explained by theories, as the generalisations of Boyle's Law and Dalton's Law are explained by the kinetic theory of gases; all that I say about the problem of comparability must be understood in this particular context. Moreover my scepticism about any alleged parallel between theorising about politics and theorising about gases will not initially be founded on the consideration of the character of human action in general. I shall not argue for example that human actions cannot have causes, not just or even mainly because I believe that this proposition is false, but because I believe that, even if its falsity is agreed, we still have substantial grounds for scepticism about comparative political science. My method of proceeding in the first part of my argument will be as follows: I shall examine in turn the claim to have formulated law-like generalisations about political attitudes, about political institutions and practices, and about the discharge of political functions. I shall then in the second part of my argument suggest an alternative strategy to that now customarily employed, although the change in strategy will turn out to also involve a change in aim.

II

The study of political culture, of political attitudes, as it has been developed, seems to rest upon the assumption that it is possible to identify political attitudes independently of political institutions and practices. There are at least two reasons for thinking this assumption false. The first derives from Wittgenstein, who pointed out that we identify and define attitudes in terms of the objects toward which they are directed, and not vice versa. Our understanding of the concept of fear depends upon our understanding of the concepts of harm and danger and not vice versa. Our understanding of the concept of an aesthetic attitude depends upon our understanding of the concept of a work of art. It follows that an ability to identify a set of attitudes in one culture as political, and a set of attitudes in some second culture as political, with a view to comparing them must depend upon our having already identified as political in both cultures a set of institutions and practices toward which these attitudes are directed. In other words, the ability to construct comparative generalisations about attitudes depends on our already having solved the problem of how to construct comparative generalisations about institutions and practices. The notion of political culture is secondary to and parasitic upon the notion of political practice.

It follows that a necessary condition of a comparative investigation of political cultures is that the argument about the comparability of political institutions should have a certain outcome; but this is only a necessary end not a sufficient condition. It is also necessary if political attitudes are to be the subject of comparative inquiry that other attitudes shall be susceptible of comparison of a certain kind. I can explain what I mean by this by citing an example from *The Civic Culture* (1965, ch. iv, pp. 102–5) where Almond and Verba argue that Italians are less committed to and identified with the actions of their government than are Germans or Englishmen, offering as evidence the fact that the Italian respondents, as compared with the English and German respondents to their survey, placed such actions very low on a list of items to which they had been asked to give a rank order in terms of the amount of pride they took in them. At no point do Almond and Verba pause to ask whether the concept of pride is the same in the three different national cultures, that is, to ask whether the different respondents had after all been asked the same question. But in fact the concept of pride ('. . . si sente piu' orgoglioso . . .') in Italy is not the same as that pride in England. The notion of taking pride in Italian culture is still inexorably linked, especially in the South but also in the North, to the notion of honour. What one takes pride in is what touches on one's honour. If asked to list the subjects which touched their honour, many Italians would spontaneously place the chastity of their immediate female relatives high on the list—a connection that it would occur to very few Englishmen to make. These notions of pride and honour partially specify and are partially specified by a notion of the family itself importantly, if imperfectly, embodied in the actualities of Italian family life. Hence we cannot hope to compare an Italian's attitude to his government's acts with an Englishman's in respect of the pride each takes; any comparison would have to begin from the different range of virtues and emotions incorporated in the different social institutions. Once again the project of comparing attitudes independently of institutions and practices encounters difficulties. These particular difficulties suggest that a key question is: what are the units in each culture which are compared to be? To this question I shall of course return; but let me note that the difficulty which I have exemplified in the preceding argument is contingent on Almond and Verba's particular procedures. It does not arise from the project of comparison as such. For the difficulty which arises over any comparison between English and German culture on the one hand, and Italian on the other, from relying on the in fact false assumption that these cultures agree in their concept of pride would not arise in the same way if Italian attitudes were to be compared with Greek, for example. Not that there would not be other and perhaps more subtle pitfalls, but these would not arise merely because concepts of pride and honour are not shared.

We can now pose our problem in the following way: we wish to find identifiable units in different societies and cultures about which we may construct true causal generalisations. Political attitudes, for the two reasons I have given, are implausible candidates; what about political institutions and practices? The first point to be made here is that in turning to the discussion of political institutions and practices we have not left behind the topic of political attitudes. For attitudes to and beliefs about institutions and practices may sometimes be purely external phenomena; that is, the institution or the practice is what it is and does what it does independently of what certain people think and feel about it. But it is an obvious truism that no institution or practice is what it is, or does what it does, independently of what anyone whatsoever thinks or feels about it. For institutions and practices are always partially, even if to differing degrees, constituted by what certain people think and feel about them.

Consider the example of a currency system: a given type of piece of paper or of metal has the value that it has not only because it has been issued by a duly constituted authority, but because it is accepted as having that value by the members of a particular currency-using population. When this condition is not generally satisfied, as in Germany and Austria in 1923, the currency ceases to have value, and thus ceases to be currency. So also with an army: an officer has the authority that he has not only because his commission has been issued by a duly constituted authority, but because he is accepted as having that status by the men serving under him. When this condition is not generally satisfied, as in Russia in 1917, an officer ceases to have authority, and thus ceases to be an officer. Since such beliefs about social institutions are partially constitutive of social institutions, it is impossible to identify the institution except in terms of the beliefs of those who engage in its practices. This fact is ignored in general by those who wish to define political science as the study of political *behaviour*, with a view to thereby providing a public, neutral subject matter for scientific inquiry. But if we identify behaviour except in terms of the intentions and therefore of the beliefs of the agents we shall risk describing what they are doing as what we would be doing if we went through that series of movements or something like it rather than what they are actually doing. Nor do we avoid this difficulty merely by finding *some* description of the behaviour in question which both the agents themselves and the political scientist would accept. For clearly both agents and political scientists might apply the description 'voting behaviour' to what they do, but yet have a quite different understanding of what it is to vote. But now what bearing does all this have upon the project of comparing political institutions and practices?

III

I take it that if the generalisations which political scientists construct are to be part of a science, then among the conditions which must be satisfied is this: that we shall be able to distinguish between genuine law-like generalisations and mere *de facto* generalisations which hold only of the instances so far observed. I understand by this distinction, as many others have understood by it, the difference between a generalisation the assertion of which commits one to the assertion of a set of corresponding counter-factual conditionals and a generalisation which does not so commit one. In the natural sciences the ground for treating a generalisation as a law is generally not merely that as a matter of fact no plausible counter-examples have yet been produced. It is also normally required that it be supported by a body of theory. But what then of these generalisations which we wish to assert as genuine law-like generalisations before we have any well-established theory? What about the generalisations of Kepler or of Galileo before Newton formulated his laws? What about Boyle's Law or Dalton's Law before the establishment of the kinetic theory? At this point the problems of confirmation theory become real.

The particular finding of confirmation theory that is relevant is that the degree to which a positive instance does genuinely confirm a generalisation is in part a matter of the kind of environment in which it is found. For the greater the extent of the radically different environments in which confirmatory instances of a generalisation are found, the less likely it is that the generalisation is only confirmed in certain contingent environmental circumstances. Now it is a matter of contingent fact that nature is so structured that this condition is normally realisable. For nature could have been otherwise. If black ravens on being taken into laboratories for pigmentation tests, or if black ravens on being observed in the Arctic—in the course of our seeking confirmation or otherwise of the generalisation that all ravens are black—promptly turned into philosophers of science or clouds of dust, generalisations about ravenly nigritude could not be as well founded as they are. But in fact the character of social life is such that in some respects it resembles this imaginary nature rather than nature as it—fortunately for natural scientists—is.

Consider for example the alleged generalisation that in two-party electoral systems the two parties will tend to move together in their policies and the alleged explanation for this generalisation, that this is because neither party can hope to win those voters attracted by the furthest opposed wing of the other party, but only those nearest to it. Hence where, for example, the parties and their wings can be placed on a Left-Right dimension, each party tends to move its policies toward the centre, having no hope of winning votes from the extreme Right or Left. Now consider two different kinds of attempts to provide counter-examples to this generalisation. An example of the first would be Greece before the *coup d'état* of the colonels. This seems to be a straightforward refutation of the generalisation, even if we remember that a single counter-example in the natural sciences is never adequate to refute a well-established theory or a generalisation with a huge weight of evidence supporting it, such as the generalisation that all solids except bismuth, cast-iron, ice, and type metal expand when heated. For here we have nothing like a well-supported theory or generalisation; it is rather as if the seventh raven we were to come across was coloured magenta. Now consider a quite different kind of attempt to provide a counter-example.

Suppose that someone were to point to the rival parties in Sierra Leone immediately before the army seized power there, and to offer them as a counter-example. We ought at once to remember what Ruth Schachter wrote of African mass parties: 'They and their cultural affiliates were interested in everything from the cradle to the grave—in birth, initiation, religion, marriage, divorce, dancing, song, plays, feuds, debts, land, migration, death, public order—and not only electoral success.' At once the question cannot but be framed: 'Why do we think of these as parties, rather than as, say, churches?' The answer, that they have some of the marks of American political parties, and that they call themselves parties, does nothing to show that in fact the meaning of 'party' is not radically changed when the cultural context is radically changed, or that even if it is not changed the description has not become inapplicable. The intentions, the beliefs, the concepts which inform the practices of African mass parties provide so different a context that there can be no question of transporting the phenomena of party to this context in order to provide a suitably different environment for testing our generalisation. Where the environment and where the culture is radically different the phenomenon is viewed so differently by those who participate in it that it is an entirely different phenomenon. In just this respect does society differ from nature. That is to say, the provision of an environment sufficiently different to make the search for counter-examples interesting will normally be the provision of an environment where we cannot hope or expect to find examples of the original phenomenon and therefore cannot hope to find counter-examples.

Note that my thesis is not that to transplant a phenomenon such as party is to subject it to causal influences which transform it. That is doubtless true. But the difficulty of studying political parties in alien social environments to test a generalisation constructed about political parties in familiar social environments is not like the difficulty of studying viruses: that their own causal properties and/or those of the environment cause them to mutate too rapidly and too often. If this were the type of difficulty that we encountered in formulating cross-cultural generalisations about politics, then we might well ask if we could not insulate the object of study in its new environment from the disturbing causal influences at work. To ask this would be to mistake my point which is not about causal interference with the phenomenon of party, but with the absence of the same concept of party, or perhaps of any concept of party, as we understand it, in the alien culture.

Let me now consider a possible objection to this thesis which would base itself upon my choice of examples. A quite different choice of examples might provide us with more plausible candidates for cross-cultural generalisation. Consider the alleged (and quite possibly false) generalisation that in the government of cities, if a single non-transferable vote for single members is the method of election, then there will be over a certain time span a tendency for a two-party system to flourish. This seems to hold in the United States. But it might hold in other alien environments, even environments of an exotic kind, where we could identify the system as two-party, even if unclear in what sense the parties were parties. But this is surely therefore an example of at least a possible cross-cultural comparison which provides us with a law-like generalisation and is therefore lethal to my entire thesis. Let me at once concede that I take this generalisation to be law-like in that it does indeed entail counter-factual conditionals, and let me further concede that the counter-factuals in question might be true. But I do not concede that it injures my thesis. Why not?

The reason for not conceding that this example, if true, would injure my thesis is intimately connected with the fact that I should not be extremely surprised if the generalisation in question did turn out to be true of cities outside North America, as well as in North America. For what could make the generalisation true, if true, is that voters prefer in general not to waste their votes in voting on matters that concern the administration of their daily lives; and it requires only a minimal and a very untheoretical understanding of the electoral system produced by such a voting procedure to understand that in the majority of cases votes for a third party will be wasted. The considerations from which we can deduce *this* particular generalisation are thus concerned with human rationality in general; they do not have any specific connection with politics and they do not belong to political science, but to our general understanding of rationality. This will be true of all generalisations which concern the formal structures of human argument, even if they appear in political clothing, furnishing us with explanations of particular political choices and actions. So it must be, for example, with all applications of the theory of games to politics.

My thesis about the legitimacy or otherwise of the project of accumulating a stock of cross-cultural generalisations about political behaviour to furnish the empirical foundation for a political science, as I have developed it so far, can now be stated disjunctively: *either* such generalisations about institutions will necessarily lack the kind of confirmation they require *or* they will be consequences of true generalisations about human rationality and not part of a specifically political science.

To complete this part of my argument I must now make three further observations. The first is that my statement of the difficulties in constructing true and warranted cross-cultural generalisations about political institutions is obviously akin to the arguments which some anthropologists—notably Edmund Leach and Walter Goldschmidt—have developed about cross-cultural generalisations in their discipline. But Goldschmidt has then argued that it is not institutions, but functions, or rather institutions only as serving certain functions, which we ought to aspire to compare; and this contention has already been advanced by some political scientists. We are, that is to say, to begin by identifying the same function in different societies and then to inquire how quite different institutions have this same effect; for I take it that to say that X performs, serves, or discharges a given function always entails that X is the cause of a particular effect, even if this does not exhaust the meaning of the statement in which function was ascribed. It is certainly not a final objection to this project that most political scientists who have tried to specify the functions in question have produced nothing but statements about institutions and their effects in which the word 'function' may appear, but could be replaced not only without loss, but with gain.

> Wherever the political party has emerged, it appears to perform some common functions in a wide variety of political systems . . . the organisation called the party is expected to organize public opinion and to communicate demands to the center of governmental power and decision . . . the party must articulate to its followers the concept and meaning of the broader community . . . the party is likely to be involved in political recruitment . . . These similarities of function . . . suggest that the political party emerges when the activities of a political system reach a certain degree of complexity, or whenever the notion of political power comes to include the idea that the mass public must participate or be controlled (LaPalombara and Weiner, 1966).

In a passage like this, the notion of function can be replaced entirely by either the notion of effect or the notion of purpose. When we so replace it, we notice also that the transition from previous to tentative conclusion requires no reliance on any factual generalisations anyway; it is merely a matter of drawing out the consequences of definition. But even if in the writing of political scientists as sophisticated as LaPalombara and Weiner the function of the use of 'function' is unclear, it does not follow that this has to be so. But the condition of its not being so is that we should have some criteria for identifying the functions served by political institutions which is other than, and independent of, the aims and purposes of political agents and the effects of political institutions. The provision of such a criteria would require the identification of a system, using the word 'system' precisely, so that concepts of feedback and equilibrium are applicable on the basis of quantitative data which will provide values for variables in differential equations. I scarcely need stress the remoteness of this goal from the present state of all political science; if we match the requirements that have to be satisfied to identify such a system—which would involve, for example, being able to distinguish between change that is part of the movement of items through the system, change that is itself part of the structuring of the system, and change that is the system decaying by providing ways of measuring rates of change for all three—then a work like David Easton's *A Systems Analysis of Political Life* (1965) looks like a mad, millenarian dream. I therefore take it that any attempt to answer my argument by suggesting that cross-cultural generalisations about institutions may be provided by means of a prior account in terms of functions is bound to fail.

My second observation is that my argument does not imply any undervaluation of the importance of the work done by political scientists in establishing both the facts about particular institutions and the very limited generalisations they do establish. That the conditions under which these generalisations hold necessarily remain unclear to us for the kind of reason that I have given does not mean that we do not need the best that we can get in this case, which is what they give us; only this kind of accumulation of data in no way leads toward the construction of a science. I shall later suggest an alternative context in which these empirical labours could perhaps be viewed more constructively. For the moment I note that it is Machiavelli who ought to be regarded as the patron saint of political studies and not Hobbes, and for this reason: Hobbes believed—as presumably Almond and LaPalombara and Easton (although Easton, in ways that I do not entirely understand, tries to distinguish his enterprise from that of Hobbes) believe—that the fortuitous, the surprising, the unpredicted, arise in politics only because our knowledge of political motions is less adequate than our knowledge of planetary motions. Given time, labour, and foundation grants—the contemporary version of royal patronage—an unpredicted revolution—but for the sheer complexity of human affairs—ought to be as disgraceful to political scientists, as an unpredicted eclipse to astronomers. But Machiavelli realised that in political life *fortuna*, the bitch goddess of unpredictability, has never been dethroned. To any stock of maxims derived from empirically founded generalisations the student of politics must always add one more: 'And do not be surprised if in the event things turn out otherwise.' The need to include this maxim follows from my argument, just as it follows from Machiavelli's.

My third observation is that in the history of political theory we have more than once been here before, and notably in the dispute between James Mill and Macaulay. James Mill argued, although in the interests of a quite different conclusion, even more that we cannot find reliable empirical generalisations about political behaviour: 'Absolute monarchy under Neros and Caligulas . . . is the scourge of human nature. On the other side, the public of Denmark . . . under their absolute monarch are as well governed as any people in Europe . . . the surface of history affords, therefore, no certain principles of decision.' Mill then proceeded to argue from this that we ought to turn instead to the type of psychology favoured by the utilitarians for our explanations, that there is no specifically political science. Against him Macaulay argued that the empirical facts about government *do* yield genuine law-like generalisations, not least generalisations of a kind which enable us to predict future actions with great confidence. And it is clear that this practical use of law-like generalisations provides Macaulay with a crucial motive. The claim to technical expertise on the part of the political scientist is closely bound up with the defence of the possibility of formulating law-like generalisations. If the latter fails, the former is gravely impaired. When in our time on the basis of *his* generalisations Lipset predicts totalitarian horrors as the outcome of widespread political participation, he turns out to be the true heir of Macaulay who, on the basis of *his* generalisations, predicted cultural ruin if 'the great number' were allowed to participate in government; 'they will commit waste of every sort in the estate of mankind, and transmit it to posterity impoverished and desolate', so that 'in two or three hundred years, a few lean and half naked fishermen may divide with owls and foxes the ruins of the greatest of European cities . . .' In both Macaulay and Lipset the claims of political science are closely linked to a claim about the political status of the political scientist, to a claim about the possession of political expertise, which entitles the political scientist to advise government. This claim too demands inquiry; but a prerequisite for such inquiry is a further development of my central argument.

IV

My doubts about identifying institutions in different cultures as 'the same' and therefore as interestingly different are of course compatible with a recognition of the massive fact that the same actions are regularly performed in quite different cultures. One class of such actions are those that derive from implicit imitation. It is of course not necessarily or always the case that if one person imitates another he does what the other does. Indeed it is sometimes the condition of successful imitation that he who imitates shall not do what the other does precisely in order to seem to do what the other does. But when the intention to perform the same action as another *is* present, we always have an intelligible question as to why, if the corresponding action or its consequences or both are not the same as those produced by the agent imitated, they are not so. Of course it may be that even a particular intention to perform certain actions cannot be intelligibly embodied in some cultures; *Don*

Quixote is the classical example. But we do have clear cases where the same intention is embodied in two different cultures, such intentions as to apply Roman Law or the Code Napoléon, or to bring about some particular course of economic development. What we shall achieve if we study the projects springing from such intentions are two or more histories of these projects, and it is only after writing these histories that we shall be able to compare the different outcomes of the same intention. We shall not, that is to say, begin by collecting data in the hope of formulating causal generalisations; we shall begin by looking at cases where a will to achieve the same end was realised with greater or lesser success in different cultural contexts.

There is of course a notable formula which seems to prescribe this approach: 'Men make their own history, but they do not make it just as they please. They do not make it under circumstances chosen by themselves, but under circumstances directly encountered, given and transmitted from the past.' But when Marx wrote these words he did not discriminate what was implied by this approach from a search for causal generalisations, and he does not do so at least in part because he treats what he calls the circumstances of action only as a causally effective and limiting environment and not in addition, or rather primarily, as a context of meaning-conferring symbols and rules. So Marx speaks of 'the burden of history' in the very next sentence and Engels speaks of history as a 'series of parallelograms of forces', and it is this model of Engels which creates for Plekhanov the problem of the role of the individual in history (since an individual can be no more than a point at which some force operates). But the question with which Marx began in the *Eighteenth Brumaire* does not require an answer in terms of causal generalisations and parallelograms of forces. For what Marx asks then is why, when someone aspires to perform the same actions as a predecessor in some earlier cultural period—as the English Puritans aspired to be Old Testament Israelites or the French Revolutionaries Roman republicans or Louis Napoléon to do the deeds of Napoleon I—the actions should be so different. A full answer to Marx's question would provide a genuine starting point for historical comparison, but such an answer could only be provided by first writing a history of each of these episodes.

I therefore take it that if we wish to have a science of comparative politics, one first step is the writing of a series of comparative histories; that comparative history is a more fundamental discipline than comparative politics. But then the crucial question arises: what can we legitimately expect the study of comparative history to yield? And one of the best ways of answering this question is to ask what the study of comparative history has in fact yielded. Consider for example Isaac Deutscher's thesis about revolutions. Deutscher asserted that in the English, French, and Russian revolutions the same 'broad scheme of revolutionary development' could be discerned. This scheme involves three stages: a first stage in which 'popular energy, impatience, anger and hope' burst out, and 'the party that gives the fullest expression to the popular mood outdoes its rivals, gains the confidence of the masses and rises to power'; a second stage in which during the war on behalf of the revolution the leaders of the revolutionary party and the people are so well in accord that the leaders 'are willing and even eager to submit their policies to open debate and to accept the popular verdict'; and a third stage in which weariness and ruthlessness divide party and people, so that the revolutionary party cannot listen to, but must indeed suppress the voice of the people, thus in consequence splitting itself between the holders of revolutionary power and the caretakers of the purity of revolutionary doctrine. This pattern holds of 'any party of the revolution, whether it be called Independent, Jacobin or Bolschevik'.

That there are such patterns revealed by the rare studies of comparative history that we already possess and that there will be more is clear. But how are we to understand them? When we assert the recurrence of such a pattern, what are we asserting? Deutscher himself, following Engels and Plekhanov, understood this pattern of revolutionary behaviour deterministically. Hence followed his very different assessment of Trotsky's relation to Stalin from Trotsky's own non-deterministic assessment of that relationship. Deutscher treats each stage, as he specified it, as satisfying both a necessary and a sufficient condition for the occurrence of the next stage, as he specified it; hence he takes it that Trotsky, the caretaker of revolutionary purity, could not but have failed to hold power, since maintaining the revolutionary doctrine and holding power are causally incompatible.

The evaluation of Deutscher's specific contentions about revolution is not relevant to my present argument; but the contention Deutscher almost takes for granted, namely that the discernment of recurring patterns in history has as its end-product the formulation of law-like generalisations, is precisely what I want to question. For when I suggested that the study of comparative politics would certainly benefit from, and perhaps require, a prior writing of comparative history, I did not intend to imply that what comparative history will provide us with is merely a stock of more adequate materials for the construction of these cross-cultural, law-like generalisations which the present methods of orthodox political science aspire to but in fact fail to provide; that the comparative history is not so much an alternative, as merely a necessary prelude to proceeding as before. What I want to suggest is that it is characteristic of the causal knowledge which history does provide us with that the antecedent conditions in terms of which we explain historical outcomes are sometimes necessary conditions for the occurrence of some specific outcome, but are never sufficient. If this is so then the patterns which we discern in comparative history will always be *de facto* guides yielding Machiavellian maxims, rather than Hobbesian laws. But is it so? Is comparative political science, even when based on comparative history, precluded from formulating law-like generalisations?

To cast light on this, compare the situation of the political scientist with that of the political agent. The political agent confronts a situation in which he wishes to produce certain outcomes. He wishes, for example, to maintain two-party democracy in a new state, or he wishes to overthrow that state by revolutionary action. The situation he confronts consists of other political agents: party politicians, soldiers, trade union leaders, trade union rank and file, and so on. Some of each of these groups are keen readers of such works as *Political Man*, *Voting*, *Permanent Revolution*, and so on. Each of these derives certain inductively grounded maxims from these works; in an earlier age the maxims had different sources—Livy, Plutarch, what Napoleon did, or political folk wisdom—but the situation was essentially the same. The difficulty in applying the maxims is that the factors in the situation confronting the agent include the beliefs of every other agent about what each agent other than himself will do in applying the maxims, including the beliefs of every agent about what every other agent believes about his beliefs. 'I know you know I know you know I know' is a crucial piece of poetic wisdom for political as well as for sexual behaviour. The perception of any pattern or regularity in the behaviour of the other actors, or in the behaviour characteristic of this particular type of situation, is what particularly invites deviation from the pattern. 'They all knew what Napoleon would have done,' said Grant of the Union generals. 'The trouble was that the rebel generals didn't know about Napoleon.'

The key part that beliefs play in defining political situations, and the fact that beliefs are always liable to be altered by reflection upon the situation, including reflection about the beliefs of other agents, has a crucial consequence: that we cannot ever identify a determinate set of factors which constitute the initial conditions for the production of some outcome in conformity with a law-like regularity. To claim that we could identify such regularities and such sets of factors would be to claim that we can understand what occurs in politics independently of a knowledge of the beliefs of the agents, for it would be to claim that the beliefs do not play a causal role in political outcomes.

It makes no difference at this point if the alleged law-like regularity is framed in probabilistic terms: when the alleged probability of an outcome is 0·7, the prediction is as vulnerable to reflection by agents as when the alleged probability of an outcome is 1. The conclusion that political agents are bound to be prone to error in their predictions of what other agents will do, and hence of political outcomes, has one important merit other than that of following validly from my premises: it would appear to be true. Nor is its truth incompatible with the fact that some political agents produce more correct predictions than others. It would perhaps be cynical to explain this latter fact by pointing out that given an entirely random relationship between prediction and outcome in a sufficiently large population of predictors, predictions, and outcomes, certain predictors would consistently predict correctly, just as certain predictors would consistently predict incorrectly. But without resorting to either cynicism or the theorems of statistics one can point out that success at prediction in practical affairs, including political affairs, can never be embodied into a method which can be taught, precisely because the maxims relied upon are open-textured and open-ended, and the sense of when which maxim is relevant cannot itself be unpacked into a set of maxims.

It may be asked: when I conclude that political agents cannot find law-like generalisations to aid them in their actions (other of course than those crucial and rock-like law-like generalisations of the physical senses which are available to us all, such that a bullet accelerates in the way that all moving bodies do, and that when a man's skull is crushed by an ice pick he dies), what is the force of 'cannot'? Do I mean only that we have at the moment no technique for identifying determinate sets of antecedent conditions of the relevant kind, but that such a technique might well be discovered? Or do I mean that there is some confusion in the nature of such a technique? Am I saying what the limits of inquiry are *as of now*, or what the limits *as such* are?

I am strongly inclined to say that at the moment we have no grounds for answering this question as it stands in either way. We lack even the most minimal theoretical background against which to raise such questions. To say this is not to ignore the empirical work done by both psychologists and sociologists on such topics as prejudice, cognitive dissonance, and the relation of roles to beliefs; it is to say that the results of empirical studies in this field (which are not always obviously consistent with each other) are exceptionally difficult to interpret and to assess, in part just for the type of reason that I have given.

What I have been arguing in this latter part of my essay is that the political agent cannot rely on law-governed regularities in his activities. But just those premises, which entail that conclusion, entail that the political scientist is in no better position in this respect than the political agent. The political scientist may claim to know more (quantitatively, as it were) than many political agents; but his knowledge is not of a different kind, and there seems no reason to believe that the chances that he will be able to apply the inductively grounded maxims which he derives from his studies in the course of political action successfully are any higher than they are for any other political agent.

If this is so, then the case for Machiavelli against Hobbes rests not merely on the impossibility of testing these law-like generalisations to which a true science of comparative politics would have to aspire; it derives also from the nature of the subject matter of political science. For the most that any study of comparative politics based upon comparative history can hope to supply us with in the foreseeable future is *de facto* generalisations about what has been an obstacle to or has facilitated certain types of course of action. There is available for the formulation of this type of generalisation no vocabulary for political scientists which is essentially more sophisticated than the vocabulary of political agents themselves. And the advice given by political scientists turns out to be simply the advice given by a certain genre of political agent, agents as partial, as socially conditioned, as creative and as wayward as any others.

To this the defender of orthodox political science might well feel bound to reply as follows. *Qua* scientist, he may claim, he has a vocabulary that is not available to political agents; and he has this neutrality precisely because he restricts himself to the facts and to theorising about them in an uncommitted way. Your redefinition of the tasks of political studies would, he might complain, destroy this neutrality. For the model of explanation implicit in your view of the relation of comparative history to comparative politics is as follows: Men in two different cultures seek to implement the same intention in action. Either their actions or the consequences of their actions may differ. If they do, by examining what was present in the one case and absent in the other, you make inferences as to what the obstacles or diversions were in either or both cases. You then explain in terms of the presence or absence of these obstacles or diversions the success or failure of the respective projects. But this is in fact a model of explanation familiar in our everyday understanding of action; and when we apply it in everyday life we cite as explanations for the success or failure of men's projects, not merely the external obstacles which they faced or the lack of such obstacles, but such factors as their reasonableness or unreasonableness, their courage or their weakness, their willingness or reluctance to commit injustice and so on. That is to say, your model of explanation is that used by ordinary men in their political and other actions to assess themselves and each other and it is of the essence of this mode of explanation that we may cite in explanation evaluations both of intelligence and of moral character. The strength of orthodox comparative political science, this objector will go on, is that it has broken decisively with the evaluative commitments of the world of action. Just because it aspires to study these scientifically, it cannot share them. It must instead be objective in a sense that requires that it be neutral and value-free.

I accept from this objection the characterisation of my own standpoint. It would certainly be an open empirical question whether it ever was in fact true that this or that project failed because of the unreasonableness or the injustice of the agents; but *a priori* nothing could rule out the possibility of these being true and relevant explanations. Political science would become in a true sense a moral science. But I do not take this to be in any way an objection. For what is the alternative, as it is exemplified in comparative political science as it is now usually practiced?

The type of comparative political science of which I have been highly critical is indeed generally and deeply committed to the view that its inquiries and explanations are indeed value-free. This results in an attempt to allow evaluative expressions into political life only in intentional contexts, in *oratio obliqua*, or in quotation marks. Hence, as John Schaar (1970) has pointed out, such notions as those of legitimacy are in fact defined in terms of belief. Lipset says that 'Legitimacy involves the capacity of the system to engender and maintain the belief that the existing political institutions are the most appropriate ones for the society' (1963, p. 77) and Robert Bierstedt writes that 'In the tradition of Weber, legitimacy has been defined as the degree to which institutions are valued for themselves and considered right and proper' (1965, p. 386). These definitions are clearly mistaken in any case; not only would there be no contradiction in holding that a government was entirely legitimate, but that its institutions were morally ill-suited to a particular society, but in a society where this latter was widely believed, it would not follow either that the government was, or that it was considered, illegitimate. But it is not mere definitional ineptitude that I am concerned with here. Suppose that we define, as Lipset and the Weberian tradition according to Bierstedt do, evaluation in terms so that where 'X' is an evaluative expression it is always defined so that 'A is X' is equivalent in meaning to an expression of the form 'A is believed by some class of persons to be Y' where 'Y' is another evaluative expression. Suppose further that, as both Lipset and some Weberians do, we try to explain legitimacy in terms of stability or vice versa. What is clear is that the original definitional move has pre-empted on a crucial causal and explanatory question: is it only beliefs about what is legitimate, what is appropriate, what is right which can be causally effective, or can the legitimacy of an institution, the appropriateness of an institution or an action, or the rightness or the justice of an action, themselves be causally effective? The definitional move of Lipset and Bierstadt removes *a priori* the possibility of a certain class of characteristics of intention and urgency being relevant in giving causal explanations.

Lipset and Bierstadt are thereby taking sides in an ancient philosophical argument: is it important for the ruler to be just, or is it only important for him to be thought to be just? What Lipset and Bierstadt do in defining legitimacy is not unlike what Thrasymachus did in defining justice and what Glaucon and Adeimantus did in developing Thrasymachus' case. We may now recall that Thrasymachus too claimed to be merely reporting how the world went, to be a neutral and value-free observer. My thesis on this last point can indeed be summarised as follows: to insist that political science be value-free is to insist that we never use in our explanations such clauses as 'because it was unjust' or 'because it was illegitimate' when we explain the collapse of a policy or a régime; and to insist on this is to agree with Thrasymachus—even if for different reasons—that justice plays no part and can play no part in political life. The insistence on being value-free thus involves the most extreme of value commitments. Hence I take it to be no objection to the methodology which I propose that it is clearly not able to purge its explanations of evaluative elements.

Note that I have offered no arguments at this point for believing that Thrasymachus is, as a matter of fact, mistaken; what I have done is to suggest that those who maintain the stance of orthodox comparative political science are committed by their starting point and not by the empirical findings to the view that he was right. And this raises one more kind of doubt about their view. For the response to my parable about the man who aspired to be the author of the general theory of holes might well have been that such a man is intellectually misguided, but practically harmless. When, however, one has to recognise that this kind of intellectual mistake is allied to a Thrasymachean attitude to morality, it becomes clear that if this type of enterprise is to be ranked as a joke, it must be classed with the more dangerous kinds of practical jokes.

REFERENCES

ALMOND, G. A. and VERBA, S. (1965) *The Civic Culture*, Little, Brown.

BIERSTEDT, R. (1965) 'Legitimacy', in J. Gould and W. L. Kolb, eds., *Dictionary of the Social Sciences*, Tavistock.

EASTON, D. (1965) *A Systems Analysis of Political Life*, Wiley.

LAPALOMBARA, J. and WEINER, M., eds. (1966) *Political Parties and Political Development*, Princeton University Press.

LIPSET, S. M. (1963) *Political Man*, Anchor, Doubleday.

SCHAAR, J. (1970) 'Legitimacy in the modern state' in P. Green and R. Levinson, eds., *Power and Community*, Vintage.

SECTION 4

Strategy and theory

Section 4 is concerned with theoretical and strategic approaches to the practice of comparative politics. It opens with two articles which have been specially prepared for this reader. In the first of them Roberts discusses the diverse interrelationships that exist between the problem that the comparative analyst addresses himself to, the strategy which he adopts to 'solve' the problem and the theory (or theories) that underpin the whole comparative activity. He argues the need for a sharper awareness of these interlinkages, for the elucidation of an explicit theoretical base and the possession of a clear strategy of inquiry, if the results of comparative political analysis are to become more meaningful.

In the second original piece of this section Looker suggests that discussion of comparative politics is too often confined to issues of methodology and that comparative political enquiry would be better served if more attention were paid to issues of substantive theory. He points out that the development of the comparative politics movement (which is discussed in the extract from Almond in Section 1 of of this Reader) cannot be divorced from the social, as well as the philosophical position in which its practitioners were situated in the years following World War II. The theoretical products of this movement thus bore the mark of their historical origin and this, as much as methodological developments, is an important factor underlying the need for a reappraisal of the practice of comparative politics.

Salamon's article directs attention to an approach which is not restricted solely to the confines of political science and which offers some hope that the pitfalls identified by Looker can be avoided. Salamon summarises and discusses three works (by C. E. Black, S. P. Huntington, and Barrington Moore) which examine the process of modernisation and attempt an explanation of it from the viewpoint of comparative history. As the label suggests, this approach emphasises the historical dimension. Those who work within it seek to explain political developments by examining the conjunction of factors in different societies at different times and paying particular attention to the sequence in which they occur. It is an approach to which a number of political scientists have turned and which has produced some of the most stimulating generalisations about political life over the past few years.

One further feature of contemporary comparative political analysis is highlighted in the article by Paige which concludes the Reader. This is the tendency, found in most of theoretical approaches which have gained currency within comparative politics over the past few decades, to view politics as dependent on, or to be explained in terms of, non-political factors. Paige argues that many questions about society and politics cannot be effectively approached and answered unless political life is seen as an autonomous force in social life. There is, for example, no other way of accounting for the differences between North and South Korea. After engaging briefly in the practice of comparative politics Paige goes on to discuss alternative strategies in political research and raises the question of the definition of politics itself. These aspects of comparative politics, which have arisen at various places throughout this Reader, thus come together in Paige's essay and provide a fitting conclusion for our exploration of the practice of comparative politics.

19

G. K. Roberts

The explanation of politics: comparison, strategy and theory

Prepared for this Reader by G. K. Roberts, Reader in European Studies, University of Manchester, Institute of Science and Technology.

Lepidus: What manner o'thing is your crocodile?

Antony: It is shaped, sir, like itself, and it is as broad as it hath breadth; it is just so high as it is, and moves with its own organs; it lives by that which nourisheth it, and the elements once out of it, it transmigrates.

Lepidus: What colour is it of?

Antony: Of its own colour too.
(*Antony and Cleopatra,* II, 7).

Without comparison knowledge and understanding are impossible; without comparison in political discourse and analysis we would know as much, or as little, about politics as Lepidus ended up knowing about crocodiles. Such comparison may be implicit, referring to some general standard or measure: we read about 'safe' and 'marginal' constituencies, 'modernising' or 'developing' states, 'autocratic' or 'totalitarian' regimes, and we gain some idea of the qualities or features of the constituencies, states or regimes as a result, because the adjective implies comparison with unwinnable seats, modernised or developed states, democratic regimes. Such comparison may be explicit: 'Sweden is more democratic than Cuba'; 'Senator P is more powerful than Senator Q'; 'Lincoln was the best President the Americans ever had'. When such explicit comparison enables precise statements to be made about one or more carefully defined variables it is even more likely that our knowledge about politics will be increased. Such comparison may be a starting point for explanation: when the degree of power of one Senator compared to another can be measured, when it is known just which constituencies would change from one party to another on a 3 per cent swing, when the levels of government expenditure on the provision of public goods in five states can be presented and compared, we may then be led to inquire why power varies among senators, why some constituencies are 'safe' and others 'marginal', or what accounts for the differences between the USA on the one hand and Canada, Britain, Germany, and France on the other, in terms of governmental provision of public goods and services (King, 1973–4). For explanation, in political science as in any other systematic field of human inquiry, requires the deliberate and explicit treatment of information, so that it can be structured, tested, amended, extended, and compared.

'All political analysis can be viewed as comparative. Thus, whenever one attempts to analyse a political situation, he uses the method of comparison in order to identify the similarities and differences between the situation being studied and other situations' (Graham, 1971, p. 139). Although comparison itself lies at the heart of all political analysis, a distinction can be drawn between what has come to be known as 'the comparative method' and other varieties of scientific method which use implicit or more controlled explicit comparison: case-study analysis, experimentation, statistical analysis. For many reasons, these alternative methods of analysis are not normally available for political analysis or else are not often suited to the furtherance of explanation (Lijphart, 1975). The 'comparative method' itself has been described as 'the method of testing hypothesised empirical relationships among variables on the basis of the same logic that guides the statistical method, but in which the cases are selected in such a way as to maximise the variance of the independent variables and to minimise the variance of the control variables' (Lijphart, 1975, p. 164). In deciding to employ the comparative method, as Lijphart has defined it, as a tool for political analysis and as an aid to explanation, a number of considerations have to be explicitly confronted and decisions reached.

First, to provide a starting point, there has to be a problem or issue, a question to which comparative analysis can, at least in principle, provide an answer: why do some working class voters regularly vote Conservative rather than Labour? (Nordlinger, 1967). What qualities predispose some states rather than others to experience military intervention in their politics? (Finer, 1962). What factors enable a national minority to seek a separate political existence, or, alternatively, to remain integrated with the majority population? (Deutsch, 1953). Why is the feeling of political competence higher among the citizens of some states rather than others?

(Almond and Verba, 1963). Second, certain decisions must be taken about strategy, about the units which are to be compared, about the temporal dimensions of the cases which are to be considered, about the ways in which data are to be gathered and analysed, about the theoretic context within which explanations are to be framed. Third, and related to both the statement of the problem and the choice of strategy, the relation of the exercise of empirical comparison to *theory* has to be considered, for theory is both the end and the beginning of comparison: theory suggests problems, but the answers given to those problems may then in turn contribute to the development, refinement, or confirmation of theory.

IN THE BEGINNING IS THE PROBLEM . . .

'Good questions are a prerequisite for good answers; good answers require that the questions be put in the proper way' (Graham, 1971, p. 15).

The problem is more than just the starting point for comparative research. It also acts as a directional pointer, to indicate what types of comparison are needed, what sort of data should be acquired, what level of generalisation is appropriate, and so on. It may serve as a necessary first step to the creation or development of theory, for no theory is formed except as the result of a question to which someone hoped in his curiosity to find an answer (Deutsch, 1971, p. 12). Clearly, decisions about data, strategy, and theory will be different in comparing the revolutions of Russia and China (Skocpol, 1976), than, for instance, if comparison is concerned with personality traits of political leaders in the third world, or with the effects of types of electoral system on the types of party system in contemporary western Europe.

To serve these functions of acting as guide to data and strategy and as stimulant to theory development, the problem must be carefully and properly formulated. It must of course be a question that is capable of an answer, first of all. 'The German Question' or 'the problem of apartheid' are not, as they stand, open to the provision of an answer or solution; one would first need to know what aspects of the German question or what particular problems of apartheid are being referred to, and what the issues are in each case. To be capable of an answer, the key terms of a problem have to be very precisely defined, if necessary in such a way that they can be *operationalised*, i.e. that their presence or absence, or their relative frequency, can be tested objectively and unambiguously. In the illustrative questions set out above (p. 288), 'working-class voter', 'military intervention', 'national minority', and 'political competence' are all instances of terms that would require operational definition (Sartori, 1970; Roberts, 1971 'Introduction'). Particularly where quantification is involved—and it frequently is involved at some stage of comparative analysis, whether the problem concerns differences in policy outputs (King, 1973–4) or expansion of bureaucracies (Parkinson, 1955)—clarity of definition is a prerequisite if a valid answer to a question is to be obtained.

STRATEGY: THE ROAD TO THEORY

'When we begin to study government with curiosity, at the same instant we begin to compare; the problem is not whether to compare but how to organise comparison' (Mackenzie, 1967, p. 311).

From the vast universe of facts, the comparative analyst must select those which are relevant to the problem he is investigating. In order to select, he requires a strategy which will guide his inquiry. Choice of a strategy involves a number of decisions, some of which are of considerable complexity.

The first set of decisions concerns the contextual setting for comparative inquiry: the focus of comparison and the level of theorising which will be undertaken, for, as Lijphart has so rightly emphasised, 'the comparative method requires the careful selection of cases that fit the research problem' (1975, p. 167).

Until very recently, there was only one recognised focus for comparative inquiry: the state. This affected the varieties of problem considered to be suited to comparative research in political science; constitutional provisions, the important offices of government, institutions and their procedures—these provided most of the problems for investigation. This focus on the state also influenced the type of comparison that could be undertaken, more or less forcing it to be institutional, legalistic, and static. Comparative studies of phenomena outside this narrow field were the province of the sociologist, and although today political scientists may claim that they recognise the significance of the contributions made to comparative politics by, for example, Marx, Weber, Michels, and Parsons, the works of these writers are still much more likely to be excerpted and discussed in volumes of sociology than in political science books.[1] Nowadays few political scientists would dispute either the utility of the concept of 'the state', or its great importance as a focus for political study (see Mackenzie, 1971, esp. pp. 14–21). But there has developed over recent years an increasing feeling of impatience with the claim that the state is the only possible or proper focus for political science. Several other possibilities have been suggested: the system (Easton, 1957); the polity (Riggs, 1970); the group (Truman, 1951); the individual actor (Eulau, 1963, pp. 14–19). There is no 'right' or 'wrong' choice to be made here, only a choice among more appropriate or less appropriate alternatives, a more useful or a less useful focus. Just how appropriate or useful the selected focus is will depend on the level of generalisation and theory required, which in turn hinge upon the type of problem under investigation. Haas has stated that the choice of focus and the level of theorising is really a matter of selection of an appropriate sampling unit, and that 'this problem is entirely a function of the research question' (1962, p. 300). Certain problems will involve focus on large-scale units, such as industrialised states, empires, or international organisations; others will deal with small developing states, the provinces of a federation, metropolitan cities or European communist parties; yet others will sample the large universe of working-class voters or civil servants or university students, possibly from several different cultures. Indeed, this aspect of the problem of strategy involves three dimensions of decision: the *unit* of comparison which may be the political system itself, as a relatively autonomous structure—for example the state, or a sub-system unit, such as a province, a political party or a trade union; the *level* of comparison, which may be intra-system, such as local government authorities in Britain, or cross-system; and the temporal context, which may be simultaneous (comparison of units at some common moment or period) or 'historical' (comparison across different periods or at dissimilar moments of time). This triple consideration problem may be presented in tabular form (Table 19.1).

Of course, one cannot compare a system on an intra-system basis at a single moment of time; to do so would be to obtain as much information as Lepidus did from Antony about the crocodile, so there is a blank cell in the table.

But the other seven possibilities all exist and examples of each can readily be found:

[1] Marx, Weber, and Parsons are all represented in Thompson and Tunstall (1971); all four writers are included in a popular Reader on political sociology by Pizzorno (1971); see also Barry (1970, esp. ch. 1).

TABLE 19.1 *Unit of comparison*

Level of comparison	Simultaneous		Historical	
	System	Sub-system	System	Sub-system
Intra-system	—	B	D	F
Cross-system	A	C	E	G

Case B—comparison of states of the USA regarding welfare expenditure for a given year, or,
Case F—historically; a series of budgetary periods;
Case D—comparison of the Fourth Republic party system with the party system of the Fifth Republic in France;
Case A—comparison of governmental provision of public goods (King, 1973–4). This will overlap to some extent with case E;
Case E—comparison of communist revolution in Russia and China (Skocpol, 1976);
Case C—comparison of communist party structure in contemporary France, Spain, and Italy;
Case G—comparison of the metropolitan government structures of third-world capitals today with cities of the industrialising countries of Western Europe and the USA in the nineteenth century.

It should be emphasised that even if the main strategy of comparison is intra-system a supplementary cross-system comparison can act as a 'control' and can offer useful guidance as to the scope and extent of the applicability of results: do findings about welfare spending in the states of the USA apply also to the West German *Lander*, for example? Similarly, a historical study may act as a control on the temporal extension of results of a 'simultaneous' comparison, to check whether results are independent of the time period from which they are derived.

The level of theorising may be influenced, if not determined, by the choice of focus that is made. If states are compared, on a world scale, then comparison may involve 'grand theory', the development of explanations concerning a small number of variables of a high level of generality: inputs and outputs, bargaining, communication, revolution or policymaking. On the other hand, the problem and the units selected may be so specified and restricted that comparison involves detailed, narrow-range theorising, using concepts of a low-level order of generality, such as the study of factors affecting negro voting registration in the southern states of the USA (Bailey, 1967, part 3), or the historical causes of communist revolutions in just two specified cases (Skocpol, 1976). Or middle-range theory may be involved, claimed by some to be the most useful in terms of the enterprise of comparative politics as a whole (LaPalombara, 1968, p. 55), where units and problems fall somewhere between the highly-generalised and the very specific: aspects of party system in industrialised democratic states, or anto-colonial revolutions, for example. The choice depends on the constraints provided by the initial formulation of the problem.

The second major decision concerning strategy is also connected with the question of 'careful selection of cases to fit the research problem': this time, the choice has to be made between a 'most similar' and a 'most different' approach (Przeworski and Teune, 1970, pp. 31–9). In the case of the most similar approach, the units for comparison, whether states, party organisation, cities, individuals or groups, are chosen precisely because they are similar to each other in most of their significant attributes. For instance, Latin American states share, to a greater or lesser extent, a history of conquest by Spain or Portugal and a struggle for independence from those imperial powers, a common linguistic heritage, a broadly similar economic structure, an unstable political culture, extremes of poverty and wealth, geographic proximity, the past influence of American economic penetration, and so forth. European higher civil servants share relatively high levels of income, somewhat similar life-styles, very similar professional duties and privileges, and often a similar educational background. London, New York, Paris, nad Tokio have in common large populations, severe problems of urban transportation, land use and budgeting, dissonance between administration and social boundaries, as well as difficulties relating to crime and mass tourism. The advantage of using a 'most similar' approach is that, where the problem is one of identifying and accounting for specific differences, selection of units for analysis which possess many similarities in terms of relevant variables makes easier the identification of variables which *do* differ, and which may thus be considered as the first candidates for investigation as casual or explanatory variables. King's comparison of governmental provision of public goods in western industrialised democracies is an interesting illustration of this strategy; of the five variables which he postulates as possibly accounting for the observed differences between .he USA on the one hand and the four other cases he investigates on the other, four (elites, demands, interest groups, institutions) do not seem to vary significantly, but his fifth variable, ideas, does (King, 1973–4). Skocpol's study of communist revolutions in Russia and China is also based on the selection of 'similar' cases in order to identify significant explanatory differences (Skocpol, 1976). Differences in the policies of communist parties in Eastern European states may be explained more easily because their relations with the USSR, the geographic locations of those states, their shared post-war histories are similar (in contrast to a random sample of states, or even, of communist states). Thus differences may be accounted for by the few remaining variables which are not in fact similar in these countries: the role of religion in the state, the structure and organisation of the economy, ethnic groupings in the population, or relations with West Germany, for instance.

Of course, there are some criticisms which may be levelled at this strategy. Lijphart has stressed three important limitations or disadvantages (1975, pp. 172–3). It tends to result in low-range or, at best, middle-range theory, since the very act of selection of similar cases restricts in advance the scope of application of such contributions to theory as finally do emerge. The infrequency of suitable 'similar' cases may tend to over-concentrate comparative research on the limited opportunities which do exist: Anglo-Saxon democracies, European communist states, the states of the USA, and so on. Most significantly of all, the selection of a small number of similar cases for comparison (and this strategy tends towards analysis of only a small number of cases) leads to a danger of over-determination of observed differences: more than one type of explanation may account for differences in the outcome of communist revolution when only two cases under comparison: Russia and China. In addition to these criticisms, there is often the danger that, in selecting a 'most similar' approach, other aspects of strategy which would be better met by use of a 'most different' approach, will be overlooked or neglected.

The alternative strategy, then, is to use a 'most different' approach, based not upon systems or cases which are similarly patterned in their main relationships, but on those where the actual patterns of relationships among variables differ. This strategy is particularly useful where not observed differences, but observed similarities, are to be explained. The rationale for using this approach is that, if, despite major differences of geographic location, very distinctive cultures, variations in economic structure, or even of the historic period under consideration, similarities in the factors under investigation can be observed these may be prima facie accounted for by the few similarities that remain. Military intervention in states of widely different geographic location and economic and cultural attributes (Finer, 1962), electoral corruption in Victorian England and post-independence Nigeria (Wraith and Simpkins, 1963), the progress of revolution in France after 1789 and Russia after 1917, separatism in the Rhineland and Bavaria after World War 1 compared to Quebec, Nigeria, Scotland, and Pakistan in recent years—these are phenomena which require a 'most different' approach.

This approach, too, does not escape criticism, In particular, it may also involve making an unguided choice amongst a large number of possible residual similarities even in otherwise differently patterned cases.

Data provide a third strategic consideration. The problem which is the starting-point for comparison, decisions about strategy concerning the selection and availablity of cases, the choice of theoretical framework, all will direct a comparative inquiry towards certain types and categories of data whilst excluding others. For the study of political attitudes and participation in five different political systems. sample surveys may be used to gather data (Almond and Verba, 1963) for a comparison of public expenditures in western democracies, aggregate statistical data may be required (King, 1973-4); for a longitudinal comparison of electoral behaviour in Britain, voting statistics coupled with questionnaires data may be the most fruitful data strategy (Butler and Stokes, 1969).

Availability and access are other problems. The 'thirty year rule' applied to British governmental records, questions of personal and official confidentiality, linguistic and cultural barriers, non-response rates in sample surveys based on questionnaires: these are some of the constraints that may operate in this area. The reliability of data may also be a problem: do countries which are being compared gather their statistics accurately? are questionnaire responses about recall of voting preferences at the past two elections reliable? are the recollections of Crossman, Brown, and Wilson about the 1964-70 Labour administrations trustworthy chronicles of what actually happened? Nor must problems of comparability of data be overlooked: not all states at any one time, nor does one state across different time periods, gather and classify data in the same way about the same topics.

Fourthly, there is a problem of strategy concerned with the linkages that may have to be made between the object under investigation (working-class voters, revolutionary leaders, nationalised industries, budgetary processes) and its broader context (the state, the electorate, the political system). Social scientists have called this the 'ecological problem'—that statements true of a political system or other contextual unit cannot be used directly to make statements that will necessarily hold true for elements of that unit. Suppose one is given aggregate data about the voting preferences of a group of the electorate, say, working-class voters (that two-thirds vote Labour, for example); no valid prediction can be made from this data about the voting preference of any sub-section or individual member of that group. Linkages must be constructed by the testing of theories at different levels, so that more generalised theories are firmly based on rigorously tested middle-range and lower-range theories. There is also always a need to test how far differences in the objects under comparison—whether voting systems, levels of political awareness, forms of constitutional court or patterns and modes of military intervention in politics—are caused by differences in the patterning of contextual systems (such as the state), and how far by factors external to the system (such as foreign intervention). And, having concluded an example of comparative analysis, there is always the further step of trying to say something valid for the system on the basis of comparison of particular aspects of the system.

There are several problems associated with the role of 'the political' in any example of research in comparative politics. There is a need anyway to define 'the political' in advance of selecting and formulating a problem. As suggested above, a narrow-gauge definition based on 'the state' limits the choice of problem as well as the focus of inquiry undertaken to investigate that problem. Broader definitions, centred around concepts of 'the political system', 'authoritative decision-making', and 'power' still provide criteria of separation from other areas of social inquiry, but also encourage a more catholic approach to problem formulation and strategies of inquiry, as well as serving as a reminder that 'the political' in real-life situations is always inextricably interwoven with economic, cultural, legal, anthropological, and many other aspects of society as a whole.

This reminder is also of importance in the search for data. If comparative politics is distinguished from other areas of study by the *type of problem* with which it is concerned,[2] it would be sterile and restrictive to limit its *areas of investigation and explanation* to political matters only. Of course, and quite correctly, writers such as Sartori (cited in LaPalombara, 1968, p. 54) and Mackenzie (1971, pp. 20–1)

---

[2] The reverse could also be argued: that it is distinguished by the type of *solutions* it seeks to problems which may or may not be political, but this position does seem less logical and less defensible.

have emphasised the autonomy of political factors—that 'the political' is not always reducible to economic or social factors. But the explanations which will result from research into a political problem will almost always include factors which reach beyond the realm of the political—educational, cultural, psychological, technological, geographic, historical, and other factors may be involved.

Other problems of strategy exist which go beyond the matters already discussed of case selection, data, the definition of the 'political', and so on. In particular, strategy will always be constrained by limitation of resources: of time, money, and techniques. The acquisition of data will bring in its wake a host of problems about the treatment of cross-cultural distinctions (Roberts, 1972, pp. 25–6, 33–4), translation methods, sampling procedures, and similar matters. But these are common to many forms of comparative social research. In comparative politics, the main danger is that of selecting strategies which prematurely exclude significant data, or close off promising lines of analysis. The remedy is a 'multi-approach' strategy (Almond, 1970, p. 22), eclecticism as far as is congruent with the advancement of the inquiry. As has already been suggested, one strategy may be pursued with regard to the selection of cases, and another strategy then employed as a check on the validity and possible extension of results (above, p. 292). The problem of over-determination of explanations which may arise in, say, a 'most similar' approach may be met by a second-stage inquiry involving a 'most different' selection of cases as a means of narrowing the range of possible explanatory factors.

THEORY: THE MAP AND THE DESTINATION

'... each theory pierces the gloom from a slightly different angle and highlights somewhat different problems' (Easton, 1965, p. 472).

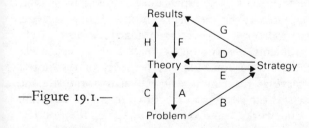

—Figure 19.1.—

Theories serve many different purposes in comparative political analysis, and are related to the formulation of problems and the selection of strategies in a variety of ways. Diagrammatically, these relationships may be represented as in Figure 19.1.

In earlier sections of this essay, the relationships between the problem and choice of strategy (arrow B) and between choice of strategy and results of comparison (arrow G) have been indicated. In this section, the significance of the two-way relationships between theory and problem (arrows A, C), theory and strategy (arrows D, E), and theory and results (arrows F, H) will be considered.

But, first, what is 'theory'? It may be defined as an interrelated set of propositions about the linkages between elements or processes, cast in terms of a particular conceptual vocabulary (which is not necessarily always or totally expressed in verbal form: symbols and digits may be involved, for instance), and offering some—perhaps very tentative and approximate—explanation for the forms and values which those linkages assume. A theory of revolutions, for example, will probably relate the concepts of government and regime, revolutionary uprising, participants—both elite and mass— in the revolution, precipitating causes and conditions (though different styles of revolutionary theory will focus on different sets of possible causes and conditions), and perhaps external factors such as imported ideologies and foreign military and diplomatic intervention. Such a theory will also proffer suggestions as to why these concepts are related in the way that the theory proposes.

'Given that the analysis should be comparative, the first step in the inquiry must be the discovery of a general frame of reference' (Blondel, 1969, p. 15). A theory, or a theoretical framework, provides this general frame of reference. Even when a theoretical framework lacks some of the qualities of a fully-fledged theory, when it is perhaps 'only a specialised vocabulary for description' (Holt and Turner, 1970, p. 27), when its heuristic value as provocation to thought greatly outweighs its likely explanatory or predictive power, as it has been suggested is the case with Marxist theory (Gregor, 1971, p. 166), it may still serve very well as a framework for research. It may generate problems, it may suggest relative priorities among problems, and certainly the vocabulary of a theory or theoretical framework may serve as the language in which to formulate the problem which acts as the starting-point for comparative research. The theoretical frameworks based on the concept of the political system, such as those developed by Easton, Deutsch, and Almond, are some of the best known examples, but others may be mentioned of varying degrees of refinement and explanatory power: exchange and bargaining theories, associated with such writers as Riker, Downs, Curry and Wade, and Olson; sociological theories, often related to electoral behaviour and political participation, such as those employed by Lipset and by Butler and Stokes; psychological theories, as described by Eulau or Greenstein; and others based on central concepts of conflict, elites or policy outputs.[3] But the relationship between theory and the initial problem in a case of comparative analysis is not unidirectional. The problem, once formulated, may point to some particular theory or range of theories which may appear to be potentially more fruitful than others, in acting as a conceptual framework for research and as a guide to strategy. An example of this is the problem of accounting for differences in the political stability of governments, regimes or states. A choice might be made among theories based on class, revolution, the input–output system devised by Easton, or a communications theory such as Deutsch developed (Deutsch, 1966). Or some new combination of elements of several of these theories might be chosen, at least as a beginning. However, at first glance, it would appear that psychological theories, or bargaining theories of a high degree of formal rigour (such as Riker's), would not be very helpful as frameworks within which to organise such a comparative analysis—though investigation of the problem of political stability might in time suggest otherwsie.

The relationships between theory and strategy are multiple and rich. Theory selection may determine the way in which cases for comparison are selected, whether intra-system or cross-system comparison shall be undertaken (cf. Peters *et al.*, 1977, pp. 327–8), whether a historical rather than a simultaneous dimension shall be selected (e.g. Skocpol, 1976, p. 288), and whether a 'most similar' or a 'most different' approach ought to be adopted. The more rigorous and the more refined the theory, the more probable that research strategies related to it will be predetermined in terms of choice of cases; in particular, if the initial problem for analysis derives from a variation or extension of such a theory, it is probable that a 'most similar' approach will be used, to limit the number of key variables under investigation.

Theory is also relevant to aspects of strategy concerned with data collection and evaluation. It has been claimed that information only acquires significance—and hence can only then deserve the name of

[3] For a review of several of these theoretical frameworks, see Roberts (1972, pp. 39–49).

'data'—when related to some theoretic context (Przeworski and Teune, 1970, p. xi), and that 'theory provides a pattern for recognising and assimilating facts' (McClelland, 1966, p. 11). The statistical information that only two out of every three females on the electoral register actually voted in the last general election may normally provoke a shrug of the shoulders and an uninterested response: 'So what?' The same information when related to a theory of electoral behaviour applied to a problem of comparative political participation may become highly relevant data. Further, theory may provide schemes of classification for data, and highlight gaps that require new or additional data in order to be eliminated.

Theory may also be of assistance in coping with linkage problems. It may suggest ways of relating data of different levels of generality (aggregate voting statistics for constituencies and sample survey responses about party preference, for example), and may provide directions for analysis, involving the suggestion of new relationships between previously discrete categories of data.

Reciprocally, strategic decisions—made imperative because of the nature of the initial problem, restricted resources or limited data— may affect the theoretical context within which comparison may be undertaken. Some theoretical frameworks may demand techniques or time or access to data sources that are not available, and so they have to be abandoned, at least initially, in favour of more congenial frameworks.

Finally, there is a dual relationship between theory and the results of empirical comparison. The theoretic framework which guided the original selection and formulation of the research problem, which constrained choice of research strategy, also acts as a structure which provides form within which to present the results of analysis in an integrated and comprehensible manner, and a mode of transmission by means of which such results can be communicated to other political scientists, even across different cultures and over long periods of time (McClelland, 1966, p. 15). It provides a ready means of comparing results: an investigation of parliamentary coalitions in western European states, conducted within the context of Riker's coalition theory, can be compared to the results of other empirical investigation into coalition formation and behaviour, at whatever level of focus and whether intra-system or cross-system, provided these too have been expressed in the conceptual language of Riker's theory.

In reverse, obviously theory is the goal, the destination, towards which comparative empirical research is necessarily directed. The results of such research, or developments of method and strategy during its course, may confirm, refute, refine, amend or cast doubt upon existing theory. Typologies may be developed, which may suggest new hypotheses or extensions of theory (cf. Peters *et al.*, 1977, esp. pp. 329–35). Temporal or cultural extensions of theoretical propositions by empirical research may suggest new boundaries or conditions, perhaps narrower than were previously considered to be the case, within which such propositions may hold, as has occurred for instance with Michels' 'iron law of oliarchy', with theories about the relationship between electoral systems and party systems, with ideas about party cohesions in Britain and the USA (see Holt and Turner, 1970, pp. 16–18). And, in turn, such revisions of theory may prompt new questions, new research . . . and so the cycle of problem, strategy, comparative research, and theorising begins over again.

Theory is not just the ivy that clings to the walls of the ivory tower. It can also be a guide to political action, a way in which 'future observations and consequences of actions in the outside world can be predicted' (Deutsch, 1971, p. 12). This imposes a responsibility on the political scientist, whether as researcher or theorist, to question and to test his propositions and his results. In the end, we must neither neglect theory, nor claim too much for it: 'All we can realistically hope is that a better theory will give us a better chance to do a better job' (Deutsch, 1971, p. 15).

THE USES OF HISTORICAL COMPARISON

'The most challenging innovation that comparative politics has produced is the idea of extending its cross-cultural comparisons backwards in time' (Thrupp, 1970, p. 345).

Although reference has been made already to the strategic significance of comparison which involves more than one time period (above, pp. 291–2), the importance of historical comparison warrants some special consideration of its purposes and utility.

There are two different reasons why comparative political analysis has recently devoted more attention to what Almond has called 'the systematic exploitation of historical experience' (1970, p. 28). Comparison across time enlarged tremendously the range of cases available for comparative analysis, whether the problem under investigation be concerned with revolutions, military coups, secession movements, elections, changes of leadership in dictatorship, crisis policymaking, or whatever. Especially if the unit of comparison is to be a single system or a small number of very similar systems, historical comparisons may be the only way to obtain sufficient cases to analyse. Furthermore, historical comparison may enrich and illuminate simultaneous comparison, identifying aspects that are affected by the passage of time: 'just as the variation in the circumstances of different periods allows us to see more clearly the role of factors that remain fixed in the short run, so the varied experience of different countries allows us to see more clearly the role of factors that remain fixed within any one of them' (Butler and Stokes, 1969, p. 533). In this way, historical comparison may act as a control, a check on the validity or extension of results.

In some instances, historical comparison is not just a matter of strategic preference; it can be required by the relationship of the problem to theory. Skocpol's consideration of the different outcomes of the Russian and Chinese communist revolutions pointed to the need to examine 'antecedent differences' (1976, p. 287). The concerns of Plato and Aristotle about the ways in which different types of regime change over time, the studies of political modernisation processes in developed and developing states, comparison by means of cohort analyses of different generations in terms of their political behaviour—these necessitate historical comparison. The historical dimension is an integral part of the research problem.

Special problems may arise concerning comparability and availability of data across different time periods, but these are in many cases being overcome, just as they have been overcome to a large extent in comparative economic history. Certainly the potential rewards of historical comparison make the effort worthwhile.

IN CONCLUSION

Three points emerge from this review of the relationships between problems, strategies, theories, and data in comparative political analysis. First, the choice of strategy or theory should be a matter for explicit and preliminary decisions before the stages of data-collection and data-evaluation are undertaken. Only in this manner can it be expected that the results of a comparative inquiry will relate to other and more general work in a cumulative fashion, and thus take on a significance beyond their own limited outcome. This does not mean that amendments may not be made to the original choices as research progresses; the diagram on p. 297 emphasised that such relationships often work in reciprocal directions. But for comparative research to be meaningful, for it to meet expected standards of rigour and validity, it must commence from an explicit theoretical base and possess a clear strategy of inquiry. Second, it must be remembered that no single theoretical framework, however general, is suited to the investigation of every single type or level of problem. Eaton's model may not be helpful in dealing with problems of the recruitment of political elites, or explaining variations in policy outcome; an inquiry into political development is more likely to be advanced by the employment of a systems-based theory than by the use of a micro-political framework which focuses on political behaviour; Marxist theory may not be a suitable context within which to conduct a comparative analysis of leadership behaviour. Hence it is fruitless to criticise one theoretical framework because it does not do the job of another. Third, strategy, theory, and the acquisition and analysis of data are all interconnected. The range of theory determines the level, as well as the types, of data with which it can cope; the strategy chosen must take account of the level of generality of the theoretical context; and so on. An investigation based on a sample survey will be a waste of time and effort if the level of data required is that of aggregate electoral statistics already published in official records, for example.

There is no one 'best way' in comparative politics, no single approach of theory or method that supersedes the rest. What is required is an awareness of the range of approaches, theories, method and techniques that are available, an appreciation of their limitations and special problems, and a knowledge of how comparative inquiry has been conducted in the past—and with what degree of success. This awareness, this sensitivity to possibilities, this knowledge, will enable comparative politics to become, if not an exact science, one that is increasingly rigorous and self-conscious, and one that helps through its discoveries to extend the boundaries of human knowledge.

REFERENCES

ALMOND, G. (1970) 'Determinacy-choice, stability-change: some thoughts on a contemporary polemic in political theory', *Government and Opposition, 5.*
ALMOND, G. and VERBA, S. (1963) *The Civic Culture*, Princeton University Press.
BAILEY, H., ed. (1967) *Negro Politics in America,* Bobbs-Merrill.
BARRY, B. (1970) *Sociologists, Economists and Democracy,* Collier-Macmillan.
BLONDEL, J. (1969) *An Introduction to Comparative Government*, Weidenfeld and Nicolson.
BUTLER, D. and STOKES, D. (1969) *Political Change in Britain,* Macmillan.

DEUTSCH, K. (1953) *Nationalism and Social Communication,* M.I.T. Press–Wiley.

DEUTSCH, K. (1966) *The Nerves of Government,* Free Press.

DEUTSCH, K. (1971) 'On political theory and political action', *American Political Science Review,* **65.**

EASTON, D. (1957) 'An approach to the analysis of political systems', *World Politics,* **9.**

EASTON, D. (1965) *A Systems Analysis of Political Life,* Wiley.

EULAU, H. (1963) *The Behavioral Persuasion in Politics,* Random House.

FINER, S. (1962) *The Man on Horseback,* Pall Mall Press.

GRAHAM, G. (1971) *Methodological Foundations for Political Analysis,* Xerox Publishing Co.

GREGOR, A. (1971) *An Introduction to Metapolitics,* Free Press.

HAAS, M. (1962) 'Comparative analysis', *Western Political Quarterly,* **15.**

HOLT, R. and TURNER, J., eds. (1970) *The Methodology of Comparative Research,* Free Press.

KING, A. (1973–4) 'Ideas, institutions, and the policies of governments: a comparative analysis', *British Journal of Political Science,* **3.** (See also pp. 101–41 of this Reader.)

LAPALOMBARA, J. (1968) 'Macrotheories and microapplications in comparative politics', *Comparative Politics,* **1.**

LIJPHART, A. (1975) 'The comparable-cases strategy in comparative research', *Comparative Political Studies,* **8.**

MCCLELLAND, C. (1966) *Theory and the International System,* Collier-Macmillan.

MACKENZIE, W. (1967) *Politics and Social Science,* Penguin.

MACKENZIE, W. (1971) *The Study of Political Science Today.* Macmillan.

NORDLINGER, E. (1967) *The Working Class Tories,* MacGibbon and Kee.

PARKINSON, C. (1955) 'Parkinson's law', *The Economist,* 19 November 1955. (See also pp. 39–45 of this Reader.)

PETERS, B. *et al.* (1977) 'Types of democratic systems and types of public policy', *Comparative Politics,* **9.** (See also pp. 70–100 of this Reader.)

PIZZORNO, A., ed. (1971) *Political Sociology,* Penguin.

PRZEWORSKI, A. and TEUNE, H. (1970) *The Logic of Comparative Social Enquiry,* Wiley.

RIGGS, F. (1970) 'The comparison of whole political systems', in R. Holt and J. Turner, eds., *The Methodology of Comparative Research,* Free Press.

ROBERTS, G. (1971) *A Dictionary of Political Analysis,* Longman.

ROBERTS, G. (1972) *What is Comparative Politics?* Macmillan.

SARTORI, G. (1970) 'Concept misformation in comparative politics', *American Political Science Review,* **54.** (See also pp. 228–65 of this Reader.)

SKOCPOL, T. (1976) 'Old regime legacies and communist revolutions in Russia and China', *Social Forces,* **55.** (See also pp. 166–201 of this Reader.)

THOMPSON, K. and TUNSTALL, J., eds. (1971) *Sociological Perspectives,* Penguin and The Open University.

THRUPP, S. (1970) 'Diachronic methods in comparative politics', in R. Holt and J. Turner, eds., *The Methodology of Comparative Research,* Free Press.

TRUMAN, D. (1951) *The Governmental Process,* Knopf.

WRAITH, R. and SIMPKINS, E. (1963) *Corruption in Developing Countries,* Allen and Unwin.

20

R. *Looker* Comparative politics:
Methods or theories?*

Prepared for this Reader by R. Looker, Lecturer in Politics, York University.

'A woman without a man is like a fish without a bicycle'
(Women's Lib Slogan)

Too much of the general literature of 'Comparative Politics' is preoccupied with 'methodology' to the neglect of substantive theory.
All too often, surveys of 'the state of the discipline' seem obsessed
with picking over the well-chewed bones of 'problems of comparative method', while actual theories of politics creep in only at the
margin, as mere illustrations of some mighty methodological
principle. The purpose of this article is to make a contribution to
rectifying this imbalance by examining a number of important
trends in the substantive content of comparative political and social
analysis in the post-1945 Anglo-Saxon 'academic' world.[1]

It would be pleasant if an article such as this could avoid problems
of methodology. Unfortunately this cannot entirely be the case. For
the above criticism isn't simply based on a belief that what the practitioners of comparative politics actually claim to have discovered

---

* Various friends and colleagues—not necessarily exclusive categories—
have helped with advice and suggestions for reading in areas outside my
own normal fields of interest. My thanks, therefore, along with the usual
disclaimers on their behalf to Arthur Brittan, David Coates, David Hay,
John Horton, T. V. Sathyamurthy, David Skidmore and Albert Weale.

[1] Our subject-matter is thus wider than post-war 'Comparative Politics'
as such, and reflects on the extent to which practitioners of that 'discipline' have often found their theoretical inspiration in work carried out
in the related fields of sociology, economics, history, and philosophy. At
the same time, it does not purport to survey the entire post-war scene in
this respect. Much continental—especially French, German, and Italian—
'social science' marched to the sounds of very different intellectual drums
throughout the period from those of British and North American analysis,
and very little by way of dialogue existed between them at least until the
1960s.

about the world should make at least as interesting a subject for discussion as the methods they claim to have used in making those discoveries; nor is it merely that some of the issues presented as matters for heuristic decision—the use of 'the nation-state' or its theoretical analogue, 'the system', as the basic unit of comparative analysis is a good case in point—are at least as plausibly regarded as substantively empirical questions. Much more awkwardly, the very practice of divorcing discussions of method from those of theory itself involves begging a number of what we might call 'meta-methodological' questions, for the problem of the relationship between the two is itself an issue in debate between rival perspectives. Thus if only to avoid begging such questions, a survey such as is envisaged here must needs pay some attention to methodology, if only to the extent of identifying some of the important meta-theoretical perspectives that have been influential in the period concerned, and indicating the empirical connections that have existed between them and more substantive theoretical schools and traditions.

I   THE EMERGENT CONSENSUS : COMPARATIVE POLITICS IN THE POST-WAR USA

Movement and method

Arguably, the use of systematic comparison in the study of politics goes back to Aristotle. What is not open to question is that Comparative Politics as a self-conscious programme, or 'Movement' in Almond's terms (p. 20 of this Reader) was the product of the bourgeoning political and social science departments of US universities in the post-war period.

To its adherents, the main impulse behind the Movement was methodological. Its programme aimed to replace what was seen as the unscientific muddle of old-fashioned political studies with the new discipline-cum-profession of Political Science. The hallmark of this discipline was its concern for, and adherence to, the canons of scientific method as they were generally understood within the predominantly Positivist[2] intellectual milieu of the time. Such a positivist Science of Politics would, through its firm adherence to proper

[2] Positivism is here used in the widest and loosest sense to embrace all those empiricist approaches which stress the essential unity of scientific method, a method which while it attains paradigmatic application in the natural science procedures, can in principle at least be equally legitimately deployed in the social sciences. See Kolakowski (1972) for a sympathetic survey of the tradition and Popper (1959) for the most generally accepted formulation of the logic of its method.

scientific procedures—precision in concept-formation, rigour in testing hypotheses, systematic data collection, quantification, etc.— ensure that it could claim its place alongside the sciences of nature as fully comparable with them in aspiration and method, if not yet in substantive achievement. Indeed, essential to such a positivist conception of methodology is the conviction that there are no differences in principle between the logics of natural and social investigation. In practice, of course, it was acknowledged that there were many difficulties in the path which led to the construction of a natural science of politics and society, most notably the impossibility and/or ethical unacceptability of using techniques of controlled experimentation in social and political life. It was here that the *method of comparison* could substitute for controlled experimentation as the foundation stone of a Political Science, for systematic comparison across a range of political contexts could provide a perfectly acceptable analogue to the laboratory experiments of the physical scientists. Thus within the largely Positivist categories within which the Movement operated, scientific politics emerged as necessarily comparative politics,[3] and the commitment to the method of comparison carried with it a commitment to the 'meta-methodological' perspectives of Positivism.

Global perspectives

Yet while this commitment to a positivist conception of Comparative Politics was an important component of the Movement, it does not of itself explain one other vital facet, namely the global aspirations of its substantive theorising. For Comparative Politics in this period aimed not simply at being a scientific politics; it was also a crucial component in a programme to construct a comprehensive—and hence comparative—social science of the entire planet, an 'universal social science' comparable in aspiration to the nineteenth-century Germanic ideal of a 'universal history'.

[3] This was, of course, the 'maximum programme' of the new scientific Politics, and within the ranks of the Movement there was plenty of room for more cautious approaches, doubts, and disagreements; for every 'enthusiast' like Macridis (1955) there were more sceptical 'traditionalists' like Heckscher (1957), just as for every advocate of overarching political frameworks like Easton (1965) one could find more modest practitioners of 'middle range theory' like Duverger (1954). But such doubts and disagreements were contained within a broader consensus on the goal of a science of comparative politics. Nor did they offer any real challenge to the dominant conception of the scientific enterprise within which that goal was articulated.

The substantive basis for this kind of global political and social science lay, simply enough, in the changed position of the USA in the post-war world. Throwing off the 'isolationism' of earlier times, the USA emerged in 1945 as the dominant super-power in the world. Faced with the facts of American power and its global reach, it was hardly surprising that questions concerning the uses and justification of that power should loom large in the consciousness not only of political leaders and commentators, and even ordinary citizens, but also in the research programme and theorisings of what Eckstein (1963) characterised as the 'policy-oriented and training-oriented discipline of political science' (p. 24). Nor is it altogether surprising that the historical context of that power—a Cold War globally fought out from Berlin to Korea, not to mention in the hearing of the Un-American Activities Committee in Washington—should have profoundly shaped and influenced the content and direction of the enterprise of a global comparative political and social science.

Briefly, we can identify three 'problem-areas' as foci of analytical concern for that enterprise, each one of which tapped into a different dimension of US world involvement. These related to (a) the advanced industrialised nations which went to make up 'the West' or 'Free World', over which the US asserted leadership; (b) the Communist bloc to the East with which the US was locked in Cold War struggle; (c) the vast mass of non-industrialised territories to the South, many only just emerging from colonial tutelage, which provided one of the key arenas for the Cold War confrontations.

A global, scientific, and comparative science could not tackle these related problem areas in an ad hoc way as separate and isolated foci of interest. Yet a fully comparative analysis required a standard against which the very different political and social experiences of these global segments could be evaluated. That standard was to be provided by the USA itself. In place of the older Isolationist tradition which had located American experiences and virtues as uniquely the property of 'God's own country', a new comparative political and social science undertook the task of formulating the categories of analysis within which the USA could serve as the universal theoretical standard of comparison.

The American standard

It is evident from the above discussion that our focus of interest here is somewhat more extensive than a narrow definition of 'political science' might allow. And it is important to stress that political analyses were only one component part of a much wider social scientific programme embracing also sociological and economic modes of discourse. Yet viewing that programme as a whole, one very striking feature of the resultant complex of ideas was the extent to which the 'American standard' was identified and articulated in terms of its politics. In place of socio-economic categories like 'capitalism' political categories like 'democracy' were assigned central importance in the characterisation of American society. The key to that society was seen to lay in its pluralistic democratic processes, and in the material and ideal circumstances which both made possible such a democracy and which sustained and reinforced that democracy.

Five facets of this analysis are deserving of further attention here. *First,* there was the near-universal acceptance of some variant of Schumpeter's (1943) re-definition of the democratic process as the competitive struggle between rival elites for the popular vote. Shorn of its author's own pessimistic prognoses for the future of American capitalism, this account was taken both as the actual description of the US political process and as the prescriptive standard of representative democracy. Critical to this account was the very considerable emphasis placed upon the creative role of political elites and leadership—and a correspondingly limited and passive role for the mass electorate—within the institutional constraints imposed by the competitive political process itself.

A *second* facet qualified the somewhat elitist implications of the above position by stressing that effective authority—and in democracies, power was characteristically legitimate and therefore consensual/authoritative rather than coercive in character, as Parsons (1963) had argued—was exercised within limits which both circumscribed the effective range of state power and ensured the effective consultation with, and conciliation of, all significant 'interests' in and through the workings of the political process itself. Put a different way, the characteristic pattern of distribution of power in an advanced industrialised democracy was pluralistic and polycentric rather than monolithic and concentrated.

The potentially elitist implications of the thesis were further qualified by our *third* and *fourth* considerations—ideal and material. The ideational factor emphasised the extent to which a common culture, a shared set of values, and a consensus on at least the means and possibly the ends of the democratic process, ensured that no fundamental of ideology or interest could emerge to disrupt the stability of the society. For, above all, American democracy was *stable* democracy, and indeed stability was one central prerequisite for a lasting democratic system. Complementing this ideational process was our fourth, material, dimension[4] which stressed the resource capacity of an advanced industrialised society to resolve the strains generated by the inequalities and deprivations of earlier, capitalist phases of development. Whether this was seen as the result of internal economic evolution (the Liberal-Democratic variant) or as a consequence of the adoption of neo-Keynesian techniques of economic management (the Social-Democratic variant), the outcome was a pattern of sustained economic growth, full employment, and rising living standards which had largely eroded the bite of class antagonisms and the radical political conflicts such antagonisms had generated in previous epochs. Class differences, on this view, were no longer the source of fundamental division and conflict, but rather, as Kornhauser (1960) suggested, the basis for a stable politics of competition for relative advantage within the framework of representative democracy.

Underpinning these four, substantive, theses was a *fifth* analytical component which served to locate the others within a wider conceptual scheme which stressed their systemic inter-relatedness. Proposals for such 'systemic' frameworks were many and varied from Easton's (1965) 'input-output' models, and Almond's (1960) 'structural-functionalist' variant of the political system, to Parson's (1951) overarching conception of the social system. One crucial functional imperative directing the construction of such frameworks was precisely the requirements of a cross-national comparative analysis. For if the claim that, say, Parsons made for his schema were correct, it could be regarded as providing a necessary and indispensable starting point for the analysis of any and every society, in terms of the functional imperatives that had to be met in order that a society could survive at all. Thus to the extent that 'systemic' analysis provided the enterprise of constructing a universally applicable comparative analysis of politics and society with an analytically necessary starting point, carping criticisms of that enterprise on the grounds of ethnocentrism or concept-stretching could be easily dismissed. A global comparative science of politics necessarily

---

[4] Of course, the balance of explanatory emphasis between ideal and material factors varied greatly. Some, like Parsons (1959) and Almond and Verba (1963) placed greatest emphasis on the cultural system in accounting for democratic stability. To others, like Crosland (1956), the material advances were much more crucial. Others again, like Lipset (1960) and Bell (1961) sought to steer a middle path, paying intellectual dues to both claimants.

required universally applicable categories and concepts and 'systems/ analysis' appeared to meet this need.

Global comparisons and contrasts

Careful readers of the above account of the American standard will have detected some conceptual slippage from the focus on US democracy towards a characterisation of the political structure and processes of advanced industrialised societies. The slippage was intentional, for it was in this latter, hypostatised form that the political and social theorists presented the post-war USA for comparison with 'the West', the Eastern bloc, and the 'underdeveloped' South.

The comparative analysis of 'the West' presented few difficulties from this point of view. If US experience could be taken as a paradigm of 'advanced industrial society' as such, then the character of its partners in 'the West' could be assessed in terms of their degrees of approximation to the American condition. On such criteria, Britain and the 'older'—i.e. white settler—Commonwealth countries were in process of 'making it', as were the Scandinavian and Benelux nations. Unfortunately from the point of view of the theory, four of the most important industrialised powers of 'the Free World'— Germany, Japan, Italy, and France—were, either by virtue of their recent fascist pasts and/or their present propensity to sustain sizeable votes for Communist parties, clearly 'deviant cases' with regard to any easy equation of advanced industrialisation with pluralistic democracy. The resolution of the problem lay in equating Left voting and Rightist regimes as facets of an essentially identical phenomena[5] to be explained as 'extremist' mass responses to the appeals of anti-democratic and manipulative elites under circumstances when, for one reason or another, the normal constraints and institutionalised processes of pluralist democracy ceased to work. For Kornhauser (1960) and other theorists of 'mass society', what was involved was a pathological mirror-image of pluralistic democracy, which could nonetheless be analysed and explained in terms of the

[5] This neat obliteration of the significance of any substantive differences between the regimes and mass movements of Right and Left also served to facilitate a reinterpretation of America's own history. Thus a range of very disparate movements, from the Populists in the late nineteenth century to the McCarthyites in the 1950s were grouped together as irrational mass reactions to the functional imperatives of American society. See, for example, Bell (1956) and Hofstadter (1955). (But see also Rogin, 1967, and Pollack, 1966, for replies.)

latter's categories of analysis, thus preserving their globally comparative usefulness.

Such observations already suggest the kind of analysis likely to be applied to the *Eastern* bloc. Communism, no more than Nazism, was to be understood in terms of its substantive programme and ideology rather both were to be comprehended, not as polar opposites, but as two faces of the same *totalitarian* coin. Thus in place of the older polarities of Left and Right, of Capitalism and Communism, the fundamental dualism of the post-war world was articulated as Democracy vs. Totalitarianism. From Arendt (1951) to Friedrich and Brzezinski (1965) the concept of totalitarianism was given a wide range of interpretations, but in at least some of its variants, it was articulated in the categories of, and by means of a contrast with, the American standard. Thus totalitarianism involved a system of elite rule which was constrained by neither the institutional framework of democracy, nor a pluralistic power structure, nor yet again by any genuine system of shared values. In place of the latter there was a state-imposed and public ideology which legitimated the regime and the system of terroristic control and mobilisation it maintained over its subject population. Such regimes were often held to be inherently expansionist, with the result that their ambitions posed continuous threats—of internal subversion as well as external aggression—to the nations of both the industrialised West and the developing South. The global role and responsibilities of American power were, on this account, reactions and attempts to contain and repel the threat to world peace and security posed by the totalitarian Communist regimes.[6]

Approaches to the comparative analysis of the nations of the 'undeveloped' *South* necessarily started from a recognition of the most stark and glaring difference between them and the nations of the industrialised West. That is, they started from the facts of material poverty and economic 'backwardness'. The key perspectives brought to bear were those of 'development' and 'modernisation', quasi-evolutionary accounts which concentrated attention on the problem

[6] This 'global' perspective might appear to suggest a shift in the conceptual framework of comparative political and social analysis from the level of autonomous nation-states to that of a 'world-system' of some sort. However, outside the relatively narrow confines of International Relations studies, the autonomous national 'system' continued to reign conceptually supreme. 'External' forces and influences, whether from West or East, thus functioned as 'exogenous' factors interfering with the otherwise endogenously determined processes of the system.

of developing such societies from their current backward and 'traditional' condition, via industrialisation, urbanisation, and the market economy, towards the attainment of the goal of 'advanced industrialised societies'. Specifically economic modes of analysis clearly played a very major part in the formulation of theories of development—Rostow's (1962) work was of very considerable influence in this respect—but not to the exclusion of comparative political and social analysis. Economic development and stable democracy were seen as intertwined goals whose attainment required dynamic modernising elites to overcome 'traditional' blockages to nation-building, mobilise the masses in the collective task of modernisation, and act as a key channel for that process of 'acculturation' whereby the values and skills of the advanced West were permeated through the cultural system of the society.[7] Once again, the experience organised in the American standard was adequate to encompass both the situation of the South and its solutions.

II THE CRUMBLING CONSENSUS: CRISIS AND CRITIQUE IN THE 1960S AND 1970S

The above account of the themes of post-war comparative political and social analysis is, needless to say, very much an 'ideal-typical' schematisation of what was in fact a complex and disputatious intellectual scene. Such simplifications should not be taken to imply that this range of ideas constituted some fully articulated 'system', still less an orthodoxy comparable to, say, the 'official Marxism' of the Soviet bloc. Yet, this said, it must be admitted that taken as a whole, such ideas came close to constituting a consensus, on both methodological form and substantive content of social science, pervading the post-war Anglo-Saxon academic world.[8] (For con-

[7] Development studies cover an enormous field. For our purposes, Hozelitz (1960), Lerner (1958), and Almond and associates (1960, 1963, 1965) are most directly relevant.

[8] The consensus had its 'darker' aspects. Its adherents all too frequently drew the parameters of their universe of discourse—that which defined what was to count as a professionally acceptable contribution to intellectual debate—in a manner that more or less coincided with the substantive and methodological assumptions embodied in the consensus. Controversy within that universe of discourse was both acceptable and welcome, but those who, like that isolated critic of the 1950s, Wright Mills (1956), sought to challenge that overall perspective from a radical position paid a substantial price in terms of professional career prospects for such temerity, as Horowitz and others (1964) have pointed out. (In the

venience, we will refer to this fusion of positivist method and liberal-democratic perspectives as 'the Consensus' for the rest of this discussion.)

Part of the strength of this Consensus, taken at its widest, lay in its ability to blend together many of the most influential theses produced by that world—political pluralism, sociological functionalism, economic Keynesianism—into interrelated and mutually supporting ranges of analyses. Such an achievement in its turn seemed to testify both to the validity of the positivist methodology articulated in the programme of the Consensus and to the extent to which that programme had been carried out and borne fruit. The goal of a comprehensively universal comparative political and social science appeared to be in process of realisation by the early 1960s.

Yet, by the end of the decade, this powerful Consensus had crumbled away, and its characteristic themes came to constitute one, highly debatable school of political and social analysis, alongside others of at least equal credibility. The hows and whys of this process will form the subject-matter of this section of our discussion, beginning with matters methodological.

Scientism—the test of practice

In recent years, whenever two or three Anglo-Saxon social scientists have gathered together in the name of methodology, sooner or later the fateful words 'conflicting paradigms' will have been heard.[9] One central feature of the dethroning of positivism as *the* 'philosophy of science' within the social science was being replaced by a situation in which many perspectives were in open competition for that title.

Yet this was as much a consequence as a contributary cause of the crisis facing the Consensus in the 1960s. Even if we confine our attention to narrowly methodological matters for the moment, then we must note that the assault on the pervasive scientism of Consensus analysis in this period was at least as much a matter of

---

changed intellectual climate of the 1960s, Wright Mills enjoyed a considerable but posthumous influence as a guru of the new radical political sociology.) More conservative critics like Strauss (1959) and Oakeshott (1962) got a more polite, but equally ineffectual, hearing from their academic colleagues.

[9] Kuhn's (1970) terminology certainly facilitated the methodological debate among social scientists in the period, though whether his conceptualisation of science is either adequate in itself or relevant to specifically social scientific experience is open to considerable doubt. See, for example, the debate in Lakatos and Musgrave (1970).

critically examining the results of the positivist programme in practice as in a rejection of that programme in principle. Three facets of this critique are worth mentioning here, for collectively they illustrate the range of dissatisfaction with that practice which were articulated.

One of the easiest targets for criticism and indeed ridicule was the cult of quantification which many practitioners of the Consensus took as the index of a social analysis which was truly scientific. This was not simply a matter of the crass and simplistic substitution of statistical correlations in place of analysis and theory, though this certainly characterised much of the worst practice of the school. It also bred the futile pursuit of mathematical models of the kind criticised by Hacker (1967, p. 214 in this Reader) and the higher lunacies of Lasswell's (1962) proposals for a worldwide data survey harnessing the energies of secondary school children.

A second and more serious facet of the critique was that the methodological commitment of the Consensus may have rested fundamentally on the formulation and testing of empirical hypotheses which identify significant causal relationships between dependent and independent variables, but the actual practice frequently fell far short of this commitment. Consensus political scientists were too often content to concentrate on the construction of taxonomies and conceptual frameworks. 'Analysis' thus often became little more than a process of allocating data to its relevant 'box' in some classificatory schema or simple re-describing reality in terms of the categories deployed by such schema.[10] The situation was made much worse by the fact that one of the most influential components within the Consensus, Parsonian structural-functionalism, had from its creator's earliest formulations (1937) treated theory in a way which came very close to identifying it with the construction of such analytical schema, in sharp contrast to dominant positivist understanding of that term and its role in scientific research.[11] Such core

[10] Classification is, of course, an important component in the work of theory construction. The criticism is directed at a practice which identifies it as the main or even sole component of such work.

[11] Many debates of the time, especially in sociology, were generated around the manifold ambiguities of the methodological status of Parsonian theorising, particularly around the key 'functionalist' explanations which appeared to substitute teleology for causality in social explanation —on which see Gouldner (1959). The basic problem was that Parsons' analysis was ultimately rooted in Idealist categories. At a methodological level, therefore, there was always an awkwardness of 'fit' between Parsons' analysis and the dominant scientistic approaches in vogue among social scientists. For a more general discussion see Black (1961) and Gouldner (1971).

weaknesses of practice along with singular minor but cumulatively damning *defects* such as errors of logic, inadequacies of definition, confusions of correlation with explanation, arbitrariness in the selection and interpretation of data, etc.—such criticisms were posed, not only by embattled ideological opponents on the Left, whether Old or New, but by sober 'moderates' like Stretton (1969) and Barry (1970). And their targets were not the tyroes and epigones of the Consensus, but works then held to embody some of its 'best practice'—Almond and Verba (1963), Easton (1965), Eckstein (1966), and Lipset (1960) among others. Regardless of whether or not the methodological standards of the Consensus were appropriate or correct ones, too many of its prominent adherents could be charged with failing to live up to them in their practice.

The third aspect of the critique concerned the question of 'objectivity' in science. There had always been a disjunction between methodological theory and substantive practice among adherents of the Consensus. On the one hand, objectivity was at the very heart of scientific as opposed to ideologically biased analysis. On the other hand, Consensus analysis revealed a clear and often explicit 'value commitment' to defend and advance the cause of 'Western Democracy'. Furthermore, the emphasis in this period on the political and social sciences as 'policy sciences', whose problem-solving capability was available to meet the needs of government and business, raised problems as to their compatibility with the requirements of a 'value-free' social science. It thus required no theoretical scepticism concerning the possibilities of such a science to be able to advance some doubts as to whether the practice measured up to such methodological standards.

Yet such doubts, by themselves, were hardly damning of the enterprise. The very emphasis that Consensus analysis placed on the role of shared values in society, if it did not resolve the tensions, at least permitted some kind of peaceful coexistence between the methodological theory and the substantive practice. The real challenge to the claims to objectivity and scientific status by the Consensus arose, not from these considerations, but emerged out of the visible disintegration of that substantive consensus both in the academic and wider community during the course of the 1960s. When, for example, critics found considerable difficulty in distinguishing between Huntington's 'academic' (1968a) and more 'policy-oriented' (1968b) views on the developing South and US involvement therein; when one of his colleagues at Harvard was heard to observe, apropos of his advocacy of strategic relocation of the Vietnamese population, 'Sam has simply lost the ability to distinguish between urbanisation and genocide'[12] then it is evident that the issues in contention were no longer confined within the bounds of what normally passes for academic and scholarly debate. It is to the manifold political and social tension, crises and conflicts of the decade which posed such serious questions about the theoretical adequacy of the consensus that we must now turn our attention.

Theories and realities—the experience

To seek to encompass the global politics of over a decade in the space of a few lines requires an acceptance of a very considerable degree of schematisation and over-simplification. Bearing this in mind, we can identify three complexes of relevant trends, relating to the East, West, and South respectively, and then consider the ways in which such trends were woven together as the data for radical critiques of Consensus theorising.

Looking to the East, the period was marked by a complex set of trends—the Sino-Soviet split, the limited 'liberalisation' of post-Stalinist Russia, the thaw in the cold war and emergent detente between USA and the Soviet Union—all of which altered the configuration of 'International Communism' and Western relationships to it in ways which the Consensus theorising of the 1940s and 1950s seemed no longer capable of grasping or explaining. To take two examples, the analysis of totalitarianism placed major theoretical blockages in the way of understanding processes of internally induced evolution within regimes so conceptualised, and required substantial modification or even abandonment.[13] Similarly, the central preoccupation with 'containing Communist aggression' in the 1960s no longer confronted a generalised and global 'International Communist' threat, but the very specific realities of relations with Communist China in South East Asia. Analysis had, perforce, to concentrate on specifically Chinese as distinct from generically Communist dimensions of the situation.

But if the developments on the Eastern front, as it were, produced

[12] Cited by O'Brien (1972), p. 364, an article which provides a very useful survey of the changing 'ideological' content of Consensus theorising on the developing nations in the period under discussion here.

[13] Thus this period saw the emergence of a 'revisionist' thesis within the Consensus in terms of a 'convergence thesis' by which the technological logic of advanced industrialisation propelled the USSR along a path towards western pluralism. See Goldethorpe (1964) and Brzezinski (1969) for discussions of this theme.

a certain 'fraying of edges' of the Consensus theorising, they did not, taken in isolation, provide a basis for disrupting the Consensus itself. That was much more the work of the interconnected trends in relationships with the South and developments within the West itself.

The Consensus analysis of the 'developing areas' in the *South* had always been characterised by a certain theoretical 'haziness' as far as certain dimensions of the historical experience of North–South relations were concerned. Thus the 'development' model, charting an endogenous processes of 'modernisation' leading such societies from 'traditional' to 'industrialised' status, effectively provided only for Western 'acculturation' or Eastern 'subversion' by way of exogenous influences in the process. The historical facts of western influence in the South, whether by way of direct colonial rule in Africa and Asia or more informal politico-economic relations in Latin America, meshed uneasily with this development model, as was also the case with the often violent history of post-war decolonisation (e.g. Kenya, Egypt, and Aden for the British; the Congo for the Belgians; Angola and Mozambique for the Portuguese; Indo-China and Algeria for the French).

Similarly and throughout the period, a minority of critics had observed that US global power and involvement—from 'hot wars' like Korea to less formal destabilisation in Iran, Guatemala, Cuba, and the like—was perhaps at least in principle capable of inter-pretations other than those explaining them as part of the defence of democracy against the International Communist threat. Yet such critics remained a tiny minority, even when, like Wright Mills (1960) on Cuba, they wrote in a context in which older Cold War perspectives had already begun to erode the 'containment' thesis.

What destroyed the plausibility of the Consensus analysis of the 'developing' South for substantial sections of the academic—and wider—communities in the 1960s were the realities of US involve-ment in the long and bloody war in Vietnam. Vietnam undermined the Consensus from many directions. The character and development of the war itself raised massive doubts as to the empirical and ethical adequacy[14] of the Consensus account of the nature and purpose of

[14] Consider the intellectual climate in which one eminent and scholarly critic of the war could write, almost uncontroversially, of American Political Science and International Relations that they were 'rather dismal branches of American scholarship, by and large, and so closely identified with American imperial goals, that one is hardly astonished to discover the widespread abandonment of civilised norms' (p. 62) in their writings (Chomsky, 1969).

American global power. Similarly, the experiences of the anti-war protest movements and associated campus unrest[15]—and of 'official' responses to them—widened the scope of those queries and doubts to encompass the conceptual heartland of the Consensus, namely its analysis of the politics of 'advanced industrial societies' in the West.

The core of the Consensus analysis had lain in its characterisation of the societies of the *West*—and paradigmatically the USA—as representative democracies whose key supports were social stability, political consensus, and economic growth. On all counts, the circumstances of the 1960s and early 1970s seemed to conspire against the expectations of this theory.

The sources of instability were complex and varied. In Western Europe, a major component was the re-emergence of labour unrest on a large scale. Whether in the form of 'unofficial militancy' of sections of British trade unionists, or the strike waves of the 'long hot summers' in Italy, or, most spectacularly of all, the mass insurgency of May 1968 in France, the working classes of Europe seemed to be raising question-marks over an analysis which had 'integrated' and 'institutionalised' them within a post-capitalist industrialised society. In the USA the escalation of 'the race issue' from the passive resistance and freedom rides in the South of the late 1950s and early 1960s to the explosions of the ghetto riots and quasi-insurrectionist politics of 'Black Power' in the North in the years that followed, destroyed the theoretical 'containment' of Black American oppression within the 'special circumstances' categories of 'civil rights'. For both Black activists and white academic commentators, that experience needed to be made central to any understanding of the essential character of American society and its politics.[16]

These and other sources of instability and conflict—religion and nationalism in Ulster and Belgium; language, culture, and separatist aspirations from Quebec and Scotland to the Basques, Catalans, Bretons, and Corsicans—inevitably generated or inspired a wide variety of parties, movements, and groupings, whose theory and

[15] The campus revolt in the USA acted as a crucial catalyst in compelling academics to confront their own responsibilities—as citizens, theorists, and participating 'policy scientists'—on the war and other issues facing America. Its impact on social scientific 're-thinking' during this period was thus out of all proportion to its 'objective' social significance. For differing ways in which academics responded, compare Lipset (1972), Dahl (1970), and Moore (1969).

[16] For some significant Black voices see Malcolm X (1968), Carmichael and Hamilton (1968), and King (1964). For radical commentaries see Genovese (1971) and Allen (1970).

practice challenged the supposedly consensual base of politics in the West. It was not simply that a multiplicty of old and new, reactionary and revolutionary, ideologies emerged to effectively deny the 'end of ideology' and 'consensus on ends' proclaimed by the Consensus. More significant, perhaps, was the adoption by many of these movements of modes of political action whose operational premiss was the fraudulence or ineffectiveness of the institutions and procedures of pluralistic democracy.[17] They therefore operated outside the orthodox political framework, in some cases as openly 'extra parliamentary oppositions' aiming at mass mobilisation and direct action to gain their ends, in other cases as conspiratorial 'urban guerrilla' or 'terrorist' groupings relying on quasi-military strategies of force and violence.

In response to such practical 'refutations' of any general 'consensus on means', the official institutions and agencies of the state in the western nations responded in ways and with means which, at least on occasion, went far beyond what was politically neutral or even legally permissible. Legal or not, the growth in the scale and frequency of officially sanctioned state violence against internal opponents was a particularly marked feature of the period (commencing perhaps with the military-assisted overthrow of the French Fourth Republic in 1958, a survey of such trends would range from the FBI's destruction of the Black Panthers, and the 'Kent State Massacre', through the British military involvement in Ulster to the 'Colonels' Coup' in Greece). To put it no stronger, such phenomena raise problems for an analysis which concentrates its attention on the consensual dimensions of state authority to the neglect of coercive state power.

And by the end of the 1960s, the two post-war decades of rapid and steady growth in the domestic economies and inter-national trade of the Western nations—the longest and most sustained such period in the history of industrialism—were coming to a close, as both trade and growth rates became more irregular and interrupted. Thus question-marks already hung over the dynamics of the western economies before the 'oil price revolution' of the 1970s acted as a catalyst, precipitating recession, stagnation, and rising unemployment on a scale not seen since the 1930s. The easy optimism of the Consensus that the old pre-war structural problems of the western

---

[17] Even where they remained within the orthodox political arena, the survival and success of parties such as the 'de-stalinised' Communists of Italy and France provided a major theoretical—and practical—headache for adherents of the Consensus.

economies had been solved in the post-war period increasingly appeared as misplaced, and its key theoretical component, Keynesianism, was very quickly displaced as the touchstone of economic policy.

The radical critiques—some themes

Out of the instabilities and conflicts of the period, a whole range of 'radical critiques' of Consensus orthodoxies were either generated or revived to win considerable intellectual assent and support within the academic, and more particularly social scientific, community. Though its sources of inspiration were by no means confined to it, the revival of Marxism (and proliferation of 'Marxisms') as both an intellectually fertile and respectable tradition of analysis and as a source of practical inspiration[18] played a very important role in shaping and influencing such critiques. By way of summary and conclusion of this section, we can attempt to abstract from the complex range of theses which crowded under the umbrella-phrase of 'radical critiques' certain characteristic themes and conceptions. For convenience, these can be grouped around the subjects of the 'internal structures' and 'external relationships' of 'the West' in general and the USA in particular.[19]

The Consensus' conception of the 'internal structures' of 'advanced industrialised societies' pivoted around terms like stability, consensus, authority, pluralistic democracy, affluence, shared interests etc. Its critics regarded such a conceptualisation as not altogether unideological glosses on a form of society whose essence was better captured in concepts like instability, conflict, power, oligarchy, deprivation, exploitation, etc. In Marxist and quasi-Marxist versions, these facts were anchored in the specifically capitalist character of such societies and thus capable of eradication through the creation of socialist alternatives; in what, for want of a better term, we might call the 'radical Weberian' variants, these were ultimately ineradicable features of all societies but which at least admitted of greater degrees of amelioration than was currently allowed for in the West.

[18] For some gauge of the development in self-confidence of this current in the 1960s compare two products of the British 'New Left' at different ends of the decade—Thompson *et al.* (1960) and Blackburn (1972).

[19] The complex of views held by the radicals on the Eastern bloc are too complex to summarise here, except to note that, insofar as they looked for sources of inspiration, it was to Third World revolutions or perhaps China rather than the Soviet bloc that they turned. The critics of the 1960s were very different in perspective from the 'fellow-travellers' of the 1930s.

(Barrington Moore, 1972, is perhaps the best known, but by no means the only, representative of this line of thought.)

If we look at the arguments about 'internal structures' a little more closely, we can identify five characteristic theses. First, Western societies are built upon systems of stratification, e.g. class structures (Westergaard, 1972), a culture of poverty (Harrington, 1962), internal colonialism in the US (Allen, 1970), which are necessarily systems of exploitation and/or oppression. Second, the system of stratification is interrelated with a dominant power structure, e.g. 'power-elite' (Wright Mills, 1956), 'monopoly capitalism' (Baran and Sweezy, 1966), or even Eisenhower's 'military–industrial complex', which acts in the protection of the interests of the dominant elite or class. Third, the state is either a component of, or acts as an agency for, the power structure, and is thus not subject to any effective or meaningful democratic control by the mass electorate. (For the range of Marxist variants on this theme see Miliband, 1969, and Poulantzas, 1973. For a very different 'Weberian' variant, see Galbraith, 1967.) Fourth, the condition of western societies ensures a marked potential for instability and conflict, which is only partially contained by a mixture of manipulative ideological controls (Marcuse's (1964) society of one dimensional men, for instance), coercive power, successful economic performance—anchored, on some views, by a 'permanent arms economy' (Kidron, 1968), or imperialist control over a world-system (Magdoff, 1969). Fifth, for a variety of reasons—the consequences for the Imperialist economies of 'wars of national liberation', and the internal logic of the capitalist mode of production itself are two alternative accounts—the ability of the western economies to generate full employment and sustained economic growth has been increasingly impaired in recent years, with potentially explosive consequences for the internal stability of their societies. (For two Marxist variants on these themes see Glyn & Sutcliffe, 1972, and Gamble & Walton, 1976).

This bald and schematic condensation of often complex and subtle explorations of the 'internal structures' of Western societies has already spilled over at several points onto a world-stage. For central to many of the radical critiques of the Consensus is a substantive perspective which locates particular nation-states within the context of a larger world-system which is itself characterised by instability, conflict, etc. The conceptual implications of this position will occupy our attention in the final section of this discussion, so for the moment we need simply observe that, within such a framework, the account of the interrelationships with East and South are now transformed into something very different from the perspective of the Consensus.

To the East, most adherents of the radical critique proved unwilling to accept the orthodox Cold War account of Soviet–US relationships, and undertook historical re-evaluation of its origins. (See, for example, Kolko, 1972, for a specific version of this thesis, and Maier, 1970, for a more general survey.) On such accounts, the West—and the USA in particular—bore an at least equal burden of responsibility for the outbreak of the Cold War, which was better understood, not as an attempt to 'contain' the 'international Communist Threat', but as a struggle between two world super-powers, the USA and the USSR, to maintain or enhance their dominant positions on the globe. Whether expressed in the language of a 'new machiavellianism' of world politics (the 'Weberian' variant) or in the more specifically Marxist categories of rival types of capitalisms (on which see Harris and Palmer, 1971) the result was a very different picture from that offered by the Consensus.

Similarly to the *South*, the radical critics stressed that the actual interrelationship between the advanced industrial West and the poverty-stricken Third World (for which see Worsley, 1964) was hardly a matter of the ideational niceties of 'acculturation'. Much more basically material interests—in markets, raw materials, strategic bases, etc.—had characterised the West's past colonial, and continuing neo-imperialist, dominance and exploitation of the dependent nations of the South. The precise conceptualisation of the relationship differs from Barrington Moore's (1972) notion of the USA as a 'predatory democracy', to Magdoff's (1969) treatment of it as Imperialism, to Frank's (1969) account of 'under development' and 'dependency', for example. However, there is a commonly shared conviction as to the direct responsibility of the industrialised West (in some variants, the North as a whole) for the condition of that mass of humanity whom Fanon (1965) terms 'the damned of the earth'.

III   THE ROLE OF COMPARATIVE POLITICS—SOME RIVAL CONCEPTIONS AND APPROACHES

In the first section of this article it was suggested that the project of Comparative Politics in the post-war years was closely tied, both in methodological conception and in substantive scope and execution, to a complex body of analysis which fused together Positivist scientism and liberal-democratic perspectives into 'the Consensus'. In the second section, it was further suggested that though the

Consensus managed to exercise a powerful intellectual hegemony over the social science departments of British and American universities, for the best part of two decades following the end of the war, that pre-eminence was effectively challenged, on related methodological and substantive grounds, during the course of the 1960s and 1970s. The result has been a proliferation of alternative perspectives within the fields of political and social analysis, both on matters of substantive empirical assertion and on broader meta-theoretical and methodological issues. The former matters have already been touched on schematically in terms of a contrast between the consensus and the Radical Critique; the latter now requires a little more attention.

Ultimately the problem of scientific methodology in the social sciences is that there is no general agreement about what it consists of or indeed whether it is possible at all. On the contrary, there are a number of competing and opposed perspectives which take issue with each other on, among other things, whether it is legitimate to regard the study of society as a scientific activity at all, and even if it is, whether the science involved is comparable in principle or in practice to the procedures of the natural sciences. Lest it be thought that such matters can be avoided in the context of a more narrow discussion of comparative politics, it must be noted that such questions also involve a number of inconvenient disputes about what types of comparison may be used in social and political science, the purposes for which we use them, the limitations inherent in comparative activity, etc.

Translating such generalities back into our own level of concerns, the problem can be posed thus. We have seen that the project for a comparative politics was closely associated with commitments to a positivist methodology and that the conception of comparison involved and its legitimation were grounded in that methodology. We have also seen that one dimension of the crisis years of the 1960s and the 1970s has been the displacement of Positivism as the dominant account of social and political analysis and the widespread renewal of interest in alternative (Idealist, Weberian, and Marxist) approaches to these matters. The problem therefore becomes: how fares the project for a comparative politics in these changed circumstances? Is it so closely tied to a positivist methodology that the challenge to the methodology is also a challenge to the project itself? Or is it that there are now not one but several competing projects for comparative politics, each of which has its own specific methodology? In this final section, an attempt will be made to indicate some of the alternative answers that have been made to these questions, both in principle and practice.

Postitivism and the consensus

The Consensus is by no means a generally discredited set of theses, though its remaining adherents have adopted a more subdued posture of late. Substantively, there has been a retreat in focus from the global sweep of earlier comparative theorising into more modest enterprises. More interestingly, perhaps, is a shift in the connections existing between positivist methodological commitment and strategies of analysis, away from comparative politics and towards a somewhat different mode of discourse. The positivist programme in politics now finds its most enthusiastic articulation in the construction and application of theories and models of behaviour derived from economic analysis and games theory. In substantive scope, such theories are much narrower in focus than those of the Consensus; not global politics, but aspects of representative democracy such as party competition (Robertson, 1976), voting behaviour (Budge and Fairlie, 1976) and resource allocation (Breton, 1974) are the characteristic concerns here. Methodologically, there is a heavy emphasis on modes of explanation favoured in micro-economic analysis—the construction of rational models of behaviour from which deductions are made which can then be compared with 'real world' situations. Thus comparison of a sort is utilised, but it is of a somewhat different character, and plays a far more peripheral role in the analysis, than was the case of comparative politics as envisaged by the Consensus. Insofar as this 'economic' analysis, therefore, occupies an increasing segment of interest among adherents of a positivist conception of political analysis, the scope and role of an explicitly 'Comparative Politics' project is minimised in practice if not necessarily in theory.

Idealism

The positivist pursuit of a *science* of politics may be less concerned today with the project of a *comparative* politics than hitherto, but it still provides the most powerful methodological underpinnings that project has yet received. Idealism, in stark contrast, poses challenges to that project at every turn. At one level, many of its variants deny the possibility of any such social *science*, or at the very least insist that it is very different from natural science. At another level, some versions of Idealism have attacked the use of systematic comparison in social and political analysis as either illegitimate or vacuous. At a third level, the central emphasis assigned to ideational and cultural levels of explanation within Idealist analyses results in practice in a marked neglect of power and 'the political' as major dimensions of interest.

If idealism is of interest to students of comparative politics primarily as a source of critiques of that project both in principle and in practice, it is unfortunately the case for such students that no simple or straightforward summary of 'the Idealist critique' can be given, since Idealism embraces not one but a whole range of often contradictory perspectives. Radically over-simplifying, however, we can focus on two major variants, the one 'historical' and the other 'sociological'. As they differ somewhat in their implications for a comparative science of politics, we will touch on each briefly in turn.

The 'historical' variant exploits to the full the well-known difficulties that Positivist methodology has in accounting for historical explanations.[20] On this account, natural-positivist-science seeks to abstract from the infinite and concrete particularly of the real world in order to discover order and system—patterns of similarities and differences, etc.—in classes of phenomena. The search for regularities in nature, and the attempt to formulate universally valid causal generalisations about them is thus inherently comparative in character.

The essence of the 'historical sciences', on the other hand, is seen to lie precisely in their particularistic focus. They are not concerned with conceptualising a specific event or culture as an instance of a general class or type but with grasping such particular societies, cultures, and epochs as unique complexes of elements whose character and significance can only be understood by 'locating' them as a part of that social, cultural, etc., 'whole' or 'totality'. Such a holism—one which identifies the relevant totality at the level of particular national or 'regional' culture epochs—necessarily emphasises the essential non-comparability of different societal wholes. In the extreme case, as with Dilthey, any comparison between cultures would involve an illicit ethnocentrism since it would inevitably result in mis-analysing one-society in terms of categories derived from, and given meaning by the context of, another society. Even the moderate variant

[20] Positivism explains particular events etc. insofar as they can be treated as instances of a law, etc. Positivist knowledge is always, therefore, general in character, and insofar as history is said to offer knowledge of particular events qua particular events, it is difficult to see how a Positivist science can account for such knowledge. Current attempts to argue that history deploys tacit generalisations—'covering laws', etc. (see discussions in Gardiner, 1959, and Hook, 1963)—haven't won much support from practising historians as a whole. For further discussions see Leff (1969).

stresses that any such attempted comparisons are more a matter of art than of science, a question of apprehending real but indefinable 'family resemblances', to use Wittgenstein's (1958) influential metaphor, rather than imposing some rigid comparative net on material too subtle to be caught therein.

In contrast, the 'sociological' variant of Idealism resolves such problems of comparison by rejecting their premiss, namely that social analysis involves a particularising science of history. Instead, they substitute a project aimed at discovering the fundamental—and hence abstract, general and ahistorical—forms or structures held to underlie all social phenomena. We have already encountered one such variant of these ideas in the ambiguously idealist categories of that Parsonian functionalism which enjoyed such hegemony in the sociology departments of the 1950s. Over the past decade, functionalism has been displaced, in British universities at least, by a bewildering variety of competing idealisms—phenomenology, ethnomethodology, symbolic interactionism, dramaturgy, structuralism, etc.[21]—most of which are focused on language as the key which unlocks the door leading to these fundamental structures, meanings, patterns of inter-action, etc.

Unlike the 'historical' variants, the 'sociological' approaches are not necessarily antagonistic to comparative political analysis, even if their conception of its scientific basis is rather different from that of 'positivism'. Indeed, they could in principle hope to provide a comparative framework similar in scope and conception to that offered by Parsonian 'systems' analysis to the Consensus in earlier decades. In practice, the work of most of the adherents of these perspectives exhibits a marked retreat from the national and cross-national societal and political concerns of the earlier period. In its place, there is an almost obsessional concern with the micro-social (the minutiae of conversational analysis for example) or remotely anthropological as with Levi-Strauss (1966). Given the often marked intellectual dependence on sociological theory which political science has exhibited in the past, this outcome is highly significant, and suggests that the latter must look elsewhere than to Sociological Idealism for its current inspiration.[22]

[21] For examples of these respective positions see Schutz (1962), Garfinkel (1967), Mead (1934), Goffman (1959), and Levi-Strauss (1966). A more general review is offered in Rex (1974).
[22] Some attempts have been made to link up these discussions with more political concerns—see for example, Clegg (1975) and Smart (1976)—but these are exceptions which prove the general rule.

Weberian themes

Paradoxically, the 'sociological voice' whose characteristic modes of thought and substantive ideas appear to be exercising a growing influence on the direction and scope of comparative political and social analysis is that of Max Weber. The paradox lies in the fact that Weber's intellectual roots lie in the 'historical' school, as a development on the neo-Kantian perspectives of Rickert (1962), and it is to his work in the field of comparative history, and the methodology that inspired it (1949) rather than his more formalistic sociology (1947) that his current influence can be traced.

Weber, like the 'historical' Idealists, held that the object of historical analysis was to locate that which was specific and particular to a given society, culture or epoch. But in Weber's view, this allowed at least some role for comparative analysis in establishing what, say, a range of different cultures shared in common and thus helping to bring into sharper and contrasted focus precisely those features which were unique and non-comparable—say the 'Protestant Ethic' in the West for example (1930). The role of comparative analysis is thus limited, but nonetheless important in historical work.[23]

When speaking of Weberian 'influences', a note of caution needs to be struck. Weber's work is permeated with tensions and ambiguities, and there are many 'voices', both substantive and methodological, which have been detected therein. Thus the Weber who 'speaks' to Parsons (1937) is very different from the one 'heard' by Mommsen (1974).[24] Nor is it a question of locating an explicitly 'Weberian', or even 'Radical Weberian' school. Rather it is a matter of the articulation of characteristically Weberian themes and modes of analysis by writers who would not necessarily identify themselves explicitly with Weber.

Given these qualifications, we can discern four characteristically Weberian themes which recur in much current work. First, there is an emphasis on the value-relevant basis of social and political analysis, and hence a rejection of Positivist conceptions of 'objectivity' (see, for example, Dawe's, 1970, account of 'the two sociologies' for direct echoes of this theme). Second, there is the stress on comparative method as pre-eminently a tool of historical analysis, as

[23] Such a position clearly has to face the charge of illicit ethnocentrism considered earlier. Weber's solution was to accept that his categories were value-based rather than derived from reality, which resolves the dilemma at the cost of accepting a 'relativistic' base for such analysis.

[24] For a debate between these perspectives see Stammer (1971).

in the case of Barrington Moore (1967). Third, there is a concern with the realities of power, conflict, and instability as central facts of all social life, which has influenced at least some strands of the 'radical critique' discussed earlier (see Rex, 1961 and 1974). Fourth, there is a deep pessimism about the bureaucratised future facing advanced industrialised societies which pervades much contemporary writing, though this version of 'the iron cage' is only occasionally developed in explicitly Weberian terms, as with Jacoby (1973).

Marxism

Of all the developments of the past decade or so, the enormous revival of Marxist analysis might have been expected to have had the most powerful impact on the methodology of comparative politics. That this has been only partially the case requires some explanation.

In the Marxist revival of the 1960s,[25] two rival 'schools', both arriving from the continent, came to the forefront of discussion. The first, the so-called 'Frankfurt School' (on the history of which, see Jay, 1973) saw one of its main roles in exposing the ideological roots of positivist modes of discourse in social science. In its place was to be substituted a 'critical theory' which, while leaning heavily on Marxist themes and methods, also borrowed from other non-Marxist influences, including Freud.

What then was this Marxist method in the eyes of the Frankfurt School? Its debate with positivism, summarised in Adorno *et al.* (1976), served to identify what it rejected, but left unresolved the ambiguities surrounding its more definite commitments. Critics have indeed argued that ultimately the School is not in fact practising Marxist empirical analysis at all but rather a form of moral philosophy. Certainly, the standards of 'the rational society' and 'human interests' which Habermas (1972) uses to anchor his 'critical' analysis of contemporary reality seem more morally evaluative than empirically grounded. Put another way, the 'Marxism' of the Frankfurt School strikes many as constituting a type of Idealist metaphysics, and this was certainly the view of the second influential School of the 1960s, the 'Structuralists'.

The 'Structuralists', whose most distinguished articulator is Althusser (1969), see the source of this kind of Idealist 'deformation' of Marxism in the stress placed by the Frankfurt School and others on the Hegelian roots of Marxist methodology. Against this, the 'Althusserians' argue that the 'scientific socialism' of Marx and

[25] See Anderson (1976) for a much more extensive and rather different survey of Marxist influences.

Engels involves a decisive epistemological break from Hegel and other Idealist philosophers. Unfortunately, the problem again is that it is easier to see what the Structuralists reject than what they accept as constituting the new epistemology of 'scientific socialism'. For all the emphasis on the distinctive character of Marxist 'science' and 'theory' in the writings of the School, it is difficult to identify what distinguishes it from the perspectives of Positivism or even—as some 'heretics' within the camp have alleged (see Hindess and Hirst, 1975) —of Idealism.

The paradox of the Marxist revival of the 1960s is thus that the two leading Schools most closely associated with it, both of whom were self-consciously preoccupied with establishing the distinctive character of Marxist methodology, adopted perspectives which their critics found virtually indistinguishable from existing Positivist or Idealist ones. The search for a specifically Marxist mode of analysis must therefore be directed elsewhere. Not surprisingly, for an orientation that is often termed 'historical materialism', its most secure anchorage can be located within the various historical disciplines.

Too great an emphasis on the Marxist Revival of the 1960s can obscure the fact that even at the height of the period of Consensus hegemony, Marxism continued to form part of the Anglo-Saxon intellectual scene, occupying an influential if subordinate niche in fields of enquiry such as labour history (see for example, Hobsbawn, 1962, and Thompson, 1963), Though its practitioners were for the most part either unconcerned with or even on occasion—see Thompson, 1965—hostile towards too 'theoretical' a discussion of the methodology of Marxist analysis, their work embodied an identification of that methodology with history. In a sense, their practice offered a better guide to the core of Marxist methods than did the self-conscious 'theorising' of the rival 'schools' of the 1960s. For our purposes, however, we still need to enquire about both the nature of that historical practice and its implications for a distinctively Marxist approach to the study of comparative politics.

We observed earlier that the character of historical explanation forms a crucial issue in dispute between Positivism and Idealism. One way of locating the core of Marxist 'historical materialism' is to see it as siding with the latter against the former in this dispute. That is to say, it rejects the use of universal laws and generalisations in history of the kind advocated by Positivism, in favour of a science which, like some Idealisms, seeks to grasp the world in its historical particularity. Put more simply, Marxism, like some variants of Idealism, aims not at a science of generalising laws but at grasping 'the historical' and its complex, particular and detailed totality. Moreover, again like some variants of Idealism, its concept of the 'totality' as an articulated whole composed of interrelated parts, stressed the characteristically 'systemic' dimension of social reality, as distinct from the Positivist conception of contingent interactions governed by invariant laws. (Dangerously oversimplifying, we can suggest that just as the mechanical metaphor illustrates the 'image' of the social world in Positivist practice, so also does the biological metaphor in the case of Marxism and Idealism. In both cases, of course, it is simply an illustrative metaphor!)

Does this mean, therefore, that historical materialism is simply a variant of Idealism? Two observations may serve to indicate that its assertion of 'materialism' against 'idealism' is fully justified. First, and most obviously, whereas Idealist approaches anchor their ultimate explanatory categories at the level of 'culture' and 'ideas', identifying material factors as 'mere' causal instrumentalities for the expression and realisation of 'values', Marxist analysis re-orders this relationship and grounds such 'values', etc., in the material intercourse of the human species with its environment. (Marx's own statement of this perspective in the first section of 'The German Ideology', 1965, still remains one of its clearest expositions.) Thus the 'totality' of Marxist analysis is material and concrete rather than idealist and abstract in its explanatory conception.

The second observation in justification of historical materialism as a distinctive methodological perspective lies in its substantive identification of the totality with the historical process itself. As was observed earlier, the characteristic 'totality' or 'whole' as conceived in historical variants of Idealism is a national, regional or epochal 'culture'. It is precisely because of this identification of the particular totality with national, etc., 'cultures' that some Idealists are able to attack not only Positivist conceptions of cross-national generalisations but all such generalisations as illegitimate indulgence in ethnocentrism. In complete contrast, Marxism identifies the ultimate 'totality' as nothing less than the historical evolution of homo sapiens in its dynamic interrelationships with its material environment. Within that 'totality', particular societies, epochs, etc., constitute more historically specific constituent 'parts' of the overarching 'whole', just as they in turn form 'relative totalities', or relatively autonomous systems composed and constituted by dynamically interacting parts, etc. On this account, therefore, cross-national comparisons are not simply legitimate but essential components of a Marxist historical analysis. They are nonetheless always concerned with historically particular statements rather than universal laws, even when the historically specific object of investigation is the history of humanity taken as a whole!

It cannot be pretended that such a brief and abstract formulation of historical materialism does either justice to its subject-matter or conveys a great deal to the reader. Limitations of space prevents us doing anything about the former, except to indicate that Goldman's (1964) discussion of the dialectics of what we might call 'part-whole' analysis is an invaluable guide, especially Parts I and V. The latter problem can perhaps be ameliorated by offering a much more concrete illustration of the approaches involved by reference to Marxist conceptions of capitalism. What is the appropriate 'concrete totality' within which to comprehend and analyse this mode of production? The answer, on this account, is only very partially and derivately, 'the various national capitalisms'. For their essential characteristics can only be grasped and explained in terms of their locations within, and inter-relationship with, an historically world-system (the totality of 'world-capitalism') as it has developed over the course of the last half millennium from its European origins to encompass the entire globe.

Capitalism is thus not, in essence, a 'type' of society whose characteristics can be discerned by comparing various nations which are said to exhibit certain similarities, though such an analysis is not of itself illegitimate, merely limited. Nor are the differences discerned between such national capitalisms best grasped as variations in relationships between particular components of that 'type', though again such attempts are not illicit. The mistake involved in both cases is that they ignore that which establishes the real and concrete connections between those nations in the first place, namely the overall world-system of which they are various, and varied, national component 'parts'. They are comparable because they are inter-connected in the real world, and not merely conceptually in the categories the analyst brings to bear on them. To take but one example; Barrington Moore's (1967) stimulating attempt to locate and analyse the 'different routes to the modern world' is ultimately flawed, on this account, by its conceptual anchorage in the categories of the nation-state. It cannot therefore explain why these different routes were distributed in time and space as they were, nor indeed can it monitor the adequacy of the account of the routes themselves against the charges of an arbitrary selection of either 'culture-bound' or 'concept-stretched' variables like 'lords' and 'peasants'. In both cases, Marxists would assert, only an adequate grasp of the very different ways in which the British, French, Russian, Chinese, Indian, etc., 'national-components' were integrated into the developing world-capitalist system over the past two centuries can hope to resolve such problems and counter such criticisms. Cross-national and cross-cultural comparisons of that kind are an integral part of the analysis of capitalism for Marxists precisely because capitalism is a world-system or totality. And such comparisons are necessarily concerned with concrete, specific, and historically changing inter-relationships within world capitalism rather than with abstract conceptual schema or universal causal laws.

Our conclusion, therefore, savours somewhat of a paradox. For the project for a Comparative Politics, most vigorously asserted in the post-war years in the Positivist totalities of the Consensus, now finds its strongest articulation in the 1970s in the very different methodological and substantive harmonics of Marxist historical materialism. In both cases the global reach and scope of such a project is a central characteristic of the enterprise, though their substantive analysis of that globe are remarkably contradictory. Likewise, they both proclaim the need for a comparative science, though their accounts of both science and the nature of comparison seem largely antagonistic to each other. It remains to be seen whether historical materialism can make a better job than the Consensus did of delivering in substantive terms what it promises in its methodology.[26]

A POSTSCRIPT

The range of issues covered by this paper has been wide, but its actual purpose has been a modest one—that of providing a sketch-map of trends in post-war comparative political and social analysis in the Anglo-Saxon academic world. Like all mapping exercises, it has selected material for emphasis in terms of its author's perspectives, in this case perspectives which emphasise that comparative political analysis is not simply a matter of utilising a variety of comparative

[26] Current indications suggest that in the coming years one major area of enormous potential from the point of view of Marxist scholarship lies in the analysis of the origins and development of the capitalist world-system. Wallerstein (1974) and, more ambiguously, Anderson (1974) among others, have already begun projects in this area whose comparative range promises much for the future. In this respect, the intellectual debts owed here to the 'Annales' school in France, and in particular to Braudel (1973) are striking, and it is to be hoped that many more works embodying this somewhat eclectic approach within the broad tradition of historical materialism will become readily accessible in English translations.

techniques within a field of enquiry which can be given a fairly neutral definition and delineation. Rather the situation is one which a whole range of possibly contradictory 'projects' for comparative political and social analysis offer competing accounts, both of the nature of the field of enquiry and of character, purpose and limitations of comparative analysis within them. Hopefully, this perspective may have illuminated the terrain—or perhaps the terrains?—which lie ahead of the student of comparative politics. But it would be misleading to claim that this article has demonstrated the validity of these perspectives, as opposed to merely exhibit their possible fruitfulness. Another map-maker, using different cartographic perspectives, might well have sketched a very different terrain, and the problem of judging between such rival maps cannot be decided in advance of advancing on to the terrain itself.

REFERENCES

ADORNO, T. W. et al. (1976) The Positivist Dispute in German Sociology, Heinemann.

ALLEN, R. L. (1970) A Guide to Black Power in America, Gollancz.

ALMOND, G. and COLEMAN, J., eds. (1960) The Politics of Developing Areas, Princeton University Press.

ALMOND, G. and POWELL, G. B. (1965) Comparative Politics: A Developmental Approach, Little Brown.

ALMOND, G. and VERBA, S. (1963) The Civic Culture, Princeton University Press.

ALTHUSSER, L. (1969) For Marx, Allen Lane.

ANDERSON, P. (1974) Lineages of the Absolutist State, New Left Books.

ANDERSON, P. (1976) Considerations on Western Marxism, New Left Books.

ARENDT, H. (1951) The Origins of Totalitarianism, Harcourt Brace.

BACHRACH, P. and BARATZ (1962) 'Two faces of power', American Political Science Review, 56, 947–52.

BARAN, P. A. and SWEEZY, P. M. (1966) Monopoly Capital, Monthly Review Press.

BARRY, B. M. (1970) Sociologists, Economists and Democracy, Collier-Macmillan.

BELL, D., ed. (1956) The Radical Right, Criterion Books.

BELL, D. (1961) The End of Ideology, The Free Press.

BENDIX, R. and LIPSET, S. M., eds. (1967) Class, Status and Power: Social Stratification in Comparative Perspective, 2nd edn., Routledge and Kegan Paul.

BLACK, M., ed. (1961) The Social Theories of Talcott Parsons, Prentice Hall.

BLACKBURN, R., ed. (1972) Ideology in Social Science, Collins.

BRAUDEL, F. (1973) The Mediterranean and the Mediterranean World in the Age of Philip II, Collins.

BRETON, A. (1974) The Economic Theory of Representative Government, Macmillan.

BUCHANAN, J. M. and TULLOCK, G. (1962) The Calculus of Consent, University of Michigan Press.

BUDGE, I. and FAIRLEE, A. C. (1976) *Voting and Party Competition,* Wiley.
BURDICK, E. and BRODBECK, A., eds. (1959) *American Voting Behavior,* The Free Press.
BRZEZINSKI, Z. (1969) *Dilemmas of Change in Soviet Politics,* Columbia University Press.
CARMICHAEL, S. and HAMILTON, C. V. (1968) *Black Power: The Politics of Liberation in America,* Cape.
CASTLES, F. G., MURRAY, D. J. and POTTER, D. C., eds. (1971) *Decisions, Organisation and Society,* Penguin.
CHOMSKY, N. (1969) *American Power and the New Mandarins,* Penguin.
CLEGG, S. (1975) *Power, Rule and Domination,* Routledge and Kegan Paul.
CONNERY, R. H., ed. (1969) *Urban Riots: Violence and Social Change,* Vintage Books.
CROSLAND, A. (1956) *The Future of Socialism,* Cape.
DAHL, R. (1970) *After the Revolution? Authority in a Good Society,* Yale University Press.
DAWE, A. (1970) 'The two sociologies', reprinted in Thompson, K., and Tunstall, J., eds. (1971).
DILTHEY, W. (1961) *Meaning in History,* George Allen & Unwin.
DOWNS, A. (1957) *An Economic Theory of Democracy,* Harper & Row.
DUVERGER, M. (1954) *Political Parties,* Methuen.
EASTON, D. (1965) *A Systems Analysis of Political Life,* Wiley.
ECKSTEIN, H. (1966) *Division and Cohesion in Democracy,* Princeton University Press.
ECKSTEIN, H. and APTER, D. E., eds. (1963) *Comparative Politics,* The Free Press.
FANON, F. (1965) *The Wretched of the Earth,* MacGibbon & Kee.
FRANK, A. GUNDER (1969) *Latin America: Underdevelopment or Revolution,* Monthly Review Press.
FRIEDRICH, C. J. and BRZEZINSKI, Z. (1965) *Totalitarian Dictatorship and Democracy,* Harvard University Press.
GALBRAITH, J. K. (1967) *The New Industrial State,* Hamilton.
GAMBLE, A. and WALTON, P. (1976) *Capitalism in Crisis: Inflation and the State,* Macmillan.
GARDINER, P. (1959) *Theories of History,* The Free Press.
GARFINKEL, H. (1967) *Studies in Ethnomethodology,* Prentice-Hall.
GENOVESE, E. (1971) *Essays in Red and Black,* Allen Lane.
GLYN, A. and SUTCLIFFE, B. (1972) *British Capitalism, Workers and the Profits Squeeze,* Penguin.
GOFFMAN, E. (1959) *The Presentation of Self in Everyday Life,* Doubleday.
GOLDETHORPE, J. H. (1964) 'Social stratification in industrialised societies', reprinted in Bendix, R. and Lipset, S., eds. (1967), 2nd edn.
GOLDMANN, L. (1964) *The Hidden God,* Routledge and Kegan Paul.
GOULDNER, A. (1959) 'Reciprocity and autonomy in functional theory', in Gross, L., ed. (1959).
GOULDNER, A. (1971) *The Coming Crisis in Western Sociology,* Heinemann.
GROSS, L., ed. (1959) *Symposium in Sociological Theory,* Row, Peterson & Co.
HABERMAS, J. (1972) *Knowledge and Human Interests,* Heinemann.
HARRINGTON, M. (1962) *The Other America: Poverty in the United States,* Macmillan.

HARRIS, N. and PALMER, J., eds. (1971) *World Crisis: Essays in Revolutionary Socialism*, Hutchinson.

HECKSCHER, G. (1957) *The Study of Comparative Government and Politics*, George Allen and Unwin.

HINDESS, B. and HIRST, P. Q. (1975) *Pre-Capitalist Modes of Production*, Routledge and Kegan Paul.

HOBSBAWM, E. (1962) *The Age of Revolution*, Weidenfeld & Nicolson.

HOFSTADTER, R. (1955) *The Age of Reform*, Knopf.

HOOK, S., ed. (1963) *Philosophy and History*, New York University Press.

HOROWITZ, I. L., ed. (1964) *The New Sociology*, Oxford University Press.

HOSELITZ, B. F. (1960) *Sociological Factors in Economic Development*, The Free Press.

HUNTINGTON, S. P. (1968a) *Political Order in Changing Societies*, Yale University Press.

HUNTINGTON, S. P. (1968b) 'The bases of accommodation', *Foreign Affairs*, **46**, No. 4, June.

JACOBY, H. (1973) *The Bureaucratisation of the World*, University of California Press.

JAY, M. (1973) *The Dialectical Imagination*, Heinemann.

KIDRON, M. (1968) *Western Capitalism Since the War*, Weidenfeld & Nicolson.

KING, M. L. (1964) *Why We Can't Wait*, Harper & Row.

KOLAKOWSKI, L. (1972) *Positivist Philosophy*, Penguin.

KOLKO, J. A. and KOLKO, G. (1969) *The Limits of Power*, Harper & Row.

KORNHAUSER, W. (1960) *The Politics of Mass Society*, Routledge and Kegan Paul.

KUHN, T. S. (1970) *The Structure of Scientific Revolutions*, 2nd edn., University of Chicago Press.

LAKATOS, I. and MUSGRAVE, A., eds. (1970) *Criticism and the Growth of Knowledge*, Cambridge University Press.

LASSWELL, H. D. (1962) *The Future of Political Science*, Prentice-Hall.

LEFF, G. (1969) *History and Social Theory*, Merlin Press.

LERNER, D. (1958) *The Passing of Traditional Society*, The Free Press.

LEVI-STRAUSS, C. (1966) *The Savage Mind*, Weidenfeld and Nicolson.

LIPSET, S. M. (1960) *Political Man*, Heinemann.

LIPSET, S. M. (1972) 'Academia and politics in America', in Nossiter *et al.*, eds. (1972).

MAGDOFF, H. (1969) *The Age of Imperialism*, Monthly Review Press.

MAIER, C. S. (1970) 'Revisionism and the interpretation of cold war origins', in *Perspectives in American History*, **IV**.

MARCUSE, H. (1964) *One-Dimensional Man*, Routledge and Kegan Paul.

MARX, K. and ENGELS, F. (1964) *The German Ideology*, Progress Publishers.

MEAD, G. H. (1934) *Mind, Self and Society*, University of Chicago Press.

MILIBAND, R. (1969) *The State in Capitalist Society*, Weidenfeld and Nicolson.

MILIBAND, R. and SAVILLE, J., eds. (1965) *The Socialist Register*, Merlin Press.

MILLS, C. WRIGHT (1956) *The Power Elite*, Oxford University Press.

MILLS, C. WRIGHT (1960) *Listen Yankee*, Balantine Books.

MOMMSEN, W. J. (1974) *The Age of Bureaucracy*, Blackwells.

MOORE, BARRINGTON (1967) *Social Origins of Dictatorship and Democracy*, Penguin.

MOORE, BARRINGTON (1969) 'Thoughts on violence and anarchy', in Connery, R. H., ed.(1969).

MOORE, BARRINGTON (1972) *Reflections on the Causes of Human Misery*, Allen Lane.

NOSSITER, T. J., HANSON, A. H. and ROKKAN, S., eds. (1972) *Imagination and Precision in the Social Sciences*, Faber and Faber.

OAKESHOTT, M. (1962) *Rationalism in Politics and Other Essays*, Methuen.

O'BRIEN, D. CRUISE (1972) 'Modernisation, order and the erosion of a democratic ideal', *Journal of Development Studies*, **8**, No. 4, July.

PARSONS, T. (1937) *The Structure of Social Action*, McGraw-Hill.

PARSONS, T. (1951) *The Social System*, Routledge and Kegan Paul.

PARSONS, T. (1959) 'Voting and the equilibrium of the American political system', in Burdick, E. and Brodbeck, Q., eds. (1959).

PARSONS, T. (1963) 'On the concept of political power', *Proceedings of the American Philosophical Society*, **107**, June.

POLLACK, N. (1966) *The Populist Response to Industrial America*, W. W. Norton & Co.

POPPER, K. R. (1959) *The Logic of Scientific Discovery*, Hutchinson.

POULANTZAS, N. (1973) *Political Power and Social Classes*, New Left Books.

RICKERT, H. (1962) *Science and History*, Van Nostrand.

REX, J. (1961) *Key Problems of Sociological Theory*, Routledge and Kegan Paul.

REX, J. (1974) *Approaches to Sociology*, Routledge and Kegan Paul.

ROBERTSON, D. (1976) *A Theory of Party Competition*, Wiley.

ROGIN, M. (1967) *The Intellectuals and McCarthy*, M.I.T. Press.

ROSTOW, W. W. (1962) *The Stages of Economic Growth*, Cambridge University Press.

SAHAY, A., ed. (1971) *Max Weber and Modern Sociology*, Routledge and Kegan Paul.

SCHUMPETER, J. A. (1943) *Capitalism, Socialism and Democracy*, George Allen & Unwin.

SCHUTZ, A. (1962) *Collected Papers, Vol. 1: The Problem of Social Reality*, Martinus Nijhoff.

SMART, B. (1976) *Sociology, Phenomenology and Marxian Analysis*, Routledge and Kegan Paul.

STAMMER, O., ed. (1971) *Max Weber and Sociology Today*, Blackwell.

STRAUSS, L. (1959) *What Is Political Philosophy?*, The Free Press.

STRETTON, H. (1969) *The Political Sciences*, Routledge and Kegan Paul.

THOMPSON, E. P. (1963) *The Making of the English Working Class*, Gollancz.

THOMPSON, E. P. (1965) 'The peculiarities of the English', in Miliband, R. and Saville, J., eds. (1965).

THOMPSON, E. P. *et al.*, eds. (1960) *Out of Apathy*, New Left Books.

THOMPSON, J. and TUNSTALL, J., eds. (1971) *Sociological Perspectives*, Penguin.

WALLERSTEIN, I. (1974) *The Modern World System*, Harcourt Brace.

WEBER, M. (1930) *The Protestant Ethic and The Spirit of Capitalism*, George Allen & Unwin.

WEBER, M. (1947) *The Theory of Social and Economic Organisation*, Oxford University Press.

WEBER, M. (1949) *The Methodology of the Social Sciences*, The Free Press.

WESTERGAARD, J. H. (1972) 'Sociology: the myth of classlessness', in Blackburn, R., ed. (1972).

WINCH, P. (1958) The Idea of a Social Science and Its Relation to Philosophy, Routledge and Kegan Paul.
WITTGENSTEIN, L. (1958) Philosophical Investigations, rev. edn., Blackwells.
WORSLEY, P. (1964) The Third World, Weidenfeld and Nicolson.
X, MALCOLM (1968) The Autobiography of Malcolm X, Penguin.

21

L. M. *Salamon*   Comparative history

From 'Comparative history and the theory of modernization', *World Politics*, 23, no. 1, October 1970, pp. 83–103.

I

One of the sorest needs in the social sciences is for clear and concise conceptual equipment to give structure to disciplines and order to the range of hypotheses these disciplines purport to explore. Perhaps nowhere is this need for conceptual equipment more pressing, however, than in that amorphous area of study that examines the broad range of social processes gathered under the rubric of 'modernisation'. Depending on one's perspective, the process of modernisation is either primarily economic, or political, or psychological, or social, or technological, or all of the above. Like the elephant in the old tale, the beast is different depending on who touches it and where.

Even when the focus is on the political aspect of the process, the conceptual confusion remains. In a 1965 article, Lucien Pye delineated no fewer than ten separate concepts masquerading under the term 'political development'. Cutting the conceptual confusion into ten neat parts was itself somewhat revealing, of course, since the same concepts could have been arranged under five headings or fifteen with no greater loss of clarity. Indeed, Pye manages to distill them into three categories that he defines as the 'development syndrome' (1966, pp. 31–48). Obviously, a field of inquiry as broad as this could profit from exposure to more rigorous conceptual models, for such models provide the leading questions necessary to guide research and make it productive.

Perhaps it is the social scientist with a firm understanding of history who can be most useful in this search for fruitful models of modernisation. Comparative history can generate readily testable hypotheses firmly grounded in empirical reality. At the very least, the social scientist concerned with understanding the process of modernisation would do well to investigate what the comparative historian has to offer before he ventures out on his own. If nothing else, this is a possible cure for the parochialism of the country or area specialist.

Fortunately, three recently published works attempt to tackle this problem of formulating empirically based models of the process of modernisation drawing on comparative historical materials. One of them—C. E. Black's *The Dynamics of Modernization* (1966)—was written by an historian turned social scientist. Another—Barrington Moore, Jr.'s *Social Origins of Dictatorship and Democracy* (1966)—was written by a social scientist turned historian. The third—Samuel P. Huntington's *Political Order in Changing Societies* (1968)—comes from the pen of a political scientist who draws heavily on historical materials.

In all three cases the combination of social science and history is a fruitful one, even though the outcomes are quite different. Indeed, in some respects, each of these three works undertakes a different task. Black and Moore, for instance, attempt to formulate theories of history, Black to explain the speed of modernisation in different countries, Moore to explain its costs. Huntington, on the other hand, tries to formulate not a theory of history but a theory of politics that attempts to specify the prerequisites of political order in times of social change.

Despite these differences, however, the three works also overlap. In particular, each author attempts to give some theoretical order to what Black refers to as 'the central problem in political modernization', that is, 'the process by which a society makes the transition from a political leadership wedded to the traditional system to one that favours thoroughgoing modernization'. It is this area of overlap in these three works that we will analyse here. In particular, we will examine the conceptual tools these three scholars use to explore this process of transition from traditional to modernising leadership.

Even a quick glance suggests that these conceptual tools are in fact different, emphasising different aspects of this historical process, generating different suggestions about further lines of exploration, and producing different predictions about the future patterns of modernisation in the world. Where Black and Huntington consider the political aspects of this process most critical, Moore focuses instead on economic relations. Where Black's typology groups Japan, Russia, and China together in one pattern and Germany in another, Moore's typology groups Germany together with Japan in one pattern and places Russia together with China in another.

What we propose to investigate in this article are the answers to two questions. First, what are the criteria for these different groupings? And second, which is the most productive and for what purposes? In other words, we propose to analyse these three works explicitly as models of the modernisation process. This means, basically, that we will concentrate less on the accuracy of the facts each author presents than on the way he organises this complicated field of inquiry. We will, in short, evaluate the *questions* they ask, not the answers they propose.

II

The use of conceptual models or typologies in thinking is not a matter of choice: it is the *sine qua non* of all understanding. As Karl Deutsch wrote in *The Nerves of Government* (1963, p. 12), 'It seems clear . . . that we all use models in our thinking all the time, even though we may not stop to notice it. When we say that we "understand" a situation, political or otherwise, we say, in effect, that we have in our mind an abstract model, vague or specific that permits us to parallel or predict such changes in that situation of interest to us.' The primary function of a model, and of theory in general, therefore, is to provide scholars with criteria that specify which facts are relevant to a particular process and which are not. Thomas Kuhn stated this point well in his book, *The Structure of Scientific Revolutions.* 'In the absence of a paradigm or some candidate for paradigm, all of the facts that could possibly pertain to the development of a given science are likely to seem equally relevant. As a result, early fact-finding is a far more nearly random activity than the one that subsequent scientific development makes familiar' (1962, p. 15). It is for this reason that Deutsch can argue that 'progress in the effectiveness of symbols and symbol systems is thus basic progress in the technology of thinking and in the development of human powers of insight and action' (1963, p. 10).

Anyone who has studied the literature on modernisation over the past decade must be sensitive to this need for 'basic progress in the technology of thinking'. A very impressive array of historical material has been gathered about a wide variety of societies, but there is still a need for conceptual equipment that can limit the field and locate the critical aspects of this all-encompassing process.

The task of a model, therefore, is not simply to describe but, more importantly, to explain by identifying the critical parts of the process under study. A good model organises facts into a meaningful framework in such a way as to generate a series of testable hypotheses with predictive power, or at least a series of insights about where to look for something interesting. The best model is the one that performs the functions most efficiently. But how can we recognise the best models? Indeed, on what grounds can we compare one model to another?

Karl Deutsch answered these questions in *The Nerves of Government*, in which he proposed three criteria for evaluating models. In Deutsch's terms, the quality of a model depends on its *economy*, its *originality*, and its *explanatory or predictive powers* (1963, pp. 16–18). Thus, in the first place, the better model is the one that is more *economical*, the one that truly identifies the more critical aspects of the process under study and thus produces a picture of reality that is significantly simpler than reality, thereby permitting selection of facts. In the second place, the better model is the one that is more *original*, the one that focuses attention on relationships that are not already obvious and are not trivial. In the third place, the better model is the one that has greater *explanatory and predictive capacities*. This is the most complicated of the three criteria. To be predictive, a model must have *rigour*, *combinatorial richness*, and *organising power*. *Rigour* is a measure of the model's ability to produce unique answers at various stages of inquiry. *Combinatorial richness* refers to the range of hypotheses the model generates, the number of interesting and important relations it identifies. *Organising power* consists of the capability of the model to explain processes other than those it was originally designed to explain.

Perhaps the best way to explain these criteria is to illustrate their utility in evaluating models in the physical sciences. Sixteenth-century astronomers faced the difficult choice between two alternative models of the cosmos. Both professed to explain the known facts about the movement of the heavenly bodies in mathematical terms. The Ptolemaic model portrayed the cosmos as a series of concentric spheres with the earth at the centre. The Copernican model portrayed instead a cosmos with the sun at the centre, encircled by a number of planets, among which was the earth. Since both models seemed to explain the observed facts, scholars had difficulty accepting one and rejecting the other. On what basis could this decision have been made? And why do scholars today accept the Copernican model?

The criteria cited above permit us to answer these questions. In Deutsch's terms, the Copernican model proved to be more *economical* and *predictive*. It was more economical because, especially after Kepler's improvements, it permitted astronomers to explain with a few brief statements what had taken Ptolemaic scholars intricate calculations to explain. The Ptolemaic model had accommodated the increasingly detailed knowledge about the heavenly bodies only by elaborating a complex system of new cycles and epicycles, each described by an intricate mathematical statement, so that Milton, by his time, depicted the cosmos

> With Centric and Concentric scribbled o'er
> Cycle and Epicycle, Orb in Orb.

The Copernican model explained the same facts, but with much greater economy. A few simple mathematical statements accounted for the whole body of accumulated knowledge about the movement of the heavenly bodies.

The Copernican model was also more *predictive* than the Ptolemaic, largely because it had greater *combinatorial richness* and *organising power*. Its greater *combinatorial richness* was evident in its ability to explain everything that the Ptolemaic model had explained and in addition account for a great many hitherto unexplained facts, such as the appearance of meteors. Very significantly, the widespread acceptance of the Copernican model coincided with the discovery of phenomena that had formerly escaped the notice of astronomers wedded to the Ptolemaic model, a development that suggests that models lead not only to the explanation of facts, but also to their discovery.[1] New models can make scholars sensitive to facts they had formerly overlooked or ignored. The model that accounts for more of these formerly ignored facts must certainly deserve our adherence.

The greater *organising power* of the Copernican model is evident in its great flexibility: the ease with which it has accommodated speculations about other solar systems, its ability to explain the trajectory of man-made bodies as they circle the earth, and the success with which it has survived the application of the theory of gravity to the movement of the heavenly bodies.

---

[1] Thomas Kuhn discusses this point in the following terms: 'Can it conceivably be an accident, for example, that Western astronomers first saw change in the previously immutable heavens during the half-century after Copernicus' new paradigm was first proposed? ... The very ease and rapidity with which astronomers saw new things when looking at old objects with old instruments may make us wish to say that, after Copernicus, astronomers lived in a different world. In any case, their research responded as though that were the case' Kuhn (1962, pp. 115–16).

The criteria Deutsch suggests thus permit us to explain the nature of the superiority of the Copernican model of the cosmos over the Ptolemaic. What we must do now is to apply these same criteria to three social science models of the process of modernisation. Even if we do not derive from this exercise a model comparable to either the Copernican or Ptolemaic one, we should nevertheless succeed in identifying where the existing models lead us and where they fall short. Let us begin with the model developed by Cyril E. Black in *The Dynamics of Modernization* (1966).

III

Black begins by identifying four ' critical problems that all modernising societies must face' (p. 67). The first is what he calls the 'challenge of modernity', and it consists of 'the initial confrontation of a society within its traditional framework of knowledge, with modern ideas and institutions, and the emergence of advocates of modernity'. The second problem is 'the consolidation of modernising leadership', the transfer of power from traditional to modernising leaders. The third is the 'economic and social transformation', the process of industrialisation and urbanisation. The fourth problem, finally, is the 'integration of society', which he defines as the 'phase in which economic and social transformation produces fundamental reorganisation of the social structure throughout the society' (pp. 68–9).

According to Black, there are significant similarities in the ways various societies cope with these four problems. He illustrates this point by elaborating a typology of the ways in which societies have coped with the problem of the 'consolidation of modernising leadership'. The typology allocates each of the more than 170 politically organised societies into one of seven patterns 'according to the characteristic political problems that modernising leaders have faced in gaining power and in implementing their programs' (p. 96). Five criteria form the basis of the typology's grouping of societies, and it is therefore on the usefulness and fruitfulness of these criteria that the worth of Black's typology must be evaluated. The five criteria can be stated in five questions as follows:

1. Did the transfer of political power from traditional to modernising leaders in a society occur early or late in relation to other societies?
2. Was the immediate challenge of modernity internal or external?
3. Did the society enjoy continuity of territory and population during the modern era?

4. Did the society experience colonial rule in the modern era?
5. Did the society enter the modern era with institutions sufficiently well developed to permit adaptation to the functions of modernity?

Essentially, this model explains two aspects of the modernisation process: (1) the speed with which the transition to modernising leadership occurs, and (2) the degree of instability that accompanies this transition. Thus, Black hypothesises that where modernisation occurred early, where the challenge of modernity was essentially internal, where no problems of territorial discontinuity plagued the modernising leaders, where no foreign colonial power thwarted modernising efforts, and where institutions existed capable of adapting to modernisation—where all these conditions existed, the transition to modernising leadership was accomplished fairly peacefully and fairly quickly. England, therefore, is the 'ideal type' of modernising society that enjoyed almost all of these blessings, and France is a close second. Together, they constitute Black's 'first pattern'. Other societies have had a more difficult time, depending on which of the five benefits they lacked. The societies in Black's 'third pattern'—including Switzerland, Denmark, Germany, the Netherlands—enjoyed the advantage of completing the transition to modernising leadership fairly early, thus escaping the application of unsuitable foreign models, but they suffered because modernisation came to them externally, and they all faced severe problems of nation-building that distracted attention from the other tasks of modernisation. Russia, China, and Japan ('fifth pattern'), on the other hand, form a distinct pattern because, although they relied on external models, their traditional institutions were well enough developed before the challenge of modernity appeared to permit them to resist outside influences and complete the transition to modernising leadership without direct outside intervention. Altogether, Black identifies seven patterns on the basis of these five criteria, the seventh including only the countries of sub-Sahara Africa, which, in Black's view, lack the traditional institutions capable of making a creative adaptation to the functions of modernity.

Black's typology provides us with a simple set of concepts around which a vast array of historical material can be organised. In the terms elaborated earlier, therefore, the model seems to be quite *economical*, as Black demonstrates when he applies it to no fewer than 170 societies. The problem, however, is that Black pays a high price for this economy, perhaps too high a price. In particular, the model purchases economy only by sacrificing *originality* and *predictive power*, the two other criteria of a good model.

The sacrifice of *originality* is evident in the operational definitions Black supplies for several of the key factors in his typology. Take the second criterion in the typology, which distinguishes between societies in which the challenge of modernity was external and those in which it was essentially internal. Black argues convincingly that this distinction helps to explain three aspects of the modernisation process: the nature of the struggle between traditional and modernising leaders, the length of time required to consolidate modernising leadership, and the extent to which stable modern institutions are established (p. 98). These are all extremely significant aspects and Black's distinction is therefore potentially important and nontrivial. But then Black explains the operational meaning of his distinction. The difference between societies in which the challenge of modernity was essentially external and those in which it was internal, we learn, depends merely on whether the society experienced a 'decisive confrontation on native soil with foreign occupying forces' (p. 98). Certainly this must be an obvious point: a foreign military invasion is bound to affect the nature of the struggle between traditional and modernising leaders. But what about the less obvious types of external challenges? What effects do they have? Indeed, do all foreign invasions have similar effects? In short, Black's formulation begs more questions than it answers; and the questions it begs seem more interesting and significant than those it answers.

In many places, to be sure, Black's model identifies more complicated and original explanatory factors. In these places, however, the model too frequently suffers from a second shortcoming: limited *explanatory and predictive capacities* caused, in the first place, by lack of *rigour*, and, in the second place, by lack of *combinatorial richness*.

Given the nature of the phenomena social science tries to explain, lack of *rigour* is almost a necessary occupational hazard. The critic must therefore be careful not to require such high standards of rigour that he forecloses the possibility for any comparative history and conceptualisation at all. The concern for rigour, however, need not be only an impediment to conceptualisation. It can also be an asset if it forces scholars to explain their conceptual categories more clearly. In the case of Black's model, several of the criteria lack this clarity.

Perhaps most striking in this respect is his fifth criterion: the existence of 'traditional institutions . . . sufficiently developed to be adaptable to the functions of modernity' (p. 103). The notion that the nature of a society's 'traditional' institutions affects its pattern of modernisation is certainly an interesting hypothesis deserving careful study. The problem, however, is Black's failure to give some objective or operational meaning to his concept of 'under-developed' traditional institutions. The division between these societies where the 'level of development of traditional institutions is on the whole not adequate to provide the basis for adaptation' and those societies where the level of development *is* adequate seems quite arbitrary, for Black supplies us with only the most rudimentary clues about how to gauge this aspect of institutional development. At the worst, therefore, his hypothesis about the level of development of traditional institutions can be reduced to a tautology: it attributes poorly developed traditional institutions to those societies that have not yet modernised, and then hypothesises that those countries with poorly developed traditional institutions have trouble modernising. What is needed is a more objective and 'rigorous' definition of poorly developed traditional institutions.

Another indication of the lack of rigour of Black's model is his failure to try to test his hypotheses about the speed and stability of the modernisation process. Even though he does not bother to make the calculations, however, his figures seem to confirm his hypotheses, at least about the speed of modernisation. Thus the societies in the 'third pattern', which faced difficult problems of nation-building, required an average of sixty-one years for the modernising leadership to consolidate itself, while the societies in the 'fifth pattern', which escaped these problems, required only an average of forty-two years to accomplish this consolidation. All of these calculations depend, however, on the accuracy of the cut-off points Black suggests for the various stages of modernisation; and these dates are, to say the least, somewhat arbitrary.

When we turn to the problem of assessing the degree of stability or instability that accomplished the process of modernisation, the problem of measurement becomes even more serious. Black copes with it by ignoring it completely. He assumes that certain societies entered the modern world with less violence and instability than did others, but he makes no attempt to support this assumption. Moreover, he makes no attempt to distinguish between the violence modernisation implies for some of the former colonial areas now attempting to modernise and the violence that accompanied modernisation in the United Kingdom in the form of the enclosure movement. The presumption is that the latter was not violence at all.

Lack of *rigour* is only one cause of the limited *explanatory and predictive capacity* of Black's model, however. The model also lacks *combinatorial richness*. It identifies only a very limited range of hypotheses. It concentrates on the speed and stability of the modernisation process, but has little to say about whether modernisation will occur at all in a society, and if it does, what specific form it will take.

When Black attempts to deal with these questions, his argument tends to fall back on a single factor: culture. Thus he explains that Russia and China became totalitarian because 'the weight of tradition pre-disposed them to extreme forms of centralisation. . . .' (p. 85). Similarly, democracy developed only in those countries that had 'a deeply rooted tradition of individual rights'. The problem with such explanations is that they fail to explain how these particular traditions became functional in these specific societies and not in others. After all, Black himself noted that all traditional societies had elements of nondemo-cratic traditions. Why did these prevail in some cases, and not in others? The model offers no clues about where to look for the answers to this kind of question. Its *combinatorial richness*, in short, is limited.

The model Black offers, therefore, provides us with a very rough sketch of the terrain of modernisation. Considering the size of the terrain, this is no mean achievement. But it would be wrong to over-state the achievement. Black's sketch indicates where the ocean stops and the land begins. Therefore, the scholar seeking to explore the interior had best begin with this rough sketch; but he would be wise not to venture too far from the shore with it as his only guide. Black identifies certain critical obstacles that must be surmounted in the course of modernisation and some of the elements affecting a society's ability to overcome these obstacles. His emphasis on the impact of foreign influences on modernisation is particularly important in this regard and is a factor all too frequently overlooked. The model is of only limited use, however, when we turn to more difficult research questions. What effects do various aspects of the pre-modern social structure have on the way a society modernises? Are there significant differences among different types of modernising elites that affect the process of modernisation? What determines the form that the transi-tion to modernising leadership will take? To comprehend these aspects of the modernising process we need additional conceptual equipment. Samuel P. Huntington undertakes to devise some of this equipment in one portion of his book, *Political Order in Changing Societies* (1968). The following section, therefore, will evaluate Huntington's effort to conceptualise the process of transition to modernising leadership.

IV

In large part, Huntington's *Political Order in Changing Societies* focuses on the political aspects of what Black would term the stage of 'economic and social transformation', the stage that follows the 'consolidation of modernising leadership'. He analyses with great insight the challenge to political institutions this transformation poses and argues persuasively for the need to understand the implications modernisation has for the durability and effectiveness of political institutions. In a section of his first chapter, however, Huntington elaborates a model dealing with what Black considers an earlier stage, the 'consolidation of modernising leadership'. It is this part of Huntington's presentation that we will envisage here.

The model Huntington develops focuses primarily on the dialectical relation between urban and rural areas—what Huntington terms the 'city-country gap'. The model divides the modernisation process into four interrelated stages, each characterised by a peculiar urban-rural relation. In the first stage, what Huntington calls the 'typical traditional phase', the countryside dominates the city socially, economically, and politically; but both city and country are fundamentally stable, with political participation restricted to a small aristocratic group of landowners in the countryside. The beginnings of economic and social change, however, lead to a second stage as urban groups develop strength and begin to challenge the rural elite: in Huntington's words, 'the urban middle class, in short, makes its appearance in politics and makes the city the source of unrest and opposition to the political and social system which is still dominated by the country' (p. 73). The third stage appears when the urban groups overthrow the ruling rural elite, producing what Huntington calls the 'urban breakthrough'. The fourth stage is perhaps the most complex, for it involves the re-uniting of the polity through the inauguration of the rural masses into politics. This can occur in any of four ways, depending on whether the sponsors of the 'Green Uprising' are: (1) nationalist intellectuals; (2) a section of the urban elite trying to overwhelm its more narrowly based urban political opponents; (3) a rurally oriented military junta; or (4) a clique of revolutionary urban intellectuals. Each of these four forms of the 'Green Uprising' has implications for the target of the uprising and the framework in which it occurs. The first three forms, however, mobilise the peasants *into the system* and thus re-establish order by 'containing' urban instability. The last form mobilises the peasants *against* the system and leads to a joint urban-rural attack on the existing social and political order. 'Thus', says Huntington, 'paradoxically, the Green Uprising has either a highly traditionalising impact on the political system or a profoundly revolutionary one' (p. 77).

The model Huntington proposes seems to satisfy at least two of the three criteria of a good model that we defined earlier. In the first place, it seems to be quite *economical*, for it seems to be capable of organising a complex array of historical material efficiently and meaningfully. In the second place, it identifies at least two very fruitful and *non-trivial* hypotheses for research: first, that 'the timing, the method, and the auspices of the Green Uprising . . . decisively influence the subsequent political evolution of the society'; and second, that 'a society is . . . vulnerable to revolution only when the opposition of the middle class to the political system coincides with the opposition of the peasants' (p. 78). Nevertheless, the model fails to satisfy our third requirement, for it has somewhat limited *explanatory and predictive capacities*. In particular, the model lacks what we earlier termed *rigour, organising power*, and *combinatorial richness*.

The limited *rigour* of Huntington's model is perhaps its least significant shortcoming, for, as we have already had occasion to observe, social science models lack rigour almost as a matter of necessity. Indeed, any model that demarcates successive stages of historical development is in danger of sacrificing rigour to clarity, and Huntington's is no exception. His four stages are archetypes that serve to underline certain important historical configurations. However, when we try to find examples of these stages in the historical record, problems immediately arise, because the separate stages have a tendency to flow into one another. The lines of demarcation in fact are not nearly so sharp as they are in theory. And Huntington supplies us with only the roughest clues about how to determine, in a specific case, which stage we are in.

More serious than the model's lack of rigour, however, is its limited *organising power*, its inability to explain processes other than those it was originally designed to explain. The problem is that it fails to account for some important alternative patterns of historical development. The 'urban breakthrough' Huntington posits as a critical stage in his model of modernisation resembles, at first glance, the concept of 'bourgeois revolution' formulated by Marx and Engels in *The Communist Manifesto*, complete with the dialectic of urban (bourgeois) and rural (feudal) conflict culminating in a revolutionary surge. According to Marx and Engels, 'We see then: the means of production and of exchange, on whose foundation the bourgeoisie built itself up, were generated in feudal society. At a certain stage in the development of those means of production and of exchange, . . . the feudal organisation of agriculture and manufacturing industry, in one word, the feudal relations of property, became no longer compatible with the already developed productive forces; they became so many fetters. *They had to be burst asunder; they were burst asunder*' (Feuer, 1959, p. 12). Thus, the urban breakthrough.

In Huntington's case, of course, it is not only 'productive forces' that provide the engine of change, but also what Marx and Engels would term the 'relations of production'. The source of the 'urban break-through' is the new political elite that takes power in a society and undertakes to transform the society's 'productive forces'. In Hunting-ton's model the initiative rests with the politicians.

The problem with this model, however, is that it applies to only a very restricted range of historical experience, namely, to those societies in which an independent urban middle class did in fact develop, and in which this urban middle class did in fact become 'the source of opposition to the political and social system which is still dominated by the country' (Huntington, p. 73). Neither of these developments is inevitable. In fact, they are far from being even probable. The weak-ness of the urban middle classes in Germany and Japan is well known. But this weakness did not prevent modernisation. Indeed, the mere appearance of an urban middle class is no guarantee that this middle class will oppose the prevailing rurally dominated social system. To the contrary, as Maurice Dobb has noted (1963, pp. 17–18), at least the commercial elements of the urban middle class are 'more likely to be under an inducement to preserve the existing mode of production than to transform it'. Politics may move to the city but still protect the country's interests. The *organising power* of Huntington's model is therefore somewhat limited because the model fails to equip the scholar both with a set of concepts that help him comprehend the pattern modernisation takes in the absence of an urban breakthrough, and with a set of criteria to enable him to determine clearly whether this 'breakthrough' has in fact occurred.

Closely related to the limited *organising power* of the model is its restricted *combinatorial richness*, the restricted range of hypotheses the model generates. Although Huntington specifies four possible patterns of Green Uprising and asserts that the particular pattern that prevails is highly important, he nevertheless fails to offer a convincing explana-tion of why one pattern occurs and not another. His model, in short, *identifies* the four patterns, but fails to provide clues about where to look to *explain* the patterns. In fact, he offers only one suggestion to explain the appearance of one pattern of Green Uprising and not another. It depends, he asserts, on the *choices* of leaders. 'Whether a society evolves through a more or less revolutionary path thus depends upon the *choices* made by its leaders and their urban opponents *after* the city asserts its role in the political system' (p. 78, italics added). From this it would appear that Huntington considers any of the four patterns of Green Uprising equally likely for any society. While no one would deny that the choices of political leaders are quite important in determining the form of the Green Uprising, it seems equally difficult to deny that at least some features of the objective situation affect the leaders' choices.

Elsewhere in his book Huntington does specify some of these features. In particular, he concentrates on the political structure of traditional society and argues that the structure of power in the traditional political system significantly affects the character of the Green Uprising. To modernise, argues Huntington, a society must have political institutions capable of innovating policy and absorbing increased political participation. The first requires the concentration of power, the latter its dispersal. Societies with highly concentrated political power, like the centralised monarchies of France, China and Russia, are best able to promote innovation, but least able to absorb the increased participation innovation invariably produces. As a result, these societies are most susceptible to revolution. On the other hand, traditional systems in which power is dispersed may not modernise so quickly, but will do so less violently because they will be able to absorb increased political participation (pp. 274–8).

This concept of the 'absorptive capacity' of a political system is a fruitful one, which Huntington develops with great skill and which he uses to explain the incidence of revolution in France, China, Russia, Mexico, Bolivia, Guatemala, and Cuba. The concept, and the model of which it is a part, are somewhat less helpful, however, in explaining why certain societies with similar traditional political structures develop so differently—why England, for instance, became a liberal democracy and Japan a fascist dictatorship, even though both societies had dispersed traditional political institutions.

A large part of the explanation of these variations seems to lie in the nature of the social forces produced by economic change, and thus in the character of this economic change itself. What we need in order to comprehend these variations, therefore, is conceptual equipment addressed explicitly to the problem of ordering the social and economic determinants of the transition to modernising leadership, much as Huntington's model orders the political factors. The work of Barrington Moore, Jr., is one attempt to formulate such equipment.

V

In his *Social Origins of Dictatorship and Democracy* (1966), Moore identifies three basic patterns of modernisation. What he terms the 'capitalist-democratic route' corresponds very roughly to what

Huntington identifies as the 'urban breakthrough cum containment' pattern. What Moore refers to as the 'communist route' corresponds in a very rough way with what Huntington terms the 'Green Uprising: Revolution'. What Moore terms the 'fascist route' corresponds to the pattern of modernisation without an urban breakthrough, a pattern that Huntington fails to consider.

This apparent similarity between the concepts used by Huntington and those used by Moore masks, however, the basic dissimilarity in the orientations of the models they develop. Where Huntington concentrates simply on the basic dichotomy between urban and rural sectors of a society, Moore concentrates on the complex set of interrelations among four critical sets of actors in the pre-modern society: the landed upper classes, the peasantry, the urban bourgeoise, and the governmental bureaucracy. Where Huntington tends to stress political relations, Moore focuses instead on economic relations. Indeed, Moore defines his three patterns of modernisation in terms of the social class that sponsors the commercialisation of agriculture. Thus the 'capitalist-democratic route' prevails where a strong commercial and industrial bourgeoisie sponsors the commercialisation of agriculture either by converting the landed elite to capitalist methods of farming, as in England, or by destroying the economic power of the landed elite, as in France. In the second pattern, the 'fascist route', the landed upper class itself sponsors the transition to modern capitalistic production on the land *before* the urban bourgoisie has a chance to establish its power. Finally, the 'communist route' occurs where, in the absence of a modernising, commercialising surge from the landed elites *or* the urban bourgeoisie, the peasantry itself, in co-operation with one or another group in the society, takes the initiative.

Four central hypotheses thus form the core of Moore's model. The hypotheses are, to be sure, rather ponderous; but this reflects as much the complexity of the underlying social processes as it does the limitations of the approach. In brief, these hypotheses can be reduced to the following, even though Moore never states them in this form:

1. Given a strong and independent urban commercial and industrial middle class, the probability is high that democratic capitalism will develop, but only if a rough balance exists between the governmental bureaucracy and the landed upper classes in the society and if the urban bourgeoisie manages to exert its control over national policy, either by converting the landed elites as in England or by destroying their power as in France.

2. In the absence of a strong and independent bourgeoisie, fascism is

likely when the landed upper classes sponsor the commercialisation of agriculture themselves and, in the process, expropriate and rationalise the machinery of government to enforce labour discipline in the countryside and secure worker identification with the state in the city.

3. Where the urban bourgeoisie is weak and the landed upper classes fail to commercialise agriculture, the intrusion of market relations into the countryside makes peasant revolution likely, but only when the peasant community is itself cohesive and the link between the peasant and the landlord is weak, and even then only when the peasants can find allies with organisational skills.

4. Where the urban bourgeoisie is weak, the landed upper classes see no incentive to commercialise agriculture, and the peasant community lacks the cohesion necessary for effective political action, the probability is high that modernisation will simply not occur until one of these conditions disappears and, particularly, until one of these social groupings makes a decisive break with the past.

The particular historical events that produce these constellations of forces, can, of course, vary. Thus the middle classes can be weak because the landed upper classes bypass the cities and retain control of commerce in their own hands (Germany), or because a foreign colonial power has monopolised the functions an indigenous middle class might have performed (India). In either case, the outcome is essentially the same: a weak commercial and industrial class and consequently a weak democratic challenge to the landed elites. Depending on other factors, therefore, the result will be fascism or communism or stagnation—but probably not capitalist democracy.

Moore's 'three routes to the modern world' conceptualise a great deal of human experience with great clarity. Compared to the other models we have considered, Moore's model, to use our earlier terminology, is somewhat less *economical*. Nevertheless, its *originality* more than compensates for its shortcomings in economy, and is in fact a prime cause of them. The simple fact is that Moore's model attempts more than the others we have considered: it attempts to explain not only *whether* modernisation will occur, but also *what form* it will take, and what consequences various forms have for human freedom and suffering. The leading questions Moore poses to guide research may, therefore, lack elegance and economy, but they more than make up for this by being thoroughly nontrivial.

Despite these assets, the model contains some shortcomings that limit its *explanatory and predictive power*. In particular, the model lacks *rigour* and suffers from some interesting lapses in *combinatorial richness* and *organising power*.

As we have had occasion to note twice already, the critic of social science models must relax somewhat his demands for rigour lest these demands foreclose all possibility of conceptualisation. In the field of comparative history, the criteria for success of a model cannot yet be how close the model takes us to definite and precise quantitative predictions, but rather how far it takes us from the position that 'anything is possible'. Moore's model takes us quite far in this direction, and it is this that gives it great value for the researcher. Nevertheless, there is reason to doubt whether Moore has provided those who wish to use his concepts with clear enough explanations of their meaning and precise enough indication about how to apply them. As a result, there is a serious danger that the hypotheses he identifies may become, in the hands of less careful scholars, mere tautologies.

The concept of a 'strong and independent bourgeoisie', for instance, is critical to Moore's argument and plays an important part in his model. Where such a group exists, the chances are good for some form of democracy; where it is absent, fascism, peasant revolution, or stagnation are more likely. But how are we to recognise such a group and to gauge its strength and independence? One way, of course, would be to determine the size of the middle classes and the share of the nation's wealth they control. A close reading of Moore's analysis, however, suggests that these measures of middle-class strength and independence are not sufficient. They must be supplemented by a consideration of the degrees of cultural autonomy of the bourgeoisie, the degree to which the bourgeoisie adopts or rejects the cultural norms and traits of the landed elite. Such a consideration, however, is difficult to make and is of necessity highly subjective. The danger, therefore, is that the strength of the bourgeoisie in any society will be evaluated by looking at what that bourgeoisie does—e.g., does it challenge the landed upper class? Does a capitalist revolution occur? Such an approach will transform Moore's hypothesis about the *effects* of having a strong bourgeoisie into a tautology, for it makes these effects part of the definition of a 'strong and independent bourgeoisie'. While the social consequences may be the same when we have a weak bourgeoisie as when we have a strong one that fails to act wisely, the explanations of these two phenomena are quite different. Moore's use of the concept of a 'strong and independent bourgeoisie' confuses the two.

The same is true of such concepts as 'a rough balance between the Crown and the landed upper classes', 'exploitative landlordism', and a 'revolutionary break with the past'. The difficulty in providing an objective definition of these concepts produces a temptation to define them, at least partly, in terms of their hypothesised consequences. Thus, there is a temptation to establish the existence of 'exploitative landlordism' by reference to peasant violence, and then to use the concept of 'exploitative landlordism' as an explanation of this very violence.

For the most part, Moore avoids these traps in his analyses of specific societies. Nevertheless, his failure to provide clear, objective, and non-tautological meanings to his concepts undermines somewhat his model's usefulness for other researchers. In the terms we introduced earlier, this failure limits its *explanatory and predictive capacities*.

Another, and closely related, limit on the explanatory and predictive capacities of Moore's model arises from a lapse in its *combinatorial richness*. For the most part, the model perceives political events as derivative. It is therefore rich in hypotheses that explain particular political events by reference to particular social and economic configurations. In a sense, politics is 'over-explained' in economic and social terms, leaving little room for political explanations of political events. Moore's model, in short, neglects precisely what is central to Huntington's—what we might term the organisational or institutional dimension of social change.

This dimension, however, is an important part of any explanation of different forms of modernisation. The appearance of fascism in Germany in 1933, for instance, must be attributed, at least in part, to an institutional breakdown, to the inability of the German middle classes and workers to develop political organisations resilient enough to withstand the shock of depression. The appearance of a Communist régime in Russian in 1917 was a result, at least partly, of the superior political organising skills of the Bolsheviks. Had a strong Communist party organisation existed in France in 1789, the same thing might have occurred there too, regardless of the vast structural differences between the two societies. The simple fact appears to be that the skills of the politician play an important part in explaining the route a particular country takes. The winner of a revolution is not necessarily the group that commits the violence, but the one that builds the institutions that survive afterwards.

Organisational skills are the monopoly of no particular social class, unless the intellectuals can be considered a social class. The route a particular country takes to the modern world may therefore be as much a function of the ideology and political skill of the intellectuals as it is a function of the strength of the landed elite and commercial bourgeoisie. A bourgeoisie that is strong in numbers and wealth but poor in organisational skill may fare far worse than one small and poor in everything but the capacity to organise. This may be one of the most important differences between the German and English middle classes: the latter had a long history of self-government through commercial guilds and urban government corporations; the former displayed a tendency for nothing so much as internecine warfare and ideological controversy. At the very least, an otherwise weak bourgeoisie can maximise its influence through effective organisation. Perhaps, in the last analysis, fascism emerged in Germany not because the landed elite was economically 'stronger' than the bourgeoisie, but because the army and the state bureaucracy were *better organised* than the middle-class political parties. If this is so, the safeguard against fascism may not necessarily be social revolution aimed at destroying the landed elite, but may rather be political organisation among the urban middle class. Moore's model goes far in explaining the context in which this political skill, this ability to organise political institutions, operates. In the process, however, he downgrades the importance of political skill itself.[2]

Political skill undoubtedly has important economic causes: it is almost impossible to organise a political party among plantation slaves. But there also seem to be other determinants of political skill, such as those deriving from the cultural values of a particular society. Where these operate, the problem a ruling class faces is much more complex than Moore concedes. It may be, as Moore argues, that a society's values reflect the economic needs of its ruling classes. However, a set of values serving the *economic* interests of the ruling class may nevertheless undermine the long-term *political* position of this class by unwittingly inculcating a set of norms conducive to political organisation. As two students of India demonstrate (Rudolph and Rudolph, 1967, pp. 17–154), the very caste system that serves so well to facilitate exploitation by the upper classes also acts as a ready-made vehicle for horizontal political organisation aimed at undermining the political power of this upper class. By neglecting this organisational and institutional dimension of social change, Moore limits the *combinatorial richness* of his model and thereby restricts its *explanatory and predictive capacity*.

A third restriction on the *explanatory and predictive capacity* of the model Moore presents is its somewhat limited *organising power*, its

---

[2] Samuel P. Huntington treats this issue skilfully in the first chapter of his book, *Political Order in Changing Societies* (1968).

limited ability to explain the processes of change in societies other than those from which the model was developed. Moore's model emerged from the comparative study of eight separate societies: England, France, Germany, United States, China, Russia, Japan, and India. Curiously, however, six of these societies shared at least one important historical characteristic, a characteristic that plays a prominent role in the typology formulated by Black. Except for India and the United States, all of these societies escaped colonial rule in the modern era; and although America experienced colonial rule, it escaped something far more significant—namely, a 'traditional' agrarian structure, either feudal or bureaucratic. It may not be surprising, therefore, to find that none of Moore's three models applies to India, even though the Indian case provides a check on the accuracy of the 'bourgeois revolution' model. Since India and most of the currently modernising societies *did* experience colonial rule or something comparable, it is important to understand the significance of this fact.

In general, those societies that escaped foreign control enjoyed the opportunity to modernise in response to essentially internal forces. Therefore, a model such as Moore's, which explains modernisation largely in terms of these internal social and economic configurations, seems to apply quite well to these cases. It fails to explain adequately, however, the evolution of the ex-colonies where outside forces interfered with what would otherwise have been their 'natural' evolution.

Surprisingly enough, this interference may have been most significant to the political sphere, where colonial powers imposed foreign political forms like parliamentary institutions and political parties. In most cases, to be sure, traditional ruling groups adapted themselves to these new institutions and learned to use them for their own purposes. The survival of these political forms imposed from outside, however, facilitates the creation of new types of power, resting, for instance, on the organisational network of a modern political party. These political institutions, therefore, open a new historical possibility, a 'fourth route to the modern world' through the creation of mass political parties.

In his discussion of India, Moore implicitly acknowledges the possibility of this fourth route, even though it depends on a form of power his model fails to allow for, partly as a result of its neglect of what we earlier termed the 'organisational dimension' of change. 'Nehru', Moore observes, 'was a very powerful political leader. To deny that he had a great deal of room to manoeuvre seems absurd' (p. 407). But Nehru's power derived not simply from his class position or from hereditary right, but from his position in a 'modern', mass, political party that had exploited to advantage the British-imposed parliamentary institution. This party created a new form of political power and a new basis of legitimacy, both of which are potentially available to leaders who wish to modernise their societies yet avoid the three routes that Moore outlines. Indeed, thanks to the changes in communications technology that make it far easier to organise mass political institutions today, this fourth route may be a common one in the foreseeable future.

The creation of mass political parties does not guarantee modernisation, however. For modernisation to succeed, the new bases of political power and legitimacy must be used, in Moore's phrase, to 'channel into industrial construction the resources that agriculture does generate' (p. 406). It was Nehru's shortcoming as a political leader that he neglected this necessity and thereby failed to exploit fully the opportunity his political power gave him. While this shortcoming was not unexpected given the social bases of the Congress Party's power, it was far from inevitable. And it need not be repeated by other political leaders who enjoy the same opportunity.

VI

It should be apparent by now that the three models of modernisation considered here are at least partly complementary. Of the three, I find Moore's model most useful in explaining the economic and social bases of the transition to modernising leadership and thereby identifying the essential processes most efficiently. Nevertheless, Black's stress on external influences on modernisation and Huntington's stress on the institutional or organisational dimensions seem to be necessary complements without which Moore's analysis falls short.

The three models discussed here do not exhaust the repertoire of comparative historical approaches to modernisation. The discussion here will have accomplished its goal, nevertheless, if it has systematically located some of the shortcomings in these three models and, in the process, developed a way to evaluate these other approaches.

REFERENCES

BLACK, C. E. (1966) *The Dynamics of Modernization*, Harper.
DEUTSCH, K. (1963) *The Nerves of Government*, New York, Free Press.
DOBB, M. (1963) *Studies in the Development of Capitalism*, New York, International Publishers Company.
FEUER, L., ed. (1959) *Marx and Engels: Basic Writings on Politics and Philosophy*, Smith Press.
HUNTINGTON, S. P. (1968) *Political Order in Changing Societies*, Yale University Press.

KUHN, T. (1962) *The Structure of Scientific Revolutions*, University of Chicago Press.

MOORE, B. (1966) *Social Origins of Dictatorship and Democracy*, Beacon.

PYE, L. (1965) 'The concept of political development' in *The Annals of the American Academy of Social and Political Science*, 358, March; reprinted in L. Pye, ed. (1966) *Aspects of Political Development*, Little, Brown.

RUDOLPH, L. and RUDOLPH, S. (1967) *The Modernity of Tradition*, University of Chicago Press.

22

G. D. Paige   The primacy of politics

From 'The rediscovery of politics', in J. D. Montgomery and W. J. Siffin,
eds., *Approaches to Development: Politics, Administration and Change*,
McGraw-Hill, 1966, pp. 49–58.

The intellectual components are now at hand for the rediscovery of
politics, or one kind of purposive human behaviour, as àn independent,
creative force in human affairs.

Oddly enough, it now seems that in the sometimes vicious but often
beneficial polemic between the 'traditionalists' and 'behaviouralists' in
American political science after World War II, both sides were 'right'
but for 'wrong' reasons. The former were right, not because the
political behaviour of mankind cannot be studied by scientific methods
or because cherished values necessarily need be sacrified in the process,
but because man is a creative being who can envision worlds yet
unknown and can strive purposively for their attainment. The latter
were right, not because they insisted on broadening the study of
politics beyond laws and formal institutions or because they insisted
upon quantification and new methodologies, but because their search
for more satisfying ways of explaining patterns of political behaviour
brought them face to face with man. In man, capable of both innovative
and patterned behaviour, the two schools met.

But in one respect both schools seem to have been 'wrong' for the
'right' reason. This was in the degree to which both trends of thought
tended to be imbued with a more or less subtle deterministic bias. This
bias was not really qualitatively different between the traditional and
the behavioural approaches, especially since most political scientists
combined both orientations in one form or another, but perhaps it
became somewhat more pronounced in the 'revolt' of the latter.

While the traditional orientation, inconsistently and unsuccessfully,
tried to keep political-legal institutions as the focus of attention, it

tended to view institutional action internally as largely the product of 'tradition' and externally as mainly the result of weighty geographic, historical, philosophical, social, economic, and cultural determinants. The behavioural orientation, on the other hand, seemed to lead to an intensified examination of the behavioural components of institutional action, a search that quickly led to more precise exploration of psychology, sociology, social psychology, and cultural anthropology—all of these viewed as related to more traditional environmental concerns. But while more and more factors such as family socialisation, education, and cultural values were rediscovered and linked to political behaviour, the degrees of freedom open to politics seemed to become less and less. It might almost be said that while political scientists had rediscovered the 'wholeness' of society (after Aristotle and Confucius) they had 'lost' politics.

Perhaps the loss of focus upon politics can be explained by one component of what James W. Fesler (1962, p. 138) has termed 'the natural history of revolts against conventional wisdom', i.e., a tendency 'to make the newly discovered element the independent variable to which *the earlier perceived part of reality becomes a merely dependent variable* [emphasis added]'. Thus, one of the largely unanticipated consequences of the revolt against the study of formal political-legal institutions has been a tendency to treat political behaviour as being a derivative of more basic economic, social, and psychocultural forces. In other words, one could say that most of the variance in political variables could be explained by variance in nonpolitical variables.

Recent American political science has been characterised by a rather strong deterministic bias. While the intellectual historian may more adequately trace the sources of this bias, at least two of major import can be suggested. First, political science could not but be affected by the ideas of the intellectual giants of the past century—Marx, Darwin, and Freud—all of whom placed man in a matrix of forces largely beyond his control. Political scientists, then, cannot be excepted from David C. McClelland's incisive assertion that 'for a century we have been dominated by Social Darwinism, by the implicit or explicit notion that man is a creature of his environment, whether natural or social. . . . Practically all social scientists in the past several generations have begun with society and tried to create man in its image' (1961, p. 391).

Secondly, there is a more specifically political reason, however, why political scientists nurtured in a liberal-democratic tradition, as in the United States, should tend to find it congenial to view political

behaviour as largely a dependent social variable. This is the representa-
tional view of politics according to which political actions both are and
ought to be predominantly the expression of more basic underlying
social forces. Thus political leaders are seen to act on behalf of and in
response to objective demands largely beyond their ability to manipulate. Politics is viewed as 'the art of the possible'; and the range of
the 'possible' is generally thought to be quite narrow. Political leaders
reinforce this view when they explain and defend major decisions they
have taken on the grounds that they were inevitable, inescapable, and
without feasible alternative. Political behaviour from this point of view,
then, tends to be seen as frothy foam on the surface of the deep social
sea.

It seems highly likely that the determinist view of politics has
conditioned much of recent American discussion about the great issues
of our time: peace; national security; and 'development' in Africa,
Asia, Latin America, the Middle East, and the American South. One
of the bases of failure to appreciate the nature and implications of
Soviet science might well have been an organic view of society in which
the characteristics of any single aspect (in this case politics) must
necessarily be characteristic of any other aspect (science). Also the idea
in foreign aid to developing countries that the improvement and
liberalisation of one variable (economics) would result in similar
political effects seems to have been based in large part on a nonpolitical
view of politics.

Appraisals of the viability of the political patterns of a free society
in developing areas have also been influenced by the deterministic idea
that without certain objective socioeconomic prerequisites they are
impossible. (But this would rule out India.) The Communist analogue
to this kind of argument is that the behavioural patterns of socialism
and communism cannot be established until certain objective economic
and technological prerequisites have been established. (But this would
rule out China.)

The policy consequences of a deterministic bias in American political
thought and analysis have been illustrated recently in a brilliant
evaluation by Tang Tsou of American policy toward China in the
period from 1941 to 1950 (1963). Specifically Tsou has concluded
that prior to the Communist victory in 1949 such a bias resulted in:
(1) overestimation of the cultural obstacles to rapid industrialisation
under Communist rule; and (2) underestimation of the ability of
innovative international and domestic political action to avert a
Communist takeover. While granting a 'kernel of truth' to the original
analysis, Tsou argues (p. 397):

Nevertheless, what these analyses failed to take adequately into account was a new political factor: The ability of a totalitarian party, using all the levers of social control, to manipulate mass attitudes, to organize social life, and to tap surplus labor as a source of capital for the paramount purpose (until 1949 at least) of rapid industrialisation. It is a new dimension which American specialists and officials, immersed in the liberal, democratic environment of a free society, naturally failed to gauge. *The trend of the social sciences up to that time, which emphasized the determining effects of social forces on political actions, also left them unprepared to appraise correctly a situation in which the political actors deliberately and methodically sought to manipulate the social environment to achieve a preconceived purpose.* This deterministic bias, which was a measure of the separation of knowledge from practice, led the West at once to overestimate the difficulties confronted by the Communists and to underestimate the ability of the free world to work out its destiny. This is one of the basic sources of its incapacity to undertake a bold program to meet the Communist challenge [emphasis added].

In general, it might be hypothesised that the stronger the elements of socioeconomic and cultural determinism in political analysis, the less the tendency of policy makers to innovate courses of action or to pursue them if created by someone else.

The main theoretical question which is raised by the foregoing considerations can now be sharply posed: Are political systems to be conceived of as largely determined by the socioeconomic characteristics of the societies in which they are found? Or are they to be conceived as capable of largely autonomous variation which can result in profound economic, social, and cultural change?

The question may not even be considered a meaningful one unless some of the confusion generated by the necessary social science distinction between relationships among 'analytical aspects of concrete social objects' and relationships among 'concrete social objects' themselves is dispersed. In the former, the idea of 'causation' may be inappropriate; in the latter, failure to recognise it may be paralysing.

Without doubt, the idea that for any concrete social object (one or more human beings) there can be an infinity of analytical aspects was a vital contribution to the development of social science. It cautioned against the reification of social concepts and challenged the remarkable creativity of the human brain to invent more powerful concepts, to posit their hypothetical interlinkages, and to demonstrate their empirical relationships. Since such analytical concepts were merely creations of the brain designed to call atention to certain aspects of what was in reality human behaviour 'in the whole', it followed that it was illogical to conceive of concept A 'causing' concept B. Thus it became 'nonsense' to speak of changes in the political aspect of society 'causing' changes in the economic aspect of society, or vice versa.

However fruitful these ideas may be for the attempt to characterise whole societies in terms of systems of action, they do not provide a satisfying explanation for the role of politics in social change. Thus to term *political actions* of the 18-million-man Communist party of China as merely an analytical aspect of Chinese society that cannot be conceived in causal terms is, to put matters mildly, misleading. One solution for this kind of problem, of course, has been the adoption of the concept of the 'predominantly X-oriented concrete social object'. Therefore, it becomes meaningful to speak of the effect of a pre-dominantly economically oriented one. It was in this latter sense that Robert Vincent Daniels (1961) concluded after a comparative study of the Chinese and Russian Communist revolutions: 'In present day communism, the political superstructure is not a reflection of the economic base, but its creator; political power and inspired willful leadership become the prime movers of history' (p. 230).

China thus seems to provide one strong case in affirmative answer to the theoretical question posed above. The works of Mao Tse-tung, like those of Lenin, are replete with recognition of the primacy of politics over objective socioeconomic conditions. In his analysis of Chinese society, Mao argued repeatedly that 90 per cent of the Chinese popula-tion consisted of peasants who were imbued with a strong sense of 'petty bourgeois individualism' because of their economic basis of small individual farms (Mao Tse-tung, 1956, Vol. iv, p. 41). This was hardly the objective basis upon which to build a collectivist society where individual and family property would virtually disappear. The significance of this fact was not lost on Mao, whose confidence in final victory seemed occasionally to sag. His remedy for despair, however, was not to counsel patience while the objective stars in the ecological firmament of politics moved to more propitious positions, but rather to call for the intensification of purposeful effort. 'If we do not win', wrote Mao in 1945, 'we will blame neither heaven nor earth, but only ourselves' (1960, Vol. iv, p. 15).

The Chinese cases, however, may not be satisfactorily conclusive. The interactions of historical variables may be viewed as so complex that the isolation of the effects of purposive political initiative may be thought to be virtually impossible. What might be more convincing would be conditions approximating those of an experimental psychological laboratory where the effects of different kinds of political stimuli might be measured in the responses of both experimental and control groups. If a people highly homogeneous in history, language, culture, economic system, social structure, politics, administration, and all other characteristics could be divided into two groups—and if these two groups could each be subjected to a different kind of political stimuli— then it might be possible to gauge the impact of purposive political behaviour or its relative independence of other aspects of society.

One of the interesting features of the mid-twentieth century, however tragic it may be for the peoples directly concerned, is that there are in the world at least three 'natural laboratories' in which the conditions specified above are roughly approximated: Korea, Vietnam, and Germany. One of the great challenges to contemporary social science is to explore the theoretical implications of what has happened in these bisected societies.

The Korean case, for example, argues even more strongly than the Chinese one for the rediscovery of politics in terms of enhanced theoretical appreciation of political degrees of freedom in the social matrix. Severance of the Thirty-eighth Parallel in 1945 effectively divided socially homogeneous[1] Korea into two 'test' groups, North and South.

In North Korea over the past eighteeen years the dominant political factor—first the Soviet Army and now the 1·3-million-man Korean Workers' Party—has changed substantially the Korean economic structure. In agriculture, purposive political action first created a highly dispersed system of ownership through a land reform in 1946 which gave 'land to the tiller in perpetuity'. Between 1953 and 1958 political action destroyed the private ownership system and organised all of North Korea's farmers into collective farms. In industry and trade, developments have been the same. Purposive political action has demolished a relatively private economy, established collectivised farms, and has subjected the economy to political and administrative control. Centralised control of the economy seems to have been carried to an extreme in North Korea, where it is reported that even a match cannot be purchased outside a state store. The main point is that North Korea's economic structure now differs markedly from that of the Japanese period as well as from that of contemporary South Korea and that the reasons for this difference lie mainly in deliberate political action: ideas, leadership, organisation, and power.

[1] There were significant differences, of course, in the non-human environment, mainly in the distribution of natural resources.

Deliberate policy has brought about marked changes in other areas of society as well including education, religion, the arts, and certain aspects of the family. The point is not the assertion of a naïve voluntarism—'to will is to achieve'—but rather to suggest that the North Korean case illustrates again that it is possible to achieve major socioeconomic changes with dramatic swiftness through purposive political action.

The politics of South Korea, however, seem to support the other side of the argument for the theoretical autonomy of politics, i.e., not that politics can bring about major social changes but that *substantial changes may take place in the political sphere without the occurrences of correspondingly marked changes in the socioeconomic characteristics of a society.* Thus in the short period of only thirteen months from April 1960 through May 1961 South Koreans lived under three drastically different systems for the making of authoritative social policy, while there appeared to be no fluctuations in socioeconomic variables of corresponding magnitude—self-legitimating political propaganda notwithstanding. First, under President Syngman Rhee Korea manifested dominant-party authoritarianism in which the president gradually expanded his sphere of government: local officials were largely appointed; elections were manipulated; the press was slightly critical but extremely cautious; fear of political persecution was widespread; no scholarly research on politics was published; the rumour networks seemed to be the best sources of political information.

After the fall of the Rhee Government, which followed the April 19 1960 student demonstrations against the injustices of the March election and its aftermath, Koreans lived for about twelve months under remarkably free and nonauthoritarian political conditions. A three-month interim government changed the constitution to a parliamentary cabinet system and held unprecedentedly free elections. During the approximately nine-month tenure of Premier John M. Chang the powers of the executive seemed to be on the decline while those of the assembly seemed ascending. In general the period might be characterised as one of multi-party liberalism: local officials were largely elected; there were few election irregularities; the press was blatantly critical; fear of political persecution was not widespread; academic research and publication on Korean politics began; few rumours were more shocking than stories which could be read openly in the press.

The military coup of May 16, 1961, swept away previous political arrangements and instituted an era of no-party military dictatorship: a thirty-man junta, or its most powerful faction, began to make decisions for Korea; assembly and parties were abolished; elections were deferred for at least two years; local officials were again appointed; an atmosphere close to political terror came to prevail; the press lost its independence; the importance of rumour grew.

Throughout all three periods of political variation, there was little marked variation in other aspects of South Korean society: private farming prevailed; there was a strong private component in industry and trade; religions flourished; there was considerable unemployment and economic hardship.

Thus while the strong Communist political stimulus greatly changed the face of North Korean society, the different (and perhaps weaker?) 'democratic' political stimulus in South Korea seemed to affect less and to be undetermined by the gradually changing nature of South Korean society. At the same time, over nearly twenty years, the two parts of Korea became markedly different from what they had been in 1945 and from each other.

To sum up the main line of argument at this point, it has been contended that political science has suffered recently from a strong deterministic bias; that this bias has involved making politics merely a dependent social variable as well as merely a prisoner of its own 'tradition'; that such a bias leads to serious policy miscalculations; and that the observed role of politics in the developing countries such as China (and especially in the natural laboratory of Korea) leads to the conclusion that political behaviour can be conceived both as a 'causal' and 'relatively autonomous' social force. The general thesis has been characterised as the 'rediscovery' of politics.

It may be that we shall have to credit the rediscovery of politics to the totalitarians such as Lenin in Russia, Mao in China, and Kim Ilsong in North Korea. If so, we shall be but returning to the insight of Franz Neumann (1957) that, 'while democracy . . . misconceived the relation of economics and politics, its enemies right and left clearly recognized the precedence of politics over economics: Fascism and Bolshevism are in agreement that politics has precedence' (p. 264).

But the totalitarians need not be our only teacher. We might also learn from democrats such as Nehru. When Clinton J. Rossiter recently returned from a trip to India with a vow that he would never give another lecture on the impossibility of the existence of a free political system because of the absence of the necessary socioeconomic prerequisites (*New York Times*, June 13, 1962), he was participating also in the rediscovery of politics. The rediscovery is also strengthened by the global historical studies of 'modernisation' since about 1600 that have been conducted by Cyril E. Black, who has concluded that while certain universal features of modernisation may be expected to take place (e.g., urbanisation, rising literacy, and the spread of mass communication), the political systems in which they shall occur are indeterminate. With special reference to China and Russia, Black (1962) has concluded:

> The victory of Communism in Russia and China may be regarded as in no sense inevitable but rather as a largely personal achievement of Lenin and Mao. . . . The eventual modernization of Russia and China was not at issue. What was at issue was the manner in which they would be modernized, and the ideologies and programs that would be adopted. This issue was decided as a result of the specific struggles between political leaders and parties which were so much a matter of contingency, chance, and accident that no general historical interpretation could predict the outcome. If a general trend exists, the role of political leadership may well determine the specific manner in which this trend is implemented (p. 15).

Politics having been rediscovered, however, the question might well be asked as to what exactly it is that has been 'rediscovered'. Here it is hardly likely that there will be high consensus among the rediscoverers. Which of the many definitions of politics is to be understood? Is it to be Lenin's 'who does what to whom' (*kto kovo*), or Mao's 'war without bloodshed' (*bu-liu hsüeh ti chang-cheng*)? Or is it to be the more familiar formulations of Lasswell (1936), 'who gets what, when, how'; of Easton (1953), 'the authoritative allocation of values'; of Levy (1952), 'the allocation of power and responsibility'; or of Snyder (1958), 'the making of authoritative social decisions'?

As a contribution to the quest for a concept for rediscovered politics it can only be suggested that such a concept may well include heightened emphasis upon *purposive organisational behaviour the object of which is to formulate and to achieve social goals by means of consensus and coercion*. Political organisational behaviour might be distinguished from other kinds of organisational behaviour (economic, social, religious, etc.) in that conflict over ends and means within and among such organisations cannot be resolved in ways binding upon all members of the society without the participation of members of the political organisation. Perhaps the definition of politics given by Professor Masao Maruyama (1961) of Tokyo University will make an especially fruitful contribution to a rediscovered concept of politics. He explains it as 'the organization of control by man over man'.

Among some of the implications for political science which might stem from the rediscovery of politics suggested above might be the following: first, greater emphasis upon the nature and role of political leadership. Political leadership is not now a field of specialisation within the discipline; virtually no graduate seminars or undergraduate courses focus principally upon it. Yet if political behaviour is conceived of as an innovating autonomous force, then increased attention might be devoted to the nature of political creativity. The growing psychological literature on creativity (Getzels and Jackson, 1962) which stems both from scientific and business interests might be brought into conjunction with political biography for this purpose.

Second, the sharpening of focus on purposive organisational behaviour which is linked to the rediscovery of politics suggests greater emphasis upon large-scale organisational behaviour—parties, bureacracies, and military organisations—and somewhat less upon the ecology of such organisations. This is its major implication for the study of comparative administration. However, this is not to deny the fruitfulness of study of the interactions, tensions, and conflicts between such organisations and their environments, but only to redress somewhat the tendency to impute rather deterministically ecological characteristics to such organisations as almost insuperable limitations on their behaviour.

Third, the rediscovery of politics suggests that the 'laws' governing the patterned regularities which political scientists seek to explain may be more microscopic than macroscopic, more Newtonian than Cartesian, and more behavioural than grossly institutional, historical, or environmental. It may be, for example, that the 'laws' governing political change are similar to those involved in social learning; i.e., from *different* (or similar) antecedent conditions, polities may proceed to different (or similar) consequent states of affairs through the *same* 'laws' of transformation.[2] This is but a suggestion and is not meant to disparage more macroscopic concerns.

Finally, the rediscovery of politics suggests a renewed focus on what might be termed potentiality analysis in political research. While political scientists have been seized by chronological questions of empirical indeterminacy (i.e., questions about 'what was', 'what is', or 'what will be'), they have as yet developed neither the theoretical rationale nor the methodology for answering questions of potential indeterminacy ('what could have been', 'what could be'). With the weakening of deterministic bias, interest heightens in probing the probable distribution of alternative outcomes which might have resulted from purposive political initiative. Perhaps this would mean merely the return to the concept of 'power' in another guise, but it

[2] For the social learning analogy see Banchera and Walters (1963, p. 253).

would be a reinvigorated power—creative, alert, flexible, both patterned and probabilistic—a rediscovered politics as purposive organisational behaviour in a conflict-filled pursuit of a 'better' world.

REFERENCES

BANCHERA, A. and WALTERS, R. H. (1963) *Social Learning and Personality Development*, Holt, Rinehart & Winston.
BLACK, C. E. (1962) 'Political modernisation', in K. London, ed., *Unity and Contradiction*, Praeger.
DANIELS, R. V. (1961) 'The Chinese revolution in Russian perspective', *World Politics*, 18.
EASTON, D. (1953) *The Political System*, Knopf.
FESLER, J. W. (1962) 'Field administration', in F. Heady and S. L. Stokes, eds., *Papers in Comparative Public Administration*, Ann Arbor.
GETZELS, J. W. and JACKSON, P. W. (1962) *Creativity and Intelligence*, Wiley.
LASSWELL, H. D. (1936) *Politics: Who Gets What, When, How*, New York, Smith.
LEVY, M. J. (1952) *The Structure of Society*, Princeton University Press.
MAO TSE-TUNG (1956) *Selected Works*, New York, International Publisher's Company.
MAO TSE-TUNG (1960) *Selected Works*, Peking, Foreign Languages Publishing House.
MARUYAMA, M. (1961) *Gendai seiji no shiso to kodo, Modern Political Thought and Behavior*. Tokyo.
MCCLELLAND, D. C. (1961) *The Achieving Society*, Van Nostrand.
NEUMANN, F. (1957) *The Democratic and the Authoritarian State*, New York, Free Press.
SNYDER, R. C. (1958) 'A decision-making approach to the study of political phenomena', in R. Young, ed., *New Approaches to the Study of Politics*, Northwestern University Press.
TANG TSOU (1963) *America's Failure in China, 1941–50*, University of Chicago.

Author Index

Skinner, G. William, 170, 180
Skocpol, T., 35, 294, 302
Smelser, Neil J., 243
Snyder, R. C., 369
Stokes, D., 128, 299
Stolper, G., 122
Stretton, H., 316

Tang Tsou, 363–4
Tocqueville, A. de, 21, 52, 142–3, 144, 158
Tönnies, Ferdinand, 25
Treischke, Heinrich von, 123
Trotsky, Leon, 186
Truman, D. B., 53
Turner, J., 202–3

Verba, S., 25, 53–4, 268–9, 316

Weber, Max, 6, 8–9, 14, 25, 243, 252, 290, 328
Weiner, M., 24, 274
Welter, R., 137
White, Stephanie, 88
Wildavsky, Aaron, 88
Williams, Philip, 83
Wittgenstein, L., 268, 327

Zawadzki, B., 145, 157

Subject Index

abstraction ladder, *see* ladder of abstraction
airlines, 103
Alexander II, Czar of Russia, 149, 150, 152, 160
American Consensus analysis, 22, 306–25, 330
 'American Standard', 308–11
 crisis and critique of, 313–21
 global perspectives of, 307–8, 311–13, 317
 internal structure concepts in, 321–2
 methodology of, 306–7
 and positivism, 325, 333
 radical critiques of, 321–3, 329
American Medical Association, 115
American Political Science Association, 23
American Revolution (1775), 146, 155
anarchy, 15
aristocracy, 1, 47, 51
Attlee, Clement, 205
authority, 7–10, 13, 16, 32

banking, 105

behavioural movement, 24–5, 70–1, 325, 361–2
Berlin blockade 1948, 159
Bevan, Aneurin, 120
bias in political inquiry, 203, 361–4, 368, 370
Bismarck, Otto von, 122–3, 129
bourgeois revolution, 350
Boxer Rebellion 1900, 146
Bretton Woods Agreement, 207
Britain, *see* United Kingdom
British Medical Association, 121
British Navy Estimates, 42
Bukharin, Nicolai, 190–1

cabinet government, 60, 89
Canada, 116–18
capitalism, 321–2, 332, 353
 definition of, 11
 see also democracy, capitalist
Catherine the Great, 147
causation, 364–5, 368
Chamberlain, Austen, 121
Charondas, 49